LYNCHING AND LEISURE

Lynching and Leisure

Race and the Transformation of Mob Violence in Texas

TERRY ANNE SCOTT

The University of Arkansas Press
Fayetteville
2022

ISBN: 978-1-68226-189-7
eISBN: 978-1-61075-761-4

26 25 24 23 22   5 4 3 2 1

Manufactured in the United States of America

Designed by Liz Lester

♾ The paper used in this publication meets the minimum require-ments of the American National Standard for Permanence of Paper for Printed Library Materials Z39.48-1984.

Library of Congress Cataloging-in-Publication Data

Names: Scott, Terry Anne, author.
Title: Lynching and leisure: race and the transformation of mob violence in Texas / Terry Anne Scott.
Description: Fayetteville: University of Arkansas Press, 2022. | Includes appendix: List of lynching victims in Texas, 1866–1942. Data table includes date, name, race, gender, city, county, alleged crime, mode of death, size of mob. | Includes bibliographical ref-erences and index. | Summary: "Comprehensive study that traces how lynchings in Texas evolved from largely clandestine acts into racialized recreation in which crowd involvement became integral to the atrocities committed"—Provided by publisher.
Identifiers: LCCN 2021029513 (print) | LCCN 2021029514 (ebook) | ISBN 9781682261897 (cloth; alkaline paper) | ISBN 9781610757614 (ebook)
Subjects: LCSH: Lynching—Texas—History—19th century. | Lynching—Texas—History—20th century. | Lynching—Social aspects—Texas. | African Americans—Violence against—Texas—History. | Leisure—History. | Texas—Race relations—History.
Classification: LCC HV6465.T4 S46 2022 (print) | LCC HV6465.T4 (ebook) | DDC 364.1/34—dc23
LC record available at https://lccn.loc.gov/2021029513
LC ebook record available at https://lccn.loc.gov/2021029514

For Warren, Ezri, Oni, Zahar, and Mom

CONTENTS

ACKNOWLEDGMENTS

I was born into a family, both immediate and extended, in which success was measured not by the expanse of one's coffers, but instead by one's ability to create and accomplish goals that positively impact our surrounding communities. The capacity to produce meaningful publications and teach others about the history of an extraordinary people certainly fits within my family's matrix for success. I thereby owe an immeasurable debt of gratitude to my parents, William and Micheline Schulte, for teaching me that no goal is out of reach, and that all goals should leave the world a better place. They instilled in me the unrelenting value of hard work, dedication, and love. I thank them for their many sacrifices and their unconditional love. I thank them for making all things possible and for allowing me to wholly believe that anything can be accomplished. I also thank them for teaching me to respect and help the least among us. My driven, talented, amazing brother, Ricky, would have lauded this work as the most masterful, awe-inspiring study ever completed in any discipline—not because it is so, but simply because I produced it. I was his infallible little sister. Everyone should have such a person in his/her/their corner. I know he is still in mine. I thank my little brother, Matthew, for his unequivocal support and encouragement, his well-timed gifts of levity in the midst of some otherwise tense moments, and his continuous ability to suggest just the right book or writer. Thank you to AJ and Jordyn for their continued support and pride, their enduring enthusiasm for all things creative and intellectual, and for the utter joy that they bring to our lives. I also thank AJ for his help with formatting issues. I thank my loving Aunt Janine for her constant support and joy in my accomplishments. She, together with Aunt Marie Jose, Angie, Jessica, and Joelle are truly appreciated for serving as incredible examples of determination, integrity, and generosity of spirit. They have shown me how to successfully and gracefully balance the demands of one's family and one's professional life. Their love, cheering, and support are true, unrelenting gifts. I would also like to extend a heartfelt thank you to the amazing Tracee, who has been an official promoter at all the right times. I also want to greatly thank Malinda, Audrey, Stephanie, Teyanna, and Tricia. Each of these women is truly inspirational. Their support and friendship have been incredibly appreciated.

Many magnificent, supportive archivists, librarians, and scholars have helped bring this work to fruition. I thank the many individuals at repositories and libraries across the country who have provided me with documents and direction that have proven imminently useful. Thank you to the staff at the University of Arkansas Press, especially Jenny Vos and David Scott Cunningham, for all of your help in making this manuscript into a book. I am grateful to archivists and librarians at the Dallas Public Library in Dallas, Texas and to Walter Hill at the National Archives in College Park, Maryland. I am grateful to Dr. Marsha Prior and Dr. Graham Haslam for their support and encouragement. Thank you as well to my colleagues in the Department of History at Hood College. A special thanks to Dr. Emilie Amt for our many conversations related to this work. Dr. Dennis Cordell, Dr. Edward Countryman, and Dr. Kenneth Hamilton at Southern Methodist University are worthy of commendation for their passion for teaching and the examples that they set for aspiring scholars. They all encouraged and ignited intellectual curiosity among their students, and they personified the joy inherent in teaching. Dr. Hamilton taught me early in my career the value of exploring how African Americans conquered seemingly insurmountable obstacles to determine the trajectory of their lives. I owe an incredible debt of gratitude to the faculty and staff in the Department of History at the University of Chicago. They have lent both intellectual and practical support during this process. Ellen Wu provided much need encouragement and laughter as we waded through the challenges and delights of graduate education. It was in Dr. Neil Harris's class that the idea for this study was born. I am particularly indebted to Dr. Julie Saville and Dr. Thomas Holt at the University of Chicago. Dr. Saville's encouraging, careful reading of this study helped immeasurably as I worked to sharpen my arguments. I thank her for her encouragement and insight. My advisor and mentor, Dr. Thomas Holt, has been a true inspiration. He supported and honed my ideas since the very beginning, even when others thought leisure and lynching should not be mentioned together. I thank him for his incredible breadth of knowledge, his generosity of time, and his constant and invaluable feedback as he read the many drafts of this work. His extensive insight and comments have been immensely valuable, and I am honored to have been able to learn from him.

My husband, Warren Earl Scott, II, and my daughters, Ezri, Oni, and Zahar, have expressed a level of pride and happiness for me that would fill the deepest of the Earth's crevasses. This endorsement, this proverbial high-five, is invaluable. Girls, you are all incredibly intelligent, beautiful, compassionate souls who have imbued my life with a joy and meaning that must be tantamount to Heaven. I am so proud of you. Imagine the world in which you desire to exist and then create it. It can be done. Ezri and Oni, thank you also for helping to research aspects of this book. Our trip to Austin, Texas, will forever be remembered and adored. Warren, you have been on this journey with me since we sat on a bench together outside the student center and debated the merits of Frederick Douglass's work. Thank you for accompanying me to varied libraries and repositories. Thank you for reading my drafts and reminding me when needed about the importance of this work. Thank you for your vital insight. Thank you for believing in me when others thought my tasks impossible. Thank you for making the everyday extraordinary.

LYNCHING AND LEISURE

Sport and Hate

O, Cruel mob—destroying crew.
Who gave the life of man to you?
Why have you gathered, small and great to
murder more through sport than hate?

—LAURETTA HOLMAN GOODEN,
"Question to a Mob"[1]

On the morning of May 15, 1916, people gathered in the southcentral Texas town of Waco were bursting with anticipation. As the sheriff's deputies escorted Jesse Washington, a local Black teenager, into the town's courtroom for his trial, a white male observer brandished a pistol and averred, "Might as well get him now."[2] Seeking to postpone the inevitable violence for a couple of hours, another man in the restive crowd wrestled the firearm from the gunman and insisted, "Let them have the trial. We'll get him before sundown, and you might hurt some innocent man."[3] The courtroom was filled to capacity with spectators occupying every pew and all the interstices along the rim. While the area only accommodated five hundred people, Judge Richard Irby Munroe allowed perhaps fifteen hundred to witness the trial. Some individuals in attendance stood on benches while others sat precariously perched atop railings to get a better glimpse of the accused. A narrow passage had to be cleared through the dense cluster of interested parties to allow Munroe access to the bench. The court reporter had trouble finding room at his desk and counsel chose to stand rather than jostle for a seat. The tumult in the courtroom produced by the overcrowding led Munroe to warn, "there won't be any court today."[4] In response, a voice from the balcony tersely bellowed, "we don't need any courts."[5]

Arrested the previous week, Washington was charged with murder in the bludgeoning death of Lucy Fryer. Her children, Ruby and George Jr., found the body of their mother, a fifty-three-year-old white woman, late that Monday afternoon on the family's property in Robinson, seven miles southeast of Waco. In the hours following Fryer's death, multiple theories circulated as to who might have killed her. None satisfied local interest quite like the one that arraigned Washington, a laborer on the Fryers' farm. Later that day, after the discovery of Fryer's body, Washington was arrested in his yard reportedly wearing a shirt with blood on it. Any presumption of his innocence was met with swift muzzling. Twenty-seven-year-old A. T. Smith, the Black managing editor of *Paul Quinn Weekly*, an organ for Paul Quinn College—one of two Black colleges in Waco—reprinted a *Chicago Defender* article that unabashedly proclaimed Fryer's husband, George, murdered his wife. Alluding to false accusations of crime often heaved upon Black men, the article further charged that "nine times of ten, the Race man accused is innocent."[6] Local white officials arrested Smith, who was later convicted of libel and sentenced to one year of hard labor on the local road gang.[7]

Within hours of his arrest, Washington was transported to a Hillsboro jail, approximately thirty-five miles north of Waco, where officers assigned to protect him promised they would prevent a possible lynching if he simply confessed to the crime. Likely frightened for his life, he complied. Fearing that a mob might forcibly remove him from the Hillsboro jail, officers transported Washington yet again, this time to Dallas, nearly ninety miles from Waco, where he confessed a second time after similar promises of protection. The entirety of his coerced, signed confession was printed in three local papers, easily accessed and possibly read by potential jurors in McLennan and surrounding counties. Illiterate, Washington could not read the confession that he ultimately signed with an *X*. By the following Monday morning, the young man was back in McLennan County before an all-white jury.[8]

Washington's speedy trial was a charade, a miscarriage of justice even before the mob violence that consumed much of the day. Jury selection itself required only thirty-five minutes because of the defense attorney's unwilling- ness to peremptorily strike any potential jurors. By 10:00 a.m., the trial was underway. A reporter in the courtroom disclosed, "when asked whether he pleaded guilty or not guilty, [Washington] replied 'Yes, sir,'" an answer that reveals with disturbing precision Washington's inability to fully understand the charges levelled against him.[9] The defense attorney did not cross-examine any of the prosecution's witnesses who took the stand, nor did he expose bla- tant inadequacies in the prosecution's case. Fewer than ninety minutes after the trial commenced, the prosecution and defense rested. Once instructed, the jury retired for deliberation only to return within four minutes. The foreman, W. B. Brazelton, penciled the verdict on a small piece of paper: "We the jury find the defendant guilty as charged in the indictment and assess his punishment as death."[10] By 11:22 a.m., the farcical judicial proceedings had ended, giving way to even more blatant mob rule.[11]

"Get the nigger," a voice commanded from the back of the court- room seconds before hands grabbed Washington and hurried him down the back stairwell of the courthouse. Munroe did not attempt to stop the mob even though he had firearms in his desk.[12] The judge's decision may have been influenced by the countless silhouettes of revolvers that could be detected through the garments of the spectators, but his later comments make that scenario seem unlikely. Elisabeth Freeman, a white suffragist and investigator for the National Association for the Advancement of Colored People (NAACP), later asked the judge why he neglected to simply "clear the courtroom" and thereby prevent the mob from intervening in the legal proceedings.[13] Dismissive of or perhaps mildly irritated by Freeman's query, Munroe quickly rebuked her seeming naiveté by informing her that she did not understand the South. "If a person is big enough, he can get up and stop the biggest mob," Freeman retorted as an indictment of Munroe's character. "Do you want to spill innocent blood for a nigger?" the judge rhe- torically countered.[14] Others shared Munroe's sentiment. When Freeman asked Sheriff S. S. Fleming why the fifty deputies he had recently sworn in were not present to shield Washington from the crowd, his response echoed that of the judge: "Would you want to protect the nigger?"[15]

Washington was dragged and delivered to the assemblage of local cit- izens, male and female, young and old. Those thronged about the court- house had been awaiting the lynching of the teenager for several hours, some for much longer.[16] Many members of the crowd had been stationed on the periphery of the courthouse for more than a day after buzz of the impending deed reached them. Freeman revealed in her report that a young manicurist in town confessed, "It was generally known that something was going to happen."[17] Those who worked in the building rushed to the win- dows to witness the torture when they heard scuffling outside. Without hesitation, members of the mob secured a chain around the Black teenager's neck, and, in what seems a cruel joke of lasting, bitter irony, towed him down Washington Avenue toward the city's historic bridge. It is likely the intended destination was influenced by the memory of Sank Majors, an African American man who was hanged from that same bridge in 1905.[18] The mob abruptly turned on Second Street, however, and headed to city hall when word arrived that many of those gathered outside the municipal building had begun constructing a bonfire on the lawn. As he was dragged towards what would become his funeral pyre, those who lined the road struck Washington with shovels, clubs, and bricks, and stabbed him with knives "until his body was a solid color of red," an observer stoically divulged.[19] Some used planks with nails protruding from the ends to strike him as he passed. "Haven't I one friend in all the crowd?" pleaded Washington.[20]

As his limp but living body neared the public square of the town, someone lassoed him with a second chain that members of the crowd tossed over the limb of an oak tree. Serving as a torturous prologue to their victim's fiery fate, the mob severed Washington's ear and then castrated him. Several men then yanked the dangling end of the chain in concert and hoisted Washington into the air. Thousands cheered as his blood-soaked body ascended. Some members of the lynch mob busily gathered combustible material to finish erecting the funeral pyre beneath the swaying teenager while others doused him in oil.[21] As his lynchers lowered his mutilated body into the hodgepodge of wooden and cardboard debris, "people pressed forward, each eager to be the first to light the fire," one observer revealed.[22] In the end, a little boy was awarded the eerie honor. Another young boy sat upon his father's shoulders "where he could get a good view," one observer recalled. When asked if the act was indecorous, the father replied, "my son can't learn too young the proper way to treat a nigger."[23] The *Waco Times* reported that other "onlookers" hung from windows, perched themselves atop buildings and trees, and "over-flow[ed] the square" on ground level. Many shouted in "delight" as "the negro's body commenced to burn."[24] Several women "laugh[ed] and chat[ted]" while the youth was reduced to a charred mass.[25] One elegantly dressed white woman cheerfully clapped "when a way was cleared so that she could see the writhing, naked form of the fast dying black," another local paper reported.[26]

Hundreds of city employees watched the lynching from the crowded windows of government buildings where they worked. Waco Chief of Police Guy McNamara and Mayor John R. Dollins viewed the affair from the less congested space of the mayor's office. The vast majority of the other fifteen thousand individuals who witnessed or directly assisted in the atrocities committed against Washington were away from work or household duties. Several students from Waco High School opted to spend their lunch hour at the lynching.[27]

Conscious of the commercial opportunities afforded at lynching scenes, some resourceful members of the mob took charge of vending body parts as souvenirs to those desirous of a more concrete memento of the day's events. A group of enterprising schoolboys were among the first to seize the opportunity to peddle a memento of the day. After a cowboy lassoed Washington's corpse from his horse and dragged it through a Black residential area, the head became severed from the body. The boys placed Washington's charred skull upon a doorstep, extracted the teeth, and sold them for as much as five dollars apiece. Others in the crowd commuted the chain used to affix Washington's remains to a telephone pole into a vendible commodity. After dismantling the chain, they sold individual links for twenty-five cents. A number of white Texans evaded the cost of a middleman and segmented Washington's remains themselves, carting off pieces of bones and toes as corporeal keepsakes. Freeman reported that some men wrapped "proof" of Washington's castrated body in a handkerchief and sauntered about the crowd displaying the "souvenir" of their exploit.[28]

Fred A. Gildersleeve, a local photographer, approached the lynching as an opportunity to profit from individuals' interests in memorializing the event they had witnessed. A telephone call furnished Gildersleeve with advance notice of the imminent exploit, enabling him to arrive at city hall in time to set up his camera and wait for the torture to unfold. Known locally as "Gildy," Gildersleeve had been in Waco since 1905. Over the next half century, he would regularly photograph varied area events. The front or reverse side of his images often bore his full name, a clear indication of the pride he took in his craft. Gildersleeve was well aware of the profitability associated with lynching photography. Prior to Washington's lynching, he conferred with Waco Mayor John R. Dollins to take photographs of the event from a window in city hall. Dollins allegedly received a share of the profits from the sale of the images. Gildersleeve's surviving photographs capture the magnitude and expectant mood of the thousands gathered around the scene of the burning. One photograph, which reveals the eagerness of some to obtain an unobstructed view, features a man lifting another man above the crest of the mob. Another arrests the wretched finality of the Black teenager's existence. The top of Washington's desiccated skull lays atop smoldering wood and other debris as the remaining portions of his body are slumped over the edge of the pyre. It is an image that at once bears the iniquity of a moment as well as a protracted reality that defined the world Washington navigated. Gildersleeve sold his images of Washington's lynching, some of which were commuted to postcards, on the streets of Waco to those eager to possess the tortuous event in perpetuity.[29]

Thirty-three years before the lynching of Jesse Washington, three white men had also met their deaths at the hands of a Texas mob. On the evening of Monday, December 24, 1883, southeast of Waco in McDade, Texas, fifty armed white men apprehended Henry Pfeiffer, Wright McLemore, and Thad McLemore, also white, at the Rock Saloon. Each member of the mob wore a mask to conceal his identity. They carried the three victims one mile into the thickets, beyond public view. The mob placed nooses around their necks and hanged them from an oak tree. Once the deed was done and the men were lifeless, the mob returned to town, leaving Pfeiffer and the McLemores swaying in the late-night air. Six relatives of the lynched men arrived in McDade the following day armed with shotguns and revolvers, ready to exact revenge. An ensuing gun fight left two of the sextet dead and another wounded. News of the trouble reached Austin, where Governor John Ireland, concerned about continued violence, ordered detachments of militia from outside of Houston to impede any further conflicts. When the two companies of men arrived Wednesday morning, all was calm; they returned home by 9:45 a.m. that same day. Relatives retrieved the bodies of Pfeiffer and the McLemores—intact—for burial.[30] There were no souvenirs gathered after this lynching; there was neither pomp nor shouts of jubilation to celebrate the event.

These two lynching episodes, separated by more than three decades, reveal a vast chasm in the modality of mob violence in Texas. There were, of course, court proceedings, however spurious, before the lynching of Jesse Washington—itself a rarity in the metanarrative of lynching African Americans in that state and elsewhere. Although mob rule was the dominant narrative in both the Waco and McDade incidents, there were clear differences in the character and general mood of the antagonists, in the spectators' experiences, and in both the symbolism associated with the violent acts as well as with the physical, social, and cultural relics of those acts.[31] Here, then, we are confronted by stark differentials: brevity, anonymity, and the absence of ceremony and commercialism in McDade, in contrast with a public performance, retreat from work, spectacle, commercialism, and recreation in Waco—a lynching protocol that would be produced repeatedly in Texas and elsewhere from the latter portion of the nineteenth century well into the early twentieth century. The race of the lynching victim was central to these divergent varieties of mob violence. Once a strictly punitive and largely clandestine form of extralegal punishment, lynching in Texas evolved into a largely racialized, publicly viewed, well-attended, frequently commercialized exhibition of mob violence. A new culture of lynching evolved following Reconstruction, one in which the victim was now typically Black, and the mob's fear of judicial retribution for its murderous efforts nearly disappeared. "In the days when people were afraid to be known to have any connection with the crime of lynching, they were always masked," Samuel Burdett maintained in his 1901 work on lynching.[32] "Now," he rued, there was "no mistake as to who were actual participants in the several lynchings which have taken place, for no masks are used, and any fear of being punished by law seems to have entirely gone."[33]

But what I refer to as a new lynching culture involved much more. By the end of the nineteenth century, white people in Texas broadened the social implications of lynching from punitive in intent—with an emphasis on the victim rather than the crowd—to recreational, with the crowd's spectatorship and enjoyment integral to and simultaneously shaping the spectacle created, the methods of torture employed, the images preserved and disseminated, and the commodities produced and collected. This study addresses lingering questions about why such transformations occurred and how widespread they were in the state between the end of Reconstruction and the early decades of the twentieth century. Transformations rooted largely in rural-to-urban migration, urbanization, mechanization, racist conceptualizations of criminality, and mass consumption fundamentally altered the value and rationale of lynching and transfigured the nature of the act. These altered lynching practices and connotations, I further argue, reveal broader changes in both race relations and the concept of crime in Texas during the latter portion of the nineteenth century, reflecting in part the rise of industrial capitalism and its impact on work rhythms and shifts in modes of racialized social control. The collective, unlawful mob that had long been part of southern and Texas mores gained a new inflection with the intensified othering of Black people through varied forms of denigration and popular entertainment. Always an extemporaneous form of social justice, the new lynching culture of the late nineteenth century—one characterized largely by race, spectacle, consumption, recreation, and modern technologies—was a visual exhibition of the sociopolitical reordering and economic transformation intrinsic to post-emancipation Texas. It was a response not simply to racist attitudes and suspicions, but also to modifications to everyday life in the wake of increasingly nonagrarian labor arrangements.

Scholars and others have for decades used statistics compiled by the NAACP and Tuskegee Institute when citing the occurrence of lynching across the country. After the NAACP courageously began tracking lynching in 1917, investigators hired by the organization searched old newspapers dating as far back as 1889 for information. They also relied upon the reporting of local citizens. The NAACP findings typically tracked the location of the lynching, the race of the lynching victim, the alleged crime, and, on occasion, the lynching victim's age. Investigators for the organization considered their count supplemental to the *Chicago Tribune*'s purportedly deficient yearly totals (the *Chicago Tribune*, which began tallying lynchings annually in 1882 and printing the statistics in its January issues, was the first agency to keep methodical records of the "work of Judge Lynch"). The NAACP counted 335 lynchings (of all persons, regardless of race) in Texas for the period extending from 1889 to 1918, a figure cited by nearly all studies that discuss lynching in the state. Tuskegee University's records place the total number of lynchings that occurred in Texas between 1882 and 1968 at 493. Both institutions ranked Texas as third among states in the number of total lynchings. Studies on varied aspects of United States history continue to rely on the figures from either the NAACP or Tuskegee when examining mob violence. As a result, the number of persons lynched in Texas has been dramatically undercounted for decades. In a study published in 2015, the Equal Justice Initiative (EJI) (an organization whose diligence in exposing the expanse and heinousness of lynching has been incomparable) reported that 4,084 African Americans, the vast majority of whom were men, lost their lives as a result of mob violence in the United States between 1877 and 1950.[34] The EJI's tally, which only focuses on the lynching of African Americans, includes approximately 800 lynchings from across the country that had not been included in previous studies. The organization places the number of Texas lynchings between 1877 and 1950 at 335.

It is a wretched reality that new studies, including this one, continue to uncover additional lynchings in the state of Texas. My research reveals that between 1866 and 1950, as many as 750 people lost their lives to Texas lynch mobs—469 were Black, 140 were white, 111 were Mexican, at least 1 was Native American, and the race of 29 persons remains unknown. It should be noted that those individuals listed as "unknown" were likely not Black as the race of African Americans was rarely ignored in the historical record. While the NAACP determined that 335 people were lynched in Texas between 1889 and 1918, I determined that 385 people were likely lynched (281 Black, 70 Mexican, 32 white, 1 Native American, and the race of 1 remains unknown) during that period. Similarly, my research has determined that Tuskegee's numbers undercounted the total number of persons lynched between 1882 and 1950 by approximately 134 people. I offer this corrective data to demonstrate that, as the EJI has emphasized, the numbers of those lynched continue to increase as additional research is conducted. It is a horrifying commentary on racial violence in America. It should be noted that the EJI has welcomed curative analyses, including the one in this study.[35]

STUDY	TOTAL LYNCHINGS OF AFRICAN AMERICANS IN THE UNITED STATES, 1877–1950	TOTAL LYNCHINGS OF ALL PERSONS IN TEXAS, 1868–1950	TOTAL LYNCHINGS OF ALL PERSONS IN TEXAS, 1889–1918	TOTAL LYNCHINGS OF ALL PERSONS IN TEXAS, 1882–1950	TOTAL LYNCHINGS OF AFRICAN AMERICANS IN TEXAS, 1877–1950
NAACP	——	——	335	——	——
Tuskegee University	——	——	——	493	——
EJI	4,084	——	——	——	335
Lynching and Leisure	——	750	385	627	437

TABLE 1.1: Number of Persons Lynched, 1866–1950

Lynching in Texas had been a prevalent part of the state's social landscape following the Civil War, one that gave it a national reputation for lawlessness and violence. In 1868, the West Virginia *Wheeling Daily Register* insisted that "lynch-law prevails in [Texas] to a shocking extent."[36] A Philadelphia newspaper printed the following in 1869: "in Texas . . . Judge Lynch cannot even wait for lawful court and jury, but hangs his supposed culprit at the first tree."[37] In 1876, the New Orleans *Morning Star and Catholic Messenger* observed, "the prevalence of lynching in Texas is astonishing,"—a charge leveled by newspapers across the country.[38] Two years later, a journalist for the Ohio-based *Cincinnati Daily Star* wrote in jest, "the trees in Texas sometimes bear other fruit than horse thieves."[39] There were several threads of commonality that marked these early Texas lynchings. The lynching victims in the first decades following the war were often white. Their alleged crimes typically involved horse theft, cattle theft, or murder. Furthermore, their bodies were frequently found hanging from a tree in the hours or days following their deaths and the parties who lynched them, if seen, were often masked. By stark contrast, starting after Reconstruction and extending well into the twentieth century, the lynching of Black bodies was done with a visibility, impunity, and fanfare that would come to define a new lynching culture. While there were still white and Mexican victims of lynching, the victims were overwhelmingly Black.

This racialization of mob violence in Texas and the attendant transformation of the practice perhaps matter more than aforementioned corrective calculations. There were some lynchings before the end of the Civil War in Texas, as I discuss in chapter 1, but the numbers and character are far from comparable when juxtaposed with the postbellum era and beyond. W. Fitzhugh Brundage notes in his influential work on lynching that "the tradition of mob violence that had taken root in the antebellum South differed both in character and frequency from the later practice of lynching."[40] He adds, "before the Civil War, whites, not blacks, were the preferred victims of mobs."[41] The practice in Texas was no exception. Notwithstanding the elevated violence against newly freed African Americans in the immediate years following the Civil War, whites would remain the primary targets of mob violence until after Reconstruction. In the 1870s, 79 people lost their lives to lynching in Texas. The racial breakdown was as follows: 46 were white (58.2 percent), 28 were Black (35 percent), 4 were Mexican (5 percent), and the race of 1 remains unknown. My research demonstrates that by the end of the following decade, the total number of lynchings in the state more than tripled. At least 211 people died by mob violence in the state during the 1880s. The percentage of Black victims also increased and outpaced the percentage of white victims. At least 94, or just over 44 percent, were African American, while 61 were white, which accounts for 29 percent of the total. At least 28 of the victims were Mexican (13 percent) and the race of 28 victims remains unknown. Mob violence became increasingly racialized during the 1890s when as many as 150 people were lynched in the state, 122 (approximately 81 percent) were Black. That trend would continue for decades. From 1900 to 1950, at least 300 people in Texas died by lynching. Just over 72 percent were Black. The vast majority of the remaining victims were Mexican. During many of those 51 years, *only* Black people were lynched. With that shift in the race of the victims of mob violence came the concurrent infusion of pageantry.[42]

With notable exceptions—such as the NAACP—social scientists, reformers and others who wrote or lectured about lynching during the early portion of the twentieth century assumed a type of southern exceptionalism—a geographic and social removal from modern, civilized cultural norms and mores—as the underlying impetus for lynching. They frequently characterized this type of social violence as an archaic expression of rural, backwoods, southern white people. More recently, scholars have investigated racialized lynching as a phenomenon partially or wholly allied with spectacle and modernity. In her study of the connection between lynching and spectacle, historian Amy Louise Wood argues that the turn-of-the-century increase in racial violence reflected southern communities' "uncertain and troubled transformation into modern, urban societies."[43] Wood builds on the work of other scholars, including Jacqueline Goldsby, Leon Litwack, and Grace Elizabeth Hale, who have collectively demonstrated how spectacle, consumerism, and modernity were linked to mob violence, and have thus greatly nuanced our understanding of the various contours of lynching in America.[44]

Much remains to be learned, however, from a deeper exploration of how varied economic, sociopolitical, and cultural phenomena in a particular locale shaped the character of lynching, and, by extension, worked to trivialize Black lives. To achieve that more comprehensive understanding of the widespread nature and pronouncements of racialized collective violence in Jim Crow America, we must continue to explore and consider regional and local variations that molded the changing character of lynching. When focusing on a particular locale, we can more fully comprehend the creation and varied manifestations—from the psychosomatic to the commercial—of a given lynching narrative. Regional differences are evident, for example, in the fact that Black Texans were far less likely than other southern African Americans to leave their native state and migrate north, in part because of local employment options offered in urbanizing or industrializing areas of the state. As demonstrated in the following study, high rates of rural-to-urban migration within the state of Texas led to racial contestation that would largely impact how local white people would exact varied modes of racialized social control, from the legal to the extralegal to the categorically violent. Much of the bitterness engendered by intrastate migratory patterns would be manifest in manners unseen in other states.

This study addresses persistent questions about why lynching assumed a particular character by the end of the late nineteenth century by examining how mob violence has been subject to regional and transnational variances. Lynching culture in the United States was not a monolith. "Much of the existing literature on the late nineteenth and early twentieth centuries dwells upon the static character of white oppression of blacks," writes Brundage. Consequently, in his investigation of the complex and changing culture of mob violence in Georgia and Virginia, he examines how variations in the practice were impacted by wide-ranging, regional phenomena:

> The regional variations in mob violence and in the responses of both black and white southerners to it affirm the degree of diversity that existed in race relations, even during a period disgraced by the most vicious white racism. The slogan of white supremacy was pervasive across the South—it was an article of faith for most white southerners—and yet political and economic forces and the conventions emerged from them generated regional variations in race relations.[45]

My work builds upon Brundage's regional variation framework. By undertaking a study about differences in the culture of mob violence over time within the vast expanse of the state, this study also responds to Michael J. Pfeifer's state-of-the-field analysis of lynching studies in which he argues that there is still a need for "serious, comprehensive scholarly treatment" of lynching in the state of Texas. [46]

My work examines how socially constructed notions about Black misconduct, misrepresentations of African Americans in material and popular culture, labor adjustments ushered in by industrial capitalism and the attendant effects of Black migration, and reactions against Black freedom expressions significantly transformed mob violence. What is most striking about how postbellum racial anxiety and hatred manifested, however, is the extent to which they were linked to and expressed through a language and performance of leisure and how the lynching event itself was often marked as a moment of leisure-time enjoyment. The new lynching culture that emerged by the end of Reconstruction in Texas was one marked by the racialization of mob violence and its transformation from "quiet violence" to acts often defined by spectacle, consumerism, and fanfare. Even when largely devoid of those overt markers of entertainment and display, racialized lynchings still often conformed to a leisure narrative as I define it in this study. In an increasingly urbanizing environment, Texans spent both their nonworking and working hours differently than in the past. Hence was born a complex relationship among race, labor, industry, violence, and recreation, all of which facilitated fundamental changes in the character of lynching from what had been true just a few decades earlier. The timing and meaning of leisure were affected by demographic, spatial, and technological changes, opening a new space for the practice of lynching in which leisure shaped its character even as white Texans carved a new form of leisure from acts of incredible racial violence.

Michel Foucault's influential study of changes in the French penal system over the course of several hundred years helps unpack the connection between lynching and leisure. Although Foucault was analyzing legal executions sanctioned by the state rather than acts of extralegal violence, portions of his discussion on public torture are applicable to the similar events in Texas. The "'excesses' of torture" Foucault describes were exercises designed to reveal and enhance the omnipotence of the state.[47] "And, from the point of view of the law that imposes it," he writes, "public torture and execution must be spectacular, it must be seen by all almost as its triumph."[48] Similarly, although extralegal, the spectacle and theatricality of lynchings in Texas also reinforced the hegemony of the extrajudicial white mob and legitimated its defense of the social order that underlay white supremacy. Recall the spectator at the Waco trial who declared, "We don't need any courts," as a challenge to the state's authority. In explicit contrast to solemn judicial proceedings described by Foucault, however, American lynch mobs fashioned spectacles designed to integrate punishment with pleasure, in acts whose very publicity amounted to declarations of their legitimacy. As in Foucault, spectacle was an assertion of the public will. In Texas lynchings, mobilizing the citizenry for pomp-filled, public displays of torture and death served as a visual manifestation of white racial dominance and Black subjugation in the midst of vast and unsettling changes that appeared to challenge the racial hierarchy.

During the post-emancipation era, a rising tide of racism threatened African Americans' already tenuous place in the sociocultural, political, and economic structure of southern society. This was especially true in Texas. At the same time, any signs of Black upward mobility and political empowerment challenged the white supremacy that normalized antebellum racial relations. African Americans in the eastern three-fifths of the state found themselves at the hub of contestation over physical, social, and political space during the latter portion of the nineteenth century that would impact the residential and racial landscape of towns and cities, the structure of work in factories, the formation of local and statewide legislation designed to restrict their freedoms, and the leisure outlets of those who thought their power and identity were vulnerable to Black advancement and encroachment. In Texas, dramatically expanding Black populations in the eastern portion of the state brought already prevalent racial concerns to the forefront of white people's consciousness. The swelling of the Black populations in towns and cities meant job competition and what historian Allen Spears has referred to as increased "social visibility," both of which grated on the already thin racial tolerance of whites. The contingent effects of an expanding wage-labor market brought freedmen and whites into ostensibly unrestricted contact, which subsequently made African Americans' presence and varied assertions of freedom highly threatening to the established order of race relations in Texas. From many white people's perspective, the boundaries of Black people's place in society were becoming increasingly elusive. A social structure that once firmly relegated African Americans to the nethermost regions of the racial hierarchy now required a new social configuration. Edgar Gardner Murphy, a white progressive reformer, observed early in the twentieth century that southern whites' racial intolerance had moved "from an undiscriminating attack upon the Negro's ballot to a like attack upon his schools, his labor, his life—from the contention that no Negro shall vote to the contention that no Negro shall learn that no Negro shall labor, and (by implication) that no Negro shall live."[49]

By the end of the nineteenth century, southern white people had constructed a romanticized view of the antebellum era. It became the Old South, a "legend of incalculable potentialities," according to historian C. Vann Woodard.[50] It was a South, the famed early twentieth century journalist W. J. Cash insisted, that "yearned backward toward its past with passionate longing."[51] This view of the Old South, NAACP Assistant Secretary in 1921 Walter White argued, in large measure encompassed the notion that "the ex-slave whom the South professed to love so tenderly" was a docile being who would do as told by his or her white enslaver.[52] By contrast, contended a late-nineteenth century white pundit, "the new negro at the South is less industrious, less thrifty, less trustworthy, and less self-controlled than was his father or his grandfather."[53]

While many southern white people considered the "New Negro" to be insolent and idle, by contrast Black people interpreted him as something entirely dissimilar. A Black Texas newspaper boasted in 1895 that a New Negro had emerged, one who "takes advantages of his opportunities."[54] Indeed, two New Negro prototypes materialized by the end of the century, one loathed by whites and another held in esteem by African Americans. It was, however, the comingling of disparate New Negro images—impudence and indolence on the one hand and ambition and prosperity on the other—not merely the image openly discussed by white southerners, that served as the nub of new racism and transformed how southerners in general and many white Texans in particular perceived African Americans. It also transformed how whites in the state and other portions of the country transformed the notion of crime. How race was constructed and considered at a precise historical moment is what rendered a particular action a crime. Black self-assertion was perceived as a criminal act. Black lives, the new lynching culture indicated, did not matter when racial boundaries were threatened.

The archetype of the New Negro has been effectively used by historians to help account for myriad social and political changes, including turn-of-the-century racial massacres, acts of violence motivated largely by jealousy, and the banishment of African Americans from political office and small towns.[55] This study explores a broadened consideration of how the implications of the New Negro, specifically the duality of the schematic, altered lynching practices. Envy and anxiety created by this new individual, one whose progress and seeming indolence unnerved local whites, devalued the lives of African Americans and helped to recreate them as objects to be ridiculed, mocked, laughed at, and even collected. "The people of the South dont [sic] think any more of killing the black fellows than you would think of killing a flea," confessed one white southerner in a letter to a member of the NAACP executive committee.[56] Whites' attempts to defend their superiority in the social hierarchy negatively impacted the already debased status of African Americans as it recreated play. In short, the complexities of this New Negro image influenced how people thought about and spent their nonwork hours.

That which renders certain activities leisure for an individual is neither innate nor static; rather, an individual's choices of leisure are a reflection of social, economic, and political phenomena and anxieties at a particular historical moment. Cultural historian Steven M. Gelber, in his exceptional study of hobbies, posits that "leisure, no less than church, state, family education, and work, is constituted in a way that generates and reproduces the structure of society. All the various relationships that form the social structure—including class, race, gender, and age—express themselves in leisure activity."[57] As noted above, the expansion of a nonagrarian labor system increased interracial contact and heightened racial discord in Texas. Meanwhile, the rise of a modern, consumer culture changed the character of that contact, since it now functioned within a matrix of long-standing racism and racial violence, a legacy of slavery, and an altered social and political structure that placed race and racial hierarchies at the center of everyday life and politics. During a historical moment when white supremacy and its economic, social, and psychological remunerations seemed to be increasingly at stake, recreational activities that centered on objectifying and debasing African Americans offered a way to ensure the rigidity of African Americans' inferior social standing while affording all classes of white Texans the ability to reestablish their place in the racial hierarchy. In short, who and what African Americans were was integral to the construction and valorization of a white identity. In Texas and the South at large, white identities greatly hinged on the degradation of African Americans.

Consequently, as the boundaries of African Americans' place in society grew increasingly unfixed, distortions in the white perception of African Americans changed not simply the practice, but the very character and display of lynching. From the landed gentry or factory owner to the near-homeless wage laborer or unemployed migrant, whites could buttress their superiority to African Americans through a new form of commodification of Black bodies, through the eerie pleasure derived from witnessing and perhaps participating in the lynching of a person perceived as lowly, diabolical, or even nonhuman. Perhaps famed cultural critic and journalist Henry Louis Mencken was correct when he insisted that to make Black degradation and suffering the focus of one's recreational activities bolstered many whites' sense of self-worth. As he wrote in 1924: "To snort and froth at a rival makes [a person] conspicuous, prominent, a man of mark; it is therefore easy to induce him to do it."[58] To partake in a lynching, he continued, "instantly makes [a person] feel that he has played an heroic role in the world, that he has accomplished something large and memorable—above all, that he has had a gaudy good time."[59]

The collective, extralegal mob that had long been part of southern and Texas mores further gained a new inflection with the intensified othering of Black people through varied forms of popular entertainment and denigration. This commodification of Black bodies was hardly a new phenomenon, of course, since African Americans had long served a performative commercial function in white society. Since the antebellum era, ludicrous images of African Americans were enjoyed as stage entertainment through the medium of minstrelsy, and later as comic figures, in coon songs, as Black collectibles, and as Black caricatures in films. The new lynching narrative thus sat squarely on a continuum of the commercial exploitation of Black bodies, a racialized design of objectifying the Black body that was reconfigured in Texas during a historical moment when white identity sought alternative means of reinforcement.[60] Decades before Mencken's commentary, contemporary observers had already begun to draw parallels between white southerners' bizarre recreation tastes and lynching. "We venture to assert that seven-eighths of every lynching party is composed of pure, sporting mob, which goes nigger-hunting, just as it goes to a cock-fight or a prize-fight," asserted a journalist for the *Nation* in 1893.[61] Charles S. Johnson called lynching a "hybrid of sport-vengeance."[62] Two decades later, Mencken suggested that "lynching often takes the place of . . . the theatre, the symphony orchestra, and other diversions common to larger communities."[63] Scoffing at southern culture's inclination toward barbarism, he recommended that bull-fighting, a sport rife with violence, be instituted in the southern recreational scheme as a substitute for many southern whites' attraction to the lynching of African Americans.[64]

Most work on leisure has concentrated on associating it with, or studying it within the context of, specific types of conventional activities, including baseball, reading, quilting, visiting, and even less pious recreational indulgencies such as gambling and drinking. Indeed, the concept of leisure is as applicable to lynchings as it is to baseball, reading, card playing, or any other self-directed, conventionally understood recreational activity that generates pleasure for people during their nonwork hours. Several conventions determine how social scientists delineate leisure from other time expenditures. Leisure activities occur in time that is separate from work. Moreover, the activity is self-directed and discretionary, whether in an active or inactive state and is presumed to foster some level of enjoyment or pleasure. Thus, the literature on leisure largely validates activity or inactivity as leisure if an individual chooses to partake in and subsequently experiences enjoyment from engaging in it. Robert Steppins, a leading scholar of leisure studies, contends, "Leisure is actively defined as such by those engaging it."[65] A definition of leisure necessarily implicates the personal significance associated with an expenditure of free time; how one interprets an activity conducted during leisure time is essential to qualifying that activity as leisure, even if it contrasts with another person's preferences and convictions.[66] Therefore, that which renders particular activities leisure for certain individuals is not static. Furthermore, individual choice is informed by a variety of socializing processes. "What participants find appealing," Steppins further maintains, "stems from socialization, from what they learned through friends, family, culture, and the like."[67]

As demonstrated in this study, individuals' choices of leisure activities are a reflection of sociocultural, economic, as well as political phenomena and concerns, the intersecting of which permeated the work and home spheres in Texas during the later nineteenth and early twentieth centuries in ways that redefined leisure and subsequently quelled anxieties over change.

W. J. Cash's celebrated and telling *The Mind of the South*, a work that, as argued by Joel Williamson, is often reflective only of the static southern setting of Cash's own rearing, nonetheless provides a glimpse into southern whites' attitudes toward lynching that are relevant when discussing the complex correlation between collective violence and gratification. Lynching, Cash argues, "figured with rising force as a very model of heroic activity, and . . . this feeling played a constantly expanding role in the complex." [68] "Enjoyment," he adds, "grew apace with practice in the business."[69]

The new lynching culture in Texas moves beyond simply spectacle or consumerism. It bespeaks more than changes in industry and labor arrangements. Intersecting economic and sociopolitical changes, together with vicissitudes in popular and material culture, transfigured the act of lynching, and rendered it, for some, a new leisure activity. To continue to neglect or dismiss the relationship between lynching, race, and leisure is to deny the very contexts within which Black lives were trivialized in a manner that made spectacular, commercialized exhibitions of violence possible. It is, furthermore, to deny how, in measures small and large, the continuous devaluation of African Americans' worth haunts modern society.

Historically, Blackness has functioned as a complex determinant of racial interaction, domination, and racial disparities in the interpretation of crime and the application of justice. Certain phenomena rendered African Americans objects for both persecution and entertainment and placed an alternate value on their lives. A seemingly unbridgeable chasm between humanistic nuances and the permanence of a socially constructed existence frequently continues to define African Americans, promoting false notions of their supposedly innate predispositions toward criminality and violence. As a result, an entire people are often placed within the restrictive, at times perilous, confines of a particular conception of their existence and inclinations. While not central to this project, my research nonetheless helps to historicize why, for instance, persistent conflations of race and criminality influence the manner in which ostensibly neutral laws and legal practices have, in many instances, led to discriminatory disparities in varied judicial processes and law enforcement patterns. These disparities often reflect and reinforce perceptions about race and misconduct that emerged from historical processes of encoding Blackness with certain markers of inferiority, worthlessness, and threat. As famed Martiniquan philosopher, writer, and physician Frantz Fanon has mockingly declared in reference to the rigidity of racial perception: "Negroes are savages, brutes, illiterates."[70] This "myth," he implores, must "be destroyed at all costs."[71] A central goal for this study is to assist in destroying this lethal myth by contextualizing, at least in part, how the conflation of Blackness and criminality has pervaded an American consciousness and has been produced and reproduced across time and space. *Lynching as Leisure* recounts and contextualizes significant developments in the white perception of Black people following the Civil War, when Black freedom expressions, together with disruptions to the racial hierarchy, transformed how Black people would be recast and subjugated. This is crucial in understanding how African Americans would be perceived of as both criminally inclined and devoid of humanistic value.

The emergence of a new lynching culture in Texas evolved from expansive and intersecting modifications in migration, mechanization, recreation, racial alterity, as well as new interpretations of crime and justice. The following chapters will analyze these changes. *Lynching and Leisure* is divided into two sections. In three chapters, part 1, "Mastery of the Mob," examines the intersecting phenomena that allowed lynching to emerge and continue as a form of racialized social violence for decades following emancipation. Chapter 1 explores how local citizens' claims to the legitimacy and necessity of mob violence were intensified by shifting social and political boundaries after emancipation. Lynching became so tightly woven with ideas about political power, racial identity, reactions to Black expressions of freedom, racialized concepts of criminality, legal processes, and eventually feminine virtue that the perceived need for the practice opened a space for vast modifications and chilling regularities in the actual act by the close of the nineteenth century. Here I largely reject the notion of vigilantism. The actions of the mobs frequently became something that moved far beyond vigilantism, for such a characterization of the type of racialized social violence that took hold in Texas would suggest that the actions of mobs functioned outside of legal convention. Instead, I argue that white Texans created a new system of judicial norms. Melding the ethos of frontier-style justice with anxieties over Black freedom and progress born from the changing and complex interplay of whites and Blacks in the absence of slavery, the emerging pseudojudicial system forged by white Texas would supplant the processes of the state's judicial system. Through the mob violence that came to define racialized social control in the state, local whites produced a new system of norms that justified the wielding of power exacted by one racial group over another. A process of defining and addressing crime as it related to African American life in a post-emancipation era transcended and at times replaced legal convention, thereby authenticating mob violence in the state as a legitimate and widely acceptable judicial process. Lynching became justifiable killing and attendance at or participation in the act was a socially acceptable engagement of one's time. If they chose to interpret and engage in that event as leisure, they were free to do so.

In chapter 2, I analyze the meaning and ceremony of burning Black bodies. My research demonstrates that there is a discernible link between mob actions that involved allegations of physical or sexual assault of a white woman and the burning alive of the accused when the accused was a Black man. By the late nineteenth century, the collective violence exacted on Black Texans accused of committing certain crimes so frequently included burning that it added a torturous, visual image to the lynching narrative and further sanctioned the authority of the mob. Burning bodies effectively transformed extralegal murder into a highly visible, public spectacle that extended the domain and authority of the mob—a melding that both created the Foucauldian triumphant punishment and collapsed distinctions between anarchical and lawful authority. A death ritual that included burning was necessarily public, and the various details of its protocol—from apprehending the accused, to transporting the mob's prey to a particular site, to the performance of execution—required that the machinery of the law be superseded and that there be adequate lead time to disseminate knowledge of the impending event.

In chapter 3, I explore the correlation between increased urbanization and industrialization and the proliferation of racialized mob violence. As African Americans migrated to urbanizing eastern Texas towns that were infused with a tradition of slavery and white domination (the eastern three-fifths of the state), rivalry for subsistence wages mounted within the matrix of already flaring white racial tension, pitting white against Black and leaving whites' economic standing threatened. Migratory patterns also heightened racial anxieties over Black residential encroachment into white communities. Thus, the rise in industrial capitalism—not simply as a matter of increased free—or leisure—time, but as a factor that brought a growing number of African Americans and whites in closer, more frequent, unaccustomed contact with one another outside of the confines of enslavement—together with what whites perceived to be an increasing uncertainty about African Americans' place in society yielded yet more tension. African Americans' migration to towns and cities, and their attendant entry into labor markets, challenged the boundaries of subordination.

The remaining chapters, which are included in part 2, "For the People's Enjoyment," examine the ways white Texans interpreted the spectacle and commercialization of lynching. The chapters chronicle by what means the tangible and experiential relics of the act came to be assimilated into the same discursive space as other racialized imageries that were acknowledged sources of pleasure, novelty, and entertainment. In chapter 4, I argue that the material and popular culture procured from the death ceremony tended to render banal the brutality of racialized mob violence, which downplayed the archaic and grotesque nature of torture, and situated it within a bizarre matrix of modern recreational activity, social acceptability, and fond remembrance in the Jim Crow South. As Elizabeth Grace Hale argues, "like all cultural forms, over time lynching spectacles evolved a well-known structure, a sequence and pace of events that southerners came to understand as standard."[72] The ceremonial nature of lynching events in Texas—the methodology that became more tightly scripted with each occurrence, each aural and printed chronicling; the public, highly visible spectacle; the social acceptability—made the commercialization of racialized mob violence possible as it allowed the material emblems and representations of the experience to communicate an eerie script and thus vicariously implicated spectators and others who were not a part of the mob.

Chapter 5 examines how modern iterations of changes in transportation transformed how people thought about and engaged in racialized forms of social control and leisure. Lynching in Texas converted ordinary landscapes into sites of identity reification and cultural production as a result of changes in racial interface as well as the expanding tourism industry. Cultural historian John Sears argues that many Americans' disenchantment with the changing, industrializing urban landscapes by the second half of the nineteenth century encouraged a search for the sublime, a longing for the peaceful enjoyment of both natural phenomena and manmade attractions. In an utterly ironic fashion, tourism frequently provided an avenue for taking advantage of modern technology to assuage anxieties ushered in by industrial capitalism. Thus, during a time when disenchantment with Black migration and the attendant contestation over labor competition, Black prosperity, residential space, and increased social visibility heightened racial anxieties in Texas, lynching sites became critical spaces of identity reinforcement for whites.

Chapter 6 reveals how journalists for African American newsprints seized upon the recreational character and material culture of lynching in Texas as opportunities in their campaign to discredit and end the practice. The language and imagery of leisure filled articles, editorials, and published satirical commentary about mob violence in Texas, revealing in riveting detail how ritual murder was so often trivialized as amusement. Thus lynch mobs unwittingly provide the fodder upon which the Black press would capitalize to reach the conscience of the nation. With their meticulously detailed narratives of lynching as a barbaric form of leisure, journalists sought to shock their reading public out of its apparent apathy and generate widespread derision and disgust that could possibly work to eradicate racialized mob violence.

« | »

The meaning of the term *lynching* has historically been subject to much quarrel among antilynching advocates, which, as historian and scholar of lynching Christopher Waldrep argues, indicates that they "understood discourse as central to their struggle and fought hard to control it."[73] They "shaped definitions of lynching in order to further particular strategies."[74] Before fully examining how the character of lynching changed over time to create a new lynching culture, it is necessary to define how the term is used in this study. My definition adheres to those used by the key antilynching reformers who have historically investigated and chronicled lynchings in the United States, including the NAACP and Tuskegee Institute. I lean heavily on the consensus aspects of the definition constructed by those two organizations as well as others at an antilynching conference held in 1940. My definition also conforms generally with that used in both past antilynching legislation, as well as that put forth by Congress in the 2019 Emmett Till Antilynching Act.

On December 11, 1940, on the campus of Tuskegee Institute, the NAACP, the International Labor Defense (ILD), the Association of Southern Women for the Prevention of Lynching (ASWPL), and other leading antilynching organizations and activists as well as scholars of lynching met for a summit conference on lynching. The tasks at hand included the creation of a consensus definition of what constituted a lynching. After much debate, those present agreed to a definition of lynching that included four criteria. First, a dead body was essential to defining lynching. Therefore, for violence to qualify as a lynching, a person must have been killed. Second, that death must have been brought about illegally, i.e., outside of standard and codified judicial processes. Third, the murder must have been carried out by a group. Participants present at the conference argued the definition of a group. Many agreed that at least three people had to be involved in the mob murder of the lynching victim. They arrived at this number by adopting the quantity used in most antilynching legislation. By conference's end, however, this aspect of mob violence failed to adhere to a consensus definition; therefore, the term *group* remained amorphous. Much antilynching legislation, however, continued to adhere to a standard that required "three or more" persons as a qualifying requisite for group or mob. Finally, the conference attendees agreed that those involved in the lynching must have engaged in this form of extralegal violence as a perceived service to tradition, race, or justice. Scholars before and since the conference have used similar definitions of lynching to inform their studies of the act. The Emmett Till Antilynching Act acknowledges: "Lynching has been generally defined as a premeditated extrajudicial killing by a group. The term has been most often used to characterize informal public executions by a mob in order to punish an alleged transgressor or to intimidate a group. Lynching can also be employed as an extreme form of informal group social control."[75]

For many white Texans, hangings, burnings, draggings or other modes of lynching Black bodies—and all of the attendant fanfare including the purchasing of souvenirs and postcards, the viewing of photographic displays, the touring of lynching sites, the taking of excursion trains chartered specifically for transport to a lynching—were at times the focal point of one's entertainment. They were a novel or merely fun thing to experience, an activity to engage in during one's spare time. White Texans' use of phrases and words such as "barbeque," "pastime," "neck-tie party," and "carnival" to describe lynching demonstrates in part how they situated this form of social violence within a matrix of leisure.[76] Axioms such as the one spoken by one minister's wife to another during the burning of George Johnson in Honey Grove, Texas—"Come, I never did see a nigger burned and I mustn't miss the chance"—capture the novelty and excitement experienced by many white Texans in reference to lynching, while simultaneously alluding to the self-directedness of participation as well as the absence of shame and disapproval in their interpretation of lynching.[77]

Of course, recognizing that lynching served as an option for leisure for countless people challenges our better senses, and almost offends our conventional notions of recreation and pleasure, even in comparison with other activities considered to be socially deviant. Thus, the idea that people would take part in the lynching of a human being as a form of leisure may seem untenable. It is perhaps, today, at odds with one's better judgment to imagine that individuals could engage in such atrocities as those committed against Jesse Washington and garner enjoyment from it. Despite modern concepts of leisure activities, and regardless of the emotional difficulty inherent in reconceptualizing lynching as such, lynching functioned as a form of leisure for many. To deny this reality further denies how, in measures small and large, the devaluation of African Americans' worth continues to haunt modern society. By thinking too narrowly about what constitutes leisure, we are ignoring how intersecting social and economic phenomena changed how people interpreted what was a socially acceptable engagement of one's time, and how they thought about pleasure, punishment, race, crime, and social arrangements. We are dismissing how individuals redrafted the boundaries of recreational expression in response to racial hatred, distrust, jealousy, the competition for work, and other challenges of modern life. In sum, notions of what constitutes leisure are not static, but are instead historical constructs. To disregard how lynching often functioned as leisure is to misunderstand how leisure has frequently been reconstituted in ways that reified racial and social norms and quelled social anxieties at a given moment.

"We do not need the story of the Roman gladiatorial shows . . . to tell us that man is the one animal that is capable of getting enjoyment out of the torture and death of members of its own species," a journalist for the *Nation* observed in 1893.[78] The analogy reminds us that lynching was hardly the first form of human torture people watched and participated in for enjoyment.

« I »

Mastery of the Mob

CHAPTER 1

"This Is a Land of White Man's Rule"

Black Freedom Expressions, Mastery of the Mob, and the Postbellum Racialization of Crime

Black scars disfigure,
the ruddy cheeks of your new mornings in Dixie
(lynched Black men hanging from green trees)
Blind Justice kicked, beaten, taken for a ride
and left for dead . . .
Your Constitution gone blah-blah, shattered into a
thousand pieces like a broken mirror.

—FRANK MARSHALL DAVIS, 1935

The post Civil War household word among Negroes—
"He's an Uncle Tom!"—which denoted reluctant tol-
eration for the cringing type who knew his place before
white folk, has been supplanted by a new word from
another generation which says—"Uncle Tom is dead!"

—RICHARD WRIGHT, 1936

When Jesse Washington's lynchers delivered him—fettered, wounded, and likely terrified—to his inevitable death on the lawn of Waco's city hall, Mayor John R. Dollins stood at the window of his office gazing on the gory scene with great concern. As the lynchers tossed the swaying end of a chain fastened to the teenager's neck over the limb of a large tree that garlanded the lawn, the city's mayor observed the affair unfold. He was "not concerned about what they were doing to the boy," reported Elisabeth Freeman, investigator for the National Association for the Advancement of Colored People (NAACP).[1] Instead, the mayor worried about the damage that the tree might sustain. By the time the mob arrived with Washington at that tree on the city hall lawn, his clothing was saturated with blood from the stab wounds and beatings sustained in the streets of Waco as he was dragged by the chain affixed to his neck. As members of the mob raised Washington into the air, the teenager extended his arm upward and hastily grabbed the chain in a vain attempt to save himself before one of the lynchers severed his fingers from his hand. All the while, the mayor was reportedly troubled only by the peril that faced the tree. Perhaps it was quite a handsome tree, strong and sturdy, with each ring—one may imagine—functioning as a proverbial guardian of some witty or blissful tale from Waco's bygone years. Possibly Dollins spent countless, contemplative moments since his inauguration the previous month gazing upon the majesty of that tree, which was situated just outside his window. The leaves conceivably provided some measure of shade for Dollins on a warm, late spring day as he sat at his desk and carried out his mayoral duties. In the eyes of the city's leading public official, the importance of the tree clearly superseded the value of a Black youth's life. As Washington's blood-stained garb clung to his near lifeless body while he dangled above a burning mass of boxes and debris that would soon filch his last breath, Dollins watched. Beside the mayor stood another representative of the majesty of the law in Waco, Chief of Police Guy McNamara. Neither did anything to halt the determination of the crowd.[2]

In New York, officers of the NAACP lamented the distressing fecklessness of Waco's legal authorities. The "names of five of the leaders of the mob are known to this Association, and can be had on application by responsible parties," shrugged W. E. B. Du Bois; yet these officers of the law did not apprehend a single individual among the estimated fifteen thousand who participated in the lynching.[3] Neither state nor local officials asked the NAACP to cooperate in any investigation of Washington's murder. Texas authorities seemed resigned to allow local citizens to exact punishment through extralegal measures without consequence. The only person ever convicted and imprisoned for alleged crimes related to the lynching of Jesse Washington would be A. T. Smith, the African American managing editor of *Paul Quinn Weekly*, who was charged with libel for reprinting an article that claimed the person who actually murdered Lucy Fryer was her husband.

Freeman landed in the midst of investigative antilynching work for the NAACP by way of association with the organization's secretary, Royal F. Nash, a white social worker and former journalist. Early in 1916, Freeman was traversing the South on a speaking tour in support of women's suffrage aboard the same train as Nash, who was in the process of investigating continued racial violence against African Americans in Georgia. As Freeman exited the dining car one evening, she heard a familiar voice calling: "Well, Miss Freeman." She and Nash, who had not seen one another for two years, chatted all evening until he disembarked in Atlanta. When the national office learned about the lynching in Waco, Nash knew to contact Freeman, who was in Texas at the time of the lynching. "Such a spectacle in the town square," he wired, "affords one of the most spectacular grounds of attack on the whole institution of lynching ever presented."[4] Nash then entreated, "will you not get the facts for us?" A white English immigrant who moved to New York City with her family at the age of eleven, Freeman was never one to cower from confrontation. She recalled that her induction into the suffrage movement began rather haphazardly one afternoon: "I saw a big burly policeman beating up a woman, and I ran to help her, and we were both arrested. I found out in jail what cause we were fighting for."[5] Freeman appeared to be a logical choice to investigate Washington's lynching. "Your suffrage work will probably give you an excuse for being in Waco," Nash wrote.[6] Her race would, theoretically, further ensure her safety as she maneuvered in the public sphere probing the details of the lynching. Nash's assurance that her "presence would not be noticed" ultimately failed to fulfill its underlying promise of security and anonymity, however.[7] Freeman's hotel was searched on at least two occasions.[8] It seemed suffragist work proved unduly threatening to local residents.

Freeman reported that there were residents of the area who considered the Washington lynching—which the NAACP dubbed "the Waco Horror"—to be a gross miscarriage of justice; they feared coming forward, however, due to their anomalous stance and possible threats to their safety. A director at the *Waco Morning News* revealed that he "deplored the whole thing," but worried that a printed condemnation of the affair could negatively impact circulation.[9] "Colonel" Charles Hamilton, a white Pennsylvania native and local railroad general manager, confided in Freeman that he also opposed the lawlessness that brutally ended Washington's life; however, he grew concerned that a public stance against the act would result in his own murder. This collective unease plainly illustrates the widespread, matter-of-fact acceptance of lynching in the area. Fear of retribution and concern over speaking out against perceived racial norms precluded most local dissenters from voicing their contempt for the brutality that seemed to, at least temporarily, define their town in the national imagination.[10]

For the better part of the post-emancipation era stretching well into the twentieth century, white Texans' attendance at and participation in lynchings were safeguarded from judicial retribution, personal liability, and societal censure, as I argue in this chapter. Often, the only socially condemnable interpretation of a lynching was one that cast inimical judgment on the members of a lynch mob. Indeed, lynching appears to have been part of a broader narrative of a people in the process of redefining fear and fury as entertainment in the wake of disorienting changes. In that process, they fashioned a new lynching storyline from a set of interrelated phenomena. I further argue that the importance of understanding historically specific interpretations of crime, justice, and accountability is paramount here. White mob violence cannot be accounted for simply as an intensification of racist attitudes and suspicions in the post-emancipation era, but rather through transformations in which the criminal justice system was enlisted to sustain a particular racial hierarchy in the absence of a master-slave dyad. Understanding how Blackness and criminality became conflated beginning in postbellum Texas is essential to determining how lynching could evolve into a publicly condoned event often enacted with pomp and fanfare, an event frequently consumed as leisure.

Since early in the nineteenth century, white Texans espoused an interpretation of *justice* that condoned both the judicial authority of localized citizens and a resistance to influences outside of the local community—a collective violence that supplanted any state or locally codified judicial protocols with the will of the people. When Thomas Williams, a Black man accused of attempting to rape a white woman, found himself in the possession of a white crowd numbering in the thousands in Sulphur Springs, Texas, in 1905, his fate could not be deterred by local law enforcement agents who sought to uphold conventional judicial proceedings. Sheriff Jerry Lewis approached the leaders of the mob and asked that he be allowed to take Williams into custody. Williams's eventual lynchers refused to relinquish their prisoner: "No, he is in our hands, and he shall not be given a court house trial," a voice could be heard insisting from the crowd.[11] "The law is helpless in the face of a public sentiment that is older than our statute law itself," admitted a local reporter in 1916 while discussing the lynching of an African American man in Upshur, Texas.[12] In the citizens' view, justice was mercurial and redemption situational.

While mob justice would continue to define judicial processes well into the twentieth century, earlier lynchings were devoid of the spectacle, fanfare, and commercialism that would come to define the new lynching culture emerging late in the nineteenth century.[13] Mob violence prior to the last quarter of the nineteenth century, often exacted to punish such crimes as horse theft or murder, was frequently committed under the cover of night and resulted in a scene in which the victim, typically a white person, was left hanging with the body intact and the members of the mob unseen by the broader public.

Edward W. Riley's encounters reveal the manner in which frontier justice defined judicial processes in Texas communities before race became instrumental in the revised character of mob violence. Born in Tennessee, Riley migrated as a child to Texas with his family in 1877. Before the war, Riley's father, James D. Riley, owned a plantation. The family relocated to Texas in large part because the war gravely impacted their finances. Riley affirmed that his father "concluded to try and rehabiliate [sic] his financial position in Texas." Early one spring morning when Riley was still a young boy, he set out on horseback to find a fishing spot along the Brazos River near his home in Hill County, Texas, approximately seventy miles south of Dallas. "Just before I arrived at the woods a desire to catnap came on me and when I reached the timber I was dozing," Riley recalled. When he awakened, he saw a man hanging from a rope tied to a limb of a tree. The rope had loosened from the limb and left the man dangling only inches from the ground. The sight startled the young traveler. He quickly came upon a small group of men who informed Riley that they killed the man for stealing horses, an offense frequently punished by hanging at the hands of ranchers who distrusted the ability of law enforcement officials to adequately—if at all—deal with such crimes. Riley noted that dozens of mock trials, in which a local man served as judge and all citizens present voted to determine the verdict, were held under an oak tree near Grandview in the Trinity Creek bottom. Of the fifty-five trials he remembered occurring over the span of two years, eleven ended in hangings. The others resulted in whippings, expulsion from the county, or verdicts of innocence. Replete with a dismissal of formal statute, this frontier justice was commonplace in Texas until a new style of lynching emerged. Following Reconstruction, lynching would evolve from this earlier, strictly punitive and largely clandestine form of corporeal punishment into wholly racialized, publicly viewed, well-attended, frequently commercialized exhibitions of violence in which the vast majority of victims were Black, and the concept of crime included any action that challenged the racial hierarchy.[14]

If whites in Texas perceived of African Americans as dispensable degenerates—as often avowed by white editorialists and other public figures of the time—then white Texans' interpretation of justice offered the additional component necessary to justify not only the taking of Black life without due process but doing so in brazen public displays without fear of legal consequences. One's participation in a lynch mob, whether for revenge or for what Henry Louis Mencken referred to as a "gaudy good time," was exacted through a particular interpretation of judicial authority. Whether exercised within the confines of formal statute or simply in accordance with local public opinion, white people in Texas redefined procedural law and applied justice on a situational basis. White Texas communities had long believed they could unilaterally supersede the law as dictated by a specific event and the general mood of the people. In 1852, a white Texan expressed local citizens' conception of law in his book about frontier life in the state: "Statute law is but the formal expression of what the larger community deems wisest and most just for the general welfare. The small, crude, remote settlement does the same for itself; only without writing down its enactments, and in the more summary way enforced by its peculiar situation."[15] This construal of formal statute fit along a continuum of a frontier scheme of justice that dated back to the early white presence in the area. Local residents did not necessarily spurn formal law, but instead shared an expansive, nonconventional view of its applications. The homily of one white Texan expresses the pseudojudicial role of the local community: "If a crime is committed the accused has the whole community for judges and jury. If he is found guilty by common suffrage they proceed to execute the verdict."[16] By the late postbellum era, the mob, contended Frederick Douglass, "had assumed all functions of civil authority."[17] Race was explicitly at the center of what allowed for the supplanting of judicial processes with such impudence.[18]

The idea that the white community could act as judge and jury was inflected by a racial ideology that made local African Americans a special target for mob violence as it firmly established whiteness as occupying the highest rung on the racial hierarchy. Near the end of the nineteenth century, the *Waco Morning News* lambasted the notion that African Americans should be afforded due process, claiming that the "lustful sons of Ham" required something more agonizing than a trial and subsequent punishment.[19] The journalist insisted that people of the South had concluded "there are no 'good Negroes;' that the entire race is morally rotten, hopelessly corrupt."[20] Advocating for a perverse type of preemptive justice, the editorialist resolved that it was "better to shoot a Negro before he commits a hellish crime against the dominant race."[21] The following year, a number of Texas citizens "petitioned the Governor to suspend all laws as far as they relate to the Negro, and allow the people to be judges, juries, and executioners of every Negro their vengeance may fall upon," reported the *Baltimore Afro-American*.[22] "They are indeed asking a good deal," the journalist mocked.[23] In his early twentieth century booklet entitled *A Philosophy of Race Relations*, Bolton Smith called into question the purported guilt of lynching victims, positing that white residents of southern communities where lynching occurred simply wanted to kill African Americans: "If this negro had been guilty he would have been tried, for the white people know they could convict him easily if he were guilty, and if they lynched him it was because they felt that he was innocent. They wanted to kill him anyway. He is dead just because he was a negro. Had he been white, he would be alive now."[24] The lynching of African Americans was perceived of as justifiable homicide and attending and even participating in a lynching was a socially acceptable engagement of one's time, leisure or otherwise. It is this virtual absence of shame and punishment associated with participation in lynching that assisted in rendering the form of collective racial violence a justifiable way to reify the racial hierarchy and helped transform the practice into a communal pageantry of carnivalistic violence.

Race and the Malleability of Crime

The racial hierarchy was in flux following the Civil War, leading to a societal instability that white Texans refused to tolerate. Their inviolable commitment to patrolling racial boundaries in the absence of the master-slave regime broadened their interpretations of legal processes and thereby transformed the character of lynching. The white populace increasingly perceived itself to be a gratis regulatory body of constituents equipped with the powers of judicial review and summary justice that manifestly supplanted statutory processes.[25] Local citizens could and did act without (and at times with) sanction from the court, law enforcement agents, and public administrators in large measure because they assumed their ultimate authority to be judge, juror, and executioner of last resort. Their claims to the legitimacy and necessity of extrajudicial popular justice intensified in the context of shifting social and political boundaries after emancipation. Consequently, lynching became so tightly woven with ideas about political power, racial identity, Black expressions of freedom, race and criminality, legal processes, and eventually feminine virtue that the perceived *need* for the practice opened a space for chilling regularities in and matter-of-fact acceptance of such acts.

Lynching in Texas became something that often moved beyond vigilantism, for such a characterization of the type of racialized social violence that took hold in Texas would suggest that the actions of mobs functioned outside of legal convention. This study rejects the notion of vigilantism as a wholly applicable type of collective violence in Texas. Instead, a process of defining and addressing crime as it related to African Americans transcended and at times replaced legal convention, thereby frequently authenticating mob violence in the state as a legitimate and widely acceptable substitute for normal judicial procedure. Lynching became justifiable murder; by extension, attendance at, or participation in the act was a socially acceptable engagement of one's time.

Racialized mob violence exhibited spectacles of torture far exceeding any conceivable need to reveal and punish crime. These murderous displays seemed designed to punish the apparent crime of African Americans' very existence more than they sought to penalize any singular offense. The singular crime as such, then, did not independently produce modifications in lynching; instead, social and economic change did. While any given crime could certainly be punished through lynching, it was the race of the lynched, and more specifically how race was constructed and considered at a precise moment in time, that rendered a crime particularly egregious and in need of spectacle torture. In Texas, ceremony exposed and punished a crime, but the concept and weight of crime itself were malleable. When and by whom the crime was committed factored more heavily into the immoderations of spectacle-driven, collective, and even recreational violence than did the transgression itself. The proliferation of racialized lynching thus represented a postbellum conflation of Blackness and criminality that continuously refashioned the public image of African Americans. Indeed, the lynching of African Americans served as visual, visceral testimony, reinforcing the perception of Black criminality.

Scholars frequently argue that the social class of an alleged victim influenced the manner in which summary judgment was meted to African Americans accused of a crime.[26] Others similarly contend that lynch mobs were comprised nearly entirely of working-class or rural whites, and that middle- or upper-middle class whites avoided and condemned such affairs. Lynchings in Texas did not follow these heralded archetypes. It was not merely the lynching of African Americans who committed crimes against socially prominent whites or white women that drew individuals en masse to the sites of lynchings; nor were middle- or higher-class whites largely absent from mobs. There is a homogenization of class and race largely at play here. When juxtaposed with Blackness, whiteness stood as a singular social class. The social status of a crime's alleged victim—whether a lowly white tenant farmer or a respected white sheriff—mattered not if the accused was Black. African Americans accused of violent or nonviolent crimes against whites of any social stature were lynched by crowds numbering in the hundreds and even thousands, and present in those crowds were all classes of whites. Moreover, the continued existence of mob violence required some level of compliance from all aspects of society. "The mobocratic murderers are not only permitted to go free, untried and unpunished," Frederick Douglass fittingly contended, they are often "lauded and applauded as honorable men and good citizens, the guardians of Southern women. If lynch law is in any case condemned, it is only condemned in one breath, and excused in another."[27]

Lynching in Texas followed a specious legal code by the late nineteenth century, a new system of judicial norms that lent uniformity and normative value to mob violence against people of all races, but only for Black victims of lynching did it come to resemble an archaic form of ritualistic torture. The tightly scripted ceremony of lynching—replete with brutalization, agony, and ostentatious display—oddly paralleled, even as it mocked, the methodical character of legally codified protocols. How the Black body was captured and slayed, when and where it should be dragged and displayed, who should be present, the devices of torture deployed, and what body parts could be transformed into souvenirs became a part of the legalistic ritual, a system of judicial norms that frequently bore the imprint of modernity despite echoes of a pre-modern era. These visual demonstrations of reprisal, this unnerving adherence to a wicked script and organized violence, satisfied and fueled the crowd as Texans created and repeatedly recreated virtually the same lynching storyline, time after time.

Any crime committed by a Black person often signaled a broad call to action. Such incidents not only encouraged but ostensibly required a suspension of due process, or more specifically the use of pseudojudicial legal processes that were continuously recreated as threats to the racial hierarchy dictated. Speaking before a crowd in 1896, W. H. Fuller, a deacon in the

Cameron, Texas, Colored Baptist Church, denounced the claims of "leading Southern Journals" that charged Black men were lynched because they raped white women. "I want to tell you that I deny the assertion," he decreed. Instead, Fuller continued, they were lynched for charges ranging from "the frivolous charge of dishonesty . . . to the capital offence of taking human life."[28] Indeed, the list of offenses that forced the assemblage of a mob predictably involved crimes committed against the white body, including murder, rape, and assault. Dubious allegations such as flippantly responding to a white man, race prejudice, writing a letter to a white woman, and being too prosperous for a Black person were also counted as impudence punishable by mob violence.[29] When eighteen-year-old Charley Scott was hanged by a Texas mob in 1908, the following message was written on a placard affixed to Scott's feet: "This is a warning to all negroes who are caught prowling around white folks' houses."[30] A mob in Crosby, Texas, burned John White to death for allegedly stealing a watch. In more than one instance, Black men in Texas were lynched when white women declared that they wanted to marry them. After a mob lynched two unnamed Black men in Pilot Point, Texas, a note was affixed to the door of a local newspaper indicating why the men were murdered. It read as follows: "Both these negroes got what was coming. Let this be a warning to all negro loafers. Negroes, get a job or leave town."[31] This gamut of offenses, wavering between modern interpretations of criminal transgressions and the fiercely ridiculous, exposes the mutability of crime.[32] The idea of what constituted a crime clearly became something subject to unbelievably racist and horrific interpretations. Crime, then, is something defined by historically specific phenomena, by the nuances of a quotidian existence, by social interactions, political changes, and ideas about race and identity.

When a local sheriff found Ben Little—an African American man arrested in Mount Pleasant, Texas, in October of 1885—dead and hanging from a tree after a mob removed him from his cell, a note pinned to Little's back featured the following message:

> This negro was not hanged for the highway robbery he committed in Titus County last Wednesday, but for the slanderous talk he has had about a certain white family in Mount Pleasant, which we deem a scandal to the white race. The family is as innocent and pure as the angels in heaven, and we feel that we have not committed a sin in the sight of God, and furthermore, we feel that we have done a great and noble act for our country as gentlemen. Speak to the dead for further information.[33]

The note was signed "CITIZENS OF MOUNT PLEASANT TO THE NUMBER OF SIXTY-EIGHT."[34] Little's alleged transgression, as evidenced by both his death and the open message, was not the breaking of state laws regarding theft, but instead the verbal disparaging of a "certain white family" and the "white race" broadly.[35]

In another incident, eighteen-year-old William Sullivan was hanged by a mob, led by Deputy Sheriff James Augus, in Plantersville, Texas, in 1892 after he claimed that a white woman was his wife. Augus chained Sullivan to a ceiling column and traveled around the area inviting local residents to witness Sullivan's death: "This young nigger is smart and talks back to white people, and now is a good chance to remove him."[36] The coroner's inquest ruled the murder as "death at the hands of parties or party to the jury unknown."[37]

What appeared as seemingly benign activities gained potency when the perceived aggressor was Black and the racial hierarchy ostensibly threatened. White domination served as the superlative entity in an algorithm for what rendered a crime a crime; expressions of freedom, sovereignty, and advancement by Black people thereby functioned as crime in the same manner as violent misconduct. When analyzing the increased number of African Americans lynched during the later portion of the nineteenth century, Frederick Douglas determined the following:

> It is proof that the Negro is not standing still. He is not dead, but alive and active. He is not drifting with the current, but manfully resisting it and fighting his way to better conditions than those of the past, and better than those which popular opinion prescribes for him. He is not contented with his surrounding. . . . The enemies of the Negro see that he is making progress and they naturally wish to stop him and keep him in just what they consider his proper place. They who aspire to higher grades than those fixed for them by society are scouted and scorned as upstarts for their presumptions.[38]

In June of 1908, the Harkrider Drug Company in Center, Texas, published a postcard that featured the hanging of five Black men in Sabine County, located in the southeastern portion of the state near Louisiana. The poem and image were dually used as a cautionary and visual portrayal of the important conflation of race and place. The poem read as follows:

> This is only the branch of a Dogwood tree;
> An emblem of WHITE SUPREMACY.

"The Dogwood Tree," postcard, Texas, 1908

SCENE IN SABINE COUNTY, TEXAS, JUNE 15, 1908.

The Dogwood Tree.

This is only the branch of the Dogwood tree;
   An emblem of WHITE SUPREMACY.
A lesson once taught in the Pioneer's school,
   That this is a land of WHITE MAN'S RULE.
The Red Man once in an early day,
   Was told by the Whites to mend his way.

The negro, now, by eternal grace,
   Must learn to stay in the negro's place.
In the Sunny South, the Land of the Free,
   Let the WHITE SUPREME forever be.
Let this a warning to all negroes be,
   Or they'll suffer the fate of the DOGWOOD TREE.

Copyrighted   — *Pub. by Harkrider Drug Co., Center, Tex.*

"The Dogwood Tree" postcard published by Harkrider Drug Co., Center, Texas. *Papers of the NAACP, Series A, Part 7, Reel 1.*

A lesson once taught in the Pioneer's school,
That this is a land of WHITE MAN'S RULE.
The Red Man once in an early day,
Was told by the Whites to mend his way.
The negro, now, by eternal grace,
Must learn to stay in the negro's place.
In the Sunny South, the Land of the Free,
Let the WHITE SUPREME forever be.
Let this a warning to all negroes be,
Or they'll suffer the fate of the DOGWOOD TREE.[39]

In total, nine African Americans—not only the five depicted in the postcard—were killed by mob violence following the murder of Hugh Dean, a white farmer. The four who were not hanged from the tree were shot by members of the mob. Dean was killed by gunfire two weeks previous to the lynching while purchasing whiskey near a Black church in Sabine County. Friends discovered his body the following morning. A local African American man was accused of the murder. Law officers arrested six African American men for allegedly attempting to help him leave town. A mob of a hundred and fifty men removed the prisoners from the Sabine County Sheriff in Hemphill. Frank Williams was shot trying to escape. The other five men were bound and hanged on the dogwood tree.[40] No one was arrested for the lynchings. Once again, a mob's justice supplanted the conventional, state-organized legal structure.

The Shifting Value of Black Lives

Black life had not always been valued so cheaply, as the evolution and destruction of slavery makes clear. When Stephen F. Austin inherited the empresario commission granted to his father in 1821 by Spanish authorities, he ensured that settlers would earn eighty acres of land for each slave they owned and brought to the area. When Texas gained its independence from Mexico in 1836, the total population of the state stood at over thirty-eight thousand, including five thousand enslaved Blacks. The Constitution of the Republic of Texas, established that same year, assured slaveholders that they could migrate to Texas with their human cargo from the United States. Section 9 of the General Provisions indicated the following:

> All persons of color who were slaves for life previous to their emi-
> gration to Texas, and who are now held in bondage, shall remain

in the like state of servitude, provide the said slave shall be the bona fide property of the person so holding said slave as aforesaid. Congress shall pass no laws to prohibit emigrants from the United States of America from bringing their slaves into the Republic with them, and holding them by the same tenure by which such slaves were held in the United States. . . .[41]

White planters moved to the Republic en masse, enslaved people in tow. Migratory patterns, together with an extensive illegal trade of people imported directly from Africa, increased the number of bondsmen in Texas to 58,161 by 1850, which constituted just over 27 percent of the 212,592 people in the state.[42] The increasing number of enslaved peopled facilitated a marked growth in cotton production the following decade. During the 1850s, production of the staple crop increased by approximately 600 percent, facilitated largely by enslaved labor. By the eve of the Civil War, the enslaved population, now just over 30 percent of the total population, rose steeply to 182,566, the vast majority of whom resided in the eastern three-fifths of Texas. In a Galveston market at that time, a field hand could garner as much as $1,800. By contrast, an aging or ill enslaved person would sell at a substantially reduced rate. Black women who were both lighter-skinned and considered attractive, frequently referred to as *fancy*, could be sold for several thousand dollars.[43]

Expectedly, a disproportionate number of racialized lynchings in the post-Civil War period would occur in the portion of the state where slavery thrived. During the antebellum period, however, "economic interests" often "sav[ed] Negroes from lynch-law" notes Walter White in *Rope and Faggot: A Biography of Judge Lynch*, his prominent 1925 study on mob violence. White's recounting of Frederick Law Olmsted's interview with an antebellum Virginia planter is revealing. Concerned that his slaves would perish while draining swamps, the planter insisted "a negro's life is too valuable to be risked. . . . If a negro dies, it's a considerable loss."[44] Of course, this anxiety over mortality rarely translated to a concern for overall health or familial ties, nor did it impede violent punishment. The culture of slavery normalized the relationship between violence and the patrolling of racial boundaries—a monitoring, however, that typically, but not always, stopped short of death. With few exceptions in the state of Texas, such as a mass lynching of African Americans in North Texas in 1860 after rumor of an impending slave insurrection circulated, the utility of bondage precluded an excess in lethal punishments such as lynching for enslaved African

Americans. Historian Michael J. Pfeifer's work on antebellum lynchings demonstrates that at times, enslaved African Americans were lynched when white slave owners or local magistrates considered the value of the statement or warning engendered by the lynching to outweigh the value of the individual slave as property. "The lynching of slaves," Pfeifer argues, "transpired when the master's claim to the protection of their investment in human property was effectively nullified, either through a slave's murder of a master or his family or by the white community's insistence that the collective execution of a slave outside of law served a good greater than the preservation of the value of the master's investment."[45] In 1859, a mob in Navarro County hanged an enslaved person who belonged to a Mr. Blanton. Under Texas law, if the state sanctioned and carried out a legal hanging of a slave, the enslaver would be financially compensated for their loss of property. The mob that hanged Blanton's slave offered compensation in recognition of the financial loss suffered by Blanton. While other similar incidents occurred in Texas prior to the end of the Civil War, they did not represent a pattern of lethal, racialized terror.[46] "Slaves' position as the investment of masters provided some protection from the legal consequences of serious crimes and the racial antipathies of non-slaveholding whites," argues Pfeifer.[47] There are several scholars now working on studies that examine the lynching of enslaved persons. Their work is sure to add significantly to our understanding of the system of slavery's unrelenting violence against Black bodies. Their work does not, however, refute nor challenge the fact that the lynching of enslaved people in Texas or the South at large was relatively rare compared to racial terror lynchings that followed emancipation. The majority of those lynched during the antebellum era in Texas, for instance, were not African American. The value of Black lives in southern society waned significantly once removed from the master-slave dyad. Following the abolishment of slavery, white Texans still had a material interest in Black bodies but could take advantage of them much more cheaply through sharecropping and convict leasing, rendering African Americans increasingly dispensable—so much so that 469 would meet their death at the hands of mob violence between 1868 and 1950, while only ten African Americans were killed by mob violence in the state between 1824 and 1862.[48]

During the winter of 1860, Texas delegates to the state convention approved an ordinance of secession by a vote of 166 to 8. Approximately 70 percent of the delegates were slave owners. By the end of March 1861, Texas had joined the Confederacy. Over the next several years, planters from surrounding southern states moved those whom they enslaved to Texas in an effort to keep them away from Union troops who could secure their free-dom. As a result, the state's enslaved population reached nearly one quarter of a million by the war's end.[49]

When General Gordon Granger, accompanied by approximately two thousand Union troops, arrived in Galveston, Texas, on June 18, 1865, he was conceivably weary. Texas had remained unoccupied by Union forces until Granger's arrival. The day after his troops landed at the littoral city—in a tale some argue is given more to legend than reality (some say he actually stayed perched on his horse)—Granger purportedly stood atop the city's Ashton Villa hotel and read the words that would level the racial hierarchy in the state of Texas. Whether or not the location from which he read is aggrandized, what remains undisputed are the words he read from General Order No. 3:

> The people of Texas are informed that, in accordance with a proc-lamation from the Executive of the United States, all slaves are free. This involves an absolute equality of personal rights and rights of property between former masters and slaves, and the connection heretofore existing between them becomes that between employer and hired help. The freedmen are advised to remain quietly at their present homes and work for wages.[50]

The federal dictate Granger presented demolished the world that white Texans had created. The *Texas Almanac for 1870, and Emigrant's Guide to Texas* printed a column on the state's cotton crop that reveals much about how African Americans were perceived in the state. African Americans, the columnist insisted, should be "indebted" to slavery for their "advancement, originally, from a state of humanity the lowest and most degraded known to mankind, to one comparatively civilized."[51] It expressed fear that, "released, as the negro now is, from the coercive guidance and control of the white man, his rapid deterioration is inevitable."[52] "An absolute equality of per-sonal rights and rights of property" between white and Black people, as described in the order Granger read, seemed inconceivable to those invested in the value of their whiteness, a value inextricably tied to the debased status of African Americans. In the now pending absence of a stark divide between white and Black, and the dismantling of a labor system that firmly subjugated Blackness, white Texans would work to restrict Black freedom and halt Black progress.[53]

Following the Civil War, white Texans vehemently sought ways to subjugate freedmen and their progeny. "Beginning with the emancipation of the Negro," antilynching advocate and journalist Ida B. Wells tutored in 1895, "the inevitable result of unbridled power exercised for two and a half centuries, by the white man over the Negro, began to show itself in acts of conscienceless outlawry."[54] Emancipation had triggered the ultimate disruption in the racial hierarchy. The short-lived black codes, implemented during Presidential Reconstruction, only vanquished Black freedom temporarily following the war. The placement of troops in Texas during Congressional Reconstruction—as well as the presence of agents from the Bureau of Refugees, Freedman and Abandoned Lands—helped to safeguard Black sovereignty, particularly Black political power, following the war, and somewhat quell white violence against freed people. It did not, however, eliminate violence, as freed people were regularly attacked by local whites before the end of Reconstruction in the state. "The reign of terror is set up in the county," Joe Easley, a freedman, wrote to the Texas Bureau of Refugees, Freedman, and Abandoned Lands from Sulphur Springs, Hopkins County, Texas, on July 17, 1868.[55] "I will not undertake to give a minute description of it; time and space is not sufficient. Suffice it to say that the history of the darkest ages of the world does not, in my estimation, afford a parallel," he averred.[56]

The postbellum period in Texas ushered in a new system of racialized control, one that incorporated frontier justice with a renunciation of the value of Black lives. This complex interplay made Black freedom expressions intolerable acts that required the firm reestablishment of white dominance and Black subjugation. Postwar social arrangements altered how many southern white people approached and exacted racialized social control as they reconfigured what qualified as imprudence. "Coupled with fear of the Negro politically," White contended in reference to the growing unease of southern whites during the post-emancipation period, "was fear of Negro's economic progress." Jim Crow laws would emerge later in the century, but the incremental nature of their implementation would leave a space for unchecked Black progress. In the midst of immense and troubling changes following the Civil War, white Texans became the saboteurs of Black advancement; consequently, attempts to arrest any appearance of Black sovereignty became one of the hallmarks of Reconstruction.[57]

Growing racial conflict in the state during the post-Civil War period presented an expansive view of a formula for the execution of mob violence without fear of judicial retribution, one in which Blackness itself stood as the key provocation for violent attack. Of course, defending the supposed and socially constructed virtue of white womanhood factored prominently into acts of violence committed against African Americans well into the twentieth century. "The manhood of this state can always be depended upon to protect its womanhood and the sanctity of the home," boasted a journalist in defense of the lynchers who burned an African American man to death in 1915.[58] Considered the ultimate offense against white southern culture, the trampling of white, female virtue was an action that did not require evidence, merely an accusation to entice a mob to act against the accused. "I can not [sic] tell if he is the negro; but I can't tell if he is not the negro," admitted Winnie Harmon in May 1909 of her alleged attacker.[59] Despite her doubts, a mob of white people hanged James Hodge. When Carrie Johnson, a white woman in Tyler, Texas, was allegedly attacked by a Black man, she could not identify her attacker. Daniel Davis was nonetheless arrested and then burned by a mob numbering approximately two thousand people after a local white man claimed to have seen Davis in the area prior to the attack. At times, even direct culpability was unnecessary. For instance, George Gay, a twenty-five-year-old Black man from Streetman, Texas, was shot and chained to a tree by a mob numbering one thousand in December 1922. Gay's alleged crime was that he was the uncle of a man accused of assaulting a white woman. The dialectic of the sex-crazed Black brute and chaste white woman, however, developed over time. Walter White's observations are significant here: "charges of rape were made with increasing frequency as a greater number of lynchings and more brutal methods of execution of the victims brought vehement condemnation of lynching from other parts of the country."[60] Indeed, his observations find credibility in an analysis of lynchings in Texas.[61] During the immediate postwar period, what mattered more than white womanhood as a factor for unchecked violence, however, was Blackness itself.

The unchecked violence unleashed on African Americans during the period provided an appearance of justice, one that recreated the idea of justice itself, with the reification of white identity and supremacy as the final determinants for punishment. Fraught with the proliferation of racially restrictive legal and extralegal measures, the postbellum era was one of mounting opposition to change, an analysis of which discloses how racialized social conflict became violently collectivized. Increasingly, the concept of a good, just, and orderly post-emancipation society incorporated an evolving rhetoric of Black criminality and attendant modes of racial control, thereby igniting a period of brutality that markedly demonstrated intensifying white resistance to change. This, in due course, gave way to a culture and variety of lynching void of shame or reprimand and frequently wrought with amusement.[62]

White Texans' commitment to firmly marking racial boundaries outside the polemic of bondage resulted in striking incidents of violence following the Civil War. To supervise concerns and discord produced by emancipation, Congress established the Bureau of Refugees, Freedmen, and Abandoned Lands—commonly referred to as the Freedmen's Bureau. Commissioned to ease the transition from slavery to freedom for African Americans, the organization frequently extended aid to poor whites as wells. Created by the War Department in March 1865, the Freedman's Bureau's duties included the legalization of marriages, the overseeing of labor contracts, the establishment of schools, and the reunification of families separated by war or enslavement.[63] By fall, the Freedman's Bureau operated in Texas and quickly began to receive complaints that reveal how the redrafting of racial boundaries engendered vicious responses from local whites. Records of the bureau are teeming with reports of brutal hostility toward freedmen.[64] Incidents from the reports of Captain William H. Horton, the Subassistant Commissioner of the 40th District, are worth recounting here to recreate the milieu of postwar racial interface. Horton's territory included the eastern central counties of Dallas, Ellis, Tarrant, and Johnson, an area that encompassed the cities and surrounding areas of Dallas and Fort Worth. Horton was clearly troubled by the occurrences of violence white Texans who ostensibly feared the destruction of white supremacy carried out against newly freed African Americans. His reports reflect how many local whites brazenly dismissed the regulatory function of a government-sanctioned entity that sought to maintain law and order. Horton's inclusion of the following incidents, a sampling of the complete record, offers a glimpse into the racial violence that defined the Reconstruction era in Texas:

> August 1, 1865—Two freedmen were killed by William Spencer [white] after he ordered them to return to their former master and they refused. When Horton commanded Spencer to report to the Bureau offices on charges of murdering freedmen, Spencer wrote to Horton that he did not recognize his authority and would not comply with the order.
>
> August 30, 1865—Charity, a freedwoman of color [appears as F.W.C. in the records], was tied to a log by George Baird [white] and given 100 lashes after she entreated Mrs. Baird [white] not to flog her daughter. The situation "really demands attention" Horton

ardently averred. He insisted that Charity and her daughter were exposed to "infernal treatment." Charity's alleged crime was begging the Bairds to protect her daughter from sexual assault from a "favorite black" man of the Bairds.

September 1865—Mr. Buchanan [white] dragged a freedman of color [appears as F.M.C. in the records] named John by horse for several miles. When Buchanan stopped and attempted to kill him, John managed to escape.

September 1, 1865—Two white men, Amos Foulkner and Mark Lively, hanged John Winn, an F.M.C., "to make him disclose things that he knew nothing about."

November 1865—Mr. Morse [white] "inhumanely" beat Margaret, a F.W.C., for desiring to leave her employ.

July 1865—A white man whipped then threatened to kill Ellen, a F.W.C., for attempting to leave his employ.

September 1866—A F.W.C. named Kate died after Mr. Coleman [white] beat her on the head with pistol.

June 1867—Mr. Barclay [white], the owner of a hotel in Dallas, whipped a F.W.C. so viciously that she was unable to work for days. Horton noted that Barclay had previously fired a servant for informing the Subassistant Commissioner that he feared for his life. Mr. Barclay insisted, noted Horton, that "he wouldn't have a servant that thought enough of a damn Yankee to inform them of any designs to kill them."[65]

Additional entries reveal extensive incidents of white men beating their Black female employees to near death for refusing their sexual advances. In one particularly contemptible encounter, a white man named Wilson shot and killed a formerly enslaved man who was standing on the steps of a church in Dallas. The freedman was carrying a child at the time.[66] Horton wrote in a remarkably telling report that of the fifty cases he took to the grand jury, he could not get a single indictment. Scornfully, he later confessed, "[i]n regard to a Freedman getting justice by the Civil Authorities where a White man is involved it's all a farce. They know no rights that the Negro possesses when in conflict with a White man."[67]

Violent attacks in other portions of the state also bear a fundamental consistency that further reveal how Texas whites waged a brutal, postemancipation struggle for the preservation of white supremacy. Southeast of Dallas, in Washington County, for instance, the former master of a freedman who was protesting his continued enslavement shot the freedman for his "boldness."[68] In the East Texas County of Rusk, a Black mother and her child were murdered for attempting to seek alternative employment opportunities. In Waco, the county seat of McLennan in east-central Texas, a white man shot his former slave because "she gave saucy words to her mistress."[69] In Grayson County, a white man fired upon a freedman after passing him in the road. Neither man knew the other, nor had they spoken a word. In Fort Bend County, near Houston, a white man fatally shot a freedman standing outside of a Freedmen's Bureau's office. With few exceptions, the recorded acts went unpunished.[70]

By 1868, mounting racial violence in Texas captured the attention of the United States Congress. Members from both houses authored a report that sought to investigate and explain the extensive racial violence that had occurred in the state during the first few years of Reconstruction. Entitled the "Report of the Special Committee on Lawlessness and Violence in Texas," it was submitted to Congress and the Texas Constitutional Convention in June of 1868. Compiled from State Department records, sworn witness statements, and Freedmen's Bureau records, the report included acts of violence which, collectively, create an impression that is hardly startling: racial tensions following emancipation kept pace with increasing assertions of freedom by formerly enslaved African Americans. The report, for example, chronicled multiple instances of freed people driven from their homes and crops by "rebel" whites. In Marion County, "bands of armed whites . . . travers[ed] the county, forcibly robbing freedmen of their arms, and committing other outrages upon them."[71] While such acts of intimidation concerned committee members, it was the homicides carried out between the end of the war and the first of June 1868 that captured most of the committee's concern. During that period, at least 373 freedmen were killed by whites, while ten whites were killed by freedmen in the state, figures which, by the committee's own admission, are likely incomplete considering the sources they used for their statistics did not include a survey of all Texas counties.[72] At least one source only included cases in which an indictment had been secured. Unsurprisingly, whites who were loyal to the Union and the Republican Party were also caught in the fold of bloody mayhem. The committee insisted "we are authorized by facts to affirm, that multitudes who participated in the rebellion, disappointed and maddened by their defeat, are now intensely embittered against the freedmen on account of their emancipation and enfranchisement, and on account of their devotion to the Republican Party, and against the loyal whites for their persistent adhesion to the Union."[73] This "feeling of animosity," they insisted, "prompts and inspires them" to murder in many cases.[74] Contempt for Union sympathizers was violently evident long before the war's end: in October of 1862, vigilantes hanged forty-one Unionists over the course of thirteen days in what would be known as the "Great Hanging in Gainesville."[75]

Attempting to deconstruct the impetuses for the genocidal nature of bloodshed in the state, the committee added that lethal hostility toward freedmen was further "unrestrained" by the absence of a concern for "retribution."[76] Some law enforcement officers wanted to arrest whites who committed crimes but were fearful of and intimidated by local citizens. When a sheriff in one county called upon his constituents to aid in the arrest of criminals in the area, citizens replied, "Call on your nigger friends."[77] In many instances, officers resigned due to the difficulty of forcing citizens to comply with the execution of laws. At other times, however, law officers aided local citizens in their vigilantism or endorsed lawlessness by simply disregarding its existence.[78] Evidence demonstrated, the committee surmised, that the "criminal laws of the State are not executed," and, consequently, "bad men do not fear the civil courts of Texas."[79] "Why should they?" they quipped, a hopeless inquiry fashioned largely from the derisory rate of murder convictions in the state.[80] During the three years that followed the close of the war, just over nine hundred reported murders occurred in the state, with 249 indictments and only five convictions, according to the State Department records ascertained by the committee. One of those five convictions resulted in a capital execution that conformed to statute: an ex-slave was executed in Harris County. The committee woefully concluded: "It is our solemn conviction that the courts, especially juries, as a rule, will not convict ex-rebels for offences committed against Union men and freedmen; neither will they award judgments in favor of Union men and freedmen as against rebels."[81] A group of ex-rebels assaulted a "loyal man" (a Union supporter) with deadly weapons on three separate occasions. The man provided a sworn statement regarding the attackers' identities, yet the sheriff refused to arrest them. A white man who viciously beat and attempted to murder a freedman was arrested by a Freedman's Bureau agent. The local authorities took over the case and sent the assailant to trial. A jury found him guilty and fined him a penny. A different case also ended in the conviction of a white man who committed a crime against a former slave. The case had an all too familiar ending: the man was released from jail. When Freedman's Bureau agents protested, the courts retorted that they "would not send a white man to jail for a nigger."[82] This fundamental consistency of outcomes led African Americans to the inescapable conclusion, according to the Congressional Committee, that the courts were "employed as engines for their oppression."[83]

There was an immeasurable confidence inherent in an awareness that there was no risk of punishment for crimes against Black people. The freedman's very presence ostensibly threatened a normative hierarchical structure in which southern white people dominated the highest rungs. An assurance that one would likely avoid prosecution, or retribution in any form, surely belied the inclination toward violent expression. Such unwillingness to arrest or prosecute white Texans who committed transgressions against African Americans—or white people who were loyal to the Union—functioned as an endorsement of criminal behavior against a definable other. Thus, Texas's judicial system served as an accomplice of sorts in the committing of certain crimes, a virtual coconspirator in a campaign designed to reprove formerly enslaved people, and at least for a time, white Unionists. This failure of the judicial system to prosecute whites who committed crimes against African Americans was hardly confined to the postbellum era. As late as 1933, for instance, a sheriff in Beaumont, Texas, told a journalist that he willingly gave the body of David Gregory to a mob of three-to-four hundred after members of the mob shot and killed him. Gregory was accused of murdering Nellie Williams Brockman, a white woman and wife of a local farmer. Officers alleged that they shot Gregory after he brandished a pistol when they discovered him hiding in a church. He died, they reported, while they were transporting Gregory to a hospital. When a mob attempted to claim Gregory from officers, the sheriff insisted, "I let them have the body. I figured I'd rather give up the body of a dead negro than shoot a white man."[84] Members of the mob then cut Gregory's heart out of his chest, burned his body, and fastened his remains to an automobile before dragging them through the town. The state's failure to enforce the law worked largely to remove shame from acts of violence, particularly when targets of that violence were Black. Not only was violence for the purpose of firmly establishing a hegemonic arrangement tolerable, violent resistance to change was increasingly being equated with justice.[85]

Black Freedom Expressions and Violent Backlash following the Civil War

White Texans' efforts to return African Americans to an existence that nearly as possible resembled slavery resulted in growing dissonance and countless acts of racialized violence, as the Freedman's Bureau records and the Report of the Special Committee on Lawlessness begin to make apparent. While Black people attempted to maneuver the postwar social and political landscapes, Black autonomy gestured toward a shift away from the hegemonic arrangements to which white Texans had become accustomed. African Americans in Texans welcomed the postwar era with a spirited readiness to further increase their social and economic autonomy. Black migratory patterns—which often situated freedmen near extant white settlements—and the attendant establishment of Black communities replete with markers of communal advancement including businesses, churches, and schools; together with freed people's mere liberated presence signaled a societal reordering that left many Texas whites stultified. In 1867, for instance, formerly enslaved people in Fort Bend County, near Houston, were hosting an event to raise funds for the completion of their church. During the festivities, two white men riding past fired pistols into the church where the congregants gathered to sing. Despite such determination to arrest Black autonomy, African Americans in the state pushed forth in their community-building. Included in those efforts was a discernible zeal to exercise newly established political power by promoting political affirmations in local newspapers, partaking in partisan activities such as national conventions, and voting.[86] Political empowerment was one of the most poignant and authoritative expressions of freedom. Through this emblem of citizenship, African Americans could direct the political current, especially as it impacted the trajectory of their personal and communal lives. This assertion of freedom proved to be all too precarious, however, as it was subject to the disabling effects of those determined to hinder any advancement of African Americans.

Events that unfolded following the war in the southeastern Texas town of Millican, located in Brazos County, were largely archetypical of the racial encounters that served as a foundation for decades of discord and violence. The political involvement of African Americans in the community, coupled with their creation of sovereign communal institutes, unnerved local whites and forged an algorithm for dissonance that begins to reveal how race was constructed and considered at a precise historical moment. Named for the river that dissects it, Brazos County was, by 1850, populated by 466 whites and 148 enslaved Blacks. By 1860, the Houston and Texas Central Railroad brought accelerated growth to the area; Millican served as the railroad's terminus. When the Civil War commenced, the white population rose to more than seventeen hundred while the Black population stood at just over a thousand; all of the latter were enslaved. Local white men formed multiple Confederate regiments, and the terminus in Millican functioned as a vital transportation center for the Confederacy until June of 1865 when federal troops marched into Brazos County, just ahead of the Reconstruction turmoil that, in many ways, served as a microcosm of the macro-level social and political conflicts that would define race relations in the state for more than a century.[87]

By the close of the war, the Freedman's Bureau operated in Millican. Both Brazos and Grimes counties, as well as a portion of Burleson County, comprised the Bureau's 20th Subdistrict, which included a near equal distribution of African Americans and whites, each group numbering just over thirteen thousand. Upon his arrival, the Bureau's agent in Millican was busy mediating multiple conflicts between ex-slaves and whites, from varied acts of intimidation toward African Americans to labor contract disputes. Racial tensions in the area culminated by July of 1868 in what historians now consider a racial massacre. The entire summer, however, was largely defined by violent skirmishes between the races beginning with a critical encounter in June. As African Americans in Millican busily established autonomous organizations following emancipation, these symbols of freedom that eclipsed false notions of incompetence maddened local whites. A Black church in Millican stood among those autonomous markers of liberty; the plot is largely complicated, however, by the political activism of both the church's congregants and its pastor. Historians have typically attributed the events that unfolded outside the town's Black church in June of 1868 to angst over Black political participation. It is nearly impossible, however, to accurately determine which of the expressions of freedom most incited racial animosity: political activism or institutional autonomy. The church and its congregants, then, embody the complex entanglements inherent in this narrative of postwar vicissitudes. Despite the challenges intrinsic to isolating impetuses for derision, what remains clear is that Congressional intervention and the consequent presence of federal troops did little if anything to dissuade violence.

General Philip Sheridan's arrival in Texas by March of 1867 ostensibly signaled the beginnings of a new era of racial harmony. Surely federal troops, empowered by a United States Congress that heralded its commitment to the civil rights of freedmen, would safeguard the newly proclaimed citizens from the animosities of former Confederates and their sympathizers. Since before the war's end, Congress stood at odds with both President Abraham Lincoln and his successor over how to most efficiently and equitably reunite the country. Following Lincoln's death, Andrew Johnson's steady aversion to extending the franchise to formerly enslave people was interrupted by Radical Republicans with the implementation of Congressional Reconstruction and the First Reconstruction Act (1867), which extended suffrage to Black men. Appointed to oversee the affairs in the fifth military district of Texas, General Sheridan's first actions included the removal from state and local office of hundreds of secessionists who had been elected the previous year. The unseated officials, considered disloyal to the Union, could not be trusted to safeguard the civil rights of ex-slaves. Federal agents replaced them with white Unionists and Republicans, both white and Black, to serve at least until the state constitutional convention the following year. Those removed from office included officials from Millican and other portions of Brazos County. Sheridan also designated three-man boards of registrars for each county in the state to supervise voter registration of African Americans and enforce efforts to prevent the registration of former Confederates. He selected George E. Brooks to head the panel in Brazos County. A former slave, Methodist minister, teacher, and organizer of the local Loyal Leagues designed to educate freed people about the political process, Brooks was considered a leader in Millican's Black community. By July, Brooks began his registrar duties, before a yellow fever epidemic that would, together with the opening of the H&TC Railroad in nearby Bryant, drive much of Millican's population to the county seat by fall.[88] He also assumed the helm of a local church.[89]

One Sunday morning in June of 1868, approximately fifteen Ku Klux Klan members marched outside the doors of the Black church in Millican. Service was underway with Brooks as the presiding pastor. The parade proved too alarming for the worshippers. Male congregants emerged through the doors of the wood-framed church with pistols drawn and a sturdy determination to halt any progression of the hooded menace. An exchange of gunfire lasted just long enough for the veiled assailants to disperse, leaving only pieces of Klan regalia scattered on the ground. This invasion, this parade of terror that sought to trample on the sovereignty of freed people, signaled to Millican African Americans that they must mobilize efforts to protect their community. Men in the town formed a militia, led by Brooks. Approximately two hundred Black men marched every Saturday for weeks. Armed and striding with military precision, the Black militia held drills in full view of local whites. The sight of these men carrying weapons and practicing military formations incited increasing anxiety among disgruntled local whites. Freedman's Bureau representatives attempted to mitigate the discord to no avail. They informed Millican whites that African Americans would dissolve the militia when the Klan ceased to harass them. After weeks of fruitless negotiations and multiple standoffs, rumors circulated that a Black member of the local Loyal League had been lynched. Brooks gathered the militia and headed to the home of the suspected lyncher, a white man who was a member of a once prominent slaveholding family. While in pursuit, they encountered groups of armed white men, many of whom hailed from the surrounding area and traveled by train to join in the fray. The ensuing "riot" or "war," as characterized by newspapers of the time, involved hundreds of people and left at least dozens of African Americans dead. Brooks went missing for more than a week. When his badly decomposing body was found, it could only be identified by his right hand, which was missing one finger. Federal troops once again occupied the area in a futile attempt to restore peace. Racial violence there ebbed and flowed for decades.[90]

Such altercations as those between African Americans and whites in Millican serve as mere episodes in a statewide saga of mounting tensions over postwar social and political changes. Conflicts in the town function, in many ways, as a primer to expose and deconstruct the complexities of collective violence in Texas during the early years of Reconstruction. Several lessons emerge from the pages. For instance, as historian Joel Williamson has poignantly argued, African Americans' calculated response to white aggression runs counter to the notion—one heralded as truth at the time and thereby dragged into our modern collective consciousness—that their euphoria over freedom was somehow imprinted with a "child-like jubilee."[91] Exultation did not stand in contrast to militaristic miens of self-preservation; indeed, African Americans demonstrated a very definable willingness to protect their homes and communities through armed resistance when necessary. Next, Black political and social autonomy revealed competency in the face of adversity as it blurred the boundaries of African Americans' place in society. W. E. B. Du Bois's imputations are noteworthy: "the white South feared more than Negro dishonesty, ignorance and incompetency, Negro honesty, knowledge, and efficiency."[92] It is what Millican exposes about the notion of misconduct and the application of justice, however, that is most significant here. What amounted to brutal retaliation for emancipation, in turn, sanctioned a reliance on violence to reestablish white dominion.

The Lynching of Allen Brooks and the Mob's Authority

On Thursday, March 3, in 1910, a mob in the downtown streets of Dallas, Texas, hanged Allen Brooks, who was accused of "criminally assaulting" Mary Ethel Buvens, a two-and-a-half-year-old white girl. "Brute's Crime;

A Mob's Vengeance. Judge Lynch Takes Possession of the Court House and Deals Out Justice to Allen Brooks," read the front page of the *Dallas Daily Times Herald* on the day of the lynching.[93] The story of Brooks's lynching, together with its presentation in the press, captures the discursive methods in which a new system of judicial norms in Texas spurned legal statute as it replaced judicial processes with primitive ceremony. Brooks was placed in the jury room of the Criminal District Court to hide him from a mob that had awaited his arrival in Dallas when word spread that he arrived in the city from nearby Sherman on a 5:00 a.m. train. By 9:00 a.m., the "corridors, stairways and entrances to the building" were filled with eager spectators, according to a local reporter sent to the courthouse to cover the trial. Brooks's court-appointed attorneys, George Clifton Edwards, H. Capers, and T. H. Lewis, asked for time to confer with their client before the court proceeded with the trial. They were granted thirty minutes. Just outside the courtroom, the assemblage of interested parties was growing restless. As they witnessed Brooks reentering the jury room for safekeeping, calls from the crowd for an immediate trial could be heard over the "wild cheering" that echoed in the hallways.[94] More than a dozen officers managed, at least temporarily, to calm the anxious audience by reaching for their guns and stretching a double-chain barrier across the hallway. By 10:00 a.m., Judge R. B. Seay ordered that the trial resume. Lewis requested a continuance to provide adequate time for him to confer with his client and subpoena witnesses who could testify in Brooks's defense. "All at once, as if by some mysterious mental telepathy," one bystander decreed, a rumor "gained credence" that a change of venue would occur as part of the motion for continuance. Proving too much for the mob to tolerate, the notion ignited fury and compelled them to take over the legal proceedings. The number of people in the court's corridors had grown to at least one thousand by this time. Outside, members of the gathered mob had positioned a ladder on the side of the building, a foreboding act that indicated to the deputy sheriffs assigned to protect Brooks that, "they're coming beyond a question of doubt," as one of them was heard uttering to his coworker. "They're here," the coworker replied.[95]

At approximately 11:15 a.m., leaders of the mob rushed past the sheriff and his deputies and seized Brooks, secured a rope around his neck, then tossed him out of a second story window to a "howling throng."[96] Upon landing on his head, Brooks was rendered unconscious. "With shouts of exultation," described an observer, the horde of two or three thousand followed Brooks's lifeless body as members of the mob dragged him down Main

Lynching of Allen Brooks, March 3, 1910, Dallas, Texas. Brooks can be seen hanging above the crowd. *Image # PA87-1/160-91, Dallas History & Archives Division, Dallas Public Library.*

Street until they reached Akard Street in Dallas's downtown business district. The crowd numbered between five and six thousand by the time Brooks arrived at the intersection. A young man clambered up a telephone pole in front of the Pacific Drug Store with the dangling end of the rope in his hand and tossed it over an iron spike that protruded from Elk's Arch. Other members of the mob grabbed the rope and hoisted Brooks into the air.[97]

Hours after the lynching, Sheriff A. L. Ledbetter gave a statement to the press. He insisted "it was impossible to protect the negro from a mob organized as it was." "It looks to me," he continued, "that the organization took place long before the mob reached the courthouse." Ledbetter's assessment inadvertently addresses the reproduction and duality of mob violence in Texas. Organized in both plot and form, lynch mobs were at once brash, quick assemblages as well as unremitting echoes from a barbarous past. Their actions became more tightly scripted through each successive lynching episode, even as mobs added components that reflected the nuances of modernity. The removal of the suspected criminal from the courthouse; the ritualistic hanging or burning—or both—of the body, frequently in a space where a previous lynching had occurred; authorities' frequent failure to conduct an investigation; the coroner's tendency to rule "death by parties unknown"; public sentiment that typically lauded the mob's actions; all coalesced to sanction reliance on violence and to reassure lynchers that they would not face punishment. "Immunity from arrest and punishment" for lynchers, noted an observer in 1881, "emboldened the offenders" and imprinted adolescents with a keen understanding of socially acceptable behavior as it reproduced a disregard for conventional legal systems. "Young boys 12 and 15 years old are imitating the example of the older criminals," he continued, "and may be seen any night armed with guns and revolvers swaggering through the streets only awaiting a year or two till they can become men and 'kill their man.'"[98] Adherence to the script gave way to a widespread acknowledgement that mob violence dually functioned as lawlessness and law. Entitled "JUDGE LYNCH HOLDS COURT," an article in a local paper at once mocked and condoned the extrajudicial actions of the mob that lynched Allen Brooks.[99] "Judge Lynch issued his decree and it was carried out to the letter by the servitors of that higher law judge who always brushes aside technicalities," read the article's subtitle. Recognizing that "mob law, for the time being superseded the law of the commonwealth," the journalist expressed regret that collective violence was used but confessed his "sympathy" was "with the living victim and not the dead criminal."[100] "A grim-faced stranger sat on the bench," he scoffed in reference to the almost fictitious authority of the judge. In a harsh and candid final affront to the integrity of the state's judicial system, the journalist validated the mob's rule by concluding "the higher law advocates had their day in court."[101]

Texas Senator Eramus Gilbert Senter penned his disgust with the state's criminal procedure following the lynching of Brooks in an open letter. "When someone spoke of the courts, in the crowd which lynched Allen Brooks, the cry was raised: 'to hell with the courts'—and this sentiment was loudly cheered," Senter lamented.[102] "An effective court, a court which stands for the law administered with justice to all without fear or favor," he insisted, "is the final arbiter between order and disorder; and there must be no indorsement [sic] in any reflective mind of the sentiment 'to hell with the courts.'"[103] Senter's calls for social order and the elimination of mob rule were largely quieted by the prodigious will of the local community.[104] A grand jury formed within days of the lynching resulted in no indictments.[105]

Days following the mob hanging of Charles Sawyer in Galveston on June 25, 1917, Judge Clay S. Briggs addressed a grand jury assembled to investigate the murder of the African American man. Briggs bitterly condemned the mob's actions and encouraged a steadfast investigation:

Every participant in that mob is subject to indictment for the offense of murder, I charge that it is your duty to make the fullest and most sweeping investigation of this occurrence and to fearlessly and faithfully present by indictment each and every person that you may find from such investigation to be connected with the death of the said Chester Sawyer. If as a result of your investigation, it should develop that there was a willful failure or criminal neglect on the part of any one charged with his safe-keeping to give the prisoner proper protection. It is against any such persons, if any you find are subject to such a charge. You will, therefore, begin your investigation at once and continuously pursue it until complete and the persons whom you believe guilty of any connection with the killing of Chester Sawyer should be presented by indictment before the court for trial and punishment.[106]

The inquest into both Allen Brooks's and Chester Sawyer's mob murders, regardless of the failure to indict any guilty parties in both cases, represented a departure from the judicial processes of the state's legal system. Typically, when steps were taken to apprehend or prosecute members of a mob after a lynching occurred, the incidents involved the lynching of whites. In 1900, for instance, James Sweeney was tried for the murder of Charles Crumbach after he plunged a bayonet into his neck. Both men were white. Acquitted of the crime, a mob nonetheless seized Sweeney following his release from prison in nearby Beaumont when word arrived via telegraph that he would be returning to Port Arthur, ninety miles east of Houston, where the murder occurred. The mob captured Sweeney at the train station and, with a hint of irony, carried him to a telegraph pole where he was bound and hanged. Beaumont's sheriff, upon hearing about the lynching, traveled to Port Arthur where he arrested two men, including the mob's supposed leader. In another incident the previous year, John Humphreys and his two adult sons, accused of helping a murderer to escape, were lynched near Aley, seventy-five miles southeast of Dallas. The mob's actions resulted in the conviction of ten white men, each of whom were sentenced to ten years in prison. The Humphreys, too, were white.[107]

In 1919, the trial of two Texas white men accused of murdering Chilton Jennings, a Black man, provided fleeting hope that Black victims of lynch mobs could receive justice. Jennings was taken from a jail on July 24 in Gilmer, Texas, for allegedly attacking a white woman. A mob of five hundred gathered in the courthouse yard, where Jennings was hanged "with a rope about his neck," reported the coroner.[108] Charley Lansday, William Long, and Tom Lay were indicted on charges of lynching in Upshur County. At least two trials were held, the first of which ended in a hung jury. During the second trial, the accused each received two-year sentences, both of which were suspended. It would take another eight decades for the lynchers of a Black man to be convicted and imprisoned for their crimes. On June 7, 1998, James Byrd, a forty-nine-year-old Black man, was walking alone on a road in Jasper, Texas, a far East Texas town with a history of racial strife. Three white men, John William King, Lawrence Russell Brewer, and Shawn Allen Berry, abducted Byrd, beat him, urinated on him, then tied him by his ankles to the back of a pickup truck using log chains. They dragged Byrd for two miles. The trio then left his body at a Black cemetery before heading to eat. In 1999, Berry was sentenced to life in prison. Brewer and King were sentenced to death. This would mark the first time there had been a conviction that resulted in prison time for any individual who aided in the lynching of a Black person in the state of Texas. Brewer and King were executed by lethal injection in 2011 and 2019, respectively.[109]

At times, local authorities endorsed the mob's will not simply through a failure to apprehend them, but by publicly legitimizing their authority. In 1895, T. D. Hightower, acting coroner at the time of Nelson Calhoun's lynching, dually exonerated the individuals responsible for the murder by publicly stating that the victim died "in the hands of parties unknown to me," and his death was "deserved."[110] "A most respected white lady, Mrs. Hughes, was assaulted and ravished by the deceased . . . " Hightower added in his report. Calhoun had been accused by Hughes of rape; however, a mob apprehended Calhoun from authorities before a trial occurred. Little changed over the course of the next several decades. In 1935, a mob took fifteen-year-old Ernest Collins and sixteen-year-old Benny Mitchell from the sheriff's custody in Columbus, Texas, located in the southeastern portion of the state. Collins and Mitchell were accused of murdering a nineteen-year-old white woman named Geraldine Kollman. The following day, Colorado County Attorney O. P. Moore admitted "I do not call the citizens who executed the Negroes a mob. I consider their actions an expression of the will of the people."[111] County Judge H. P. Hahn insisted that he opposed mob violence, but nonetheless echoed a sentiment similar to that expressed by Moore: "The fact that the Negroes who so brutally murdered Miss Kollmann could not be adequately punished by law because of their ages prevents me from condemning those citizens who meted justice to the ravishing murderers last night."[112] Had Collins and Mitchell stood trial,

"Colorado Co. Protects 'Womanhood' ": Ernest Collins and Benjamin Mitchell hanging from a tree. Columbus, Texas, November 1935. *Gresham Marmion Collection (MS 61), Nesbitt Memorial Library.*

the maximum sentence they would have received was confinement in a reformatory until they reached the age of twenty-one. This did not sit well with local citizens.[113]

In the main, whites' attendance at, and participation in, lynchings was not subject to judicial retribution, personal liability, or societal sneering during the late nineteenth and early twentieth centuries. The relative absence of public condemnation associated with participation in lynchings in Texas communities assisted in rendering the form of racialized, collective violence a suitable means of communal control, as well as a socially acceptable way to engage one's time. Local whites typically venerated the members of lynch mobs as civic heroes whose righteous actions assured the preeminence of whiteness, the honor of white womanhood, and the subjugation of African Americans. The lynching of Will Stanley labors the point.

"As the chimes of the clocks of Temple tolled twelve, midnight, a mob of ten thousand people formed a wedge and went by the officers en masses, gaining control of...a negro," began a printed chronicling of the events of July 30, 1915, in Temple, Texas.[114] The day's denouement would be the burning alive of Will Stanley. He was brought from nearby Rogers and marched down Temple's Main Street to his inevitable cremation. People lining the route beat Stanley as he approached the public square where a pyre of "dry goods boxes, barrels and other flammable stuff secured from the rear business houses in nearby alleys" had been constructed, according to one observer.[115] Initial reports indicated that an intruder entered the Grimes family home the previous Wednesday. W. R. Grimes and his wife were the only survivors of the attack. Their three children were killed. The assailant "wore two pairs of trousers, the under pair bearing the name of W. R. Grimes."[116] While "semi-conscious," Grimes insisted that he had a "dim recollection of a negro being in the room," reported a Texas newspaper.[117] The mother was not conscious enough to provide any details about what had occurred. Stanley proclaimed that he had not committed murder nor assault. A "heavy-set white man who owns a dun horse and a good big buggy" paid him to hold his horse, suggesting that the white man was the perpetrator. His declaration was dismissed by the mob. Members of the mob bound Stanley by a chain and tossed him atop the burning pyre. He was then "dragged through the fire backwards and forwards," observed one journalist who recounted the day's activities.[118] Stanley's remains were hanged to the Chamber of Commerce street sign with a loincloth covering his groin area. Evidence of those who participated in his murder was captured in photographs taken by Katy Electric Studio, H. Lippe Proprietor. Despite this visual evidence, no one was prosecuted for the lynching of Will Stanley.[119] "Tragedy of Temple Now Old History," the *Dallas Daily Times Herald* headline read the day following the lynching. "General Verdict Is Guilty Negro Met His Fate…" it continued.[120] The paper declared that public sentiment in the area indicated Stanley "got what was coming to him."[121] "It only proves what we have always contended," a Texas newspaper printed two weeks following the lynching, "that the people are supreme. Public sentiment is the law."[122]

While some local white journalists condemned the "uncivilized" behavior and indiscriminate lawlessness of fellow townspeople, members of local communities rarely criminalized lynchings during the late nineteenth and early twentieth centuries, at least not publicly. The dictate of one observer belabors the point:

Public sentiment endorsed the action of the people of Paris, Tyler and Corsicana when they applied the torch to the negro brutes for unspeakable crimes. That accounts for the fact that no conviction has ever been secured in cases of this kind. Public sentiment endorsed the action of the good people of Bell County and no indictment will ever be found against any man who participated in the burning of Stanley. It is a closed incident.[123]

The ability to avoid judicial consequences for one's actions seemingly encouraged participation in lynchings, and at the very least did not dissuade it. If the conclusive improbability of judicial conviction safeguarded whites' involvement in the lynching of African Americans, then local citizens' reverence for summary justice at once further absolved any related wrongdoing and cast the actions of lynch mobs into a heralded social position.[124]

Dan Kelly, a white NAACP agent sent by the national office to Kirvin, Texas, in 1922 to investigate the mob torture and murder of five Black men (three of whom were burned to death—one at a time while the remaining men watched), interviewed several members of a mob that numbered five hundred. Members of the mob piled wood boxes around Snap Curry, the first man to burn, before dousing him with crude oil and gasoline then setting him aflame. Mose Jones was then dragged by ropes into the fire. Jones died in minutes. John Cornish, the third man burned, was then forced into the flames. Distressingly, Kelly concluded in his report, "it would seem to me that the people of Texas in general are utterly unconcerned that there is a problem involved in lynching, that there is any shame or disgrace attached to it."[125] Such sentiments were often echoed and subsequently reinforced in local papers. After visiting Kirvin, one reporter noted that the "general mood [in the town] was that the mob of 600 did a 'good thing'" because their alleged victim was a white female adolescent.[126] Although the Kirvin men were accused of rape and murder, as mentioned earlier, the lynching of African Americans who committed other crimes, including arson, cattle theft, "race prejudice," and "being troublesome," were similarly lauded. In any form, attacks on white society were intolerable, and swift, extralegal justice was praised.[127]

CHAPTER 2

"Black Brutes ... Will Be Burned"

Race, Gender, and the Uninterrupted Staging of Death by Burning

For the good of all races,
We intend to daily strive,
Treated unjustly in many places,
We are Lynched and Burned alive.

—WILLIE C. BROWN, 1935

As Reverend Ambrose Hubbs approached the pulpit in Galveston's First Missionary Baptist Church, with the November breeze in the coastal city cool and a bit damp from the rains, Robert Henson Hilliard's death weighed heavily on his mind.[1] Hilliard had been chained to a pole and set ablaze in Tyler, Texas, just a few weeks before the pastor's address to those who filled the sanctuary. Every seat was occupied that Friday evening by some curious or troubled local resident, forcing many in attendance to stand to receive the words delivered by invited speakers. African Americans in the area gathered at the church to find some relief from the fear and anger that beleaguered them—to understand how they could commute their distress to action, or perhaps simply to peace. One can imagine that as Hubbs, the forty-two-year-old pastor of the storied church where enslaved African Americans once worshipped, gazed upon the fretful, sullen faces of woefully concerned attendees and raptly clenched the edges of the lectern, he reflected upon the seemingly endless milieu of racialized violence in his state. Hilliard was far from the only Black person who had died at the hands of white mobs in Texas during the months preceding the meeting at Galveston's Avenue L, as the church was frequently called. Thousands of white Texans witnessed the lynchings of Isaac Manion, Nelson Calhoun, William Johnson, Alexander White, and John Cherry during the winter and spring of 1895. By the end of the summer, an additional thirteen Black people in the state had lost their lives by way of lynching. In total, during 1895 alone, at least twenty-six African Americans—more than twice the number of the previous year—had met their deaths at the hands of mobs in Texas before the fatal burning of Hilliard, who was accused of the murder and sexual assault of a white woman. Hilliard's suffering, however, seemed particularly gruesome and wholly implausible. From the moment a flame set the pyre ablaze under his feet until his last breath of smoke-filled air on October 29, a full fifty minutes had passed.[2] One onlooker in the crowd of approximately seven thousand oddly espied, "Hilliard's power of endurance was the most wonderful thing on record."[3] Hilliard continuously begged for mercy, an appeal that was met with laughter from the mob. Before he lost consciousness, Hilliard's "lower limbs burned off . . . and his body looked to be burned to the hollow," observed an onlooker.[4] Within days of the grisly burning, the lynchers' inconceivable actions were available in stereographs—with dramatized images of the alleged murder and sexual assault—and placed on display at a local drug store to satiate the ghastly desires of a curious and malfeasant public. It had all proven too much for Black residents of the littoral city. Hubbs began to speak: "Friends, the object of this meeting is to put ourselves on record against mob violence, the lynching and burning of defenseless negroes."[5] "We are here," he continued, "to pray God to take the part of the people who are being oppressed and mobbed and burned."[6]

Beyond a collective experience of terror, anger, frustration that aligned him with others who were far too aware of unchecked racialized violence, Hubbs was fully sentient of the dangers that faced the young Black men in his own family. He stood before the crowd, conceivably imagining the faces of his sons, Eddie and Willie, thinking about the increasing vulnerability they would encounter as Black men. Willie, his youngest, was turning eleven in just a few weeks and would perhaps remain buffered from the perils of racialized violence for only a bit longer. Eddie, however, had turned fifteen that past February. He was becoming a young man, one who could easily fall victim to the terrors of lynching. Hubbs's sons-in-law, Peachey and Leon, further placed the possibilities of death by mob in stark relief for the family. To undoubtedly complicate the strata of emotions that worked to burden and inspire the pastor in concert, Hubbs and his wife, Winnie, assuredly understood that their five daughters were not exempt from the dreadful fate to which so many had succumbed: at least two Black women—Mary Phillips and an unnamed woman—were lynched in Texas that year. Hannah Phillips was also lynched. She was only twelve years old.[7]

Hubbs and the other orators who addressed the assemblage of troubled citizens that evening sought "to resort to proper methods to put down these things that are constantly causing innocent men to suffer and filling the eyes of the helpless with tears of grief," a visiting pastor resolved.[8] Another applauded the valor of Dr. James Cranfill, a white Baptist editor who had recently charged that the men who burned Hilliard committed a worse crime than the murder of which Hilliard was accused. Other white ministers and politicians, however, had failed to condemn racialized mob violence: "That's why we find ourselves in the condition we are in to-night," Hubbs contended.[9] The compulsory viciousness of boxing encouraged several white clerics in the state to pressure the governor into stopping an upcoming match between James Corbett and Bob Fitzsimmons. As one orator that evening declaimed, those clerics took no such oppositional stance against the wretchedness of burning Black men at the stake.[10]

One perhaps could not help but stare at the striking white cloth that hung behind each person who spoke from the pulpit; the Ten Commandments were scrolled across the front in large Gothic lettering—"Thou Shall Not Kill," an optical, celestial admonishment of sorts serving as a sensible background to an evening dedicated to seeking a solution to unchecked violence, to a particularly ghastly form of murder.[11] Clergy who gathered to speak at Hubbs's church thereby positioned themselves as a vanguard for revolutionary action, the guardians of decency whose courage and equally adamant wisdom would restore the blindfold to Lady Justice. As each purveyor of sentience and warden of racial justice approached that pulpit and stood robustly framed by the chiding banner, one by one they spoke impassionedly about the unconscionable nature of a particular brand of racialized mob violence—the roasting of a person to death.[12]

The burning of Black men had become so prevalent and visible in Texas by the late nineteenth century that the act became synonymous with the state and ostensibly served as a primer for mobs across the country. "Burn him, burn him, as they do in Texas," a Colorado Springs, Colorado mob yelled on July 26, 1893 at the site of an extralegal hanging.[13] When discussing the mob burning of a Black Georgia man that same year, a Midwestern newspaper proclaimed, "Georgia has followed the example of Texas in burning a negro murderer."[14] In June of 1894, when a Black man was accused of raping a white woman in Missouri, a newspaper in the state reported the following: "the neighbors declare that a repetition of the Texas negro burning scenes will occur if the villain is discovered."[15] In 1899, a journalist in California half-humorously wrote in reference to the mob burning of a Black man in Georgia that the state "seems to have gone Texas."[16] The journalist designated this form of mob death the "Texas method."[17]

Following the end of Reconstruction and continuing through the early decades of the twentieth century, the collective violence exacted on African Americans in Texas frequently included burning, a torturous form of racialized control that reveals much about mob violence in the state. While lynching in Texas could include shooting, hanging, burning, or any combination of the three, for white victims of lynch mobs, death by burning was an option never exercised.[18] Much the opposite, as apparent in the murder of Hilliard and many others, death by burning could be exacted with boundless impunity against Black men in the state. I argue in this chapter that mob burning underscored the mastery of the mob due to the element of time necessary to execute this type of summary justice. By extension, the requisite time demonstrated how the amnesty associated with this extreme form of mob violence could render it a socially acceptable space for leisure expressions. I further argue that mob burning granted a heinous element to the new style of lynching, an element typically added due to a certain kind of alleged transgression—the violation of a white body, particularly that of a white female body.

While the lynching of enslaved African Americans had been highly uncommon in Texas, it nonetheless occurred on occasion (see chapter 1). There is only one recorded burning of an enslaved African American in Texas, however: a white mob in Tarrant County burned a Black man in 1859 after he allegedly murdered his master for not purchasing the Black man's wife. All other mob lynchings by burning occurred following emancipation in the state. My research indicates that forty-five people were burned at the stake by mobs in Texas between 1876 and 1933. It was a gruesome death reserved almost entirely for Black men. Of the 45 people lynched by burning, 44 (approximately 98 percent) were Black men and 1 was a Mexican man. My research further indicates that of those 44 Black men lynched by burning, 42, or over 95 percent, were accused of a physical transgression against a white body. The other 2 were accused of burglary and arguing with a white person over a promissory note, respectively. The vast majority of the 42 burned for assaulting the body of a white person were accused of misdeeds specifically involving white female bodies. Thirty-four of the 44 (77 percent) Black men lynched by burning at the stake in

Texas were accused of physically or sexually assaulting a white woman or youth (see appendix).[19] While any accusation of contravention against white women or youth could be met with swift, extralegal violence, when Texas mobs choose to burn their victims at the stake, those victims were almost always accused of physical assault or sexual assault against the white female body, as my research demonstrates.

Burning and Lethal Stereotypes of Black Male Sexuality

The dialectic of the sex-crazed Black brute and the chaste white woman factored significantly into how the Black body would be destroyed. "The negro is a creature of passion, and not of reason" a Texas commentator publicly charged in 1876, "and no influence but that of force can control him; and this lasts only as long as the application is present and imminent."[20] A *Waco Morning News* journalist insisted in 1894, "There is not today in all the south a white woman who is safe an hour beyond the reach of her husband's rifle" from the "black rape fiend."[21] "There is not a white female child secure from brutal ravishment" of Black men, he added, the "moment she is beyond her father's sight."[22] After advancing these pronouncements, the journalist then condoned the preemptive murder of African Americans as an acceptable scheme for the protection of white womanhood: "If self-preservation of the home is the first duty of man . . . the homes of the people of the south [sic] must be protected in their purity, even if to do so it be necessary to annihilate the black race in America—to kill every Negro between the two oceans."[23] Such declarations were hardly anomalous. In a stricture scrolled across the margins of a newspaper clipping mailed to the white antilynching activist Jessie Daniel Ames, an anonymous sender lambasted "the Black african [sic] Brute" for "molesting our Godlike pure snowwhite [sic] angelic American women."[24] The Texas resident then gibed, "God will burn him in Hot Hell."[25]

Playing on fears engendered by stereotypes of the oversexed Black "beast," "fiend," "brute," or any other signifier of sexualized animalistic tendencies, crimes perceived as trampling on white female virtue did not require evidence but merely an accusation of wrongdoing to entice a mob to act. "The whites of the south [sic] will defend the virtue and honor of their women with the last drop of blood in their veins," insisted a speaker at Hubbs's church that November evening. "It is well know that when a Negro is mobbed for this crime there is not even an investigation of the mobbing," he continued, "and this is such an easy way to get rid of an objectionable Negro."[26] After a young white woman was allegedly attacked in Streetman, Texas, in December of 1922, nearly two hundred and fifty cars lined a road outside the building where officers were keeping George Gay, a twenty-five-year-old Black man, for protection from mob violence. Law enforcement officers reported that the evidence was circumstantial, and the alleged victim failed to identify Gay as her attacker. Nonetheless, members of a mob numbering approximately a thousand seized Gay from the sheriff's custody, chained him to a tree and shot him multiple times. Jesse Thomas was shot in Waco, Texas, that same year by the father of a white woman who accused Thomas of attacking her. The purported necessity of burning the Black body in the face of charges of impropriety against a white woman was so great that a mob removed Thomas's body from the morgue so a fiery ending could be exacted.[27]

Informed by fear and insecurity over Black progress and freedom expressions during the post-emancipation era, the characterization of Black men as rapists worked to undermine their humanity and elevate whiteness in a society absent of slavery and the institution's inherent racial hierarchy. "Is it not at least strange that the negro was never accused of this heinous crime when he was a slave?" queried Samuel Burdett, a Black, late-nineteenth century writer.[28] "When he was left as the protector of the 'Mistress' while the husband was away in the army," Burdett contended, "he was found to be strictly trustworthy, and was not afraid of being burned at the stake, either."[29] Frederick Douglass, who advanced similar charges against southern whites in "Lynching Black People Because They Are Black," argued that accusations of sexual assault against white women purposefully worked to "cloud the character of the Negro with a crime the most revolting, and is fitted to drive from him all sympathy, and all fair play, and all mercy. It is a crime that places him outside the pale of the law."[30] The crime, he added, "has been largely invented, if not entirely trumped up . . . to blast and ruin the Negro's character as a man and a citizen."[31] It was a charge "not so much against the crime itself, as against the color of the man alleged to be guilty of it," Douglass opined.[32]

Little, if any, evidence was needed to execute summary justice on a Black man accused of physically assaulting, raping, or attempting to rape a white woman. Even alarmingly peculiar evidence could be used to condemn a Black man to death by lynching. In August 1886, a white woman in Whitehall, Texas, by the name of Mrs. Heitmiller accused Bill Harris of raping her. Harris sat near two other Black men as Heitmiller attempted to identify her attacker. She could not positively do so by his face alone; therefore, she asked that he be stripped naked and made to assume the "posture" he was allegedly in "when he struck a match to search for the money on the mantel-piece after he had outraged" her, reported an observer.[33] Members of the mob complied with her wish. After seeing him naked and in the requested position, she insisted that he was the guilty party. Harris was immediately murdered by the mob.[34]

An attack on a white woman by a Black man was perceived as the ultimate offense against white supremacy; it enraged local citizens and frequently prompted them to implement a punishment that not only killed but annihilated the Black male body. As a wicked prelude to this visual manifestation of racialized power, lynching victims accused of attacking white women were often castrated before they were murdered. An agonizing, methodical execution reified domination over the Black male body as it restored white male southern honor local citizens believed had been assailed when a white woman was allegedly attacked by a Black man. The tortuous act of lynching by burning reduced a Black man's body to a benign, asexual mass. Burning removed signs of male genitalia, if the lynching victim was not already castrated, and destroyed any suggestion of sexual prowess as it rendered white men victorious. Death was not enough; the Black body must be destroyed. After a mob in Coolidge, Texas, hanged Alex Winn—an African American man accused of assaulting a white youth—his body was taken to a local mortuary. Dissatisfied that Winn's body remained intact, a mob broke into the mortuary, removed Winn's remains, and burned them atop a pyre erected on a nearby street.[35]

For many white southerners, their notion of a ravenous fiend with a sexual appetite for white women must be met with as much potential agony and pageantry as possible. When Dudley Morgan, tears running down his face, begged someone to shoot him as he commenced to burn in Longview, Texas, in 1902, members of the mob roared, "Let him die slow."[36] Morgan had been accused of assaulting a white woman, but just before he was tortured to death, his alleged victim was unable to identify him. Nonetheless, the gathered crowd seized the opportunity to dominate and destroy a Black male body in retribution of an alleged attack on white feminine virtue. "I wish some of you gentlemen would be Christian enough to cut my throat," pleaded twenty-five-year-old Dan Davis the following decade, as the flames began to burn his extremities in front of a mob numbering two thousand.[37] Days before Davis uttered his distressing last words, a white female teenager was discovered near the side of the road outside Tyler with her neck cut. The girl survived the attack and provided a description of her assailant, which local residents circulated on paper throughout the region. A farmer in Navarro County, seventy-five miles southwest of Tyler, claimed he recognized the description as that of a farmhand he had recently employed. The girl never personally identified her assailant. Davis was arrested and brought to a jail in Tyler. Hundreds gathered outside the jail, demanding that the law officers deliver their prisoner to them. Outwardly disappointed by officers' refusal, some men climbed the walls of the jail and entered through open windows to apprehend their prey. Davis was seized and carried to the town square where he was chained to a steel stake. Members of the mob piled dry goods cartons and wood around him, then drenched the items in kerosene and set them ablaze. People in the crowd made remarks that one observer indicted as "suggestive of a cannibalistic spirit."[38] Davis died within twenty minutes, but in a scene reminiscent of a campfire jubilee, some in attendance periodically applied kerosene to the pyre to keep the fire burning for nearly two hours. Others, it was reported, "danced and sang to testify to their enjoyment of the occasion."[39]

The Mob's Preeminence and the Element of Time

"Gentlemen and brothers, the time has about arrived for the final scenes in this tragic affair," announced one of the four or five hundred people initially gathered to lynch twenty-year-old Steve Davis, an African American man accused of assaulting a white woman near Howard, Texas, in September 1905. The group had already established that burning would be the mode of death; the location, however, remained undetermined: "A place for doing the job has not yet been agreed upon. Where shall it take place?" a man queried those gathered to watch the events of the day.[40] After some debate, those present selected the meadow. Davis was then fastened to a stake moments before his accuser and her husband tossed a flame onto the pyre that would reduce Davis to ashes. Members of the mob contacted Davis's brother and sister hours before the burning to inform them of their brother's fate. At least one report suggested that the siblings were forced to watch their brother burn. The affair, planned and executed over the course of an entire day, ultimately garnered the interest of approximately three thousand individuals. A commentator revealed, "the galleries and roofs of prairie farm houses and farm buildings for miles around were covered with people watching the blaze."[41] This callously obstinate deed, from the planning to the execution, demonstrates both the authority of the mob and the measures many local whites in the state would take to exhibit their mastery over conventions of the law and the Black body.[42]

Months later, eighteen-year-old Henry Gentry would meet a fate similar to that of Davis. A white widow and her daughter accused Gentry of breaking into their home during the early morning hours of July 23, 1910. Neighbors contacted the local constable after they saw a man lingering about the home. By eight o'clock that Saturday morning, Gentry allegedly resisted Constable Jim Mitchell's pursuit and shot him. Mitchell lived only a few minutes after being shot, but told those who came to his aid the identity of whom he believed shot him. Officers and local residents pursued Gentry to an open field near Belton, Texas. As the posse surrounded him, two shots rang out and ended his life. In an ardent exhibition of authority and influence over Gentry's existence, his lynchers stripped his body of clothing then secured his body by rope to a horse and dragged him through the public square. The eerie and unthinkable display functioned as a parade of sorts, replete with a corporal float that bespoke the wicked and bizarre determination of a mob's desire to create a superfluous exhibit of racialized domination. Members of the mob removed Gentry from the horse, heaped his naked body atop a pile of coal and wood then set him ablaze. The collective acts of violence and ceremony—from the stripping of Gentry's clothing to the parading of his bloodied corpse about the town square to his eventual cremation—sought to humiliate and disempower the accused beyond death. While in this case it is challenging to determine which act—the death of the white constable or the alleged attempt to break into the home of white women—factored more significantly into the death ritual exacted upon Gentry, it is quite likely, as evidenced by other incidents in the state, that the burning of his body had more to do with the charges involving the white women.[43]

In the state's new culture of lynching, burning imposed a gruesome progression of pain, an archaic display of command over the Black body that, in varied manners, validated and bolstered the mob's might and impudence in the policing of racial boundaries.[44] Michel Foucault's enquiry into the importance of spectacle torture is striking here: "from the point of view of the law that imposes it, public torture and execution must be spectacular, it must be seen by all almost as its triumph."[45] For Foucault, "'excesses' of torture" existed within a hegemonic arrangement in which the accused was subjected to torturous punishment in an exercise that revealed and enhanced the omnipotence of the state. The authority of the Foucauldian state parallels the pseudojudicial arrangements of racialized lynching in Texas, which, in turn, mocks the legitimacy of Texas's judicial mechanisms. Burning served as excessive torture, a death scheme that bolstered the preeminence of a ruling body—in this case, not the state but the lynch mobs that murdered African Americans. Such excesses of torture revealed manifold elements of power. Mobs were in control, and the ritualistically torturous and pomp-filled levying of death by burning functioned as a very precise formula for supremacy that sought to dominate as it emasculated Black men.

For allegedly killing a white woman, Abe Wilder was chained to a tree and burned by a mob of approximately fifteen hundred people on August 20, 1901. One observer reported that the burning, which occurred in Dexter, Texas, "took about half to three quarters of an hour, and he was badly charred and burned before life was extinct. In some places the flesh was burned to the bone."[46] As he died, he "groaned and moaned several times, and when in the midst of his misery he cried out and begged the men to shoot him and end his misery, but the men looked on grimly and did not stir to . . . allay his pain."[47]

The act of burning a Black body demonstrated the failure of the criminal justice system, or perhaps more accurately revealed the mob's de jure and de facto authority. The element of time is crucial to clearly understanding the heinousness that defined, and the influence wielded by, mobs in Texas that burned Davis, Gentry, Wilder, and other Black men to death. Victims of lynching by burning were not bodies hanged by faceless crowds and left swaying in the night for discovery at dawn, absent of pageantry and the ability to easily discern responsible parties. Instead, Black men who met their death by burning were murdered by unmasked individuals who were seemingly unafraid of having their lethal acts interrupted, as evidenced by the slow and highly visible murder of Wilder and many others. Setting a fettered human ablaze, then watching and waiting until the body is reduced to smoking ashes so corporeal souvenirs can be retrieved requires myriad investments, among them the benefit of time. The mob that captured Wilder, for instance, wired individuals in Dexter that they were en route with their victim. By the time Wilder and his captors arrived by train, more than a thousand people received the group at the depot. After Wilder's body "burned to a crisp," a commentator reported, "the mob discussed the disposition of the body" and voted unanimously that it should be hanged for two days from a tree: "A guard was detailed to see that the decision was carried out."[48] Burning made the extralegal murder highly visible as it prolonged the lawlessness and extended the domain of the mob—a melding that both created the Foucauldian triumphant punishment and distorted distinctions between the anarchical and the lawful.

In a death ritual that included burning, various details of the death protocol—from apprehending the accused, to transporting the mob's prey to a particular site, to the performance of execution—required the ability to dismiss the machinery of the law; it required a knowledge that the deed would not be interrupted; it required time. Indeed, time is essential to this algorithm for burning. A mob of a thousand white citizens from Hunt County, Texas, overpowered law officers and removed Ted Smith from his jail cell at approximately two o'clock in the morning on July 28, 1908. The African American eighteen-year-old had been accused of raping or attempting to rape a white woman. Several of Smith's lynchers affixed a rope around his neck and dragged him to the middle of Greenville's public square. His lynchers placed him atop the wooden pyre, then doused him in oil before applying the flame. Smith's cries for mercy were met with cheers from the mob. Those who witnessed his death kept the flames burning for much of the day. His body remained in the public square "until the middle of the afternoon and all of the bones were consumed, not a piece as large as a man's finger being left," reported another observer.[49] A train from nearby Farmsville delivered a curious crowd too late to see the lynching unfold in its entirety. They arrived only to witness the burning of an already unrecognizable Black body. A mob comprised of two thousand local citizens burned three Black men to death, one after the other, in the town of Kirvin, Texas, in 1922. Once the third man succumbed to the flames, individuals gathered at the site piled the bodies atop one another and burned them all once again. Those participating in the summary judgement of the men did not exhibit any fear of arrest nor concern that law officials would interrupt this protracted atrocity. Members of the mob in Kirvin enjoyed the advantage of taking their time, in part evidenced by their ability to burn their three victims twice each.[50]

There seemed to exist among mobs who used fire in their murderous endeavors little to no fear of disruption nor culpability. They were consistently unmasked; they posed for pictures while their charred targets cooled; members often organized and acted out a procession of the remains to a neighboring Black community or portion of town. Events were frequently publicized in advance: "Niggers caught," read signs throughout Paris, Texas, in 1920 announcing the imminent lynching of brothers Herman and Irving Arthur, twenty-eight and nineteen years old respectively. The notice continued: "Black brutes who killed Hodges will be burned in the fairgrounds. Be on hand."[51] Tenant farmers, the brothers shot their white landlord and his son after an alleged argument regarding financial payments and crops. A

The burning of Ted Smith. Greenville, Texas, July 28, 1908. *Graphic Arts Collection, Rare Books and Special Collections, Firestone Library, Princeton University.*

witness to the events that led to the lynching told a different story regarding why the brothers killed their landlord. The witness drafted an anonymous letter to the National Association for the Advancement for Colored People that read, in part, as follows:

> Herman and Irving Arthur, Negroes, with their parents were tenants on the Hodges' farm. They were working on halves, a system whereby the landlord furnishes his tenants and at harvest time takes the crop and the amount with interest which furnished his tenants during the year. Against the usual custom here Hodges compelled his tenants to work all day Saturday. They did this for a time, washing and ironing clothes Sunday. When they refused to work longer than noon Saturday Hodges became angry and went to their home on the farm three days before the murder and took their dinner off the stove and threw it in the yard. He also kicked their stove and household goods out in the yard. During the time Hodges son held a gun on the Negroes. He also compelled the boys to pull off their shoes and clothes; their sisters to pull off their dresses and give them to him claiming the Negroes were in debt to him. After this they decided to move from his farm. When they

(By Pacific & Atlantic)

Otis C. King, uncle of slain girl, and bloodhound used in tracking slayers.

Where three Negroes were burned at stake.

VENGEANCE.—For their alleged complicity in slaying of Eula Ausley, three Negroes were burned at the stake in Kirvin, Tex. Mob rule prevailed several days and was subdued yesterday.

"Vengeance." Newspaper clipping about the burning of several Africans Americans in Kirvin, Texas, May 6, 1922. *W. E. B. Du Bois Papers (MS 312), Special Collections and University Archives, University of Massachusetts Amherst Libraries.*

had began loading a truck Hodges and his son came up and began shooting to them. Herman Arthur ran into the house and secured a gun and came out and killed both men who were yet firing at them. A mob lynched both Negroes.[52]

When Herman and Irving's three sisters—ages twenty, seventeen, and fourteen—objected to their brothers' arrest previous to the lynching, the sisters were beaten and placed in jail. That evening, in a monstrous display of iniquity, they were taken to the basement of the jail and raped by police officers and approximately twenty other white men. More than three thousand people arrived early at the fairgrounds, the eventual lynching site of the Arthur brothers, to watch while both were doused in oil and set aflame. Their burnt corpses were fastened to the back of an automobile and dragged through the Black residential portions of the area while members of the mob repeated: "Here are the barbequed niggers . . . you niggers come out and see them and take warning."[53]

The burning of African Americans in Texas—the excess of torture; the conspicuousness; the prolonged ceremony; the pageantry; the procuring of charred, corporeal souvenirs—revealed not the omnipotence of the state, but that of the mob and its ability to function. It exposed the failure of the state to prevent mob violence as it authenticated pseudojudicial processes that produced and reproduced a particular lynching narrative. Burning, then, functioned as both epilogue and prelude beyond the site of justice. This ceremonial torture of a single body became a visual portent in a process that wove punishment and caveat, spectacle and threat—a portmanteau chronicled in print, in both public and private dialogue, in the collective memories of communities that served as arenas of torture. It added a vicious finale and a graphic warning to the real and potential targets of racialized mob violence. Finally, it allowed time for members of a mob to engage in the affair in any manner they pleased due in large measure to the virtual absence of any notion of wrongdoing or fear of retribution among local white people. Events that unfolded in Paris, Texas, labor these points with remarkable precision.

The Death by Burning of Henry Smith

On Wednesday, February 1, 1893, Ida B. Wells, the intrepid journalist and antilynching activist from Tennessee, stood before an audience of reformers at the Metropolitan Church of Washington, DC, to give a public lecture entitled "Southern Mob Rule." She was speaking at the behest of Frederick Douglass who invited her and other "leading women," such as Anna Julia Cooper and Lucy Morten, to the meeting.[54] Mary Church Terrell, writer and by then founder of the Colored Women's League, introduced Wells as a woman with "undaunted courage."[55] Wells took the stage and delivered a courageous and candid examination of racialized mob violence in America. "Contrary to what white Southerners claim about Black men and rape," Wells lectured the crowd, "lynching is nothing more than an excuse to get rid of Negroes who are acquiring wealth and property. In this way, they try to keep us terrorized."[56] Wells's oration, replete with statistics and compelling narrative, was so moving that those in attendance donated "nearly $200 to aid in the cause," she remembered.[57] The morning following her speech, newspapers carried the gruesome details of a mob burning in Paris, Texas. Wells learned about this example of unthinkable human torture while still in DC and felt compelled to act at once. She used the donations to hire a Pinkerton detective to investigate the dreadful murder. "Never in the history of civilization has any Christian people stooped to such shocking brutality and indescribable barbarism as that which characterized the people of Paris, Texas, and adjacent communities on the first of February, 1893," she later penned in her pivotal *The Red Record*, a work that sought to expose the monstrous contours of racialized mob violence.[58] Smith's cruel, slow death—the strange mix of pageantry and exhibitionist violence—foregrounds burning by mob as a performative, recreational, despotic, and racialized scheme that discloses much about the correlation between the ritualization of death by burning and alleged transgressions against white women and girls. Race stood as central to this algorithm for dominion. While whites were often harassed, threatened, or even hanged by mobs, for whites in the state accused of crimes—even crimes against white women and girls—burning was never a feasible option in the state of Texas.[59] To be sure, several years before Smith's burning, a white man in Paris, Texas, named J. E. Robinson was accused of attempting to rape an eight-year-old white girl. A mob forced him to the banks of the nearby Red River and instructed him not to return to the area. The man left, alive. Smith, by stark contrast, would not be allotted such a fate.[60]

The body of Myrtle Vance, a three-year-old white girl and daughter of Henry Vance, a local police officer, was found in the woods of Paris, Texas, on Friday, January 27, 1893. Individuals who viewed the girl's body after it was discovered swore that one of the only indications of any type of assault was the presence of "abrasion and discoloration . . . about the neck."[61] Nonetheless, within days of Smith's death, journalists reported that Smith "ravished," or sexually assaulted, the child, despite the observations of those who saw the child's body and reported there was no such evidence.[62] Atticus Haygood, a well-respected white bishop in the Methodist Church, publicly reported woeful inaccuracies regarding the murder. "So eminent a man as Bishop Haygood deliberately and, it must also appear, maliciously falsified" the details of the crime, lamented Wells.[63] Haygood charged that Myrtle had been "outraged with demoniacal cruelty and then taken by her heels and torn asunder in the mad wantonness of gorilla ferocity."[64] Haygood's use of the word gorilla in describing the viciousness of the girl's assailant seemed to intentionally evoke a racist discourse, one that seized upon the interplay of savagery and Blackness to fashion a narrative that convicted a Black man as a murderer in the absence of due process.[65] Some scholars have reported that Haygood's inflammatory story, one replete with unthinkable sexual assault and the horrific dismembering of a child, plunged the townspeople into a crazed state as they pursued Smith and then tortured him. This is not the case. The inflammatory words of the venerated cleric did not incite the ire of the mob. Haygood delivered his incendiary comments more than one week following Smith's burning. The misleading notion that Haygood leveled this racialized and embellished tale of sexual assault and murder before Smith's burning lends a suggestion of provocation for the mob's grisly actions. Instead, Haygood's intention seemed one governed by the desire to absolve the mob of their horrible deed: "Sane men who are righteous will remember not only the brutish man who dies by the slow torture of fire, they will think also of the ruined woman, worse tortured than he."[66] Haygood leveled his supposition for months. "Unless assaults by negroes on white women and little white girls come to an end," he insisted in October of 1893, nearly nine months after Smith's death, "there will most probably be still further displays of vengeance that will shock the world."[67]

The accusation of rape was an oft-repeated means of countering arguments of barbarism hurled at mobs who burned their victims. As in the case of Smith, many of those lynched by burning were not accused of rape until after their death as an attempt by those stating rape as the cause to somehow exonerate the atrocious and murderous actions of mobs. At other times, accusations of sexual assault were often added to the narrative long after the arrest without evidence, but just before the act of lynching, which further aroused the mob to brutal action. Walter White's observations in 1921 are significant here: "charges of rape were made with increasing frequency as a greater number of lynchings and more brutal methods of execution of the victims brought vehement condemnation of lynching from other parts of the country."[68]

Considered a "roustabout" but "harmless" and "weak-minded," Smith supported himself through odd jobs at the homes of local white people. His reportedly extensive drinking habits frequently put him at odds with Myrtle's father. Vance had beaten and harassed Smith repeatedly. Smith's encounters with the murdered child's father seemed to make him an easy suspect. Vance, a man known for his "bad temper," "overbearing manner," and mistreatment of prisoners, had arrested Smith and beaten him quite severely for disorderly conduct and drunkenness just days previous to Myrtle's murder.[69] Local residents contended that the crime against Myrtle was exacted by Smith in revenge. Smith's hat was reportedly found near the murder site, which sealed his fate in the public imagination. After discovering that he was named a suspect, Smith absconded to Detroit, then boarded a freight train headed for his previous residency in Hempstead County, Arkansas. He was finally captured in Hope, Arkansas, more than one hundred miles from Paris.[70] News of Smith's impending return spread across portions of Arkansas and Texas. Citizens of Paris "deliberately determined to lay aside all forms of law," according to Wells, announced the day and time that Smith would be tortured and burned for the "delectation and satisfaction" of "Christian people," she mockingly added.[71]

When the train carrying Smith en route to Paris pulled into the station at Texarkana, five thousand people awaited his arrival. The previous year, a Texarkana crowd numbering close to fifteen thousand burned Edward Coy, a Black man accused of assaulting a white woman, on the Arkansas side of the border. Concerned that Texarkana residents would detain Smith, lynch him, and subsequently dispossess Paris residents of their ability to exact a perverse form of justice as many garnered some level of amusement from the ceremony, a delegation of Paris's "prominent citizens," the district attorney among them, gave speeches at the depot and "asked that . . . the guard be allowed to deliver [Smith] up to the outraged and indignant citizens of Paris," one observer disclosed.[72] It seems the Texarkana residents obliged. The train continued, with Smith aboard, to the station at Paris where, it appeared, the mob's actions would nevertheless be influenced by the murderous affairs of Texarkana's neighbors ninety miles to the east, as the deaths of Coy and Smith would parallel one another in both pageantry and scope. An eyewitness account offers a glimpse into Smith's disposition along the way: "The Negro, for a long time after starting on the journey to Paris, did not realize his plight. At last, when he was told that he must die by slow torture, he begged for protection. His agony was awful. He pleaded and writhed in bodily and mental pain."[73] Once Smith arrived in Paris, he was positioned atop a platform, described by some as a float in a parade, that carried him to a scaffold erected for the day's events. A scathing absurdity that featured the moniker *justice* across the front, the scaffold functioned as both a visual dismissal of the sanctity of the legal process and confirmation that the mob's authority reigned supreme. Perched atop this shoddy wooden platform, Smith and his executioners stood before ten thousand people or more. Men and children straddled the necks of spectators to obtain an unobstructed view of Smith and his lynchers. Two knives were produced and used to cut Smith's shirt "piece by piece" from his body, reported a member of the mob. His lynchers tossed the "relics" to the crowd as souvenirs just before the torture commenced.[74]

A published eyewitness account provides unparalleled details of the events surrounding Smith's lynching. It includes a comprehensive chronicling of the entire affair, as well as photographs of Myrtle and Henry Vance, the site where Myrtle's body was discovered, the men who captured Smith, and scenes that featured varied stages of the lynching. Entitled *The Facts in the Case of the Horrible Murder of Little Myrtle Vance, and Its Fearful Expiation, at Paris, Texas, February 1, 1893*, the book was widely distributed following the lynching. The author's portrayal of the lynching episode, from the unrelenting search for the missing child, to the discovery of the accused's personal effects, to Smith's capture and torture, is cast as a performance of sorts, a play replete with opening credits, exposition, and a proscenium upon which the climax unfolded. His description of what happened on that stage, where Smith was surrounded by the father, brother, and two uncles of Myrtle Vance, conveys the anguishing manner in which fire was instrumental to the suffering imposed on Smith:

> Mute actors, yet most potent, now appeared as the grim fire-buckets, belching forth the smoke of newly lighted fires, were placed on the platform at his feet, and the deadly soldering-irons thrust among the heating charcoal. It requires but a few moments for the irons to become heated, when one is simultaneously inserted under the sole of each bare foot, and the throe of pain forces the brutal nerves to weaken and roars of agony rend the frozen air. Too dreadful would it be to follow in detail the further steps in the process of torture. We can only refer the reader to the press reports recorded later and which are sufficiently full.[75]

Smith bellowed in agony as red-iron rods were rolled up and down the front and back of his torso, then plunged down his throat. As a final prologue to Smith's fiery death, Henry Vance and his son plunged red hot rods into Smith's eyes.[76] The eyewitness description continues:

> All now have retired but one, who pours the oil over the body, swaying in darkness and in agony, and then the wind fans into flame the smouldering [sic] pantaloons and fires the body into scorching flames. The torch is at the same time applied below, and in another moment the smoke and flames hide the wretch from sight. It takes but a short while for all the clothing to disappear before such a holocaust, and the ropes that bind him in an upright position soon follow, when rigid and half unconscious, he falls heavily to the floor of the platform. Any human being, unsustained [sic] by the genius of evil, must have been overcome ere this, but not so with Smith; with a tenacity unequaled, he clung to his unshallowed life, and, after some time of futile effort, he found a corner post, braced himself against it, and with a supreme effort raised his roasted hands in air, hung his wrists over the guard-rail, put one leg after the other clear of the platform, and swung himself out and dropped the full ten feet to the ground, escaping, momentarily, the anger of the flames.[77]

Crowd gathered in Paris, Texas, before the lynching of Henry Smith. Photo by John L. Mertins, 1893. *Library of Congress Prints and Photographs Division, Washington, DC.*

At one point during the torture, Smith was roped and dragged back into the fire by members of the mob. Reports suggest that he may have removed himself from the pyre at least one additional time before he finally succumbed to the inferno.[78]

Details about Smith's alleged crime and lynching—published in the 185-page first-hand account, told and retold by newspapers across the state, captured in photographs, relived through tête-à-têtes, distributed as corporeal souvenirs—outwardly served as fodder for an eerie script of sorts that promoted a racialized torture and death intended as both deterrent and primer. The presence of children in the crowd was a calculated judgment on the part of local citizens, a move that likely extended two distinct yet overlapping lessons for white and Black children—one a harsh tutorial, the other an ominous warning. "Fathers, men of social business standing, took their children to teach them how to dispose of negro criminals. Mothers

Crowd gathered to watch the torture and burning of Henry Smith. The following appeared with the image in the historical record: "Photo taken about 200 ft. from platform." Photo by John L. Mertins, 1893. *Library of Congress Prints and Photographs Division, Washington, DC.*

were there too," an onlooker disclosed.[79] Another member of the crowd relayed his observations of the day to a reporter. Present at Smith's lynching, Reverend King, an African American minister and resident of Paris, Texas, whose first name is unrecorded in the historical record, grew distraught and "wept aloud" when he noticed Black children following the procession and taunting the condemned man. King sorrowfully observed:

> Even at the stake, children of both sexes and colors gathered in groups, and when the father of the murdered child raised the hissing iron with which he was about to torture the helpless victim, the children became as frantic as the grown people and struggled forward to obtain places of advantage. It was terrible. One little tot

scarcely older than little Myrtle Vance clapped her baby hands as her father held her on his shoulders above the heads of the people. "For God's sake," I shouted, "send the children home." "No, no," shouted a hundred maddened voices; "let them learn a lesson."[80]

Once the burning commenced, King "dashed through the compact mass of humanity" to the front of the crowd and yelled, "In the name of God . . . I command you to cease this torture[!]"[81] His admonishment was met with an immediate pistol-whip to the head, which knocked him to ground. "Rough hands" lifted King to his feet, and then several white men escorted him at gunpoint to his home, where they permitted him to gather a few things and then forced him to leave town. Exiled, King relayed his recollection of the lynching from New York City. "I was ridden out of Paris on a rail because I was the only man in Lamar County to raise my voice against the lynching of Smith," King told a local journalist days after he arrived in the north. "I opposed the illegal measures before the arrival of Henry Smith as a prisoner, and I was warned that I might meet his fate if I was not careful; but the sense of justice made me bold, and when I saw the poor wretch trembling with fear, and got so near him that I could hear his teeth chatter, I determined to stand by him to the last." As King's train pulled away from the station in Paris, "some one [sic]," he reported, "thrust a roll of bills into my hand and said, 'God bless you, but it was no use.'"[82]

The eyewitness published account of Smith's lynching did much to illuminate the recreational aspects of his torture and death. Multiple members of the crowd attended and interpreted the lynching as a leisure activity, replete with the elements of self-directedness, time away from work, and pleasure required to render it as such. "Hundreds turned away in horror at the awful spectacle," the writer acknowledged, "while thousands gazed on with evident satisfaction and many with demonstrations of delight."[83] Many members of the mob, or those who visited the site of his lynching during the following days, carted off pieces of clothing or bone found in the ashes as souvenirs. Still others fondly remembered what they witnessed during the days and weeks that followed, demonstrating both the pleasure they had experienced as well as their desire to extend the realm of experience to others.

The legal system's brazen failure to stop the burning or to arrest any of Smith's murderers did not escape the attention of a national audience. "If the law has any majesty, it is time at least for these advocates of public morality and acknowledged guardians of order and peace, to so declare," pleaded a journalist for the Black-owned, Philadelphia-based circular

Christian Recorder. The article characterized those who remained silent about or endorsed the mob's actions as cowards. The author then questioned the value of a legal system that allowed such an atrocity to occur: "Of what use is the strong arm of law or the balance wheel of a reason but to suppress the animal and brute in an excited populace as well as in an enraged individual? To say that the law in such cases is too powerless to assert its supremacy, is an inference of guilt and self-condemnation, as inexcusable as the most deliberate deed of the foulest criminal."[84] Benjamin Orange Flower, a white investigative journalist and founder of a social reform periodical entitled *Arena*, penned his contemplations in an editorial published in the *Christian Recorder* a few months following Smith's burning: "There is something fatally demoralizing in the lawlessness which sneers at law and oversteps all bounds of common decency and humanity in order to glut insane frenzy."[85] With a superbly rhetorical tone, Flowers opined that race was a clear determinant in the execution style: "Hence, let us notice the case from the plane of conventional justice. If a brute . . . had been a white man, would he have been burned, much less tortured? Most certainly not."[86]

Governor James Stephen Hogg dispatched a telegram to the Sheriff of Lamar County the day following Smith's burning entreating him to seek redress for the "lynching of the negro Henry Smith."[87] In a separate wire, Hogg reminded the District Attorney, "the laws of the state have been openly defied."[88] "Every good citizen is interested in maintaining and enforcing the law of the land," the governor insisted: "Either law and order or anarchy must prevail, and there can be no compromise or middle ground."[89] He then demanded, "mob violence in Texas must be stamped out."[90] What Hogg failed to openly concede is that the prevailing, increasingly normative order of judicial processes was, indeed, enforced. The day following Smith's lynching, a reporter observed, "all who participated in the torture of the negro . . . boldly proclaim the part they took in the affair and say that they have not fear of arrest."[91] In a revealing endorsement of Smith's lynching, Col. C. J. Hodge, a "leading" criminal lawyer in the state of Texas, said days following the burning: "As a lawyer and law-abiding man I deplore mob law at all times, but there are two sides to this thing. Smith's death was simply the will of the people and they cannot be blamed . . . The deed has been done and as good citizens we must indorse [sic] it."[92] Hodge's complacency with the actions of the mob wade through the strict dichotomy of legal versus extralegal punitive action. His approval expressly heralds the will of the people as the apex of a normative legal processes when the accused was Black. Despite the governor's consigned pleas for justice, and irrespective of the very public nature of the crime, no one was ever arrested for the torture and murder of Henry Smith. It seemed the will of the people would prevail as a pretext for unchecked mob violence in the state.

Nearly two weeks following Smith's death, a group of white men hanged William Butler, Smith's stepson, in nearby Hickory Creek for allegedly concealing information regarding Smith's location. "This young man," Wells notes, "against whom no word has ever been said, and who was in fact an orderly, peaceable boy, had been watched with the severest scrutiny by members of the mob who believed he knew something of the whereabouts of Smith." [93] Butler maintained from the beginning of the search for Smith that he did not know the location of his stepfather. Butler's murderers were never arrested.[94]

Malfeasance and the Mob in the Burning of John Henderson

The unabashed, self-proclaimed authority of mobs in Texas surpassed and suppressed judiciary proceedings during the later nineteenth and early twentieth centuries. The burning of John Henderson—an event that took hours to execute and remained uninterrupted—demonstrates that local sentiment and the intemperate power of white citizens ruled irrepressibly, particularly when white women were the victims of a crime.

On Thursday, March 7, 1901, W. D. Robinson, the Navarro County Sheriff, wired Governor Joseph A. Sayers: "White lady murdered by negro name unknown throat cut ear to ear. Breast and face badly cut. Posse out. Please offer reward."[95] Valle Younger, the wife of a white Corsicana area farmer, was found murdered at her home the previous day. Police officers and bloodhounds reportedly pursued the murderer's scent for forty-five miles before apprehending John Henderson, a twenty-two-year-old African American man. The officers placed Henderson in a McLennan County jail. Robinson again wired Sayers: "Complaint for murder just filed in Justice Court against John Henderson party arrested for murder. . . . Have him in . . . jail. Mob gathered here last night and still organized."[96]

Fearful that Henderson would surely be lynched should he attempt to transport him back to Corsicana, Robinson asked for counsel from the governor. From his office in Austin, Sayers ordered that the sheriff "put the prisoner in the jail of the county where he can be most secure against mob violence."[97] "Such is your duty," he reminded Robinson, "fearlessly perform it."[98] The following day, Luther A. Johnson, Navarro County Attorney, reported to Sayers that he "decided it would be best to collect evidence and have the trial as soon as possible, in case of threatened violence to the prisoner."[99] Robinson wanted Young's children, ages one and three, to identify Henderson before he potentially perished at the hands of a mob.[100] On Friday, March 8, citizens of Corsicana held a mass meeting and demanded that Henderson be returned to the city. They drafted a letter to Robinson that read as follows:

> We your petitioners, who are tax payers, and law abiding citizens, of Corsicana and Navarro County Texas, do, most respectfully ask, that the Negro John Henderson, who was arrested on our streets, and accused of murdering Mrs. Valle Younger, and who was taken to some unknown point, be, returned at once to Navarro County, that he may stand his preleinary [sic] trial, for the purpose of establishing his guilt or innocence, and for the further purpose of enabling [sic] the officers and people of Navarro County if he is innocent to continue their efforts, to find the guilty party.[101]

More than six hundred of the city's approximately nine thousand residents signed their names to the letter. Robinson, either given to false hope or untimely complacency, conveyed the following to Sayers Monday morning via wire: "I believe prisoner can be brought here and given an examining trial. The best citizens guarantee this. I think this best under the circumstances."[102] Sayers found Robinson's assessment of Henderson's welfare should he be taken back to Corsicana "unsatisfactory."[103] He insisted that the sheriff more definitively determine if Henderson "would be safe from mob violence."[104] The evening before Sayers's inquiry to Robinson, Johnson reported to Sayers: "two thousand men are here from this and adjoining counties and I fear if [Henderson] is brought back that the sheriff could not save him." Johnson's words proved prophetic, or simply mundane given the character of mob violence in the state. Robinson had told a different story. As the day commenced, however, Robinson's erstwhile confidence in the committee that swore to help him protect Henderson began to wane. He and Johnson pleaded for assistance from Sayers:

> Situation growing worse every moment. Sheriff and his force would be unable to protect this prisoner. If brought here today we do not believe that you could summons militia enough to protect him from mob violence even with the sacrifice of human life. Two thousand couraged [sic] people from the [county] and other counties are here threatening violence to the peace officers for not

bringing prisoner back. Send such telegram as can be read to mob now assembled in order to relieve the situation.[105]

A subsequent telegram sent that day from Corsicana Mayor Samuel Wistar Johnson and four other local officials reported "great excitement" in the city and an "immense crowd on the streets" that was steadily growing.[106] The mayor closed the saloons as a precaution against any additional fray that could be engendered by drunkenness.[107]

Sayers's response seemed to evade full recognition of the concerns raised in Mayor Johnson's message. He directed the mayor, sheriff, and county attorney to send notice immediately as to "whether or not the prisoner would be safe from mob violence, if brought to Corsicana."[108] The quintet unequivocally responded to Sayers that Henderson would be subject to harm should he be returned to the city.[109]

As a result of the mounting concerns expressed by various elected and appointed officials in Corsicana, Henderson found himself aboard a train with officers of the law Tuesday evening, March 12, en route to Fort Worth. The move came despite a message sent to the governor by O. C. Kirvin, the District Attorney, earlier in the day that informed Sayers "citizens in mass meeting . . . give assurance which I believe that John Henderson can safely stand his preliminary trial."[110] He asked that the governor order officers who were housing Henderson to return him to Corsicana. Not trusting the veracity of Kirvin's assessment, the governor ordered that Henderson be transported to Fort Worth instead. He never arrived. Wednesday morning, Kirvin sent word to Sayers: "Henderson is [in Corsicana] in the hands of the citizens and the sheriff is powerless."[111]

An untold number of local whites arrived from Navarro and adjoining counties at the Hillsboro depot that Tuesday evening, just before Henderson's train pulled into the station. Upon its arrival, they boarded the train and rode together with their eventual captive until the train approached Itasca—about ten miles from Hillsboro. The party then began to wrestle Henderson from the officers who were escorting him. At least one officer brandished the weapon he was carrying to stop the kidnapping, but to no avail. C. C. Weaver, the mayor of Itasca, informed Sayers in a letter penned a few days later that the men "disarmed the officers and took charge of the negro."[112] According to a journalist for the *Dallas Daily Times Herald*, the mob that apprehended Henderson had been constantly informed of his whereabouts by a person with access to the telegraph wires. Henderson was taken to a livery stable "where they ordered [horses] for their trip to Corsicana," according to the mayor who reported to the governor that he was "at home asleep and knew nothing of the occurrence" until the morning.[113] Henderson's captors then transported him on horseback the approximately fifty miles to Corsicana, where he arrived in the early morning hours of Wednesday, March 13. In a move that then noticeably conflated the authority of the mob with that of the state, the mob placed Henderson in a Corsicana jail cell for safe keeping. The oddity of that action is glaring. They did not wrestle Henderson from local authorities at the jail, nor did they hide him in some obscure location out of the reach of established law; instead, they housed him in a space that seemingly required cooperation with law enforcement. The act calls into question local authorities' role in the matter. It seems that culpability for the lynching likely lay with both local citizens and law enforcement. Further obfuscating the legitimacy of the judicial system, Justice of the Peace and Acting Coroner H. G. Roberts conferred with a committee formed from Henderson's soon to be murderers before securing a written confession from him Wednesday morning. Illiterate, Henderson signed the confession with a simple mark. The mob planned to burn him that afternoon, but word spread that Texas Rangers were headed to the area to impede any mob violence.[114]

By eleven o'clock that morning, members of the mob, which now numbered near five thousand, removed Henderson from his cell and delivered him to an unlit bonfire that had been erected on the lawn of the local courthouse. Several individuals secured Henderson to a post with a chain. Others doused his clothing with oil. In a near final moment of pageantry and torture, Conway Younger, Valle Younger's husband, used a knife to slash Henderson's face just before "dozens" of lighted matches set the pinewood planks under his feet aflame—it seems multiple members of the mob vied for the peculiarly coveted role of setting the debris ablaze. The local fire bell rang in that instance, causing throngs of people to empty stores and clamor to the courthouse in time to witness Henderson's torturous, fiery death. The fire bell was a call to the event—a notification not to flee, but instead to freely gather and decide to witness death. The curious, the vengeful, the thrill-seekers all stood shoulder to shoulder and watched as Henderson was reduced to a smoldering mound. Several men then posed for photographs with Henderson's ashen remains. Some of the images were commuted to postcards. A train arrived at noon from southern Navarro County filled with citizens who, an observer reported, "expressed disappointment at being too late" to partake in the lynching.[115]

Per Sayers's orders, Adjunct General Thomas Scurry sent a telegram to Colonel G. W. Hardy, stationed in the Corsicana area, that Wednesday

John Henderson removed from the jail by a mob. Texas, March 1901. *Texas/Dallas History and Archives Division, Dallas Public Library, Dallas, Texas.*

morning ordering Hardy to "assemble certain companies" in an effort to thwart the murderous efforts of the mob.[116] "I proceeded at once to notify officers . . . to assemble and report to me . . . then mounted first horse and went to run to court house," replied Hardy within hours, "only to see the lifeless charred form of the mob's victim chained to a post amidst the hottest fire."[117] "As it is too late to afford any protection to the prisoner," Scurry replied, "[my] former order to you is hereby countermanded. by [sic] command of the Governor."[118] Robinson later wired Sayers an update that included an attempt at personal exoneration: "Henderson was burned this morning he was brought here by Citizens & was never in my custody since taken from officers I was powerless to prevent results."[119]

During the days following Henderson's death, local residents purported

The burning of John Henderson. Corsicana, Texas, March 1901. *Texas/Dallas History and Archives Division, Dallas Public Library, Dallas, Texas.*

that their actions represented the will of Navarro County citizens. In a performance that brazenly exposed the irreverence and mastery of the mob, a note featuring the words "every white man in Navarro County pleads guilty" was affixed to a portion of Henderson's charred remains and mailed to the governor. A state law enacted in 1897 empowered the governor to order the arrest of individuals believed to be associated with a lynching. The law further permitted the governor to enlist state rangers to apprehend any individual connected with murder by mob violence. District

Attorney Kirvin arrived in Corsicana from nearby Mexia Wednesday to find "Henderson burned by citizens after confession."[120] He then declared local police officers were "blameless and powerless" in Henderson's lynching.[121] In direct contrast to Kirvin's proclamations, at least one report suggested that an officer actually led the lynching. Kirvin added that residents of Navarro could identify the lynchers, who made no effort to conceal their identities. As many as five thousand people witnessed Henderson burn, a burning that occurred at noon in the "Court House yard, the most public spot in Navarro," according to a local journalist.[122] "All those who engaged in the violation of the antilynching law seemed proud of their connection," the journalist observed.[123] Despite mounting evidence that allowed for easy identification of Henderson's assailants, Sayers did not order the arrest of a single person. Given his earlier efforts to prevent mob violence, the latter lack of action seemed at the very least odd, or perhaps a sad display of political entanglements that placed limits on the value of Black lives.[124]

After completing a formal inquest into Henderson's death, Justice of the Peace H. G. Roberts, sworn to uphold the majesty of the law, drafted his ruling: "I find that the deceased came to his death at the hands of the incensed and outraged feelings of the best people in the United States, the citizens of Navarro and adjoining counties. This evidence, as well as the confessions of guilt by the deceased, shows that his punishment was fully merited and commendable."[125] Roberts's striking suppositions, which were reprinted in newspapers across the country, cast the authority of the mob as something more than simply acceptable. The judge's acquiescent and "qualified defense," as one reporter characterized it, together with what appeared to be the conspiratorial role of law enforcement in the lynching of Henderson, publicly privileged vigilantism over judicial processes, thereby ostensibly authenticating as legal the extralegal pronouncements of the mob. No one was ever convicted for the murder of John Henderson.[126]

The Confession: Justification of Death by Burning

"Burned at the Stake: Negro Pays a Fearful Penalty for Murder and Assault—Crime is Confessed" read an August 1901 headline in the Weatherford, Texas, *Weekly Herald*.[127] The journalist relayed the story of a crowd in Whitesboro, Texas, that burned Abe Wilder to death for allegedly raping and murdering "Mrs. Caldwell," a white woman. As described earlier in this chapter, Wilder was apprehended from Constable Davis and M. W. Witt by local citizens, then chained to a tree and set aflame before a crowd numbering near fifteen hundred. "Take the fire away and I will tell you all about my past crimes and this one," Wilder implored.[128] Men subdued the flames, but Wilder fell silent. The burning commenced once again. Wilder gasped occasionally, moaned infrequently as he burned for nearly thirty minutes. While the flesh on his lower limbs melted from his bones, he begged that someone shoot him to end his misery. Silence. No one acknowledged nor answered his plea. They simply gazed on, seemingly unmoved as Wilder perished in the flames. White men lingered near the charred remains of Wilder long after death overcame him. Young boys dotted the scene, some donning straw boaters, often referred to as "Panama hats," with sharp brims that shaded their curious stares from the intensity of the late summer sun but did nothing to shield their fading innocence from the grotesque, melting mass exhibited before them. The governor dispatched thirty soldiers to Whitesboro, under the command of Major C. J. Nimon, but they arrived too late to save Wilder. Davis reported that when a mob first surrounded Wilder, Witt, and himself after Wilder's arrest, he voiced that he wished "to know whether or not the man under arrest was guilty" before he surrendered the prisoner.[129] According to his lynchers, Wilder reportedly uttered the following words, which were printed in the Denison *Sunday Gazetteer*: "I murdered Mrs. Caldwell. I laid in wait until her husband left home and went to the house. I tried to [rape] her and she was too strong for me, and I cut her throat. I went there for the purpose of [raping] her."[130]

One particular type of commentary—the confession—produced an essentialism that reified the conflation of Black criminality and the sexual fiend prototype as it worked to transport the reading public to the scene of the alleged crime. Printed details of supposed sexual attacks were frequently inflammatory or exaggerated, countenancing what historian Jacqueline Dowd Hall characterizes as a "public fantasy" that "implies a kind of group participation in the rape of the woman."[131] Reports of rape, Hall contends, "became a kind of acceptable folk pornography" across the South.[132] Printed as the purported exact words of the accused, the confessions of lynching victims in Texas often included details of sexual assault and murder that seemed to function as a complex, public engagement and exercise in the folk pornography described by Hall. But the confession also greatly facilitated the production of racial alterity. Confessions intensified the anger and resolve of potential members of a lynch mob as they worked to authenticate widespread suppositions. Any assumptive notions about Black men's hyper-sexuality and their predisposition to violence were reified in the public mind once supposed revelations from the accused were accessible, thereby making death by burning a more probable end for the accused. On many occasions, local African Americans expressed concerns that Black men were being blamed for crimes against white women that white men had actually committed. Such possibilities of white culpability were quelled by glaring headlines that presumed the guilt of Black men in the absence of due process. Even newspapers outside of the state perpetuated the practice of indicting African Americans accused of crimes through the prejudicial captions. "Negro Rapist Lynched In Texas: His Companion In Crime Will Be Lynched As Soon As Caught," read a headline in a Wichita, Kansas paper regarding the hanging of Esseck White in 1897. White, like most other victims of mob violence in the state, was never given a trial.[133] The headlines offered the first entre into determining guilt and subsequently legitimizing the tortuous death of lynching victims. Then, the seemingly careful transparency of the confession, printed in newspapers as a first- or third- person account, sealed the fate of the accused as it worked to acutely carry readers to the site of the alleged sexual deeds in absentia.

A discourse that assigned disparaging physiognomies such as the sex-crazed 'black brute,' 'rapist fiend,' or 'negro ravisher' who sought to sexually assault a chaste white woman became a template of sorts for newspaper descriptions of events that preceded the burning or hanging of a lynching victim, articles that included alleged confessions of the eventual Black victims of lynching. Perceived as the ultimate offense against white southern culture, the trampling of white female virtue was an action that did not require evidence, simply an accusation for the metering of swift, retaliatory action. Once the accusation of assault against a white woman by a Black man was levied, "no matter by whom or in what manner, whether well or ill founded, whether true or false," contended Douglass, the accused was "subject . . . to immediate death . . . He is bound with cords, hurried off . . . to the scaffold, and under its shadow he is tortured till, by pain or promises, he is made to think he can possibly gain time, or save his life by confession. . . ."[134] When William Sullivan proclaimed that he was married to a white woman, white citizens of Plantersville dismissed his assertion and publicly accused Sullivan of rape. Texas miscegenation laws, enacted as early as 1837, prevented interracial unions; however, the Black teenager's insistence that he and the white woman were husband and wife could have been born from a multitude of scenarios. Perhaps the two lived together and considered one another husband and wife in the absence of their ability to legally marry in the state. Or perhaps the two were married in a state that did not forbid interracial unions, or were married in a religious ceremony without a state issued license. Regardless of their legal status, it was local citizens, not the woman in question, who accused Sullivan of rape. The sheriff, himself a member of the mob that eventually murdered Sullivan, promised the young man that if he confessed to raping the young white woman, he would "come out all right," a journalist for the *Herald*, an Austin-based African American newspaper, reported.[135] It seems that such promises were commonly used among law enforcement agents and citizens to make Black men, fearful of lynching, admit to crimes that they had previously insisted that they did not commit. Sullivan allegedly confessed and was nonetheless lynched shortly thereafter. In the aggregate, such a promise and adversative outcome were commonplace. "I know it is often alleged that the Negro brute, as he is called, confessed his guilt before he was executed," acknowledged Francis James Grimke in 1899. Grimke, a Black Presbyterian minister, wholly doubted the veracity of confessions related to alleged crimes against white women perpetrated by Black men:

> In regard to all such alleged confessions, I have this to say: They are always to be received with the greatest amount of allowance. I have very little faith myself in them. Criminals do not as a general thing confess their guilt. Even where the charge is true, the plea almost invariably is, not guilty. Occasionally, we find a criminal turning state's evidence where others are implicated beside himself, but even then, it is because pardon is promised, because he sees in his confession the hope of escaping the punishment of his crime. No such motive as this, however, can have any influence with a Negro charged with rape or attempted rape of white women in the South; for he knows that death is inevitable whether he confesses or not. Is it not strange that the Negro rapist, unlike all other criminals, should always confess his guilt? Besides, the motive for the publication of these alleged confessions of guilt is apparent to anyone who takes the time to think. They are put forth purposely by the lynchers, in order to furnish a kind of excuse or justification for the lynching.[136]

Again and again, as Grimke argued, the confession was ostensibly used to justify lynching, particularly mob death by burning.

The accused was frequently assured safety from a lynch mob if he confessed to the crime in question; notwithstanding, the authenticity of those confessions would largely go unchallenged. On occasion, however, people publicly doubted that the confessions were authentic. When a young Black man was arrested in 1903 for the murder of a white woman, inconsistencies in the man's story led a local sheriff who interrogated him to publicly declare the man's likely innocence. The arrested man confessed to the crime but could not offer any details regarding it other than that which was already popularly known. When the sheriff asked him why he confessed to a crime he eventually swore that he did not commit, the man replied that another Black man "told me that if I told you I did it, you would let me out, and I thought he meant it."[137] Similar to the sheriff, a journalist for the *Herald* would stand as another exception when he published his doubt that the confession given by William Sullivan, a man accused of raping a white woman, was factual: "Members of the mob said after death had sealed Sullivan's mouth, that he 'confessed' that he outraged the woman, but strange to say no one knew anything about the confession of Sullivan but those that murdered him."[138] Sullivan was hanged by a mob on September 10, 1892.[139]

The printed confession allowed for a perverse, empirical reliving of sexual violence, a separate sentient narrative of experience that worked to preemptively justify any extralegal, torturous actions imposed upon the accused. Recall Jesse Washington, who hours after his arrest in May of 1916 for the murder of Lucy Fryer, was transported thirty-five miles to a Hillsboro jail from Waco by law officers who promised they would protect him from mobs if he confessed to the crime. Officers moved him yet again, this time to Dallas, out of fear that a mob in Hillsboro would remove him from their custody.

Jesse Washington was the eldest child of Lewis and Martha Washington. The couple had eleven children by the time of the 1910 census. Most historians have listed Washington's age as seventeen; this, however, might be inaccurate. Primary source accounts vary as to Washington's correct age. Several newspaper articles published during the time of his death listed him as eighteen, others gave his age as seventeen. NAACP investigator Elisabeth Freeman's report to the NAACP reveals additional confusion regarding his age. She writes, "the colored boy confessed that he was 17 or 18, but the judge says he was 23." Washington's death certificate lists him as eighteen. By contrast, the 1910 census indicates that he was fourteen when the census was enumerated in April of that year; therefore, his age at the time of death in May 1916 would have been twenty. Despite variations in the historical record regarding his age, what remains consistent in documents related to the incident is that Jesse had a quiet disposition and was likely mentally challenged. He had not been working for the Fryers long before he found himself in the custody of local law enforcement agents.[140]

The day following Fryer's death, Washington allegedly confessed to the murder multiple times, in Waco, Hillsboro, and Dallas. Freeman charged, "the [Waco] sheriff got a confession from the boy because he promised to the boy protection and a trial."[141] When asked if he feared that a mob would lynch him, Washington replied, "they promised they would not if I tell them about it."[142] In Dallas, Washington dictated the confession to Mike T. Lively, a Dallas County attorney. The teenager was likely terrified over the possible fate that lay before him. Under the easily accepted illusion that officers would protect him from mob violence if he signed the written confession, Washington, who could not read nor write because he was illiterate, marked an X on the document.[143] Three McLennan County newspapers printed Washington's signed confession, thereby convicting Washington of both murder and rape in the public mind before any trial took place. The published version of the confession, likely accessible by all literate residents of the area, as argued by Patricia Bernstein, eliminated some of the more graphic details for its readership. Washington's confession reads as follows:

> On yesterday, May 8, 1916, I was planting cotton for Mr. Fryar[144] near Robinsonville close to Waco, Texas, and about 3:30 o'clock P.M. I went up to Mr. Fryar's barn to get some more cotton seed. I called Mrs. Fryar from the house to get some cotton seed, and she came to the barn and unfastened the door and scooped up the cotton seed. I was holding the sack while she was putting the seed in the sack, and after she had finished, she was fussing with me about whipping the mule, and when she was standing inside of the door of the barn, and still talking to me, I hit her on the side of the head with a hammer that I had in my hand. I had taken the hammer from Mr. Fryar's home to the field that morning and brought it back and put it in the barn at dinner. I had picked up this hammer and had it in my hand when I called Mrs. Fryar from the house, and had the hammer in my right hand all the time I was holding the sack.
>
> When I hit Mrs. Fryar on the side of the head with the hammer she fell over, and then I assaulted her. I then picked up the hammer from where I had laid it down, and hit her twice more with the hammer on top of her head. I saw the blood coming through her bonnet.
>
> I then picked up the sack of cotton seed and carried it and the hammer to the field, where I had left the town. I left the sack of cotton seed near the planter and went about forty steps south of

Mob watching Jesse Washington burn to death. Fred Gildersleeve was the photographer. Waco, Texas, May 15, 1916. *Wiki Commons.*

Charred remains of Jesse Washington. Waco, Texas, May 15, 1916. *United States Library of Congress Prints and Photographs Division. Call Number: LOT 13093, no. 34.*

the planter and the mules, and put the hammer that I killed Mrs. Fryar with in some woods under some hackberry bush.

I knew when to the barn for the cotton seed that there wasn't anybody at the house except Mrs. Fryar, and when I called her from the house to the barn, I had already made up my mind to knock her in the head with the hammer and then assault her.

I had been working for Mr. Fryar about five months, and first made up my mind to assault Mrs. Fryar yesterday morning, and took the hammer from the buggy shed to the field with me, and brought it back and put it in the barn at dinner time, so that I could use it to knock Mrs. Fryar in the head when I came back for seed during the afternoon.

I planted cotton the rest of the afternoon, then put up the team and went home to my daddy's house, where I was arrested.

There wasn't anybody else who had anything to do with the killing or assaulting of Mrs. Fryar except myself.[145]

It seemed that the newspapers, in all the explicit strivings for coverage related to the alleged crimes of Black assailants, had some tacit publishing restrictions on acceptability as they removed or altered the more graphic details of sexual assault in the original printed confession.[146]

A Dallas County grand jury indicted Washington the Thursday following his arrest. That Monday morning, Washington found himself in a McLennan County courtroom for his trial. While much of Waco read the confession and, according to Bernstein, "knew that he was supposed to have 'criminally assaulted' [raped] Lucy Fryer," there was no mention of rape during the proceedings.[147] "Even Dr. Maynard, who testified about the wounds to Lucy's skull, was not asked about the rape," Bernstein notes, which, she concludes, strongly suggests that there was little, if any, evidence of rape.[148] At the end of the trial, a mob seized Washington, dragged him to the lawn of city hall, suspended him from a tree by the neck, then burned him until his body was reduced to a charred mass. Elisabeth Freeman decided within days of the attack, after thoroughly investigating the incident for the NAACP, that Lucy Fryer had not been raped.[149]

Renderings of Black criminality through printed confessions were not simply disseminated to southern audiences. Papers across the country carried purported admissions of guilt by Black lynching victims in Texas, allowing notions of Black sexuality and violence to influence the public image of African Americans. The casting of Black men as sex-crazed criminals would thereby become part of a national narrative in part through

Marked as "Nigger Photos, Sherman Mob. Before Lynching." George Hughes before he was burned by a crowd in Sherman, Texas, 1930. *Briscoe Center for American History, UT-Austin, CN 03113, Aldrich (Roy Wilkinson) Papers, 1858–1955.*

the reprinting of dubious confessions. Robert Henson Hilliard's alleged confession to rape and murder was featured in a Massachusetts newspaper under the subheading "Confessed His Crime." The *Lowell Daily Sun* printed Hilliard's confession as follows: "I was coming down the road and saw Mrs. Bell in the road. She was scared of me, and I knew that if I passed her she would say I tried to rape her, and I concluded that I would rape her and then kill her. I cut her throat, and cut her in another place and left."[150]

The Paradox of American Democracy and Death by Burning: Appeals for Federal Intervention

The unrestrained lynching of Black men in the state brought into question the sheer dismissiveness of any wrongdoing associated with the act in which masses of white people across the state engaged. It also demonstrated the varied forms of agency displayed by countless Black citizens who sought

George Hughes's corpse burned and affixed to a tree in Sherman, Texas, 1930. *Briscoe Center for American History, UT-Austin, CN 03114, Aldrich (Roy Wilkinson) Papers, 1858–1955.*

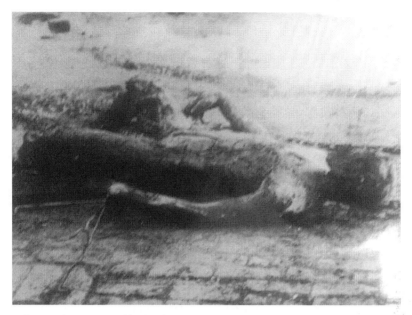

"After Lynching." Burned body of George Hughes in the street, Sherman, Texas, 1930. *Center for American History, UT-Austin, CN 03115, Aldrich (Roy Wilkinson) Papers, 1858–1955*

Abe Wilder tied to a post. A mob burned him to death. His lower limbs shown burned off in this image. Grayson and Cooke Counties, Texas, 1901. *Texas State Library and Archives Commission, Austin, Texas.*

innovative ways to address and halt this particularly grotesque form of racialized social violence and control. At times, that agency took the form of calling the federal government into account for failing to address the murder of Black people by lynching. The Department of Justice files are filled with letters from citizens, hailing from various portions of the country, writing to presidents, United States attorneys, and federal judges. Spanning decades, the letters—with tones ranging from highly impassioned and laden with clear distress to the sadly perfunctory in the recounting of a lack of federal action related to racialized mob violence—repeatedly emphasize the failure of the nation-state to even moderately uphold democratic tenets. A committee of one hundred and fifty Black ministers from Washington, DC, for instance, drafted a letter to President William Howard Taft during the late summer of 1910 urging him to address lawlessness in the nation. Prompted by the lynching of more than twenty Black men in Palestine, Texas, on August 1, the committee averred:

> We believe in democracy: which we interpret to mean government
> by suffrage and protection of law. The mission of the law is: justice
> to every man at any price . . . God's arbiter for humanity Is justice;
> not for any one race or nation above another, but for human race.
> Humane treatment, establishing the guilt of evil doers, as a part of
> the justice, is absolutely necessary.[151]

"The federal Constitution guarantees us 'life, liberty and the pursuit of happiness[']," read a letter to US Attorney General George Woodward Wickersham in December 1911, which urged him to help end the practice of lynching African Americans.[152] "I am but an humble citizen," Louis G. Gregory suppliantly wrote to President Woodrow Wilson in January 1917, days before the president's inauguration, "but am still persuaded to point out to you, the occupant of an exalted station, a service you can render ten million or more of your fellow-citizens without injury to yourself or others." Gregory had visited fourteen southern states during the previous few months, speaking with local Black leaders and assessing the gravity of racial oppression and mob violence. He advised the president to "use the moral influence" of his post and publicly "urge the equal enforcement of laws, regardless of race and color."

White citizens also made appeals to presidents for justice. "May I make a very simple suggestion?" Max Eastman, founder of the socialist magazine *The Liberator*, queried of Wilson the following year.[153] By the time Eastman's letter arrived at the White House, America had been officially involved in World War I for nearly a year. Nearly four hundred thousand African American soldiers would fight in a war that purported to make the world safe for democracy; yet the hypocrisy of the stated mission would encourage countless Americans to question how the unchecked lynching of Black people in the country could be reconciled with purported democratic ideals.[154] "The number of American negroes lynched . . . in the past year amounts to more than one every two days," Eastman made clear to Wilson, pointing out that "practically none of the murderers have been punished."[155] He then beseeched the president to issue a "public rebuke, upon grounds of patriotism and the honor of democracy, to the mayor and citizens of each town in which such an atrocity occurs."[156]

On July 26, 1918, Wilson, perhaps given to public pressure, issued a condemnation of lynching in the country. "I say plainly that every American who takes part in the act of a mob or gives it any sort of countenance is no true son of great Democracy, but its betrayer."[157] "Lynchers," he charged, "emulate [the] disgraceful example" of the enemies in the war. He then urged governors, law enforcement agents, and all other citizens "of every community in the United States, all who revere America and wish to keep her name without stain or reproach," to "cooperate—not passively merely, but actively and watchfully—to make an end of this disgraceful evil. It can not [sic] live where the community does not countenance it."[158] Beyond the statement, Wilson did little to thwart mob violence in the country. In Texas alone, at least thirteen Black men and one Black woman were murdered at the hands of white mobs in 1918. Jim Brown was hanged from a tree in Ben Hur, Texas, the day following Wilson's address. Nearly half of those who died as a result of mob violence in the state that year were burned by their murderers. It was, however, the burning death of Bragg Williams, arrested in December 1918 and lynched in January 1919, that further captured the fury of folks across the nation due to the heinousness, timing, and irony of his death. Williams's murder came only weeks after America had helped win a war for the preservation of democracy. "We proudly proclaim to be the champions of democracy," Wilson declared in his statement against lynching. Williams's lynching demonstrated otherwise.

When the eighteen-year-old Williams heard the unyielding roars echoing down the corridors of the Hillsboro jail where he awaited trial, locked in a cell, he likely knew the fate that awaited him. He had already sat, perhaps restless and consumed by fear, in a cell approximately sixty miles southwest of Hillsboro near Dallas where law enforcement agents kept him. Such precautions would serve to stave off a fiery destiny for only a few days. There he awaited his fate in Hillsboro on his final day of imprisonment when the silence of the winter morning quickly gave way to the clamor of determined citizens who sought absolute control over his body. *Boom! Boom!* Several men from the mob had cut down a telephone pole, which they were using as a battering ram to proceed down the vestibule and strike heavily at the door that barred their entrance to Williams's cell. *Boom!* As the door swung open, only the sheriff remained to halt the determination of the mob; like the door to the cell, however, he faltered.[159]

Annie Wells, a thirty-six-year-old mother of six and wife of George Wells, a local white farmer, was found in her home the morning of Monday, December 2, 1918, with her head bludgeoned and stab wounds about her chest. The body of her four-year-old son, Curtis, lay beside her. Williams, who was employed by the family, was arrested the same day. He denied committing the murders. Williams was nonetheless convicted by a jury and sentenced to hang.[160]

Moments after the trial ended, Williams would meet his end in an inferno created by the resolute mob that forcibly removed him from his cell and led him to the public square. Members of the mob chained him to a safety post as others piled wood, hay, and coal around him, then doused the hodgepodge of combustible items in oil and set it aflame. Williams died within five minutes, much faster than most lynched by fire. His body burned for forty minutes, however. "Help me, Cap," he reportedly uttered three times before his death.[161] The state attorney general leveled charges against a group of the lynchers for contempt of court because they apprehended a prisoner who had already been sentenced to hang. However, a grand jury formed at the end of the month to investigate the murder of Williams returned no indictments.[162]

The unyielding horror of Williams's lynching captured the heavy concern and sympathy of many. "Mob Violence Must Be Ended," the *San Antonio Express* headline read following his burning.[163] The paper offered a $1,000 reward "for information which results in the conviction and punishment of any member of the mob which participated in the lynching of Bragg Williams."[164] The circular promised to pay the reward "for each individual conviction and punishment."[165] Walter W. Paris, William King, and J. W. Dobbs of the First Congregational Church of Atlanta, Georgia, drafted a letter on behalf of the African American congregation to Woodrow Wilson less than a week following Williams's death. "Only last week," the trio bewailed, "a man was burned alive at the stake in Texas in broad open daylight."[166] It was, they contended, "a peculiar violation of the spirit of democracy."[167] Chiding and hypocritical, the failure of the Wilson administration and the nation at-large to protect its Black citizens from the "American habit of lynching" came on the heels of Wilson's denunci- ation the previous year.[168] Little had changed between Wilson's July 1918 affirmation and the letter drafted by Paris, King, and Dobbs. Their admon- ishments, sent six months later, bespoke a fundamental inconsistency in the nation's ability and willingness to uphold the tenants of democracy: "We do not make this appeal because this last victim was a colored man; but the fact that he was colored adds to the enormity of the offense in view of the fact that he belonged to a defenseless group."[169] "Bring to bear upon the mob the strong arm of the nation," the group implored before rebuking Wilson: "A nation that cannot protect its own is weak! If it will not, is it not wicked?"[170] In closing, the church's members insisted, "we are making this plea because we are loyal Americans and desire the best things for American democracy."[171] Reminding the president about the service of African Americans in the recent world war, they closed by boasting, "our record at home and across the seas in the world conflict now happily ended testify to our sincerity."[172]

People nationwide would level similar charges against a federal gov- ernment wholly dismissive of Black participation and sacrifice in World War I. During the summer of 1919, a white mob in Huntsville, Texas, shot Sarah Cabiness and her six children to death, then burned them in their home. As a response to the violence, John Shillady, Secretary of the NAACP, drafted a telegram to Texas Governor W. P. Hobby: "At a time when one hundred fifty-seven thousand Negroes are in France or preparing to go, offering their lives for the preservation of our country, it behooves Texas to do everything through its officials to stamp out mob violence."[173] In a preface to the telegram sent to newspapers across the country, W. E. B. Du Bois echoed Shillady's sentiments: "Negroes are offering their lives for the preservation of the ideals of democracy, the [NAACP] wishes to know if the Negroes of Texas are to be given their share of the democracy for which they are fighting."[174]

Similar appeals for federal intervention continued for years. A Black resident of New York, repulsed by David Gregory's monstrous death by burning, attached an article about the murder to an impassioned plea for justice addressed to President Franklin Delano Roosevelt early in his admin- istration. The letter, drafted on Christmas Day of 1933, insisted that the nation would in some way be called to account for its lack of action against the barbarism that plagued areas of the South:

When a race of people become so low as to do a trick so much lower than the lowest animal then I know that race cannot be the ruler of the world much longer. Many years ago, your race brought my people from Africa you taught us about a God now don't you think that same day in the near future this same God will measure out a fitting reward for such injustice. There shall be a day of reckoning. Might and injustice has never conquered "Right" need I state this fact, because you have studied the rise and fall of countries and know that these three qualities play an important part in the progress or regress of a nation or a race.[175]

The Roosevelts occupied the White House in the midst of unsettling changes in 1933. The Great Depression stood at the forefront of national concerns. Much has been written by scholars about the letters sent to both Franklin and Eleanor Roosevelt from citizens across the nation who longed for relief from the anguish engendered by unemployment, homelessness, starvation, and despair. Flooding the White House at a rate of hundreds per day by the end of 1933, the letters were filled with requests for everything from a pair of football shoes to loans to immediate employment. The letters revealed a considerable amount about the starry-eyed view many residents of the country harbored regarding the Roosevelts. The couple represented hope and a prospect for uplift from the dire conditions that marked the Great Depression. While most letters sent to the Roosevelts focus on ways to mitigate financial despair, those found in the Department of Justice files enjoin President Roosevelt to address a different problem that engaged the lives of too many—the unrelenting issue of mob violence. They were certainly not the first of their type written to United States presidents by African Americans, as evidenced by the appeals of citizens troubled by the burning of Bragg Williams and many others. But Roosevelt was perceived as the guardian of uprightness, as perhaps the eradicator of wrongdoing who would expose and eliminate the abject horror and injustice of lynching, particularly the inhumanity of death by burning.

The first year of Roosevelt's presidency witnessed a marked increase in the number of lynchings, as compared to the previous year. During 1932, the number nationwide had fallen to about eight. By the end of 1933, however, the year that Roosevelt took office, at least twenty-eight Black men were murdered by mob violence—two in Texas, one of whom was burned to death. By the end of 1935, the year that Willie C. Brown penned his letter to Roosevelt addressing the lynching of Black men in Texas, at least four additional Black men were killed by mob violence in the state.[176] In his letter, which wavered between prose and poetry, Brown tersely insisted from his home in Fort Worth, Texas: "It is time for you, Mr. President, to speak and speak in no uncertain terms!"[177] "Shall justice sleep and mercy weep forever in the National Capital," he rhetorically inquired, reminding Roosevelt of the sacrifices Black men and women made in defense of the country:

> We were loyal to Old Glory,
> Knowing life was just a chance,
> Mother weeping and wife heartbroken,
> We left all and went to France.
> Fought until foes was [sic] taken,
> Fought as only Black men Can,
> It seems now that we are forsaken
> Yet a man is just a Man.[178]

Brown pleaded that Roosevelt do everything within his "power and might" to ensure the passage of the Costigan-Wagner Anti-Lynching Bill, drafted by United States Senators Robert F. Wagner of New York and Edward Costigan of Colorado. The bill proposed that state and local officials who failed to properly protect a victim of mob justice or refused to arrest members of a lynch mob could be jailed or fined. It further proposed that counties where lynchings occurred could be fined $10,000, a sum which could be forfeited to the families of lynching victims. Referencing the hundreds of thousands of Black soldiers who served in the United States Army during the previous decades, Brown then challenged Roosevelt to rise above any potential hypocrisy by reminding the president of his own words regarding parity, justice, and a "square deal" for those who risked their lives in service to their country. Brown closed the letter with a heart-wrenching free verse poem that pithily captured both the barbarism of racialized mob violence and the sheer injustice of failing to act on behalf of Black people in America:

> For the good of all races,
> We intend to daily strive,
> Treated unjustly in many places,
> We are Lynched and Burned alive.[179]

Fearing the loss of southern support, Roosevelt never publicly endorsed the 1935 Costigan-Wagner Anti-Lynching Bill. Such a lack of support was quite an insult to antilynching advocates such as Mary McLeod Bethune and Walter Francis White, who had helped campaign for Roosevelt during his presidential run.

Texas Mobs, Burning, and the Legislation of Antilynching Measures

Within days of the 1922 Kirvin burnings, James Weldon Johnson, the Florida-born writer who become Executive Secretary of the NAACP in 1920, sent a telegram to President Warren G. Harding requesting a federal investigation "of what we are convinced are serious disorders in Texas in the environs of Kirvin and the dispatch of Federal troops there if necessary to protect the lives of American citizens."[180] He also wrote to members of the United States Senate Judiciary Committee while they had possession of the Dyer Anti-Lynching Bill. Drafted in 1918 by United States Congressman Leonidas Dyer from Missouri, the bill proposed punishments for local and state officials who failed to protect individuals from mob violence, prosecute lynchers in federal court, and require counties to pay $10,000 to the families of lynching victims. Johnson enclosed a newspaper clipping of the Kirvin burnings and urged the representatives to move forward with passage of the bill:

> This fresh demonstration of inhuman cruelty and barbarism is added emphasis to the menace of the mob to all orderly government and the dire need for quick and effective action. The roasting alive of three human beings, one after the other, in civilized country seems incredible. We ourselves would not believe it except for the positive proof that it did occur.[181]

M. F. Cyrus, a Black resident of Corsicana, Texas, wrote an impassioned letter to President Warren G. Harding urging him to help facilitate the passage of the bill. Like Johnson, Cyrus included a newspaper clipping about the Kirvin burnings. "Had they been given a trial," Cryus optimistically insisted of the lynched men, "they could have proved their innocence."[182] "It could easily been [sic] proven two white men committed the crime," he added.[183] The despondent nature of his plea was glaring: "I am but a Poor Colored American with no Proliction [sic] for my life and Property."[184] The Dyer Anti-Lynching Bill was passed by the House of Representatives in January, 1922, but was never enacted due to a filibuster in the Senate.[185]

Many similar bills sought to address the unchecked violence of lynching; approximately two hundred antilynching bills were presented to the United States Congress during the first half of the twentieth century. Representative George Henry White, an African American member of Congress from North Carolina, presented the first federal antilynching bill in 1900. The US House of Representatives approved an antilynching bill on three total occasions; the Senate never approved a single one. Thomas Terry Connally, a United States Senator from Texas, would be one of the senators who worked earnestly to prevent passage of antilynching legislation. Connally led charges against the Dyer Bill. He similarly led other senators against the 1935 Costigan-Wagner Anti-Lynching Bill and subsequently caused its demise. By 1937, Connally would co-lead a filibuster against yet another antilynching bill with Mississippi Senator Theodore Bildo after it passed in the House. Connally blazingly charged in a speech delivered on the floor of the Senate:

> If trouble makers [antilynching advocates] will but turn their preachment to the colored race, from political and social relations, toward instilling in that race observance of law, good citizenship, industrial education, industry, and frugality, the black man will move far down the pathway that leads to happiness—along that roadway the gates stand ajar.[186]

The bill was subsequently abandoned.

Connally's condemnation of African Americans revealed much about how Black lives were devalued by those who wielded the power to affect change. His opposition to antilynching legislation would be reproduced for years to come as not a single one of the aforementioned approximately two hundred antilynching bills would pass both houses of Congress. The failure of the federal government to pass legislation that would work to eradicate acts of mob violence served as an unyielding reminder, one directed at African Americans in Texas and across the nation, that their lives were systematically degraded and considered unworthy of protection.[187]

In 2005, the Senate approved Resolution 39, which apologized for their predecessor's past failures related to lynching. Following the voice vote, Senator John F. Kerry of Massachusetts lamented, "I am personally struck, even at this significant moment, by the undeniable and inescapable reality that there aren't 100 senators and co-sponsors. Maybe by the end of the evening there will be, but as we stand here with this resolution now passed by voice vote, there aren't." By the close of the evening, twenty senators had not signed on as cosponsors.[188]

On June 28, 2018, three African American United States Senators—Kamala Harris of California, Corey Booker of New Jersey, and Tim Scott of South Carolina—introduced S.3178, "to specify lynching as deprivation of civil rights, and for other purposes," according to the bill. The senators acknowledged the apology issued by their predecessors in 2015, but insisted, as written in the bill, "it is wholly necessary and appropriate for the Congress to enact legislation, after 100 years of unsuccessful legislative efforts, finally to make lynching a Federal crime." The bill described lynching as an act committed by two "or more persons" who "willfully cause bodily injury to any other person, because of the actual or perceived race, color, religion, or national origin of any person." It made the crime of lynching punishable with a sentence that can include life in prison. On February 26, 2020, the Emmett Till Antilynching Bill, as it was named, passed the United States House of Representatives with a vote of 410–4. Those who voted no cited "government overreach." Senator Rand Paul of Kentucky blocked the Senate version of the bill from passing months later.[189]

CHAPTER 3

"Love the Negroes, All Right, but in Their Place"

Race, Work, Migration, and Lynching

> *"High Visibility" actually rendered one un-visible—*
> *whether at high noon in Macy's window or illumi-*
> *nated by flaming torches and flashbulbs while under-*
> *going the ritual sacrifice that was dedicated to the*
> *ideal of white supremacy.*
>
> —RALPH ELLISON, 1952

In August 1905, Richard Turner, an African American resident of Waco, Texas, penned a despairing letter to the United States Attorney General William H. Moody in Washington, DC: "Conditions here has [sic] become in Such a State until I as a private citizen think you [sic] authority Should be appealed to for help."[1] "The colored people," he arraigned, "of the Town of Waco McClellan [sic] County and adjoining counties are [being] terrorized and panic stricken they are being abused freely by peace officers and citizens whipping them over the head with six shooters and not allowed to resent it."[2] He goes on to describe how at least a dozen Black men were whipped in neighboring Bruceville. In one instance, several white people ten miles from Waco administered a hundred and fifty lashes to a local Black man, a beating that left the man so severely injured he was unable to work, Turner bewailed. Several other abuses ensued in the area as well. African Americans were targeted by the local magistrates and fined fifty to one hundred dollars "for nothing [but] simply conversing on the streets." "No justice in the courts," Turner lamented. "A colored man is afraid to open his mouth" for fear of reprisal.[3] Turner's heart-wrenching grievances were validated repeatedly throughout the late nineteenth and much of the early twentieth centuries in incident after incident. An ostensibly benign act could result in varied forms of punishment. After bemoaning the dismal lack of protection afforded African Americans in the state, Turner's letter referenced the recent lynching of twenty-year-old Sank Majors, who had been apprehended from the sheriff by a white mob in Waco. The mob dragged Majors through the streets before attempting to burn him. His lynchers opted instead to hang him from the Waco Avenue Bridge, cut him with knives, then castrate him.[4] Majors was one of at least twenty-two people lynched between 1889 and 1922 in McLennan County. In 1889, the area had seen its first lynching when a mob murdered Henry Davis, an African American man. In 1893 alone, white mobs in McLennan County lynched five Black men, four of them in the city of Waco. Indeed, the vast majority of the murderous acts took place in Waco (see appendix). All but one of the lynching victims were African American. No one was ever convicted for these murders.

Located in central Texas, McLennan County, named for an early settler, was established by the Texas legislature in 1850 with Waco as the county seat. The area is traversed by the Brazos River, which served as an important steamboat route until the Waco and Northwestern Railroad reached Waco in 1872, followed by the Houston and Texas Central. Electric cars ran through the city by 1891, and at least two electric trolleys were erected within a decade to transport the city's citizens. McLennan's population stood at over 13,000 by 1870 and nearly doubled by the following decade. The county seat grew at an even greater rate. The city's population surged to 20,686, nearly triple what it had been just two decades prior. By 1900, Waco boasted 6 banks, 163 factories, and the yearly addition of 1,300 homes. In 1912, the Young Man's Business League characterized Waco as "a true Southern city which is possessed of all the business possibilities of the metropolitan cities in the world."[5] By 1914, approximately 35,000 people resided in what had become a bustling urban center and the sixth largest city in the state. Boosters in the area dubbed Waco "The Wonder City" while stressing the city's "progressiveness."[6]

African Americans began migrating to the area immediately following emancipation. Many worked as agricultural laborers but by the end of the century would increasingly find employment in the area's growing industries. Others would migrate to the urbanizing area to take advantage of entrepreneurial and educational opportunities. By at least 1875, Black-owned businesses appeared in Waco. The city operated schools for

Black children the next year. In 1881, the historically Black institution Paul Quinn College relocated to the city and provided elementary, collegiate, and vocational education for area African Americans. Just over a decade later, a second Black college opened its doors in the city; Central Texas Academy graduated its first class of African Americans in 1896. By 1900, the percentage of African Americans in Waco stood at nearly one third as migrants continued to arrive from rural areas to take advantage of the city's varied economic opportunities.[7]

Turner's candid, heartfelt letter captures the tenor of race relations in and around Waco in the midst of vast changes that worked to redefine the everyday lives of Black people. Even the hurried, almost breathless nature of his prose is revealing: "I wish I was in your office so I could explain every detail of this affair its awful we are Disfranchised no protection in the courts everything mean being thrust upon [us] we are accused by our enemies tried and convicted by them."[8] Perhaps the structure of his letter is simply evidence of an inadequate education, or perhaps it is demonstrative of a raw urgency and panic felt by area African Americans in the face of mounting racial tensions that seemed to keep pace with increasing Black populations. He closed the letter by lamenting that African Americans were not selected for jury service, then he entreated the district attorney to investigate the recent lynching in the area.[9] The acting attorney general forwarded Turner's letter to Henry Terrell, the United States Attorney for the Western District of Texas. Writing from his office in San Antonio, Terrell reminded the Department of Justice in his response that race relations remained a local matter: "The race question in the south [sic], as you are well aware, is a political one, and the offenses committed against the negro can only be punished, if at all, by the local municipal. The federal officials are powerless to aid or protect the negro against assaults by his fellow citizen, either black or white."[10] Concluding the letter with an almost indignant tone, Terrell questioned why he had ever been made aware of the situation: "I do not understand that I am called on by the Department to express my own views or to make any recommendations in the premises."[11]

The hopeless exchange between Turner and the attorneys-general reveals much about the region's response to the increasing social interaction of Black and white people in a post-emancipation society. Neither in the courts nor in the public streets were African Americans safeguarded from the ire of local white people who resented the presence of expanding Black populations. It seemed that increasingly discriminatory practices and racialized collective violence as well as the attendant implications—from the simply injurious, some of which is evidenced by Turner's letter, to the unrelentingly lethal—moved in tandem with Black migration to the area.

I argue in this chapter that exploring the shifting position (both perceived and real) of African Americans in the social hierarchy by the end of the nineteenth century, together with white Texans' subsequent attempts to reconstitute their own supremacy, lends further understanding to how and why racial contestation in the work and home spheres mounted and often collectivized in various discriminatory or violent actions, such as lynching. This also lends to our understanding of how lynching became a viable option for leisure. In Texas, increasing industrial development created new sites for African American employment that ultimately led to intense racial contestation over space. White people in the state frequently feared that Black migration surely meant the racial invasion of neighborhoods, schools, parks, and other safeguarded private and public domains. Black migration in Texas thereby helped to engender a resentment and rage that frequently gave way to unchecked mob violence against Black people. Indeed, there is a discernible link between the increase in Black populations in Texas towns and cities and increased mob violence, and other forms of racial terror, in those areas.

Thousands of African Americans boarded trains and fled the South during the late nineteenth and early twentieth centuries and headed largely for northern urban centers that boasted employment opportunities and the absence of overt Jim Crow; others hopped on steamships or traveled in carriages to western settlements that promised landownership. Large numbers of rural Black people opted instead to resettle in some southern cities and towns, including those across the state of Texas. The greater number of employment opportunities in Texas factories, together with the precariousness of agricultural work, encouraged African Americans to flee rural Texas and relocate in the state's growing towns and cities. Thousands of new wage earners hailed from agricultural areas where fluctuating agricultural prices and yields left many unemployed or financially wary, forcing them to seek less mercurial opportunities in factories. Even when the availability of agricultural work did not impact employment opportunities, Black migrants nevertheless traded in the fields for the factories, longing for relief from the socially and economically restrictive nature of sharecropping, tenant farming, and other plantation work. African Americans migrated to cities and towns in the region at an unprecedented pace to work in the cottonseed oil, flour, rice, shingle, and sawmills; packing houses; coal mines; brick manufacturers; the lumber camps of the hinterlands; or the eastern Texas wharves that housed expanding fish and oyster foundries. Others migrated to establish businesses or practice professions to serve expanding Black communities.[12]

Black Texans, nearly 90 percent of whom lived in the eastern three-fifths of the state by the end of the nineteenth century, were far less likely to leave their native state as compared to those in other southern states due in part to employment options offered in urbanizing areas. On average, 20 percent of African Americans born in the South did not reside in their state of birth in 1920, as compared to only 10 percent of native-born Texans. In 1930, nearly a quarter of African Americans born in Mississippi, 29 percent of those born in Georgia, and 19 percent of those born in Louisiana lived in another state as compared to only 13 percent of Texas-born African Americans. The state's towns and cities offered a viable option for Black Texans who longed for the employment, social, and/or financial opportunities available. Industry-based Texas cities such as Dallas (Dallas County) and Houston (Harris County), for instance—where railroads became the largest employers until World War I—as well as the surrounding areas attracted thousands of Black migrants in search of employment. The Black population of Dallas nearly tripled between 1900 and 1920, for instance.[13] Houston's Black population more than tripled during those same years. People who already resided on the periphery of urbanizing spaces remained where they had previously been but left the fields for the factories. The number of wage earners in the eastern region of the state more than doubled within ten years at the turn of the century and grew even larger in some areas of the state.[14]

As African Americans arrived in Texas towns and cities where slavery had existed (largely the eastern three-fifths of the state) and white domination continued, rivalry for subsistence wages mounted and racial tensions flared, pitting white against Black and seemingly threatening white people's socioeconomic standing. In September 1909, the *Southwest* reported that several mills near Waco were temporarily inoperative because Black employees of the mills "had gone cotton picking where they could make more." [15] Their white coworkers were therefore non-voluntarily unemployed, a situation which did nothing to improve race relations in the area. "Fears of labor competition in San Angelo" during 1909 caused "whites to beat a black janitor and drive other Negroes from the town," according to one observer.[16]

Even the toil of those who remained in the fields was eased by industrial growth as mechanization rendered farm work less time-consuming. Mechanization facilitated increased output, which typically ensured amplified productivity. As a result, workers achieved more free time. As famed sociologist William F. Ogburn argued, "science and technology, especially the production of machines, paved the way for many other achievements, including free time."[17] The average number of days that the lumber mills operated in Texas was 260.3, for instance, five fewer than the national average. By the first decade of the twentieth century, people in some Texas counties worked an average of 7.5 hours per day. Thus, industrial development and mechanization, not simply as a matter of migratory patterns that produced or enhanced racial contestation, reduced the number of work hours for those who escaped agricultural drudgery as wage-earning labor, thereby increasing their expenditure of free time.[18]

How people spend their non-working hours is often conditioned appreciably by the dynamics in their environment. The delineators of leisure expenditures are wholly connected to and reconstituted by the rhythms of everyday life. Early twentieth century cultural critic and journalist Henry Louis Mencken insists that "the nature of the work [a man] does in the world conditions every thought and impulse of his life, and his general attitude toward it is almost indistinguishable from his general attitude toward the cosmos. A man's politics, theology and other vices engage his attention, after all . . . in his moments of leisure."[19]

Black Progress and White Disdain

By the late nineteenth century, the increased presence and success of a new generation of African Americans brought already prevalent racial concerns of many white Texans to the forefront of white consciousness. A "New Negro" had emerged, one who, as a Black Texas newspaper described in 1895, "takes advantages of his opportunities."[20] The sons and daughters of formerly enslaved people were coming into adulthood and prospering, consequently challenging white supremacy in Texas and the South at-large. Increasing prosperity, however relative, of the first several generations to reach adulthood following emancipation challenged white supremacy and rendered social control of Black people a principal concern. The swelling of Black populations in towns and urban centers during the period meant job competition, Black progress, and what historian Allen Spears refers to as "increased social visibility," all of which grated on the already thin racial tolerance of white people as they threatened racial purity of an ostensible white space. Those who remained in areas where agriculture dominated where no longer bound to the hegemony imposed by slavery.

White people in the state frequently feared that Black migration surely meant the racial invasion of neighborhoods, schools, parks, and other safeguarded domains. From the perspective of many whites across the state, the boundaries of African Americans' place in society were becoming increasingly elusive, a perception created and sustained by the changing sociopolitical and economic roles of African Americans. W. E. B. Du Bois insisted in the *Crisis* that white people "feared more than Negro dishonesty, ignorance and incompetency [sic]," they feared "Negro honesty, knowledge, and efficiency."[21] Du Bois would repeatedly advance such critiques of the fear of Black progress; his words would incite the ire of many across the state, including a journalist for the Texas Ku Klux Klan organ *100% American*. In "The Real Black Menace," a 1923 article aimed at reproving both Du Bois and the commentaries he published in the *Crisis*, a white journalist charged that "the negro, in his place, is a man rightfully where he belongs, but one out of his place is the most out of the place thing in creation."[22] He then lambasted Du Bois—"the real Black menace"—for decrying the horrors of lynching, claiming Du Bois "and his kind are the real criminals who put the Imps of hades [sic] in the half-baked brains of the black devils who despoil their helpless victims. A negro, in his place, never does these diabolical deeds; a negro out of his place does."[23] The same issue reprinted a letter penned by Du Bois as a response to one received from E. M. Edwards of Waco. "We want to call your especial attention to the deliberate and studied attempt at insult in this black negro's letter," the editor counseled. Du Bois steadfastly reminded readers, "the white race is not superior to the black race."[24] Characterized by the paper as an "insult to Anglo-Saxons," the Du Bois letter offered the following as a concluding dictate: "If you think you are going to stop the advance of the black race by burning and mobbing, you have only to remember that you have done a good deal of that in the past and you haven't stopped us yet."[25]

Everett Dean Martin insisted in his examination of crowd behavior early in the twentieth century, "the mobs who attack Negroes are uniformly made of people who . . . find no other social support than the mere fact that they happen to belong to the white race."[26] If a "nigger puts on airs," white people "find their self-feeling injured," he added; "The presumptuous negroes who serve as such unpleasant reminders 'must be put in their proper place.'"[27] When a "misdeed is committed by a black man," Martin further contended, it "provides the whites with just the pretext they want."[28] Mary Church Terrell insisted in 1905, "no language is sufficiently caustic, bitter and severe, to express the disgust, hatred and scorn which Southern gentlemen feel for what is called the 'New Issue,' which, being interpreted, means negroes who aspire to knowledge and culture, and who have acquired a taste for the highest and best things in life."[29] White Texans often felt personally assaulted by Black prosperity and autonomy, a racist ideology that defined how they interacted with Blacks even when outside the state. In December 1906, two white Texas cowboys attempted to lynch John E. Lewis, a Black man, aboard a train traveling from Lawrence, Kansas to Wichita, Kansas. Three times they attempted to place a rope around Lewis's neck before he leaped from the train to escape. When passengers attempted to come to Lewis's aid, the cowboys brandished weapons as a clear warning to others. Lewis was donning a Knights of Pythias pin that indicated his membership in the fraternal order. The cowboys were offended by a Black man "putting on airs," according to an observer.[30] Indeed, the racialization of lynching is largely reflective of the shift in race relations in Texas following emancipation and demonstrates the growing importance that white people placed on controlling the social, economic, and political mobility of African Americans. Edgar Gardner Murphy, a white progressive reformer, observed early in the twentieth century that southern white people's growing racial intolerance shifted "from an undiscriminating attack upon the Negro's ballot to a like attack upon his schools, his labor, his life—from the contention that no Negro shall vote to the contention that no Negro shall learn that no Negro shall labor, and (by implication) that no Negro shall live."[31] In his early twentieth century investigation of lynching, Walter Francis White, the national NAACP assistant secretary at the time, observed that the lynching of African Americans was "much more an expression of Southern fear of Negro progress than of Negro crime."[32] In this he echoed an earlier comment by Frederick Douglass, who averred: "The Negro meets no resistance when on a downward course. It is only when he rises in wealth, intelligence, and manly character that he brings upon himself the heavy hand of persecution."[33] A reporter for the *Charleston News and Courier* in 1915 leveled similar contentions:

> There is an element of white people who find expression of race superiority only in keeping the inferior race as stupid, uninformed, and inefficient as individuals as it is possible. Their adoption of this course is spontaneous and it is inspired by the first flash of an unthinking instinct for self-preservation without sitting down intelligently to figure out how best to accomplish it. To so fit themselves that they can turn the increased efficiency, the high standard of the apparently encroaching inferior race to their own profit, comfort and increment and the general enrichment of the community, does not occur at all. The only impulse is to kill what appears to be a dangerous competitor. It is unthinking, suicidal and disturbingly stupid.[34]

Scholars, activists, reporters and others who wrote or lectured about lynching during the early portion of the twentieth century often cited a type of southern sequestration—a geographic and social removal from modern, civilized cultural norms and mores—as the underlying impetus for lynching. They frequently characterized mob violence as an archaic expression of backwoods, southern White people. Some recent studies have nuanced our understanding of where and why racialized social violence collectivizes. For instance, James H. Madison argues in his study of the lynching of a Black man in Marion, Indiana, on August 7, 1930, that the lynchers interpreted the act as a type of reform necessitated by changes in the social landscape. Industrialization and urbanization in Marion created fears of immorality, corruption, and increases in crime. Work and migratory patterns brought Black and white people in closer and more frequent contact and competition with one another, which subsequently threatened what white people perceived to be an increasing elusiveness of African Americans place in society. It seemed economic development was reconfiguring racial interplay and giving way to increased acts of racialized social violence. The statistical data collected for this study reveals a linear correlation between the rise of urbanization and the racialization of lynching in the state of Texas. My research demonstrates that mob violence against African Americans in Texas occurred frequently in urbanizing or growing areas rather than simply in rural, remote communities as increased rates of migration and the resultant racial contestation over space often facilitated lethal expressions of white racial superiority.

Changes ushered in by the rise in industrial capitalism facilitated the spectacle of the acts as well. Increased population density attendant to expanding economies gave way to mass lynch mobs numbering in the hundreds or even thousands who frequently witnessed lynching in the downtown public spaces of the state's towns and cities. The crowd that burned Will Stanley in Temple's public square on July 30, 1915, numbered over five thousand. "All about," reported a journalist for the Black-owned *Chicago Defender*, "the streets were filled with pedestrians and automobiles loaded with fascinated onlookers."[35]

Industrial Growth, Race, and Migration

By the turn of the twentieth century, the worth of industrial products in Texas more than tripled and manufacturing's value grew at nearly the same rate. Touting the state's industrial growth during the period, the *Texas Almanac* noted in 1904:

> The past six years have been the golden years in Texas history. They have been years of great industrial activity; hopes long cherished have been realized; plans long nurtured have brought success . . . Manufacturing in the five principal [sic] cities of the State increased 47.2 per cent in the number of wage earners and 48.4 per cent in the value of products from 1890 to 1900; in the thirty principal towns, 65.1 and 59.3 respectively, while the increase in value of products for the entire State was 69.5 per cent. These figures indicate a rapid increase in manufacturing in the rural districts.[36]

Resources manufactured from flour, sugar, and cotton seed became staple products of varied mills in the middle and eastern portions of the state. By 1900, the cottonseed oil industry product value in the state reached more than fourteen million dollars, a figure that ranked it second among other Texas industries. The average number of wage-earners in the state increased from 38,604 in 1899 to 70,230 in 1909.[37] Across the region, the rapid proliferation of industry broadened employment opportunities. Some towns, such as Texarkana in northeastern Texas, could boast of a mingling of industries. The 1904 *Texas Almanac* maintained that in the city, which "was on its way to being a manufacturing center," existed: "two furniture factories or large capacity, one handle factory, one barrel factory, one cotton press, two cotton seed oil mills, numerous lumber companies, one ice plant, several bottling concerns, two iron foundries, two gas companies, electric light system." The area also boasted four newspapers, a sewer system, and brick schools. "This town is becoming a very important jobbing center," the almanac claimed.[38] City status was conferred upon Texarkana in 1907. In 1900, white residents numbered 3,292 and Black residents numbered 1,964. By 1910, the white population nearly doubled while the Black population increased by nearly 50 percent.[39]

As African Americans migrated to Texas towns and cities, rivalry for subsistence wages mounted within the milieu of flared white racial tension. Such events pitted white against Black and left white people's economic standing and social identity threatened. Take, for instance, the attitudes of white citizens when African Americans migrated to the region east of Houston to work as longshoremen or in oil refineries. The Magnolia refinery monthly newsletter revealed, as Bruce A. Glasrud and James Smallwood posit in their study on Black labor in Texas, that many whites experienced "animosity" toward the expanding presence of Black labor and their community leaders.[40] At the Beaumont refinery, white employees grumbled in 1921, "mules, niggers, wheelbarrows, and a few white men" comprised a significant portion of the plant's workforce.[41]

W. E. B. Du Bois's pivotal 1935 study entitled *Outline of Report on Economic Condition of Negroes in the State of Texas*, recounts and analyzes how racialized capitalism in Texas, subject to the contours of white supremacy, grossly challenged Black laborers' ability to thrive. Unpublished in its entirety until 2019, the study, which Du Bois first delivered as a speech at the Sixth Annual State Conference on Negro Education held at Prairie View State College, corroborated the experiences of countless African Americans in the state regarding the gravity of the economic hardships that plagued their existence. As scholar Phillip Luke Sinitiere emphasizes, Du Bois's lecture "offers additional documentation of his more robust engagement with Marxist thought in which he proposed a socialist solution to the economic travails of White supremacy and imperialism."[42] Using a combination of census data, reports from business owners who employed over five thousand Black workers, various studies on working conditions among Black factory and agricultural laborers, as well as empirical observations, Du Bois's *Outline* presaged a near disastrous future for African Americans in the state, one fraught by mounting efforts to stymie Black advancement. Du Bois emphasized the necessity for Black colleges to teach "what is technically necessary for present human existence."[43] But "until the matter of income and the character and division of labor, and the whole social relation of the worker to the home is settled by institutions outside the school," they would not be able to train people to move beyond their marginalized posts in industry.[44] Du Bois had openly advocated for a society aligned more closely with socialist ideologies: "I talked socialism but they didn't know it," he later seemed to lament to his wife in a letter.[45] In closing, Du Bois reminded those in attendance at the symposium that "poverty stricken and inadequately paid industrial workers whom we have studied in the conference spend every month a quarter of a million dollars."[46] He then enjoined them to recognize the unfulfilled power of this pecuniary arrangement: "Conceive what this means in economic power if it is used with intelligence and under organized direction."[47]

Eastern Texas was increasingly converting its varied natural resources into industry by the postbellum era, consequently attracting migrant workers and altering the breadth of industrial capitalism for Texans. Texas's hinterlands created a large wage earner employment base for the eastern

Rocks painted with warnings to Black people to stay out of the Texas town. Edwards and Kimble County line, 1911. *Texas State Library.*

portion of the state by the end of the nineteenth century. The expanse and importance of the industry during the late nineteenth and early twentieth centuries contrasted sharply with the antebellum era. The editor of the *Houston Morning Star* bewailed in 1840 that the city was forced to "import the commonest varieties of lumber at the exorbitant price of from forty to fifty dollars a thousand" feet.[48] The lumber was imported from the northeast and commanded high prices due to the cost of transportation. Contemporary observers frequently commented on the inherent irony in having to purchase lumber outside of the state when such rich resources existed locally. Jacob DeCordova, a Texas writer, observed in 1856, "It must indeed seem strange . . . that we should be compelled to import so large an amount of lumber into Texas . . . Not only to Mobile are we indebted for timber and lumber, but large quantities are brought from the State of Maine."[49] During the antebellum era, few sawmills operated in the state due to primitive equipment and an inadequate supply of workers. "The cutting, transport, and sawing of timber required a considerable work force, even for a small mill," note Thad Sitton and James H. Conrad in their study on Texas sawmill communities.[50] After the Civil War, expanded railway lines; innovations in sawing equipment, power generation, and feed carriages; and northern entrepreneurs who recognized the vast financial opportunities available in lumber for the country's rapidly expanding population, coalesced to transform a meager trade into a major employer and revenue-generating industry in the state of Texas. Following the repeal of the 1866 Homestead Act, southern legislatures made public lands available for purchase, which lured investors to the woods of Texas. "The door to the Southern timberland was thrust wide open," historian Thomas Clark averred: "Land speculators of every stripe rushed into the region in search of virgin tracts of timber to lay low."[51] In 1870, East Texas's lumber-producing plants yielded $2 million in total value. Ten years later, the reported worth doubled. By 1890, lumber and sawmills were worth approximately six times what they had been just two decades prior, rendering the "gross and net values of products of these mills . . . first among manufacturing industries in Texas and tenth in the nation," notes historian Ruth Allen.[52] The industry grew at similar rates during subsequent decades. In 1900, in the eastern portion of Texas there were 637 lumber- and sawmills, which were steadily becoming several counties' "greatest source of wealth."[53] A study of 294 sawmills in the state in 1905 determined that, within five years, the number of laborers had nearly doubled. By 1907, board feet of lumber produced annually reached 2.25 billion, which ranked third in the nation. The expanding lumber industry prompted the proliferation of industries and manufacturers that were wholly dependent upon the production of lumber. Coffin and casket, wooden container, and furniture were among the new auxiliaries of timber. At least seventy-three furniture-making establishments operated in the eastern portion of the state by 1900.[54]

The growth of the lumber industry was so rapid that between 1870 and 1930, it was the top employer of wage earners in Texas.[55] Men across the state decided to vacate farms and seek employment in the proliferating lumber camps and sawmill towns. The migration resulted in a 202 percent increase in Texas timber industry wage earners by 1910. Revealing the importance of the lumber mills to the livelihood of Texas towns, one Texas Bible-belt newspaper chortled, "in Texas a smokestack is as sacred as a church steeple."[56] Work in Texas mills and camps could be treacherous, leading in many cases to maiming and death. The United States Bureau of the Census cited sawmilling and logging among the most dangerous occupations in the country. The wages, however, easily topped those earned through sharecropping, tenant farming, and work in a number of other industries.[57] Tens of thousands of workers traded low wages and exceptionally long hours for the safety hazards of the lumber industry by the early twentieth century. Over eighty thousand African American men across the South found employment in the camps and mills by 1910, a rate that far surpassed their employment in southern cotton textile mills, iron, and steel.[58]

Texas camps and towns erected segregated housing, schools, and other institutions for its workers, a special ordering that reflected and reinforced contemporary, discriminatory mores. Many workspaces, however, as a matter of logistics, remained integrated. This spatial binary hardly worked to lessen racial tensions. One observer grunted that some Texas companies were concerned "one little spark" might ignite a grave racial clash.[59] When violence erupted at the Call Mill after a Black sawyer was hired to replace a white one, the general manager at the Kirby Lumber Company mill sent a letter to his company official to warn against such actions: "I don't believe it is good policy to keep an extra negro sawyer. In other words, I doubt whether the white men will ever stand for a negro doing the sawing. A negro is all right as long as he is held within certain bounds, but it will not do to let him get to the top job."[60] Within a week, a Kirby company official penned his endorsement of the general manager's counsel: "Wish to advise that I have already instructed that we discontinue using this negro or another one as an entire sawyer or any other job which is termed a white man's job . . . We have enough trouble without doing something that is liable to bring on more.[61]

The Black populations in industrializing mill towns and lumber camps often generated enmity among white farmers and stockmen from the surrounding communities. The *Southern Industrial and Lumber Review* carped in 1908:

> Cases of trouble between the sawmill companies and the farmers owning the land close to the mills have been the cause of a great deal of trouble during the past year. In most cases the trouble seems to be purely malicious on the part of the farmers. They sell the timber on their lands to the sawmill companies, and when these concerns send their crews to cut the timber, the farmers refused to allow the Negro workers of the company to venture on their land to cut the timber. During the past month, there have been reports of trouble of this nature from the mill of the Carter-Kelly company at Manning. It was found necessary to get officers to protect the colored laborers while they were doing their work.[62]

The Diboll school house in Angelina County, Texas, educated African American children from the local mill town. Circa 1907. The teacher in the photo is J. W. Hogg. *The History Center, Diboll, Texas.*

The camps and towns' stores, schools, churches, and housing kept workers isolated from local communities, but local residents nonetheless resented the presence of non-white workers. To maintain goodwill among their neighbors, however, the lumber towns and camps offered varied services, including medical help and machinery maintenance, for outsiders. As Thad Stitton and James H. Conrad argue, however, "isolation and friendly gestures failed to overcome local people's distaste for strange blacks and Mexicans in their midst."[63] One Black man insisted the town of Slocum, Texas, near the Fastrill Southern Pine camp, was wholly unwelcoming of African Americans: "You couldn't even stop there to buy gas."[64] Historian Flora Bowles contends that white residents of Groveton, Texas, resented the presence of both African Americans and Mexican Americans in the local lumber camps: "Sometimes the residents would object to the foreigner or the strange negro coming among them."[65] It was not unusual for signs to appear in Trinity County trees threatening Black lumber industry workers. One such sign read: "Nigger, don't let the sun rise on you here tomorrow morning."[66] Racial tensions from whites in and surrounding the camps often forced Black workers to seek employment elsewhere. Some opted to move instead to bustling urban centers such as Houston, Fort Worth, and Dallas where Black migratory patterns brought racial hostilities to the forefront of local consciousness, policy creation, and the reification white identity.

Black Migration and the Codification of Residential Spaces

Following Reconstruction in Texas and continuing until well after the middle of the twentieth century, white citizens and municipal entities worked to firmly establish a color line that ensured the racial purity of white space through conventional and non-conventional segregationist measures. City ordinances and state laws had only slowly started to codify residential segregation by the early 1890s as municipalities were increasingly concerned about the location of Black residences. By at least 1892, Sanborn insurance maps that provide information about the edifices (construction materials; whether or not they had windows, etc.) tracked Black households in cities across the state on maps by denoting "Negro Dwellings." The maps did not, however, indicate the location of dwellings where whites or Mexican Americans, the other two sizable populations, lived. Racial earmarkings were not endemic to Sanborn maps across the country. Sanborn maps of Chicago, for instance, did not disclose the racial dispersion in area neighborhoods during the same time period. The anomalous racial denotations on Sanborn maps in the state indicate a clear desire among Texans to track the presence of Black dwellings as a regulatory measure.[67] Not only did the municipalities strive to keep informed about the location of African Americans, city officials at times also promulgated concerns over the potential for Black population surges in the city. In 1890, for example, local city officials demonstrated a clear preoccupation with the potential for Black migration to Dallas. When debating whether or not to institute a citywide eight-hour workday, a member of the city council and opponent of the eight-hour ordinance declared to a crowd gathered in support of the statute, "The idea of eight hours in Dallas will go all over the state and every laborer will rush to Dallas. Yes, every negro will rush here."[68] The councilman's comment suggests a binary concern over Black migration—Black migrants, he likely feared, would take jobs local whites believed inherently belonged to them and move into white neighborhoods.

White Texans across the state interlinked residential space with racial identity; thus, invading the former necessarily functioned as an effrontery to the latter. Residential segregation practices codified during the early twentieth century were in large measure a reactionary contrivance to increasing local Black populations and subsequent encroachment on white residential areas. As Black populations in towns and cities swelled by the end of the nineteenth century, local whites grew ever more anxious about the racial purity of their neighborhoods and workplaces, and by consequence, other private and public sites. Racial contestation over Black migration rendered residential space a highly charged and violently eruptive commodity. Defending white neighborhoods from Black invasion articulated white supremacy in an extremely home-based fashion. Black presence in or near white neighborhoods brought social tensions between whites and African Americans dangerously close to the white home-sphere. Public transportation, schools, stores, and neighborhoods had remained virtually uncontested racial spaces in Dallas and many other Texas towns and cities until an increase in Black migration. Individuals' identities were wholly entangled with their home-based accomplishments; thus, their neighborhoods not only represented an achievement, an impressive ability to attain homeownership and perhaps elevate their class status via a propertied status, but it also stood as an extension of their identity. The invasion of a racialized other threatened the worth of white identity. If a Black person could achieve homeownership in a white neighborhood, open a local business, learn a vocation, or graduate from college, the perceived merit of whites' accomplishments diminished. The manner in which many local whites defined themselves was largely tied to the identity established by their neighborhood. As their neighborhoods increasingly became a hotbed of Black encroachment, whites found new ways to articulate and safeguard the importance of their residential spaces as they expressed and reconstituted their racial identity.

Inequitable treatment of African Americans was apparent on the physical landscape of Black communities in cities and towns across the state. In 1900, a Black-owned circular in Texas charged that "the wards in which the majority of our people reside are generally the wards most poorly looked after. The streets are generally paved less [than in white neighborhoods], and as a rule, it is the fault of the [all white] aldermen."[69] Despite the lack of public works maintenance in Black sections of cities and towns, African Americans continued to strive for autonomy. Although most sought employment in downtown businesses or in the homes of whites, local African Americans relied on one another to provide other necessities for survival, thus promoting the continued proliferation of Black-owned businesses, churches, and schools by the turn of the century.[70] In turn, the existence of these institutions further promoted African American migration to those areas. The growing Black populations encouraged the migration of Black professionals to towns and cities to service African Americans who were typically barred from white institutions or unwelcome at best. These individuals joined, and in some cases swelled, the extant ranks of business owners and other Black migrants who savored the financial and social mobility inherent in bustling towns and urban centers, and who preferred to stay in Texas rather than join the throngs of African Americans who escaped north. Consequently, the consortium of African Americans equipped with the financial means to enjoy homeownership increased, which engendered statewide debates over racial integration. Encroachment consequently beckoned the alarmist reactions of whites who pleaded with state and city officials to prevent integration in white neighborhoods. Texas policymakers thus codified segregation practices as both preventative measures against, as well as responses to, the threat posed by racial integration. [71]

Black Mobility and White Backlash: Dallas, a Case Study

Evelyn Howell Carter moved to Caddo Street with her family in 1927, just before violence erupted. "White people were living on Caddo and they really didn't want the blacks," Carter recalled.[72] Her father, Jasper Louis, was a well-to-do Black undertaker in Dallas—a position yielding a salary that afforded him the luxury of homeownership. After being displaced by the forthcoming construction of North Central Avenue in Freedman's Town (a Black community adjacent to the central business district often referred to as "North Dallas"), Louis purchased a home on Caddo for his family. Shortly after the family moved into their new home, two houses were bombed. Concerned that his home was next, Louis courted the assistance of two of his friends to help "watch" the home "to see if [the bombers] came."[73] The watchers were local Black doctors, both of whom had contemplated purchasing homes on Caddo prior to the bombings. Louis and his wife toted Carter, only six at the time, along with her siblings to Carter's grandmother's house in South Dallas to ensure their safety. After several nights of standing guard, Louis grew increasing aggravated. "I'm going to . . . get my money back and go as far away from over here as I can go," Carter remembers her father vowing just before he sold the house and relocated his family to a Black portion of South Dallas.[74] She vividly recalled the remorse she and her siblings felt over having to move to South Dallas: "We had to leave all our friends in North Dallas. We hated it."[75] Louis preferred the familiarity of Freedman's Town adjacent to Caddo Street, but few homes were available for purchase in the enclave, except for those along the periphery in predominantly white areas such as Caddo Street. For Louis, the risk of living on Caddo Street far outweighed the benefits; thus, relocation proved the only feasible option for him and his family.[76]

During the early twentieth century, Caddo Street in and near Freedman's Town attracted Black professionals like Louis who were equipped with both the financial means to better their living conditions and the desire to remain close to the communal core of Dallas's Black community. While moving to outlying streets offered evasion from overcrowding and the blight subsequent to residential congestion, tumult accompanied relocation. White residential areas typically encircled Black communities; thus, increased Black migration inevitably resulted in encroachment into white neighborhoods and provoked vehement—and at times violent—objections from whites unwilling to endure integration. White residents occupied all of Caddo Street from Watt Street to Ross Avenue subsequent to the inception of the residential area. By 1927, however, African Americans began to occupy the 2300 block of Caddo, inciting the violent reaction of whites who were committed to halting integration. During February and March 1927 alone, four African Americans homes, which taken together constituted one-half of the block, were bombed.[77]

Police launched an investigation into the bombings, but the culprits were never apprehended. While the violent resistance to integration did prevent some African Americans from residing on Caddo Street, others nonetheless continued to migrate there, which, in turn, compelled white residents of the area to vacate their homes. Whites who resided on streets that encircled the Freedman's Town area, as well as those who lived on predominantly Black blocks within the enclave, continued to flee to white portions of the city that boasted an absence of Black presence and encroachment. By the 1920s, State Street and Thomas Avenue (popularly referred to as "State-Thomas"), two previously all-white, upwardly mobile streets located north of Freedman's Town, were known citywide as the residential district of the Black elite, thereby definitively forging the separation of economically diverse African Americans who were already subjected to Dallas's residential segregation customs and laws.[78]

Attempts to restrict the geographic and social mobility of African Americans in Texas during the late nineteenth century and extending well into the twentieth century assumed various implicit and explicit expressions, including cartographical markings that tracked Black households, the barring of African Americans from businesses and other institutions, the legal segregation of educational facilities, and violence. While moving to outlying streets offered evasion from overcrowding and the blight subsequent to residential congestion in some Black areas, tumult accompanied relocation, as evidenced by Carter's experiences. By examining the growth of a local Black community—in this case, Dallas—we can more fully understand how and why late nineteenth and early twentieth century assertions of white supremacy positioned the racial contestation over space in the vanguard of white consciousness. Understanding the contours of white resistance to Black geographic mobility is paramount in fully gauging the disdain and subsequent violence engendered by shifting work and residential patterns during the era.

Dallas, together with many other cities and towns across the state, was quickly industrializing late in the nineteenth century, consequently safeguarding itself from the potential perils of agrarian economies. Dallas city directories vaunted the copious "manufactures" in the city, listing various commodities manufactured and reporting annual monies yielded in any given industry. Directories further exalted Dallas enterprises by boasting, "products produced are equal to the finest in the entire land." The 1884–1885 volume asserted, "the future outlook for Dallas is a brilliant one" for the city's "growth has been steady and above the average of Texas cities." The information was far more than mere boosterism. Dallas was in fact the most industrialized city in the state by the 1880s. Had a prospective resident not perused the city's directories, or not been well-versed in Dallas's industrial ranking and gross productivity, they would still have likely been aware that a growing urban center had plenty of jobs. Whether lured by potential employment opportunities or the general appeal of an urban center, migrants arrived in Dallas and moved to those areas that were already occupied by their racial group.

On July 16, 1872, the Houston and Texas Central (H&TC) Railroad became the first to traverse the city of Dallas. Because it spurred employment and economic opportunities at an unprecedented rate, the railroad had a tremendous impact on the location and development of African American enclaves in the city and county. Railroad depots frequently hired African Americans as porters, railroad technicians, and janitors. The railroad also allowed easy access to outlying farms, which enabled day laborers to live in African American enclaves within the city along the tracks. Furthermore, much of the land adjacent to the tracks was unsettled and therefore open for Black residency. As a result of employment opportunities and vacant lands, an archipelago of African American communities dotted the railroad line from where it intersected with downtown all the way north to the city limits.[79] For instance, the H&TC was directly responsible for the development of Stringtown, an African American enclave north of downtown. Consisting of a row of shotgun houses "strung out" along the grade of the H&TC, Stringtown laid along the tracks where they intersected with Bryan and San Jacinto, and reached northward to Hall Street. The city made several other land purchases by the 1880s in an effort to accommodate Dallas's rapidly increasing population, which by 1880 had reached 10,358—an increase of approximately 7,000 people from the previous census count. During the following decade, the population surged, climbing to 38,067 by 1890. The bustling urban center had become the largest city in the state. Such unprecedented increases beckoned the addition of land to accommodate the population. With the population rapidly increasing in both the city and surrounding unincorporated areas, developers were motivated to buy tracts of land to incorporate into the city and profit on the housing needs of Dallasites. Land was developed and added so quickly that by 1890, the city had tripled in size.[80] Although the Black and white populations of Dallas had nearly quadrupled between 1880 and 1890, rendering both in need of additional housing, land additions made to the city during the period primarily served to fulfill the residential needs of the white population. Residential options for African Americans who migrated to the city prior to the turn of the century were largely limited to the areas previously occupied by other African Americans.[81]

In 1900, the number of Black residents in the city reached 9,035 of an overall population that numbered just over 42,000. By the beginning of the next decade, 18,024 Black people resided in the city. Ten years later, the Black population had increased to more than 24,000 of the city's approximately 158,000 residents. The population increases led to greater residential density within extant Black communities. Considering that several African American areas of the city were become increasingly overcrowded early in the decade, large portions of the Black enclaves quickly fell to disrepair. The lack of housing led African Americans to fill hotels and rent rooms in homes as residential alternatives. Property owners converted many single-family homes to multiple-family dwellings due to the high demand for African American housing. African Americans continued to migrate to Dallas during the decade, despite the limited residential options within the confines of segregated communities. Deterioration and the lack of homes for sale forced a substantial number of African Americans to seek residency along the outer portions of established Black communities where housing was more plentiful and more aesthetically appealing. They desired relief from the increasing deterioration of portions of Black neighborhoods where municipal neglect of public works merely exacerbated the effects of over-crowding. Most who sought housing on streets that bordered already established Black communities were those equipped with the financial means to purchase rather than rent dwellings.

Limited room for geographic expansion led many white residents of the city who lived in neighborhoods adjacent to expanding Black communities to flee from the growth; they sold or rented their homes to African Americans and moved to racially homogenous areas of the city and county.[82] Attempting to capitalize on the depressed state of many African American neighborhoods in Dallas and other urban centers, land developers and real estate companies purchased large portions of white residential districts. In turn, purchasers made the property available to African Americans who were otherwise subjected to overcrowded, unsanitary conditions in segregated districts of the city. Investors typically rented or sold these areas for substantially more than the market price, making the business of buying white-owned property and selling it to African Americans extremely lucrative. To further increase the potential for profit, investors announced to local whites that certain areas were being sold to African Americans, thus shrewdly playing off whites' concerns and their racist beliefs. In response, whites sought escape from their slowly integrating neighborhoods. Investors then purchased the property of worried whites for substantially lower prices than those they asked of African Americans who were in search of decent housing and willing to pay the markups.[83]

In 1916, a group of Deere Park white property owners insistent upon halting the migration of African Americans into their neighborhoods brought the issue of residential segregation before the Dallas City Council. William Connor, an African American man, purchased a home in the neighborhood "notwithstanding the protests of members of the Deere Park Improvement Association," noted a journalist at the time.[84] The association promised to reimburse Connor if he vacated his home. After Connor refused, his home was bombed. The assailants were never apprehended. Alarmist racial doctrines of white residents who opposed a Black presence in their communities dictated that neighborhood integration assuredly meant integrated schools, churches, and other facilities. Whites feared that the presence of African Americans in their environs would dismantle whites' racial superiority. Whiteness in America at once naturalized privilege while providing a hegemonic order to society in which African Americans were subjected to white delineations of societal structure. Being white afforded one a privileged status, entitlement to those things denied African Americans. Those African Americans who could afford to live in the same middle- and upper-middle-class neighborhoods as whites necessarily challenged the privilege associated with whiteness, lowering the prestige of whites' accomplishments. Black encroachment in white residential areas suggested that African Americans could occupy the same social status as their white neighbors, blurring the line that separated white from Black. Encroachment also demonstrated that African Americans were objecting to the established order of southern society. African Americans such as the man who moved to Deere Park denounced white objections to integration by the very act of moving to white neighborhoods. Such acts infuriated white citizens and consequently prompted city officials to address the increasingly volatile situation.[85]

Armed with a sufficient number of signatures on a petition that called for residential segregation, the Deere Park property owners presented their concerns to the city council in 1916. Noting that "there is now no ordinance prescribing and requiring the use of separate blocks by white and colored races, for residences and for other purposes," the Council argued, "such a situation creates an urgency and an emergency for the immediate preservation of the public peace, health and safety. . . ."[86] The city council drafted a segregation ordinance and placed the issue in the hands of voters. Dallasites approved the measure, which the city council adopted as Ordinance 195. Incorporated into the 1916 amended city charter, the ordinance made it,

> unlawful for any white person to use as a residence or place of
> abode, any house, building or structure or any part thereof, located
> in any colored block, as the same is hereinafter defined; and it shall
> be unlawful for any colored person to use as a residence or place
> of abode, any house, building or structure, or any part thereof,
> located in any white block.[87]

Ordinance 195 defined the "colored race" as "all persons of African descent," and the "white race" as "all persons not of the colored race as colored race is herein defined." Hence, Mexican and Asian Americans—the other two sizable nonwhite populations in Dallas—were theoretically not restricted from using facilities or residing on blocks reserved for whites. This, however, did not preclude the groups from experiencing racism in the city. In addition to block-by-block residential segregation, the measure further prescribed that "no building in the city should be used as a church, for the purpose of conducting religious services, or for a school, a dance hall or an assembly hall by white persons in a colored block or by black persons in a white block."[88]

Such measures were not restricted to Dallas. Local governments across Texas and the South at-large instituted racial zoning laws during the early twentieth century. In Louisville, Kentucky, a racial zoning ordinance similar to that implemented in Dallas mandated that a Black person could not own a home on a block where the majority of residents were white. In 1917, an African American man filed suit against Louisville after the city rescinded the purchase of his property under the local zoning ordinance. Although the lower court and the Kentucky Court of Appeals upheld the ordinance as valid, the United States Supreme Court outlawed racial zoning in *Buchanan v. Warley* (1917).[89] Passed pursuant to the Fourteenth Amendment, the ruling resolved, "all citizens of the United States shall have the same right, in every State and Territory, as is enjoyed by white citizens thereof, to inherit, purchase, lease, sell, hold and convey real and personal property."[90] Despite the Supreme Court's ruling, the racial zoning decrees mandated in Ordinance 195 remained in the Dallas City Charter and continued to be used as a segregation measure. Racially zoned areas in Dallas only existed, however, when residences of a particular locale petitioned to restrict residency.[91] The size of a locale in question could be one or several blocks in area; and considering that not every section of every neighborhood in Dallas petitioned for such restrictions, numerous residential areas in Dallas were racially unrestricted. To further complicate the efficacy of local segregation, while restrictive covenants that mandated property be sold to and occupied by white people only could affect the sale of individual properties, not all deeds bore such stipulations. Enforcing the racial restrictions on one property would not necessarily prevent African Americans from moving into adjacent properties without covenants, which minimized the citywide effectiveness of this particular means of racial segregation. When only certain properties had restrictions in a particular locale, if the area was becoming integrated, some individuals ignored deeded restraints in an effort to escape integration and simply sold their homes to the highest bidder. Furthermore, enforcing the racial restrictions on properties could be quite costly when considering attorneys' fees, thereby possibly discouraging some residents from filing suits when neighbors ignored racial covenants and sold to African Americans. If willing to endure violence precipitated by their migration to white neighborhoods, and able to secure housing from a resident or real estate broker willing to sell to them, African Americans could reside in various areas of the city where some whites left quietly while others put up a fight.

Although racial zoning, restrictive covenants, and violence were not wholly successful means of segregation, they nonetheless minimized the residential mobility of African Americans. Moreover, overcrowding was not as severe prior to World War I which minimized the need for African Americans to seek residence elsewhere. Wartime and postwar population increase, however, and the subsequent residential congestion in Dallas's Black neighborhoods soon gave way to increased Black migration to white neighborhoods. African Americans frequently petitioned the city council for improvements in African American communities during the early portion of the twentieth century, which were frequently granted with a very specific intent. Greatly opposed to residential integration, Dallas city officials—encouraged by the segregationist sentiments of local whites—granted some neighborhood improvements, such as paved streets, in area Black neighborhoods to as a means of thwarting what was perceived as Black invasion in white neighborhoods. African Americans' efforts, however, were hardly conformist; indeed, by petitioning for improvements in public works, African Americans reappropriated the racism that pushed city officials to concede to such demands and used it as a means of racial uplift.[92]

As the Black population, along with their need for decent housing, in Dallas steadily increased, the city turned again to legal segregation when it appeared that their neighborhood beautification measures failed to produce the desired effect of containing African Americans in established Black communities. This time, however, Dallas city officials and planners sought to buttress their ability to legally separate the races by weighting their efforts with the force of state statute—a task which, if successful, would extend the option for residential segregation to municipalities across the state.

Residential Segregation for Dallas and the State At-Large

When the Liberty Annex Corporation (a for-profit residential development company) attempted to develop some property for Black inhabitance in the northern portion of the city in 1926, the city's objection ultimately and unwittingly challenged Dallas's continued use of unlawful racial zoning practices. A prior agreement between white petitioners and the city in 1924 restricted the area in question to white residency. The city granted residents' requests for the racial restraint on residency under Dallas Ordinance 1106, entitled "An ordinance providing for the segregation of white and colored races in accordance with an agreement entered into by the representatives of such races concerning the hereinafter described territory and decreeing an emergency."[93] Liberty Annex filed suit against the city of Dallas (*Liberty Annex Corporation v. The City of Dallas*) in 1926, seeking an injunction to prevent the city from enforcing the local segregation ordinance. Attorneys for the plaintiff argued that "the property is not fit for the residence of white people," and thereby suitable for Black residences.[94] Charging that Liberty Annex attempted to "foist Negroes on a white neighborhood," the city countered with a plea that the racial restriction on residency resulted from an agreement, which the city argued legitimized their attempts to prevent African Americans from residing on the property.[95] Implicit in the plaintiff's stance was an acknowledgement of the disparate conditions of residential areas for whites and African Americans. The city did not directly challenge the assertion of Liberty Annex that the area was not fit for whites, but instead sought the preservation of already extant residential restrictions. Removal of the restriction on one area, the city feared, could result in the unregulated residential dispersion of African Americans citywide.[96]

Much local sentiment supported the stance of the city, despite the unconstitutionality of the ordinance. Zoning measures that allowed for the drawing of residential lines based on race were ruled unconstitutional in *Buchanan v. Warley* (1917). The ruling mattered little to local residents. Supporters did not view the situation as one of race prejudice, but instead as a necessary means to achieve racial accord. The *Dallas Times Herald* acknowledged the ordinance's illegality, but insisted, "the real purpose for which it was adopted is meritorious"—the promotion of "harmony" between the races.[97] Instead of wholly implicating African Americans, however, supporters placed much of the blame on white developers who "sometimes sell to negroes without exercising discretion, and the negroes find that they cannot live harmoniously with their neighbors." One observer warned that "total abandonment of the segregation ordinance will not help matters," but would instead "lead to numerous complaints and arguments from both Whites and negroes."[98]

Judge Wilson in the 44th District Texas Court supported local sentiment and sustained Dallas's right to enforce its segregation ordinance. Citing the invalidity of the plaintiff's charge, Wilson dismissed the case in 1926. Liberty Annex appealed the decision. The Fifth Court of Civil Appeals ruled in favor of Liberty Annex, advancing an edict that recognized "the right to occupy, purchase and sell property may not be prohibited solely because of the color of the proposed occupant." According to the court, the segregation ordinance violated the Fourteenth Amendment. Dallas appealed to the Supreme Court.

While the case, *City of Dallas et al. v. Liberty Annex Corporation*, awaited ruling, Dallas city officials did not abandon their efforts to legally restrict the mobility of African Americans. Instead of heeding the Fifth Court of Civil Appeals 1926 decision as indicative of the unfeasibility of residential segregation through legal decree, local officials approached the ruling as a formality in their continued pursuit to ensure the racial homogeneity of white area neighborhoods. Indeed, since the case had not yet reached the Supreme Court, city officials deemed the issue of racial segregation judicially undecided. Rehabilitating the physical landscape of Black neighborhoods failed to prevent Black encroachment on white neighborhoods due to the nominal nature of improvements, as well as the continued lack of available housing for growing Black populations. Furthermore, rehabilitative efforts were costlier, and potentially less effective, than ensuring segregation through legal decree. The city thus opted to pursue alternative legal mandates to ensure separation of the races.

In 1927, the Kessler Plan Commission, in conjunction with the Dallas Civic Plan Commission (both composed of local businessmen and elected officials), drafted a five-measure piece of segregation legislation to "foster a separation of White and Negro residence communities in the interest of peace, safety and welfare, fixing a penalty and declaring an emergency."[99] To avoid the illegality of drawing the boundaries of neighborhoods based on color, Section 1 of Texas Senate Bill 275, House Bill 371, granted municipalities statewide the right to withhold building permits from corporations and individuals who intended to construct a house or houses "to be occupied by white people in a negro community inhabited principally by negro people."[100] The act further prohibited "any negro [sic] to establish a home or residence on any property located in any white community inhabited principally by white people, except on the written consent of a majority of those belonging to the opposite race inhabiting such community."[101] Violation of the directives carried a $100 fine and up to ninety days in jail; every seven days in contravention of the act constituted an additional offense. The act also enabled municipalities to remove buildings that violated the terms set forth in Section 1. Concerned about potential objections from legislators and other members of the Kessler Plan Commission and the Dallas Civic Plan Commission lobbied on behalf of the bill in the state capital. Lobbyists quickly discovered that the measure "seems to have all friends and will get there as it should for it is badly needed."[102]

The segregationist mandates set forth in Senate Bill 275/House Bill 371 were part of a series of "enabling acts" presented to the Texas legislature geared toward enhancing the functionality of the state's urban environments. Included among the enabling acts was a zoning act that granted municipalities the right to condemn property for expansion, and legislation that mandated the regulation of building lines. All of the acts had decided opposition from members of the legislature except the racial segregation act. According to the *Dallas Express*, the lack of opposition to racial segregation enabling acts demonstrated that "the consensus of white opinion is to the effect that it is more necessary to get Negroes into 'their places' even in the matter of residence than . . . the regulation of the line of buildings so that the streets may be more wide; it is more necessary than the granting of park space in which the little children may play."[103] Admonishing city officials for their continued efforts to thwart Black encroachment on white neighborhoods by legislating segregation, the *Dallas Express* reminded local policymakers, "instances are on record of the practical solution of the housing relations of the two races without the invoking of legal procedure." Surely Dallas "might do well to study these cases," the circular insisted, and added that "[Dallas] can depend definitely upon the ready co-operation of its Negro citizenry with its efforts in this direction." Seeing past the camouflage of withholding building permits, African Americans recognized the act as another measure created to zone African Americans in extant Black communities, which were typically devoid of sewage lines, paved streets, and sidewalks. One observer declared that African Americans "have all to gain and nothing to lose by realizing that every future generation of their children is menaced by this sentiment in favor of legalized ghetto districts."[104]

The act passed the Texas legislature in March 1927 by a vote of 104 to 1.[105] Dallas officials thus successfully reinstated racial zoning in modified form, and legalized the system for municipalities statewide so long as local voters approved of the measure.[106] With a purportedly legal basis for localized racial zoning, a Dallas citizens' committee, chaired by city planner Charles E. Ulrickson, included a proposition for creating "Negro Districts" in a nearly $24 million bond package for various city programs. Entitled the "Ulrickson Plan," the bond program was presented to voters in December 1927.[107] The Ulrickson Committee, jointly appointed by

Mayor Louis Blaylock, the chairman of the City Plan Commission, and the presidents of the Kessler Plan Association and the Dallas Chamber of Commerce, for the purpose of "investigating and recommending a program of public improvements" for Dallas, published suggested improvements in 1927.[108] The committee recognized the "value of ample library facilities in the educational system and cultural life of the city," and recommended that of the four proposed branches, one be established for African Americans.[109] Ulrickson's recommendation met with much disdain from local whites averse to publicly funded facilities for African Americans. In conjunction with the *Dallas Express*, the Negro Chamber of Commerce, and the local African American Parent Students and Teachers Associations encouraged local African Americans to vote in favor of the Ulrickson Plan while simultaneously urging Black voters to vote "No" on Proposition 13 which, if passed, would grant the city authority to pass residential segregation ordinances. The coalition used the local Black newspaper as well as the postal service as mediums for communicating with African American voters. Despite their efforts to dictate the outcome of the 1927 election, Proposition 13 passed, thus granting local officials the power to legally confine African Americans to designated "Negro Districts." The City Planning Commission quickly mapped existing Black residential sectors of the city and filed them at city hall as public record of the boundaries of Black neighborhoods which, in accordance with Proposition 13, were the newly designated Negro Districts to which Black residency was to be confined. Such measures were by then unconstitutional due to *Buchanan v. Warley*. Proposition 13 further decreed the violation of racial restrictive covenants a penal offense punishable by one year in prison.[110] In response to the threat imposed by a growing African American population in search of housing, property owners across the state began to include racial restrictive covenants on the deeds to their homes by the early twentieth century. The practice increased in popularity until the United States Supreme Court ruled racial covenants unconstitutional in 1948. Similar to deeds in other cities across the nation, such clauses mandated that property could be "sold to or used by white person[s] only."[111] While many deeds read as above, others took pains to avoid the potential transfer of land to individuals who might have regarded themselves as white yet had Black relatives in their ancestry. Property owners evaded property sales to such individuals by specifying that the "property is not to be sold, rented or otherwise disposed of to any person of African descent."[112] If whites disregarded the deed restrictions and attempted to sell to African Americans, the Black property owner would thereby "forfeit all his or their right, title, and interest in and to said property," hence relinquishing ownership of the property to the previous owner.[113] The 1916 amendment to the 1907 Dallas charter legalized restrictive covenants already in use in the city by declaring, "all agreements made prior to the amended charter are hereby fully ratified and confirmed as though passed under the terms of this Charter amendment."[114]

Progressivism and the Codification of Black Subjugation in Texas

The formidable segregation of African Americans in Dallas and Texas at-large was part of a continuum of reforms throughout the Progressive Era. The period, which arguably extended from the 1890s to the 1920s, was marked by the dismantling of monopolistic businesses, regulation of railroads; betterment of living and working conditions; and education, health, and labor reforms. By 1905, many politicians ran for office on platforms promoting "progressive" political reforms, while many government officials as well as reformist citizens characterized themselves as "progressives," prompting historians to refer to the period as the Progressive Era. Along with the political reforms executed by predominantly male politicians, the period was inundated with the civic-minded reforms instituted by middle- and upper-class women. Women from across the county assumed responsibility for the welfare of marginalized and disadvantaged Americans in industrializing urban centers, frequently concentrating their efforts on the influx of "new immigrants" from eastern and southern Europe. Even benevolent reformers and image-conscious politicians, however, haphazardly or strategically neglected to address the needs of all individuals. White progressives' narrowly defined constituents in need of reform rarely included African Americans. Indeed, some white reformists—particularly white women (both national and local)—of the era sought to improve the lot of African Americans by including them in organizations, and/or implementing reforms that targeted African Americans' social ailments. Typically, however, reformist efforts of whites disregarded the needs of African Americans, and in some instances victimized them. Consequently, social and political reforms only incidentally, if at all, assisted African Americans, lending substantial credence to historian John Dittmer's assertion that "where black America is concerned . . . there remains a consensus that the progressive era was 'for Whites only.'"[115]

While Progressive Era reforms nationwide tended to ignore the social urgencies of African Americans, progressive measures in the South assumed a decidedly racist framework. Southern progressivism was not only imbued with a systematic neglect of African Americans, but also rested on a foundation of political paralysis and social immobilization of the group. Jim Crow and Progressivism therefore coalesced in the South. Reform efforts by white southerners unfolded in the segregation and disfranchisement of African Americans, which rendered them the victims rather than the benefactors of reform. White progressive reformers in the South thus forged a symbiotic relationship between progress for whites and the political, geographic, and subsequently social stalemate of African Americans. Progressive reforms in Texas were no exception.

Although Progressivism in Texas largely resembled those instituted nationwide (heavily focused on the establishment of railroad regulations, antitrust measures, and other economic, social, and political reforms), they also markedly exemplified *southern progressivism* defined by the attempted geographic, political, and subsequently social immobilization of African Americans. Thus, a form of Progressivism that was customarily southern and undeniably racist governed Texas political and social dynamics during much of the period. By the early 1890s, the Texas legislature mandated the separation of African Americans and whites in most arenas of public and private life where segregation was usually practiced but not yet decreed.[116] Legalized segregation, together with the restrictive suffrage measures enacted after the turn of the century that principally disfranchised African Americans in Texas, aligned the state's reformist activities with those of its southern cohorts.[117] Because progressivism for whites often translated into the social and political relapse of African Americans, the Progressive Era was characterized by a very subjective notion of progress. Progressivism can be conceptualized as a movement of individuals and institutions endeavoring to accomplish reforms deemed significant—significance defined according to individuals' experiences and expectations, allegiances and prejudice. Progressivism was an eminently successful movement for some, and a disastrously harmful one for others.

Although antitrust measures, warehousing laws, the creation of a railroad commission, and railroad regulations exemplified progressive strides made by the Texas legislature during the era, other Texas reforms rested upon a foundation of southern progressivism. Segregation and disfranchisement placed severe limitations on the social and political advancement of African Americans. As in other southern states, Texas legislation included numerous laws that restricted suffrage and codified existing segregation practices while extending the discriminatory procedures to most aspects of public and private life. Two judicial factors laid a legal foundation for the hardening of the color line in the South: the Supreme Court's rejection of the 1875 Civil Rights Act and *Plessy v. Ferguson* (1896). In 1883, the Supreme Court nullified the Civil Rights Act of 1875 that had protected African Americans' rights to access public facilities. African Americans in the South often met with resistance when attempting to frequent white-owned businesses previous to the 1883 Supreme Court decision. With the overturning of the 1875 act, however, business owners were no longer legally obligated to accommodate African Americans and far less likely to do so. The 1896 United States Supreme Court ruling *Plessy v. Ferguson* mandated that separate facilities for whites and African Americans must be equal in quality. This federal sanctioning of southern segregation practices legally fortified segregation in Texas and much of the nation. Despite the "separate but equal" ruling, facilities for African Americans were rarely, if ever, commensurate to those established for white people. In 1901, for instance, the Texas State Colored Teachers Association adopted a resolution, "protesting against alleged discrimination against negroes in the separate coaches of railroads, the claim being made that while Whites were given entire coaches, negroes were only given a half coach."[118] African Americans charged again and again that there were apparent racial disparities in facility maintenance and availability, and individuals regulating facilities often violently enforced segregation practices. In one Texas city, a white man shot a Black man on a streetcar after the Black man refused to sit in the colored section.[119]

While the primary focus of this chapter is white reaction to Black migration, labor, and progress in an effort to contribute to an explanation of collectivized and racialized violence by the late nineteenth century, it must be emphasized that local African Americans assumed a proactive stance during the Progressive Era in the face of discriminatory and oppressive reforms. They struggled to better the lives of their brethren and the conditions of their communities. Black reformers and organizations sought to eradicate the socioeconomic and political dilemmas of African Americans across the state, particularly in Texas towns and cities. Characterized by an exchange of benevolence and self-help extending beyond the boundaries of any one local African American community, African American Texans initiated social, educational, and economic reforms during the era, both for advancement of the race and as a response to the racially exclusive agendas of white reformers. African American churches functioned as settlement houses, proffering welfare services to parishioners and others.[120]

Local African Americans established colored chapters of the Young Men's and Women's Christian Associations; erected kindergartens and libraries; opened charity houses for the elderly; engaged in temperance work; petitioned city councils for improvements in street paving, sewage lines, and education; and instituted several other reforms in response to the problems of rapid urbanization and that plagued increasing Black populations in Texas towns and cities.

Long before Progressive Era reformation, the Texas legislature passed laws designed to minimize or altogether thwart the interaction of whites and African Americans. In 1858, Texans banned interracial marriages. The legislature instituted a series of Black Codes (reminiscent of slave codes) after the close of the Civil War in Texas to reify authority over African Americans who were no longer subjected to the restrictions inherent in slavery. Although the United States Congress abolished the Black Codes in 1866, local edicts—such as vagrancy ordinances, which were aimed at controlling the mobility and labor of African Americans—continued to exist in local communities. The Texas legislature legally separated white and Black children in educational facilities by 1876, and the Texas Central Railroad adhered to a recommendation by the Texas governor in the early 1880s that railroad cars be racially segregated. In 1889, the legislature approved a measure that allowed the legal segregation of races in railroad coaches and made the practice mandatory in 1891. Although segregation existed in most Texas cities prior to the Progressive Era, the Texas legislature passed the majority of the state's segregation measures during this period, thereby legalizing segregation in nearly every arena of public and even private life. The state legislature passed nearly twenty statewide segregation laws during the Progressive Era, as well as several suffrage laws drafted with the primary intent of limiting the political power of African Americans. Local communities passed countless additional ordinances, which further regulated interaction between whites and African Americans.[121] Laws made the adoption of white children by Blacks and Black children by whites illegal, prohibited Black porters from sleeping in railroad cars or using bed linens intended for white passengers, established that the baths and lockers for Black and white coal miners be separate, and created a hospital for "negro insane" at which only whites could occupy the administrative posts. These as well as other segregationist measures legalized segregation where the interaction of African Americans and whites had captured the concern of those alarmed by contact between the races.[122]

While African Americans' presence spurred the codification of segregation practices or increased racial violence in various parts of the state, the potential for Black political power served as an additional affront to white supremacy. Countless pundits and newspapers lamented Black political achievement and power as iniquitous and in opposition to the tenets of democracy at the time—or what was in fact and in practice white supremacy. "Let us reorganize the Republican party in Texas on the basis that all Republican primaries shall be conducted and participated in by white Republicans alone and exclusively; thus depriving the negro leader of his power of making denominations and selecting delegates" the *Fort Worth Weekly Gazette* encouraged in 1890.[123] White Democrats in the state echoed similar sentiments. The White Democratic Primary in Texas would work to strangle Black political power for well over half a century. The poll tax and threats of violence further dissuaded Black participation in the political processes of the state. In spite, or in some instances as a result, of these racist and restrictive measures, African American residents of Texas welcomed the twentieth century with a spirited readiness to further increase their social and economic autonomy, as evidenced by their continuous community-building efforts. Equally zealous were their continuing efforts to exercise political power by promoting political affirmations in local newspapers, partaking in partisan activities such as national conventions, and voting. The franchise was one of African Americans' most poignant and powerful expressions of freedom. Through this hallmark of citizenship, African Americans could direct the political current, especially as it impacted the lives of their local communities.

Even this precarious assertion of freedom, however, was subject to the disabling effects of white Texans determined to hinder the advancement of African Americans. Racialized voting restrictions were considered reformation and widely brought into the fold of Progressive Era reforms by the turn of the century to prevent the "negro domination" that defined Reconstruction-era politics. Reconstruction in Texas, similar to other southern states, opened vast opportunities for African Americans to serve as elected officials. For instance, forty-one African American men served in the state's legislature from 1868 to 1900.[124] Countless others served as registrars, jurors, and other public servants. Of the 78,629 Black voters in Texas in 1885, the majority subscribed to the Republican party—the party of Abraham Lincoln. At least 50,000 of the 60,000 Republicans in the state during the previous year were African American, according to the editor of the *Galveston Speculator*. Such figures provoked many white Republicans to grow increasingly concerned that the party would be referred to as the "nigger party." The politically influential Norris Wright Cuney, an African American Galveston native and implicit leader of Black Republicans in Texas following the death of E. J. Davis in 1883, further intensified the already pronounced fears of white Republicans that the party's leadership would be seized by African Americans. As a result of Cuney's rise to power, together with leadership roles assumed by other African Americans within the party, particularly their stations as delegates to state and national conventions, the contemptuous sentiments of many white Republicans were exacerbated. Such disdain for Black political power caused the Republican Party in Texas to fracture along ideological lines, while some white Republicans altogether abandoned the party to affiliate with the Democrats. In an effort to control the election of county delegates to state and national conventions, and to ensure the nomination of white men for local and state offices, "lily-white" Republican clubs constructed on the basis of white membership emerged across the state.[125]

The close of Reconstruction in the state paved the way for white Democrats to gain control of state politics. The overarching concern of the predominantly Democratic state legislature that white solidarity should inundate political affairs diminished the already limited political power of African Americans in the state. Patricians and newly rich legislators also longed to ensure that those on the lower rungs of society did not direct the political affairs of the state, which led in part to measures that targeted the political power of poor whites. During the postbellum era, some local whites already attempted to prevented African Americans from voting by threatening to raise rents, evict them from their homes, or fire them from jobs should they vote for Republicans. Other means of restricting the voting power of African Americans included violence. Legally limiting the political power of African Americans, however, would prove far more feasible, and simply easier, than continued methods of intimidation. Such restrictions were achievable in part by instituting a poll tax payable prior to an election. The failure to pay the tax would result in the inability to vote.[126] In 1901, Senator A. B. Davidson of Dewitt, Texas, passed his poll tax bill through the legislature. Although Populists charged that the bill would deprive "the laboring people . . . of their liberties at the ballot box," and some African Americans and white Republicans stated their opposition to the measure, their negligible influence in state politics failed to halt the passage of the bill. The senator's proposed law passed in the House with a vote of 87 to 15, and the Senate 23 to 6.[127]

On February 27, 1903, Representative Alexander Watkins Terrell

(Democrat), with the support of the Texas governor, presented his Terrell Election Bill to the Texas legislature. The representative's bill included specifications for the poll tax passed two years earlier, such as requiring that $1.50 be collected from "every male person between the ages of twenty-one and sixty years who resides within [Texas]" six months prior to an election to be eligible to vote. It also further restricted suffrage by privatizing primary election guidelines.[128] Terrell had encouraged the poll tax and propagandized its necessity since 1879 when he first unsuccessfully submitted a poll tax bill to the legislature. He presented similar measures in subsequent years that were defeated again and again as his restrictive suffrage bills yielded to opposition by Republicans, some Democrats, and later, Populists who regarded the bill as a noxious measure aimed at their sizably poor following. Although the poll tax would disfranchise both poor African Americans and whites in Texas, Terrell's efforts to eliminate "The thriftless, idle and semi-vagrant element of both races" were charged with a particular contempt for African American suffrage. A former slave owner and Confederate general, Terrell once stated the most injurious mistake made in the nineteenth century was "forcing the ballot into the hands of the negro."[129] During a political debate in 1891, Terrell admitted in regard to his proposed poll tax, "the chief object in view was to collect the tax on the wooly scalp."[130] So virulent was his disdain for African Americans that Terrell, once a practicing lawyer, retired from the profession prior to his career as a politician because of his aversion to being in courtrooms where African Americans served on juries. With Democratic dominance in Texas politics girded by disdain for Black political power, Terrell once again presented his election law to the Texas legislature in 1903. The time proved ripe for limiting the franchise of those deemed undesirable by the state legislature. The measure passed by a vote of 22 to 8 in the Senate and 66 to 46 in the House.[131]

Representative Thomas B. Love voted in favor of the Terrell bill and actively pursued legislation that would further curtail any African American power at the voting booth. Love had long professed the incongruous relationship between African Americans and voting rights, especially in primary elections, and proposed "that the county executive committee of each party may prescribe further qualifications."[132] Love's wishes materialized in his 1905 amendment to the 1903 Terrell Act that enabled the executive committees of parties to establish criteria for party membership, effectively determining eligibility for voting in primary elections and tacitly establishing "White primaries," which would not be ruled unconstitutional until *Smith v. Allwright* in 1947. The 1905 amendment to the Terrell Act also deemed it a misdemeanor for anyone to pay the poll tax for African Americans. The Terrell election law and amendments thus severely disfranchised Black Texans and eventually barred them altogether from Democratic primary elections. As a result of the poll tax, white primaries, and other disenfranchising efforts including intimidation and literacy tests, voter participation among African Americans in Texas plummeted to about five thousand in 1906 from approximately a hundred thousand in elections during the previous decade.[133] As these examples make evident, Texas African Americans were forced to endure legal and extralegal measures that severely limited or altogether halted their voting rights and political power. The loss of the right to vote stood alongside other measures aimed at restricting the social and political mobility of Texas African Americans. By the time of Terrell election law passed, vast aspects of both private and public life had been segregated. In the absence of slavery, African Americans' place in the racial order could be reestablished through the use of statute. As indicated previously, racialized mob violence executed in the midst of disorientating changes ushered in by shifting migratory patterns and work rhythms in an industrializing era did the same. The lynching of a Black man in Sherman, Texas, followed by the burning of Black portions of town, labors this point. In 1936, sociologist Durward Pruden published his findings regarding the case after conducting "hundreds of interviews," reading "two volumes of secret testimony taken by the Military Court of Investigation," and researching newspapers and other published materials. The charges issued against the lynching victim were "only an excuse for overt conflict that would eventually have come anyhow," he insisted, "because of the irritation of the poor whites at the increased prosperity of the business and professional Negroes."[134] Pruden argued that all local whites, however, were culpable: "The lynching . . . was more than an economic struggle at the bottom. It was aided and abetted by the passive attitude, indifference, or open approval of the upper economic classes, and was therefore, a community phenomenon."[135]

Work, Race, Migration, and a Racial Massacre in Sherman

An early twentieth century observer described Sherman, located in Grayson County, as a "leading Texas city financially, industrially, and culturally"[136] Before the turn of the century, Sherman was home to multiple flour mills, several newspapers, a public school system, and at least two colleges. The

Houston and Texas Central Railway reached the area by 1872. Several railway lines traversed the city within a few decades. The arrival of railroads spurred employment and economic opportunities at unprecedented rates, which, in turn, had a tremendous impact on the location and development of African American enclaves in the northern portion of the city. Railroad depots frequently hired African Americans as porters, railroad technicians, and janitors. The railroad also allowed easy access to outlying farms, which enabled day laborers to live in African American enclaves within the city along the tracks. Much of the land adjacent to the tracks was unsettled and therefore open for Black residency. As a result of employment opportunities and vacant lands, it was not unusual for an archipelago of African American communities to dot the railroad line from where it intersected with downtown spaces and extending to the city limits in areas across the state.[137] Sherman became a retail and shipping hub as a result of the railway. By 1890, the city boasted approximately a hundred businesses, multiple churches, and two schools and banks. In 1891, the city was home to the world's largest cotton seed oil mill. As a result of economic growth, whites and African Americans steadily migrated to the area. By the turn of the century, the city's population reached over ten thousand. Neighboring Denison experienced similar population growths. It was, by most measures, a bustling, industrializing space. Before the turn of the century, a flourishing stone quarry operated on the outskirts of town. By the 1920s, the city hosted more than fifty industrial plants that produced hardware, flour, cottonseed oil, and other products. Five railroads, over four hundred businesses, and several colleges serviced the area by the time. The area was widely known as an epicenter of industry and education in the state. The population of Grayson County reached over 74,000 in 1920 but dropped to just under 66,000 by 1930. Industry and agriculture declined during the period, stirring racial anxieties among area residents. Pruden's disclosure in his investigation of the 1930 mob torture and death of George Hughes is revealing, "Negroes are not allowed in many communities near [Sherman]."[138] "They are excluded from work at most industrial institutions," he continued, and "have to content themselves with what money sifts down from the wealthier Whites for such odd jobs as car washing, lawn mowing, shoe shining, and day labor on the farms."[139]

Despite these challenges, many African Americans in the area had become "quite prosperous" and accumulated property. Others who worked in unskilled or low wage positions competed with or worked among whites in local businesses. Black professionals, including physicians and at least one lawyer, migrated to Sherman to service the needs of local Black residents. Racial tensions engendered by Black migration, labor competition, and progress proved detrimental to local Black citizens, as evidenced by events that unfolded in May of 1930.[140]

On May 9, Hughes, an African American farmhand in Sherman, Texas, sat—likely overcome with torment—in a Grayson County courthouse awaiting trial. A mob of angry white citizens gathered inside the corridors of the courtroom and outside on the lawns, waiting for an opportunity to lynch him. Charged with the attempted rape of a white woman, Hughes had been locked in the court's vault as a preventative measure by Texas Rangers, the famed Frank Hamer among them, assigned to protect him from mob violence. Just days before, Hughes had allegedly gone to his employer, a white farm owner, to collect money owed to him. The farmer's wife reported that when she informed Hughes of her husband's absence, he became enraged. She later claimed that Hughes returned armed. She told officials that Hughes tied her to a bed, assaulted her, and left, promising to return. She then reported that she freed herself and ran for assistance from a neighbor. Many local African Americans and some whites reportedly questioned the veracity of the woman's story, and charged that if anything sexual occurred, it was consensual and the woman was afraid her husband might discover the affair. Others maintained that nothing happened. Despite questions about Hughes's supposed guilt, and in the absence of due process, an overwhelming number of white citizens from Sherman and the surrounding areas gathered outside the courthouse to apprehend their prey. Determined to gain possession of Hughes, several men and women, led by a boy toting an American flag, entered the courthouse and ascended the stairwell to the second floor. National guardsmen deployed to Sherman by a district judge to protect Hughes and maintain order tossed tear gas into the stairwell. The mob's efforts were only temporarily thwarted.[141]

Hughes's ostensible refuge was quickly commuted to a crematory as a woman and a group of teenaged boys broke the windows with rocks and threw a firebomb into the vault. As Hughes burned inside the courthouse, members of the mob cut hoses that arrived to distinguish the blaze. Some attacked the firemen as they battled the fire. Rangers assigned to protect Hughes escaped to contact the governor. By the time National Guardsmen arrived to end the lynching, Hughes had perished. Pruden interviewed many of the individuals somehow involved in the events. In his published report, he describes the determination of the mob to retrieve Hughes's body following the arrival of troops:

About 6 P.M. a . . . unit of 52 soldiers from a large city to the south arrived. Leaving a detachment to garrison their headquarters at the county jail three blocks west of the courthouse, the remainder deployed around the smoldering courthouse ruins to push the crowd back from the hanging walls. As darkness fell, the spirit of the mob became uglier. They reasoned that if the governor would not let the Rangers shoot at them, he surely would not let soldiers shoot either. They began to abuse the soldiers, and soon a pitched battle ensued in which the troops were forced to retreat the three blocks back to the jail, followed by the angry mob throwing bricks, rocks, pieces of timber, chunks of concrete, broken bottles, sticks of dynamite, etc. The mob then withdrew and returned to the courthouse square to open the vault and get the Negro.[142]

Reports vary as to what condition Hughes was in when his lynchers retrieved him from the vault. Some say he was simply unconscious. Most others argue that he was already dead. The latter seems more probable given he remained in what was likely an unbearably sweltering iron prison, which was engulfed by flames for more than ninety minutes, with little oxygen. Whether alive or deceased, Hughes was secured to the back of a roadster once removed from the vault. Several members of the mob then led "a procession back to town . . . across the railroad tracks to the negro section," reported one witness.[143] Shouts of "on to nigger town" rang out as they marched.[144] Thousands followed in what Pruden characterized as "a frenzied midnight" with "yelling, singing" and "tooting horns of automobiles" providing an aural backdrop to the scene.[145] Women and young girls "rapturously sung" "Happy Days Are Here Again," an observer reported.[146] It was "A REAL FOURTH OF JULY HOLIDAY," read the caption of an *International Newsreel* photograph depicting the raucousness in the streets.[147]

Members of the mob then turned their attentions to the living and pillaged the local African American community. Rioting whites promised to "run all the damn niggers" out of town, one observer recalled.[148] After securing Hughes's corpse to a tree that stood near a Black-owned drug store, they burned a hotel, doctor's office, two dental offices, barber shops, funeral parlors, cafes, and an insurance business, all of which were owned by African Americans. William J. Durham, an African American lawyer for the NAACP who was instrumental in desegregating the University of Texas Law School years later, was also targeted. Local white citizens burned his office to the ground as he stood across the street and witnessed the tragedy unfold.

White people in the mob also destroyed Black homes and gathering places, including the Knights of Pythias building and the Odd Fellows' Hall. As firefighters arrived to extinguish the blazes, mob members stopped them unless fires threatened adjacent white properties. The targeting of Black-owned establishments demonstrates the bitterness local whites harbored against Black prosperity. They resented propertied African Americans, as demonstrated, Pruden claimed:

> by the destruction of Negro property, the plans to burn all Negro homes, the mob slogan of 'run all the niggers out of [Honey Grove],' the posting of notices on the Negro shacks warning the occupants to leave, the notice on the establishment of a White employer warning him to discharge Negro help and employ Whites, and the period of persecution of the Negroes during the months immediately following the lynching.[149]

As a result of the violence from whites, as many as two thousand African American residents of the area absconded that evening. Many boarded wagons or hopped on mules. Others climbed into automobiles and left for neighboring cities. Some were provided protection in the homes or businesses of local whites. Those with few options for safe harbor found cover in ditches or under bridges. Just a few days following the lynching, the national guardsmen deployed to Sherman to reinstate order found type-written notices posted on the homes of Black residents of Sherman, warning that they had one day to leave the city or face the destruction of their property. A threatening notice was also found on a building of a contractor who employed African Americans. It insisted that the contractor fire his Black employees within thirty-six hours. For months following the burning and dragging of Hughes, Black citizens faced similar forms of persecution and mistreatment.[150]

For the People's Enjoyment

CHAPTER 4

"The Best Possible Views of the Torture"

Experience, Enjoyment, and the Material Culture of Lynching

"Tell my wife good-bye," Dudley Morgan muttered to a restive crowd in Lansing, Texas, minutes before flames garmented his body and smothered his life.[1] Accused of assaulting a white woman known as "Mrs. McKee" (whom some primary sources also refer to as "Mrs. McKay")—the wife of a railroad foreman—Morgan fled town when he discovered that he was a suspect.[2] He remained at large for nearly two weeks. When word of Morgan's eventual capture spread that Friday morning in May 1902, throngs of people from various parts of the state gathered at the town's depot in anticipation of the prisoner's arrival. The train carrying Morgan to his barbarous fate stopped at numerous stations en route to Lansing. Hundreds of passengers boarded and traveled along with Morgan in what seems an odd spatial coupling. There sat Morgan, forlorn and undoubtedly aware of the torturous protocol that would consume his last moments, occupying the same, cramped railcars as hordes of white spectators traveling forth to watch the execution of their fellow passenger. One wonders what filled Morgan's thoughts as he faced these last moments of freedom, perhaps staring out through the cloudy windows of the train while each passing tree, blurred and fading in the distance, delivered him closer to the fate that had befallen him. The anticipation would send even the most resilient among us into the darkest abyss of terror. When the train pulled into the Lansing depot, the large number of waiting citizens must have gravely concerned the engineer. He attempted to move the train forward before Morgan's lynchers led him off the railcar, but the actions of the engineer and his crew were halted by the barrels of several firearms. Escorted by at least two hundred men armed with Winchester rifles, Morgan was taken from the train depot to a nearby field where an iron stake had been erected. Ignitable materials surrounded the base.[3]

More than four thousand people congregated around the staging area to watch Morgan's suffering unfold. McKee arrived at the scene atop a carriage, escorted by four other women who were present as a cadre of support. The driver attempted to maneuver the carriage and its huddled consignment close enough to Morgan for McKee to garner a clear glimpse of her alleged attacker, but the expanse of the crowd prevented her from seeing the area where Morgan would meet his final moments. Instead, McKee and her band of enthusiasts remained on the periphery of the dense mob. Once Morgan arrived at his funeral pyre, members of the mob quickly fastened him to the stake using a chain and railroad ties. He was allotted a few moments to pray before the husband of the alleged victim tossed a burning match onto the pyre, which ignited the blaze and commenced the torture. Witnesses took turns sitting atop one another's shoulders to gain an unobstructed view of Morgan's burning. Many in attendance stridently barked for a slow death, a demand that seemed easily and methodically fulfilled. Once the flames scorched the railroad ties, a few members of the mob removed them and plunged them into Morgan's eyes. They then applied burning pine timbers to his neck and clothing. Writhing from the pain, Morgan implored that someone shoot him. No one obliged. More than thirty minutes after McKee's husband lit the beacon, Morgan's head finally slumped forward. Once the heat tempered, all that remained was a charred torso. People began to sift through the ashes with sticks in search of a memento from the day's events. Portions of Morgan's body and skull were collected and toted away from the scene. Remaining members of the crowd pitched the two men lauded for capturing Morgan into the air with jubilation. The yelling and cheering that had served continuously as an aural backdrop to the torturous exhibition flowed as the men, placed in a triumphant posture with their rifles held firmly in their hands, posed for photographs with the remains of their captive.[4]

Seven years prior to Morgan's lynching, Robert Henson Hilliard had met a similar fate in Tyler, Texas, about forty miles northeast of Lansing, when a mob set him ablaze and watched his body roast until it was commuted to a mass of vendible products. As many as seven thousand people gathered that day to witness his burning. "The city made holiday," a journalist observed as "large crowds of ladies and children were congregated on the awnings surrounding the plaza. Wagons, carriages, trees and buildings were converted to grandstands."[5] The International Great Northern Railroad (I&GN) carried hundreds of strangely curious witnesses from surrounding towns to the scene. Hilliard was tied to a scaffold in the town's commercial district, just in front of a purveyor of whiskey and other spirits, a drugstore, and Yoakum Seed Company. Before Hilliard's death, he penned a note to his wife and handed it to the sheriff, who took part in his lynching. The *Daily Hesperian*, a newspaper based in Gainesville, Texas, reported that the note read as follows: "I am arrested by Wig Smith. Don't know what they will do with me. If I don't see you any more [sic], goodbye."[6] Another article, printed in the *Chicago Tribune*, revealed that the second line of Hilliard's message differed in context considerably: "You know what they will do with me."[7]

Accused of raping and murdering a white woman, Hilliard's story was photographed from his capture to his death. In theatrical fashion, dramatic recreations of the alleged attack—with actors playing the roles of assailant and victim—were photographed and printed. One of the staged black-and-white images, entitled "Cutting Her Throat," included hand-applied red color intended to simulate the look of blood.[8] Breckenridge & Scruggs Company, a local drug store, ran an exhibit of the real and dramatized images, reproduced as stereographs, shortly following the lynching. An advertisement published in the local paper by the drug store read as follows:

> We have sixteen large views under powerful magnifying lenses now on exhibition. These views are true to life and show the Negro's attack, the scuffle, the murder, the body as found, etc. With eight views of the trial and burning. For place of exhibit see street bills. Don't fail to see this.[9]

Try as one may to rule the grotesque collectibles and print images produced as a result of these and other lynchings as nothing more than a catharsis of sorts, or an interval of psychosis created by a mob mentality; the centrality of entertainment—the souvenirs, pictures, dramatizations, travel, commercialized exhibits—to Morgan and Hilliard's lynchings is inescapable. The accounts are undoubtedly troubling, but what seems today an awkward, medieval-like recreation of ghastly, transgressive merchandise, images, and memories was once a carefully constructed part of the process of lynching African Americans in Texas. I argue that beyond torture, beyond punishment, the creation, preservation, and sharing of mementos and images from the sites of lynching helped shape the leisure narrative of racialized social violence in the state and worked to firmly establish schematized notions of Black denigration. Despite these prominent features of a new lynching culture, social scientists (with a few notable exceptions) have paid scant attention to the meaning and implications of the culture, both material and intangible, produced at sites of lynching.

From memories of events witnessed or discussed, to images preserved in black-and-white photographs and postcards, to other tangible vestiges of experience, including fragmented bones, burned pieces of organs, and shards of torture devices, the existence of items of reminiscence have been fairly well documented by scholars and others. However, many questions are left unanswered regarding what the procurement and dissemination of such objects reveal about how the Black body was imprinted with lethal and enduring notions of racial alterity, or why and how such terrorism was indelibly linked to an expansive leisure culture.

The meaning of memorabilia from an event is inescapably subject to the overarching variables of space and time. How one might interpret or share a print image, memory, or souvenir is shaped immeasurably by the historical moment in which the item is created and viewed. As a means of reminiscing, the production and consumption of objects and imageries from a lynching site during the late nineteenth and early twentieth centuries borrowed from and helped promote the performative role of African Americans in the post-Reconstruction era; it aided in firmly establishing an entanglement of material culture, participation, pleasure, and racial production that determinedly and visually reinforced a new, post-emancipation racial caste structure as it further objectified the Black body. The consumption of these misrepresentations enabled some southern whites to imagine themselves as something defined in stark opposition to Blackness. Black lives could be trivialized by lynching emblems and representations in a manner unachieved by other forms of terrorism. The collection and dissemination of lynching memorabilia functioned broadly as a white conquest and mastery over the Black presence, thus normalizing white domination and the brutality deemed necessary to sustain it as it informed an evolving ideology that encompassed a growing culture of racialized entertainment.

Objectified Blackness and the Reification of Whiteness

The commodification of Black bodies as a means of entertainment was hardly a novel phenomenon by the time it became part of a new lynching culture in the state of Texas. African Americans already and increasingly served a theatrical and commercialized purpose in white society. By the antebellum period, Black stereotypes were captured in minstrel stage performances and sheet music of minstrel songs, and by the end of the century in print ads, slogans, magazines, and collectibles. Entertainment mediums ushered in by early twentieth century advances in technology—early films and radio, for example—further cast African Americans as objects of entertainment. At times, when not featured as distorted or stereotypic caricatures, items were simply given racist appellations that converted ordinary things to particularly perverse forms of Black memorabilia. A slingshot was commonly referred to as a *nigger-shooter*, for instance, during the late nineteenth and much of the twentieth centuries.[10] "Gee mister, will you show us how to use a nigger-shooter," implored one Texas youth of a local expert marksman.[11] "All I want is a nigger-shooter," he added.[12] As late as the post-World War II era, a Dallas, Texas, carnival included a dunking game that promised attendees they could dunk the "nigger" if they could "hit the trigger."[13] Such designations worked to denigrate African Americans and trivialize their very existence, rendering their lives negligible and highly dispensable.

Lynching memorabilia existed alongside familiar tokens of an imagined Blackness that was becoming a cultural commonplace by the turn of the century. In turn, the material and popular culture created out of lynchings became acceptable in the midst of other entertainment mediums that utilized and objectified Black bodies. The collective mob that had long been part of southern and Texas mores gained a new inflection with the intensified othering of Black people through popular entertainment and other forms of denigration. The meaning of lynching representations was not, however, simply informed by extant and developing ideas about the Black body as a purveyor of entertainment but was largely instrumental to the creation and reproduction of these ideas. Each lynching informed the next as it coalesced with existing notions of Blackness and entertainment—a vicious cycle of give and take.

Examining the culture and associated commercial attributes of lynching in Texas, I argue, enables one to glean not only how the lynching spectacle was experienced, but more significantly how such experiences came to be assimilated into the same discursive space as other racialized imagery that were acknowledged sources of pleasure, novelty, and entertainment. Generating material and popular culture from the death ceremony tended to banalize the brutality of racialized mob violence, downplaying the archaic and grotesque nature of its rituals of torture, and situating it within a matrix of modern recreational activity and social intolerance in the Jim Crow

Carnival in Dallas, Texas, 1946. "Duck" is likely a misspelling for "dunk." *Marion Butts Collection, Photographic Archives, Dallas Public Library, Dallas, Texas.*

South. Material images and collectibles procured from the lynching scene helped reframe murder as a source of pleasure as they infused notions of play into a lynching narrative. The ceremonial nature of lynching events— the methodology that became more tightly scripted with each occurrence, each aural and printed chronicling; the public, highly visible spectacle; the social acceptability—made the commercialization of racialized mob violence possible as it allowed the material emblems and representations of the experience to communicate an eerie paradigm and vicariously implicate spectators and others who were not a part of the mob. What was done to the victims of lynching at the sites of death, and the emblems and representations produced by that violence, I further argue, functioned as socializing mechanisms in the same context as other racist memorabilia or performative mediums. The material and popular culture extended the province of experience; the dissemination and screening of the items provided people the opportunity to be involved with the events without the physical work of traveling to the sites of the lynching, which thereby made the experience available not only to those who encountered the material representations, but also to individuals with whom others shared their observations and recollections.

Revered intellectual and social critic Walter Lippmann once wrote, "The subtlest and most pervasive of all influences are those which create and maintain the repertory of stereotypes. We are told about the world before we can see it. We imagine most things before we experience them."[14] Lippmann's cautionary valuation of how varied influences lend considerably to the interpretive contours of our encounters illuminates the power and the danger of what precedes those encounters. The racist portrayals of African Americans on the radio, for instance, were so pervasive that some Black radio stations created programming during the late 1920s and early 1930s, according to Robert Weems, to "counteract mainstream radio's stereotypical depictions of African American life."[15] *The All Negro Hour* and *The All Negro Children's Hour*, first airing in 1929 and 1931 respectively, attempted to reinforce a positive image of Black people.[16] During the 1920s and 1930s, the highly popular and decidedly racist radio show *Amos 'n' Andy* helped forge an image of Black otherness in the white mind by portraying African Americans as ignorant, lazy, and at times roguish. One observer maintained that he was a regular viewer of the televised version of the radio show during its short run in the early 1950s, which further reified the stereotypes featured in the radio version by adding the visual of Black bodies to the molded caricatures. He recalls that he and his brother found the era's civil rights speeches humorous because *Amos 'n' Andy* had made African Americans into comical figures whose strict role in society was one of entertaining whites. The Black body served a static purpose for too many.

In the aftermath of the cataclysmic 1917 East St. Louis race riots, W. E. B. Du Bois scripted a pointed indictment of the visceral interpretation of Blackness shared by many whites, an indictment that echoes the core implications of Lippmann's contentions and the aforementioned observer's experiences. When unionized white workers at Aluminum Ore Company went on strike for higher wages, company officials courted nearly five hundred southern Black migrants as replacement labor. Lured by wartime employment opportunities in the city's industrial plants, more than ten thousand

African Americans had already left the South for East St. Louis by the eve of the riot. The hiring of a cheap Black labor force undermined strikers' efforts and exacerbated already heightened racial tensions in the city caused by employment competition, expanding Black communities, and concerns that the influx of a group that typically voted Republican would marginalize the political influence and power of local Democrats. Moreover, local newspapers frequently modulated the reporting of crimes committed by whites against African Americans while sensationalizing crimes in which the victim was white and the alleged assailant Black. On July 1, rumor circulated in the city that a white man had been killed by a Black man. White strikers as well as other white residents of the area summarily canvassed the city looking for Black people to attack. One eyewitness professed with impunity:

> There was no attempt at avenging specific misdeeds upon selected individuals. A black skin was a death warrant . . . Each man slain was frightfully abused as a lesson to all others of his color. A murdered man wasn't allowed to die after he had been partially pierced. He was kicked and beaten with fists, feet and clubs, hanged, shot some more, kicked and beaten again.[17]

W. E. B. Du Bois arrived in East St. Louis shortly after the murderous rioting ceased: "I rode in this city past flame-swept walls and over gray ashes; in streets almost wet with blood,"[18] Du Bois penned his analysis, which wavered between the sublimely wretched and the distressingly direct, for the NAACP's organ, the *Crisis*. As he had been in past commentaries, Du Bois remained doggedly critical of the occupants of the nation, from those whose exclusionist ideologies about citizenship necessarily ignored nonwhites, to those whose more recent transoceanic or transnational journeys delivered them to East St. Louis virtually devoid of personal encounters with African Americans. These occupants, these socioculturally diverse masses, encoded Blackness with an eternal, at times seemingly Biblical, mark of inferiority and static purpose:

> What did they see? They saw something at which they had been taught to laugh and make sport; they saw that which the heading of every newspaper column, the lie of every cub reporter, the exaggeration of every press dispatch, and the distortion of every speech and book had taught them was a mass of despicable men, inhuman; at best, laughable; at worst, the meat of mobs and fury. What did they see? They saw nine and one-half millions of human beings.[19]

Du Bois's poetic, candid prose discloses the epic tragedy of racialized alterity. He lyrically describes the archetypes of three men who occupied the physical and economic landscapes of the city: the merciless capitalist; the credulous, ironically xenophobic new immigrant; and the exploitable southern Black migrant. Despite labor arrangements that should have closely aligned white workers with southern Black migrants, the workers nonetheless envisaged an existence abruptly dissimilar. White workers and Black migrants "might have logically found common cause and community in their basically similar relation to capital," historian Thomas Cleveland Holt astutely notes, "but instead white labor came to see its interests and itself as somehow fundamentally different from those of black labor."[20]

Blackness operated as a complex determinant of racial interaction and domination that worked to shape how white people interpreted and reacted to encounters such as the one in East St. Louis. Born from fear, envy, and threat, the perception of Blackness was an indelible creation. Like Ralph Ellison's invisible man—dejected, angered, at times empowered by this seemingly unbridgeable chasm between humanistic nuances and the permanence of a socially constructed existence—the deauthenticated self became authenticate in the public mind. Fashioned from legacies of slavery; sensationalized headlines; white supremacy political campaigns; convict leasing systems; judicial opinions; from songs, novels, advertising cards, movies, and collectibles, the East St. Louis attackers' concept of Blackness trounced any version of reality. The lamentation of Ellison's nameless central character is substantial on this point: "When they approach me they see only my surroundings, themselves, or figments of their imagination—indeed, everything and anything except me."[21] "That invisibility to which I refer," he continues, "occurs because of a peculiar disposition of the eyes of those with whom I come in contact. A matter of the construction of their inner eyes, those eyes with which they look through their physical eyes upon reality."[22] The "inner eyes" are an avisual depository for every construal of Blackness, every algorithm for skewed perception and harmful interpretation of African Americans that slips between one's subconscious and conscious renderings. The Black body—whether lean and amber, muscular, chestnut, rotund and cocoa brown, puce or beige, tall, sturdy, slight—was objectified: a singular embodiment, an inhuman screen upon which the dominant group projected meaning—drawn from what Frantz Fanon poignantly characterized as "a thousand details, anecdotes, stories."[23] It is this interpretation of Blackness as a reductive concept that served a fundamental role in the configuration of a racial hierarchy that infused whiteness with enduring value.

When Ellison's nameless protagonist arrives in the North, increasingly forlorn and regrettably naïve, he seeks employment at a Long Island paint factory. "KEEP AMERICA PURE WITH LIBERTY PAINT" the electric sign seems to loudly bellow above the persistent, unforgiving flapping of American flags.[24] Ellison uses the scene as an allegorical display of patriotism that begins to reveal how the making of race coalesced with restrictive ideas about citizenship. The young migrant's tutorial from his brusque supervisor, Mr. Kimbro, lends further literary imagery to the realities of racial production. Kimbro presents his apprentice with a murky, black liquid and befuddled instruction: "the idea is to open each bucket and put in ten drops of this stuff."[25] The directive perplexed Ellison's central character who quietly questioned how the addition of a black substance could produce "Optic White," a glossy, vibrant paint that Kimbro boasted was "the purest white that can be found," as "white as George Washington's Sunday-go-to-meetin' wig."[26] In the absence of black, the normative value of white wanes—like Liberty Paint's "Optic White," it loses its luster, its perceived purity and resultant benefits. The avowed worth of a white identity wholly relies upon the very presence of Blackness. In short, white finds its elevated value because of the existence of black.

Leisure and the Lynching of Henry Smith

When Henry Smith arrived at the train depot in Paris, Texas, around noon on that Wednesday in February 1893, he was anxious, even sullen—a state that was likely intensified when he saw a massive crowd gathered near the platform awaiting his appearance. Thousands of people—Paris residents and others who poured into the city from across the state—chose to situate themselves in the midst of the occasion absent from work or other formal constraints, free to participate in the events as they unfolded, to direct the expenditures of their own time. Paris, an already busy railroad depot with three lines traversing the city by 1893, was swiftly transformed into a raucous gathering place more reminiscent of a state fair than a bustling commercial center. Witnessing the activity at a local depot hours before Smith's death, a relative of Myrtle Vance, his alleged victim, later stated, "every train that arrived from any direction was crowded to suffocation by the aroused people of neighboring towns at even considerable distances from us."[27] "The sidewalks, windows, awnings—in short, every available inch of space," he continued, "from which a view of the street could be had, was filled by a human being."[28] Local business owners closed their establishments for the day, and "owing to the intense excitement in the city," Mayor Alexander Cate cancelled school.[29] "All parents are requested to keep their children home. I do this as a matter of safety to the little ones," the mayor announced, a dictate lost on some as evidenced by the presence of children in the crowd.[30]

Smith "was placed upon a carnival float in mockery of a king upon his throne" and delivered to the stake atop a shoddy wooden platform, according to one observer. By the time Smith and his executioners mounted that platform, upwards of ten thousand people had gathered to watch the lynching. Men and children straddled the necks of some spectators to obtain an unobstructed view of Smith. An African American resident of Paris, known as Reverend King, witnessed the expectant disposition of the mob firsthand: "the father of the murdered child raised the hissing iron with which he was about to torture the helpless victim, the children became as frantic as the grown people and struggled forward to obtain places of advantage."[31] King was forced by local residents to permanently leave the city after begging to no avail for the lynchers to end their torturous antics. Smith shouted in anguish as the son and father of his alleged victim slowly immersed hot irons into his heels, and up his legs and back. The torture continued for fifty minutes. Then, as a final overture to his fiery death, they gouged his eyes with irons. One witness noted that many in the crowd watched with "delight."[32] Several photographers vied for coveted vantage points that would enable "the best possible views of the torture and final cremation," according to one of Smith's lynchers.[33] The photographers had been informed of the imminent deed hours before its occurrence. J. L. Mertins, a photographer from Wolfe City, Texas, would sell images of Smith's lynching for fifty cents apiece from his office days following the lynching. One of the photographs he produced, entitled "Little Myrtle Vance avenged" and copyrighted by Mertins in 1893, features juxtaposed images of Myrtle Vance and Smith in a seeming effort to entreat the viewer to feel satisfied that justice was secured.[34]

While people from surrounding towns purchased the pictures of Smith's lynching to commemorate the day, others carried off free corporeal souvenirs. One eyewitness reported that "hunters visited the spot and raked the ashes" of Henry Smith's remains: "pieces of his bones were found and taken away."[35] Some took remnants of charcoal from the pyre.[36] Residents from Sherman, Texas, who traveled by excursion trains to witness the lynching,

View of crowd gathered to watch the lynching of Henry Smith, who can be seen on a platform in the background. Photographer: J. L. Mertins, photo copyrighted 1893 by Frank N. Hudson, Paris, Texas. *LOT 2839 [item] [P&P], Library of Congress Prints and Photographs Division, Washington, DC.*

"No. 14. Where the Body Was Found." Photographer: J. L. Mertins, photo copyrighted 1893 by Frank N. Hudson, Paris, Texas. *LOT 2839 [item] [P&P], Library of Congress Prints and Photographs Division, Washington, DC.*

returned with "splinters of the scaffold" upon which Smith was tortured as "mementoes."[37]

During the late nineteenth and early portion of the twentieth centuries, lynching in the state of Texas encompassed the spectacle, recreation, and commercialism represented in Smith's torture and killing. His death reveals in microcosm how expansive elements of the changing character of lynching in Texas were often interpreted and consumed as something more than simply punishment. With little apprehension, the Black body could be repurposed as fun, entertaining, a source of pleasure. The exhibition of Smith's redemptive killing—the production of body parts procured to commemorate the event, the tourism and time off work, the expressions of enjoyment by members of the crowd, the purchasing of photographs that captured Smith's suffering, the phonographic reproductions of the sounds heard at the site of the lynching, the self-directed nature of people's attendance—all coalesced to help craft a narrative of leisure. As discussed in previous chapters, this transformative process relied upon significant, foundational elements that would allow the Black body to be considered and collected as a form of entertainment: the ending of a master-slave dyad that had firmly fixed the dichotomy of race and place; the virtual absence of societal shame and fear of prosecution associated with acts of racialized mob violence; the creation and reproduction of a conflation that rendered Blackness and criminality a prejudicial and grossly destructive entanglement; Black advancement and labor competition. The collection, parceling, and viewing of artifacts from the site of a lynching that promoted and profited from the lethal othering of African Americans sat squarely on a continuum of the commercial exploitation of Black bodies. It was a racialized design of objectifying African Americans that was transfigured in a particular historical moment—one when a search for alternative means of racial identity reinforcement sharply intersected with the increased consumption of Black misrepresentations in popular and material culture.[38] Lynching representations helped suture any disconnect between Blackness and entertainment as they facilitated the forging of an intimate relationship among transgressive items, pleasure, and the reification of white identity.

Black Misrepresentations and a Longing for an Imagined Past

The creation and dissemination of lynching images and tangible collectibles in the new lynching culture were systemically related to changing patterns of mass consumption and racialized disparagement in popular and material culture by end of the nineteenth century. Black collectibles of varied sorts had emerged as a way to manage, malign, and commercialize Black bodies while allowing whites to sentimentalize a pre-emancipation South in which African Americans served a manageable, deferential function. These misrepresentations thus reflected and buttressed racial stereotypes and worked to normalize a popular culture that could be woven into the performance of death and remembrance. Expanding urban markets and advances in manufacturing shaped an increasingly homogenized commercial culture by the end of the nineteenth century. Consumers could and did purchase standardized manufactured goods that advertisers packaged and sold as a means to obtain a better life through the consumption of material goods. Manufacturers and advertisers largely succeeded in forging what historian William R. Leach has characterized as a "future-oriented culture of desire that confused the good life with goods."[39] Through colorful ads, window displays, trade magazines, and other modern advertising mediums, purveyors of consumer items projected an idea that the good life could be attained through material gains—happiness was just a purchase away. Manufactured items often reflected and reinforced the social mores and evolving consciousness of real and potential consumers. As such, items that strengthened an extant racial hierarchy and the attendant self-aggrandized identities of a white southern culture could and did become very popular. Social scientist Susan Pearce argues, "collecting is close to our social mind and our ability to understand ourselves and the world we live in."[40] As discussed in chapter 1, the world white southerners lived in was one defined by anxieties over Black freedom and progress and the attendant challenges that threatened a sociracial hierarchy.

Black misrepresentations in popular culture settled questions and quelled concerns over the meaning and threat of Black expressions of sovereignty. Manufacturers and advertisers were well aware that the tangible goods that encapsulated racial alterity in one form or another would appeal to a white southern consumer. Black collectibles, such as the "jolly nigger" piggy bank—produced as early as 1882—allowed white audiences to harken back to an imagined past while trivializing and commercializing the value of Black lives. These Black collectibles would capture and reproduce a longing for a mythical Old South—the Old South that historian C. Vann Woodard once characterized as "a legend of incalculable portions." The Old South functioned as an ephemeral, reinvented self, defined by a culture in which a *noblesse oblige* considered themselves a nurturing class that cared about their slaves, and in turn, the docile and subservient slaves cheerfully served them.

The strict dichotomy of white goodwill and Black congeniality would, alas, be tainted by a Union army and a divisive war, according to those who reproduced and were emotionally invested in the romanticized concept of Dixie. Famed journalist W. J. Cash, a white southern from South Carolina, argued that the South "yearned backward toward its past with passionate longing."[41] "The ex-slave whom the South professed to love so tenderly," Walter White propounded in 1921 (while serving as the NAACP's assistant secretary), gave way to what white southerners would classify as an insolent, dangerous, untrustworthy Black person who was prone to violence, political corruption, and sexual assault.[42] The musings of a reporter in 1923 for a Dallas-based Ku Klux Klan organ labor the point: "When the negro race was brought over here as slaves they were loyal to their masters, and the white women were never despoiled. The negro was in his place as a drawer of water and hewer of wood."[43] By contrast, "the new negro of the South is less industrious, less thrifty, less trustworthy, and less self-controlled than was his father or his grandfather," insisted a late-nineteenth-century white observer.[44] It was a lamented archetype of tameness and manageability—a reinvention of past events that worked to create a cynical interpretation of contemporary society by juxtaposing an imagined Blackness of yesteryears with a new, allegedly menacing reality.

By the era of Reconstruction and beyond, African Americans were considered less controllable, insolent, given to criminal activity. According to contemporary white observers, the "New Negro" was a menacing, unruly individual who was a threat to white society. An Austin paper charged in 1895 that a "New Negro Society" was being formed by African Americans in the state for the sole purpose of ensuring that African American men could marry white women.[45] Some white newspapers drew a scathing and undocumented connection between the rape of white women and increased education among African Americans: "You can't cite us to an outrage by a negro and a white woman in slavery time," the journalist insisted before plaintively claiming that education caused African American men to "outrage . . . white women."[46] Education, the article purported, "gives a negro an equalizing feeling and a hatred toward the white race."[47]

While many southern white people considered the "New Negro" to be impudent and menacing, by contrast Black people interpreted him as something entirely dissimilar. For African Americans, the New Negro image was informed by Black success and self-sufficiency during the Reconstruction era. However, in Texas and the South at large (as well as in other portions of the country), Black advancement, whether economic, political, or educational functioned as a danger to white supremacy and the socioracial hierarchy. For many whites, African Americans' success signaled change that threatened white status and achievement. If, according to the reasoning of many whites, a Black person could advance—perhaps even beyond the financial, educational, or political status of a white person—then white supremacy was weakened. "A new Negro," argued the NAACP early in the twentieth century, "he has been able . . . to see that the ballot is the sine qua non of citizenship. . . . The Negro everywhere is determined to press his right to the citizenship guaranteed him by the federal constitution and to resent as un-American all discriminations against him as a United States citizen."[48]

Two New Negro prototypes materialized by the end of the nineteenth century, one detested by many whites and another held in esteem by African Americans. It was, however, the melding of disparate New Negro images—impudence and indolence on the one hand and ambition and prosperity on the other—that engendered heightened racism and changed how southerners in general and many white Texans in particular construed Black people. "Negroes," the *Texas Republican* charged in 1868, were "assuming airs, becoming insolent and self-important."[49] White anxiety created by this new individual devalued the lives of African Americans and helped to recreate them as objects to be feared, ridiculed, and eliminated. At times, the new perception transformed African Americans into objects that could be easily laughed at, and even collected.

Sambo and Uncle Mose were the preferred caricatures among many late-nineteenth-century white southerners. The black brute and fiend, however, were the perceived new images of Black masculinity in Texas and across the region following emancipation. All such caricatures were less than human, the new and the old, and both were perceived as wholly dispensable, but the black brute and fiend were considered sociopathic, overly sexualized monsters who sought to ravish white women. Headlines or articles that featured such descriptions as "black rape fiend" or "black brute" promoted the image. They were tropes that rendered it both possible and, according to the convictions of many white Texans, necessary to control and destroy, or even collect, the Black body.[50]

The "Sambo" stereotype as both a collectible and an exemplar of Black male corporeality became an increasingly popular part of the era's material and popular culture. The derogatory character cast Black men as simple, jovial, sycophantic imbeciles who pandered to the whims and desires of dominating and superior whites. Historian Leon Litwack charges that

Sambo, "unresentful" and eager to please, flattered the egos of whites who invented the stereotype in the antebellum era to characterize a "model slave."[51] In postbellum America, the enduring image would be represented as marionettes, salt shakers, piggy banks, noise makers, and other tangibles that worked to romanticize an old, southern past just as it served as a primer for how African Americans should perform in society.[52] A literary column entitled "Sambo and the Cooter" that ran in newspapers across Texas by the late nineteenth century depicted a daft, easily frightened, childlike imbecile who was exceedingly content with his debased societal standing—a caricature, accentuated by broken English, that rendered him wholly unimposing, benign, even ridiculous. In one installment of the series, Sambo fears that the devil has taken ahold of his heel while he is wading through water. "Lim'me loose! Lim'me loose! O Lordy! O Lordy! I'll neber go fishin' no mo' on a Sunday of you'll lim'me loose dis time!" he exclaimed, fearful that his decision to go fishing rather than attend a church service caused the devil to intervene.[53] "What de matter, Nigger?" inquires Dick, his perennial companion.[54] "Hit's de debble and, an' he's got me by the toe. Don't you see me a sinkin'? Lim'me loose! Lim'me loose!" he replies.[55]

The Mammy and Uncle Moses misrepresentations were particularly ubiquitous portrayals of Blackness in the era's popular and material culture. Appearing in many forms from salt and pepper shakers to cookie jars and cartoons, the portrayals typically featured a smiling, robust female domestic worker donning a kerchief, and a white haired, balding, male butler with hat in-hand—both standing permanently at attention and ready to serve, images that sought to commemorate and romanticize a past of racial docility and servitude. A *Dallas Daily Times Herald* comic published at the beginning of the twentieth century depicts the Mammy and Uncle Moses figures, both with absurdly enlarged white lips, admiring the musical talents of a young Black boy who appears with overtly simian characteristics. Similar to the "Sambo and Cooter" column, the comic includes an exchange of broken English, a referent that casts the duo as grossly ignorant. Referring to the feral boy, the Uncle Moses character, Deacon Shanghai, expresses to the Mammy: "Dat boy certainly is full ob music," to which she replies, "Yes, deacon: Thit comes nachel toe dat chile, His pap war un ovah by one ob dem street planners."[56]

Such misrepresentations of Blackness were regular features of late nineteenth and early twentieth century periodicals across the state. *Southern Mercury*, the journal of the Texas Farmers Alliance, frequently published sketches that highlighted racist, demeaning tropes. An article in the June 27, 1895, edition, for instance, included a fictionalized exchange about watermelons between a Black man and a white man. Replete with stereotypical syntax and racist identifiers, the column, entitled "First Sight of the Melons," worked to normalize Black misrepresentations and further trivialize Black existence: "'Youse er lookin' mighty happy dis mawnin',' says a latter day darkey." He was then referred to as "nigger" multiple times in the column.[57]

Crude, undignified distortions of Black speech and imagery, printed en masse and disseminated through widely read mediums from newspapers to almanacs, ensured that degrading, unseemly portrayals of African Americans entered the homes and minds of readers across the state and the region. In the Jim Crow South, these published depictions functioned as fixed renderings of a Black existence, imbued with the power to craft a banalized image and situate African Americans and their bodies as caricatures that debase the Black body in perpetuity. Kimberly Wallace-Sanders reminds us that Black misrepresentations in popular and material culture pervade varied systems of socialization and culture.[58] The mammy image, which first emerged during the early antebellum period, for instance, serves as a "signpost pointing to concepts and ideals extending far beyond the stereotype."[59] It reflects, she argues, "the various ways in which this image has shaped and continues to influence American concepts of race and gender."[60] Through the Mammy or auntie images, Black women became happy servants—replete with hyperbolic pleasantries; rotund, Black bodies; and broken English falling from full, smiling, rubicund lips—who adhered to every need and concern of their white employers, never decrying the social arrangements that maligned them. Other tropes of Black women in material and popular culture, such as those featuring the Jezebel or Sapphire misrepresentations, reduced them to overtly sexualized objects, available and eager to satiate the most primal needs of men—particularly white men. Often, they were featured as brash, overbearing, and emasculating wenches. The Sambo and Uncle Mose caricatures produced and disseminated images of Black men who were ignorant, imbecilic half-wits who neither challenged authority nor suggested any discontent with the status quo. Instead, the caricatures accepted their status and served as examples for others. By contrast, the black brute and fiend emerged as the antithesis of Sambo and Uncle Mose. They were neither submissive nor unwieldly, but instead given to aggressive, sociopathic behavior that included the rape of white women. The complexity of such dueling depictions (i.e., mammy and auntie versus

Newspaper cartoon of Mammy and Uncle Moses stereotypes. Dallas Daily Times Herald, *December 9, 1901.*

jezebel and sapphire or black brute and fiend versus Sambo and Uncle Mose) speaks largely to the binary perceptions of Black people, particularly Black men as related to lynching, during and even beyond the era. Wavering between weak and seedy, the contrasting images reveal much about how victims of lynching were perceived by many white people in Texas.

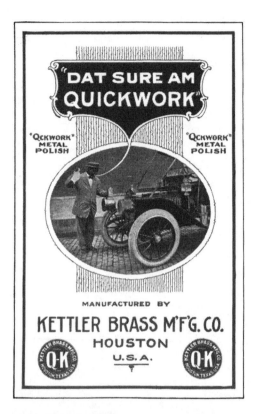

right: Advertisement from *Texas Magazine*, June 1910. *Courtesy of Texas State Library and Archives Commission.*

below: Two Black men with a wagon. *Identifier: 1975070_1753, William Deming Hornaday photograph collection, Texas State Library and Archives Commission.*

Items of Remembrance and Racialized Lynchings

Souvenirs procured at the sites of lynchings functioned as tangible forms of Black misrepresentations. They were collectibles that converted a heinous expression of racialized social control and collective violence into something more acceptable, something that worked to normalize and legitimize the relationship between lynching and leisure. As noted previously, this type of material culture created from the lynching ceremony tended to banalize the brutality of racialized mob violence, downplaying the archaic and grotesque nature of torture, and situating it within a matrix of recreational activity, social acceptability, and fond remembrance in the Jim Crow South. Brutalized Black bodies could be transformed into benign objects beyond the horrid sights and stenches of lynching. For many white Texans, wide-ranging forms of tangible items of remembrance collected or purchased at lynching scenes, or simply acquired some place following the event, served as ardent reminders of the episode they either partook in directly, or experienced vicariously. Procurement of these myriad souvenirs from the sites of lynching points to a desire on the part of individuals to commemorate the occasion; it creates a memorial, material link between the activity and the possessor of the article of remembrance.

Souvenirs are recollections of what one witnessed or helped to create. They allow people to grasp a tangible relic of their vacation, tour, encounter, or other activity and bring it home for private remembrance or show it to others as a means of boasting of what they witnessed or experienced, thereby widening the sphere of influence. Pieces of lynched Black bodies and the devices of their destruction in Texas were transformed into objects to be obtained as corporeal mementos of one's experiences by the end of the nineteenth century. Body parts segmented to pocket-sized portions; pieces of ropes used to strangle the life from Black persons and center them atop combustible materials; links of chains that anchored Black bodies to poles or automobiles—all were transformed into souvenirs, the purchase or collection of which was woven into a changing culture of lynching in Texas. Few things were left behind at the scenes of lynchings.

Individuals in the state frequently sifted through the ashes of lynching victims' funeral pyres for keepsakes. Already reduced to ashes, burned bodies made the discovery and removal of souvenirs easy when contrasted with the potential bedlam of segmenting bodies that had only been hanged or shot. "Every scrap of his clothing was eagerly sought by relic hunters," one observer disclosed after the burning of Henry Smith. Following the

1902 burning of Dudley Morgan in Lansing, Texas, several people from the crowd of four thousand who burned him "searched the ashes for parts of Morgan's body for souvenirs," according to one witness.[61] Members of the mob carted off parts of his burned skull and body after the fire expired.[62] Women in Temple extracted pieces of Will Stanley's bones from his ashes after he was burned before a mob of five thousand on July 31, 1915 for allegedly bludgeoning the children of a local white farmer.[63] Some of the women were observed standing on the shoulders of men to obtain an unobstructed view. Witnesses—some pedestrian, others in automobiles—lined the streets as Stanley was pushed into the fire before his death. He made six attempts to remove himself from atop the pyre, each attempt thwarted by chains that confined him to the flames. Many in the crowd cheered as they watched. Stanley's remains were hanged from a Chamber of Commerce sign that read "Progressive Temple."[64] Prior to the burning of nineteen-year-old Wylie McNeely in Leesburg, Texas, on October 11, 1921, members of a mob laid claim to corporeal souvenirs. They "drew lots" for the parts of McNeely's "anatomy which they regarded as the choicest souvenirs," according to one observer. As they waited to burn McNeely, many laughed and joked with one another.[65] In May of 1922, after the charred bodies of three Black men cooled in Kirvin, Texas, several white men located the lynched men's hearts, sliced off pieces, and disseminated them to the crowd. Later that month, Jesse Thomas met his death in Waco when he was accused of murdering a white man and attacking a white woman. The woman's father shot Thomas after she identified the twenty-three-year-old Black man as her assailant. Thomas's body was seized from the morgue by a crowd, burned in the public square, then dragged through town as men attempted to obtain souvenirs from the charred remains.[66]

Members of mobs did not, however, need for the body to be burned in order to procure souvenirs from it or from the site of the lynching. When a mob of two thousand hanged Sank Majors from a bridge in Waco, Texas, in 1905, several individuals stripped away pieces of his clothing and cut off portions of his fingers to keep as souvenirs. Buddy Evans, an eighteen-year-old African American accused of murdering a white man, was hanged by a mob in Center, Texas, on May 21, 1928. A local craftsman fashioned gavels from the limb of the tree used in Evans's lynching and distributed them to others. One must note the form of the craftsman's whittlings. Forging a gavel—a symbol of justice and order—from the machinery of murder is a maddening representation of the irony associated with lynching, or perhaps for the craftsman a lauding of a wicked form of justice. The same tree limb used to hang Evans was used by a mob in 1920 to hang Lige Daniels, who was sixteen years old.[67]

Similar to the craftsman from Center, others found unnervingly inventive ways to display evidence of lynching escapades. One white Texas man converted the kneecap of a Henry Smith to a "watch charm."[68] Another man discovered one of Smith's rib bones, took it home, and "placed it over his door for good luck," according to a member of the mob that murdered Smith.[69]

Possessing these items of remembrance allowed access not simply to the Black body or devices of its destruction, but to countless opportunities to relive how the possessor came to acquire the keepsakes. One could certainly find a sense of pleasure or pride in possessing these lynching representations, but without an associated storyline, the souvenir would likely cease to function as relevant—it would cease to be a souvenir. Harvey Young examines the relationship between tangible items of remembrance and a necessary retelling of the represented event: "Incomplete in itself, the souvenir requires an accompanying narrative furnished by its possessor in order to fill in that which is missing and to allow the fragment to reflect the event or experience of which it is a part."[70] A souvenir is inherently "incomplete" and finds a "sense of wholeness . . . through an embrace of an accompanying narrative."[71] A sliver of a charred organ from a lynching victim could be mistaken for a number of items when considered independent of an origin story. Similarly, a strip of clothing may be viewed simply as a sewing scrap by an observer if the possessor of, or someone familiar with, the souvenir fails to situate it in a broader, narrative context. Lynching representations "function to preserve the act in perpetuity" and "allow the act to be committed again," argues historian Jaqueline Goldsby.[72] When, for instance, the time piece fashioned from the knee of a Black lynching victim in Texas was observed or complimented by a friend or passerby, the person wearing the eerie accessory was provided an opportunity to boast about how they came to acquire it. One could relive the sounds and smells of the event, the fervor of the crowd, the feeling of accomplishment gained at the end of the deed. The possessor of the item could impart a descriptive narrative that conceivably allowed the inquirer to exist, if only momentarily, in the event while in some way being influenced by the retelling.

The sphere of a lynching experience broadened with each personal reflection or aural act of remembrance; thus, the political work and acceptance of lynching relied heavily upon memory, fostered both by the narratives that accompanied tangible relics and by recollection as a novel iteration of popular culture. Memories of events witnessed firsthand could assist in commuting racialized torture and violence to something acceptable, novel, communicable, and even entertaining. As Goldsby notes, it is not necessary to view lynching representations "to experience the power of the event."[73] When Laura Dainty-Pelham, a white female reformer from Chicago, was visiting Texas a year following the burning of Henry Smith, her hotelkeeper's wife frequently shared her memory of her presence at Smith's lynching "as if it were something to be proud of," according to Ida B. Wells in her retelling of the story.[74] On one occasion, the hotelkeeper's eight-year old daughter "who was playing about the room, came up to her mother and shaking her by the arm boasted, 'I saw them burn the nigger, didn't I Mama?'"[75] "Yes darling, you saw them burn the nigger," the mother dotingly confirmed.[76] It was not merely the possession of tangible items of remembrance, then, that extended the sphere of influence and molded how people interpreted lynching. Indeed, the events observed by those present at the lynching scene became intangible relics, they became tokens of experience that could be shared and reshared in a similar context to postcards or other representations. The visual and the aural scenes consumed by an eyewitness were collected evidence of experience that could be disseminated in the same discursive manner as tangible items of remembrance. Those who were told about the lynching could then widen the audience and experience by sharing the details with others; infinite retellings could thereby create an expansive audience for mob violence. Thus, multiple, interwoven forms of memory worked to extend and reproduce the firsthand and protracted experiences of a lynching.

Memories forged from lynching scenes and representations helped fashion the public roles of Black people as they promoted the ascendance of whiteness in a post-Reconstruction era. Each memory of Black denigration could reproduce and reinforce a destructive, partisan reality that wavered between at least two tragic perceptions of Black people: a mixture of novelty, amusement and race at one extreme and the conflation of criminality and Blackness at the other. This dialectic of criminality inscribed onto the Black body and its performative iteration in lynching required memory and its use as a socializing agent to hierarchicalize racial difference. From the reminiscences of empirical or material evidence, one could imagine and then speak about the events long after they occurred, which ensured an unlimited reproduction of truth. With each recollection or retelling, the events themselves often took on increased degrees of embellishment: the "brute" may be imagined as larger or darker; the victim of his crime may become younger, more angelic; the details of the crime committed by the lynching victim became increasingly appalling. The embellishments in turn helped legitimize the perceived need for racialized mob violence as they continuously worked to diminish apprehensions over the modality of the shift in the state's lynching culture.

Modern Entertainment Mediums and the Experiential Lynching

Approximately two thousand people gathered in September of 1905 to watch the burning of an African American man in Howard, Texas. Perched atop the roofs of farm buildings and along the streets, spectators arrived at the site of the lynching after advance notice was given of the impending event. The victim was provided two hours for prayers and visitation with his siblings, a request perhaps granted to allow more spectators time to arrive at the scene. "The negro's moans were pitiful," wrote one journalist. As "he struggled, his great muscles swelling and throbbing in an effort to break the chains which bound him," he continued.[77] John R. Spears, a resident of Northwood, New York, read about the mob death in Howard and was moved to disgust. He penned a letter to the newspaper with a derisive tone that at once encompassed his revulsion and mocked the perverted appetites for leisure espoused by whites in Texas. Spears derisively suggested that it would be "good business enterprise to organize a stock company and send a kinetoscope to the next lynching of the kind" to "portray to people just how such work is done."[78] He lamented that it would fail to capture the "zest given by the screams and prayers of the 'nigger,' but in spite of this," he continued, "it is fair to suppose that if 2,000 people will gather in a small community like Howard to see the real thing, at least 1,000 would pay 25 cents each, in an average town, for an evening with a series of photographs showing vividly the 'nigger's' contortions."[79] Spears then sardonically insisted that the kinetoscope recordings would show "the work of the modern Texans" and provide "public instruction" in the interest of "public entertainment."[80]

Though suggested mockingly in the letter described above, this analogous relationship between the lynching display and the leisure associated with cinema is reflective of modern viewership during the late nineteenth century and says much about the relationship between lynching and leisure. Viewers' increasing familiarity with Thomas Edison's Kinetoscope (large cabinets that exhibited moving pictures through peepholes on the top portion) and Vitascope (a related technology that allowed for projection to larger audiences), for instance, provided an ideal medium for experiencing a lynching after the event occurred. Austin, Texas, had one of the state's first Kinetoscope parlors by November 1894. Projected film arrived in the state as early as February 1, 1897, when the Dallas Opera House used Edison's Vitascope to play footage that included Niagara Falls, a heroic rescue, and a lynching. Modernity and the shifting culture of lynching coalesced in these hauntingly modern entertainment mediums, forging a seemingly contra-dictory display of technological advancement and archaic expressions of violence. One-reel films that played recordings of lynchings ran across the South during the end of the nineteenth century. The audiences for this form of entertainment were somewhat self-limiting due largely to the costs and logistical difficulty inherent in both purchasing early movie projectors and finding or building spaces to feature the films. Other types of recordings of Texas lynchings, however, proved far more accessible and reached audiences across the nation.[81]

The Phonograph

Within weeks of Henry Smith's death, Samuel Burdett was strolling through the streets of Seattle, Washington, "whiling away an idle hour seeing the sights," when he happened upon quite a fracas "on one of the crowded thoroughfares of this thriving little city."[82] There stood a crowd, huddled together "attending some sort of entertainment on the street."[83] Burdett admitted that, "like the curious everywhere," he "too, wanted to see what the 'show' was, and, accordingly, pushed through the crowd to where a man was mounted on a stand or platform of some sort."[84] Burdett promptly paid a five cent admission and put the phonograph upon his ears. What he was about to hear, the horrific shrieks of a man condemned to unimaginable suffering, would change the very manner in which Burdett—thousands of miles from the site of the occurrence—would come to understand both his new environment as well as the expanse of racial terror.

A native Kentuckian, Burdett had been in Seattle just a few years before he encountered the display of human malevolence extant in his new, provin-cial surroundings. Assigned to the all-Black Ninth Calvary during the Civil War in 1866, Burdett remained in that regiment until 1883 before becom-ing a doctor of veterinary medicine. He and his wife, Belle, arrived in Seattle in 1890. Burdett established a veterinary practice and quickly rose to prom-inence. Within months, he was nominated as the city's veterinary surgeon.

By the following year, Burdett cofounded Cornerstone Grand Lodge of the York Masons. He had, perhaps, by 1893 settled into the notion that in the Pacific Northwest, he and his family would be buffered from the atrocities of racialized mob violence that plagued their native South. It seemed, one day in the spring of 1893, that the space between his southern place of birth and his new northwestern residence had been suddenly collapsed as the wicked sounds of the South had found their way through phonographs to ostensibly "civilized citizens" of Seattle. [85] A seemingly archaic display or human torture and suffering was rendered very modern by the technological advancement that allowed sound to be recorded and reproduced by the end of the nineteenth century.

When Burdett noticed the crowd on the street of his adopted city engaging in some type of entertainment, he wanted to see the "show."[86] He made his way through the throngs and alas, upon hearing the sounds, his curiosity rapidly gave way to disbelief and repulsion: "Oh the horror of horrors!" All at once, as the aural realities of racial terror perforated his newfound security at the edge of the nation, Seattle became for Burdett a self-aggrandized space "where we pretend that we are educated, enlightened, and on advance ground in everything which tends to advancement."[87] Henry Smith, the Black man who met his fate by burning in Paris, Texas, on February 1, 1893, could be heard writhing and imploring, suffering "in an agonizing, heartrending manner," Burdett grieved.[88] "Oh, Lord, Mr. _____, for God's sake don't burn me; don't burn me—Oh, oh, kill me, kill me. Shoot me, shoot me!" Smith wailed.[89] Burdett expressed untiring astonishment at both the thuds of human suffering and the joyous manner in which people consumed the display as entertainment: "Here we are selling the dying groans and pitiful pleadings for mercy of a man as he suffers the awful irony of having his eyes burned out one at a time with hot irons. Think of it! So much—only five cents per groan—so much per shriek as the excruciating pain and awful suffering strikes terror in his heart."[90] Burdett's carefully crafted indictment included not simply those who listened to the phonographic renderings, but all individuals. "Here we [emphasis added] are" he deftly reminds his readers, encouraging a collective responsibility for the mob death by burning of a Black man in Texas.[91] It was an impeachment of society in its entirety. "If someone would be good enough to tell me what good end this sort of inhuman exhibition can or would possibly [serve] the information will be gratefully received," Burdett rhetorically requested near the conclusion of his account.[92]

Phonographic enumerations of Smith's gruesome death were used as entertainment around the country by the turn of the century. In 1900, a county fair in Iowa boasted of its attractions, which included Turkish dancers, gambling, and "a phonographic recital and photographs of the burning of a negro in Texas, with a lecture telling how his eyes were burned out, ears burned off, a hot iron thrust down his throat, etc.," reported an Iowa newspaper.[93] In 1901, Children's Day at an exposition in Omaha, Nebraska featured myriad merriments, including "big bundles of childish presents," sweetbread, music furnished by a junior military band, and a phonographic lecture "relating the burning of the negro Smith in Texas."[94] It seems that young or old could engage in this form of racialized violence as entertainment.

Closer to the site of lynching, the desire to harness the theatrics of mob violence were expressed in writing by Judge John M. Duncan in 1895. Duncan, characterized as "master of ceremonies" of Robert Henson Hilliard's mob death by burning in Tyler, Texas, on October 29 of that same year, had penned an open letter to the governor of Texas urging him to ban prize-fighting due to the violence inherent in the sport. After a group of Dallasites lost money in the Corbett-Fitzsimmons fight, which occurred two days following the lynching of Hilliard, they sent a telegram to Duncan sardonically expressing that the amphitheater where the fight occurred was "still standing," and "if he wishes to pull off any more negro roastings it is at his service, including the tar."[95] Duncan's letter imploring the barring of boxing was thus clearly seen by some as an ironic dictate. Further, it unmistakably delineated the lives of African Americans as worthless.

The shrieking sounds and disturbing sites of Hilliard's lynching were captured and consumed by audiences as far as Boston, Massachusetts. "A thrilling exhibition was given yesterday at Wonderland, 11 Tremont row, when a 'Phono-optic' reproduction of the burning at the stake . . . of Robert Henson Hilliard was presented before large crowds, who were spellbound by the terrible vividness of the representation," reported the *Boston Globe* the year following the lynching.[96] Visitors were able to listen to phonographic recordings and view enlarged photographs of Hilliard's burning. Frank J. Pilling, said to have been present during the lynching, provided the Boston crowd with graphic details of the events that unfolded in Tyler the previous October. It seems a fascination with Texas largely defined Wonderland's entertainment lineup for the day. In what one observer described as the "more jovial portion of the program," visitors also watched Texas Ann and Texas Ben "give a graphic portrayal of life on the plains."[97]

Print Images and Changes in a Lynching Culture

People's increased attendance at lynchings by the end of the nineteenth century kept pace with their interest in preserving and disseminating the lynching experience. Photography offered just the medium necessary to satisfy this longing. This modern mode of lending perpetuity to experience captured the grotesque and archaic in a medium often reserved for the practical and mundane. Photographs of lynchings rendered the event "somewhat familiar," according to Amy Louise Wood.[98] White southerners quite likely would "have posed for and interpreted these images through their experiences with other, more typical photographic forms and practices, such as portraiture and hunting photographs."[99] A novel opportunity for photographers to employ their medium in the pursuit of profit emerged with the creation of the changing culture of lynching in Texas. Lynchings could be profitable affairs. Photographers were well aware of the demand for memorabilia and seized the occurrence of lynchings accordingly. One Texas photographer reported that if he received advance notice of a lynching, he endeavored to attend due to his certainty that pictures produced of the event would assuredly be purchased by an interested public.[100] Lynch mobs frequently desired a photographic artifact of what they witnessed, experienced, or helped create. Others may have desired an image of an incident that they heard about but did not witness; the images allowed them to view the event *in absentia*. Still others simply succumbed to curiosity and traveled distances short and long to view photographic displays that posited Black criminality as absolute and offered an opportunity to engage in an activity that could be easily interpreted as leisure. The 1895 mob burning of Robert Henson Hilliard underscores the point. Set ablaze before a crowd in Tyler, Texas, one spectator observed that his "lower limbs burned off before he became unconscious and his body looked to be burned to the hollow."[101] The dreadful nature of his torture and death were arrested in print by C. A. Davis, a local photographer who made the images, which were commuted to stereographs, accessible to the public through both individual sale and exhibition. Printed on verso of at least one of the stereograph images was a message from Davis: "If you want anything in my line call and see me at Iron's Studio on North College Street. C. A. Davis, Tyler, Texas."[102] Davis's enterprising interests also led him to partner with Breckenridge & Scruggs Company, the drugstore that ran an exhibit of the pictures shortly following the events and boasted, in the local paper, that they had "sixteen large views under powerful magnifying lenses now on exhibition."[103] Street bills directed interested parties to the exact location of the stereographic exhibit, which featured the alleged attack and murder of a white woman and the swift punishment visited upon Hilliard, including his body chained to the scaffold. The remaining images were staged to recreate unseen portions of the events.[104]

Stereo cameras captured two images on a single plate, which were intended to be viewed simultaneously through a stereoscope. The device, which became increasingly popular by the 1880s, creates an illusion of depth, a three-dimensional view infused with a level of realism unavailable in other photographic ephemera at the time. The stereographic display created by Breckenridge & Scruggs skillfully situated viewers in each motif, both imagined and real, which thereby allowed for and authenticated a sensory engrossment as it reinforced Hilliard's guilt in the public mind. The stereo views, from "Waiting for His Victim," to "The Attack" and "Scuffle," to "The Murder," of the woman and Hilliard's "Trial and Burning," stood as absolute, undeniable truth of Hilliard's guilt.[105] Much like one would view and interpret an early motion picture replete with distinct acts—each given an evocative title and specific role in a larger narrative—the storyline delivered in the Breckenridge & Scruggs's stereographic display conceivably allowed viewers to consider the totality of the images alongside other, more familiar entertainment mechanisms, including early cinema. Of the sixteen stereographs, fifteen surviving images are housed in the Prints and Photographs Division of the Library of Congress. Notwithstanding the missing image, a copy of which may be lodged between the pages of some family photo album or in a box filled with letters and other personal items, the remaining shots collectively weave a layered account of terror and entertainment, a performance reminiscent of a Shakespearean tragedy that transcends restrictive notions of pleasure and enjoins the viewer to experience death as entertainment.

Several of the images also present an underlying, intriguing commentary on the complexities of gender and racial interaction in Jim Crow Texas. In image two, entitled "The Assault," the woman chosen to represent the white alleged victim appears to be a fair-skinned Black woman posing with her arms extended upward, away from her body and her fingers flattened in a self-protective, yet vulnerable, stance. Hilliard's stand-in is depicted as lunging toward the woman, readied for attack. The next several scenes, including "The Struggle," "Cutting Her Throat," and "Washing Himself," invite the viewer to further read the staged images as visual, visceral testimony to the inevitability of Black criminality.[106] The dialectic of the sex-crazed Black villain that increasingly permeated narratives of Black criminality by the end of the nineteenth century is authenticated through the use of these images. "The Body as Found" depicts a dramatization of a slain white woman, strewn across a trench. This black-and-white image, as briefly mentioned in a previous chapter, features a red coloring applied to areas of the body that were mutilated in some manner. A splotch of red in the woman's vaginal area is used to mimic the aftermath of a violent sexual assault.[107] Collectively, the reenacted scenes render Hilliard's guilt absolute; his trial and sentencing were carried out in a court of public opinion. Even what appears to be the selection of a Black female performer to act the part of the deceased white woman presents an apparent annotation on the heralding and perceived purity of southern white womanhood and the dangers of Black men. To place a white woman in a staged scene that featured a Black man in an aggressive stance likely seemed patently unacceptable to those taking the pictures. The choice of a Black actress thereby reflected and reinforced an ideological stance that posited the necessity of protecting white women from interaction with Black men, no matter how controlled or benign the environment.[108] The actress appears in four of the first six images, all of which feature staged scenes. What follows is a series of actual images, not reenactments, of the capture, torture, and burning to death of Hilliard. "Don't fail to see this," the newspaper ad implored.[109]

The existence of images that created a roll call of sorts of those who were responsible for lynching a person, in some cities of the state, could serve as a harbinger of culpability. When the occasional sheriff earnestly worked to bring lynchers to justice, the images could prove useful in identifying members of a mob. Despite clear photographic evidence of wrongdoing, however, arrests rarely resulted in conviction. On September 21, 1917, a mob of approximately eight hundred hanged Burl Smith, an African American man accused of attempting to rape a white woman the previous day in Goose Creek, near Houston. Deputy Constable J. D. Hunnicut and Deputy Sheriff Bert Veal arrested Smith and placed him in a Goose Creek jail cell. Between three hundred and four hundred white men arrived at the jail to seize Smith. Hunnicut and Veal attempted to thwart the advance of the mob but were overpowered. The mob secured Smith to a tree by rope and hanged him. In total, perhaps 800 people witnessed the murdered. Several pictures of the lynching were taken by local citizens and disseminated throughout the area. "Later [local citizens] confiscated all the pictures because they didn't want the authorities to see . . . these people," recalled

Dramatization of Henson Hilliard. *"1. Waiting for His Victim," Library of Congress Prints and Photographs Division.*

Dramatization intended to be Henson Hilliard attacking a white woman. *"2. The Attack," Library of Congress Prints and Photographs Division.*

Dramatization of Robert Henson Hilliard and his alleged victim. *"3. The Struggle," Library of Congress Prints and Photographs Division.*

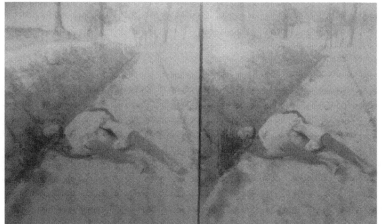

Dramatization of Robert Henson Hilliard's alleged victim after the attack. The original image includes red color on the neck to simulate the look of blood. *"5. The Body as Found," Library of Congress Prints and Photographs Division.*

Dramatization of Robert Henson Hilliard after alleged attack. *"6. Washing Himself," Library of Congress Prints and Photographs Division.*

This image features Robert Henson Hilliard and his captors. *"8. After the Trial," Library of Congress Prints and Photographs Division.*

Garrett R. Herring, a resident of the area at the time. "They arrested a few people and tried them," he added, "but they didn't do anything with them because they couldn't prove anything." The sheriff's department arrested fifteen white men for the murder of Smith. None were convicted.[110]

Postcards and a New Culture of Lynching

Other mediums for the dissemination of lynching images proved far more wide-reaching. Picture postcards, for instance, would broaden the audience for mob violence. They afford expansive insight into how mob torture and death were interpreted by spectators and others; picture postcards both disseminate a view of what one sees and, by extension, provide an intimate assessment of what the viewer experiences.

Produced in the antebellum period, envelopes with pictures on the outer portion were an early form of the modern postcard. The popularity of picture postcards in the United States would develop during the latter decades of the nineteenth century. The United States Congress enacted legislation early in 1861 that allowed cards weighing no more than one ounce to be mailed. In 1872, Congress allowed the government to print cards that included a message on one side and an address on the reverse. Private entities could produce the cards, but the legislation restricted the use of the descriptor "postal card" to government-printed mailings, which could typically be sent for one cent instead of the two cents charged to mail non-government-issued cards. Subsequent legislation passed in 1898 equalized the cost of mailing privately produced cards but restricted the inclusion of messages to the converse side of the card that bore the address. These non-government-issued cards could not bear the phrase "post card" until the Postmaster General issued Post Office No. 1447 in 1901. By 1907, postcards could also include messages on the side of the mailing that bore the address. The inclusion of images on postcards experienced a similarly segmented appearance. Postcards reached a broader audience by the 1876 United States Centennial International Exposition in Philadelphia when fairgoers could purchase photographic tokens of the images they witnessed. While the renderings could be shared with others should the consumer choose, they were not initially intended to serve as postal *objet d'art*. Address lines on the posterior side of the images would appear later in the century, a move by publishers that broadened the consumer appeal and intended use of the pictorial, experiential medium. By the early 1890s, a once-fledgling

Crowd surrounding Robert Henson Hilliard before his burning. *"7. In the Hands of the Mob," Library of Congress Prints and Photographs Division.*

Tyler, Texas before the burning of Robert Henson Hilliard. *"9. Building the Scaffold," Library of Congress Prints and Photographs Division.*

Robert Henson Hilliard praying before he was tied to the stake. *"10. Praying on the Scaffold," Library of Congress Prints and Photographs Division.*

Robert Henson Hilliard chained to a stake. *"12. First Fire Withdrawn," Library of Congress Prints and Photographs Division..*

postcard industry benefited from advances in photography and mass printing technology as well as an expanding tourism industry. The picture postcard in America had become a popular, descriptive, illustrative medium for communication used often as a tactile method to commemorate leisure outings and activities.

This mass-produced, modern form of visual communiqué found vaunting expression among consumers nationwide. Marketed largely to white audiences, pictographic collectibles grew quickly in popularity by the beginning of the twentieth century. One trade magazine commented in 1905, "Illustrated postal cards have gained considerably in the public's favor. . . . They have passed the fad stage and appear to have become a permanent feature."[111] The United States Postal Service determined that during their fiscal year ending in June 1908, approximately 677 million postcards were mailed. That number increased to nearly one billion in 1913. In noting the dramatically increasing interest in postcards across the country in the early twentieth century, *American Magazine* averred that postcards represented "one general gasp of relief—'See for yourself; I can't describe it.'"[112]

Used as advertisements, or simply as greetings, postcards that featured African Americans—mostly southern—engaged in stereotypic activities quickly rose in popularity. Created largely by white illustrators, the racialized iconography displayed in this genre of cultural artifact worked to present visual, enduring, disseminated evidence of supposed intellectual and physical inferiority, evidence authenticated with each viewing. African Americans happily eating watermelon or posing as "A Typical Coon" while working in kitchens arrested images of an imagined Blackness, one that reflected and reproduced a romanticized Old South as it borrowed from and helped to firmly establish racial alterity. The postcards frequently featured captions with a minstrel-like dialect: *th* at the beginning or end of a word was replaced with *d*; the word *Lord* appeared as *Lawd* or *Lawdsy*. The illustrators also relied on racialized physiognomy to convey commentary that postulated the omnipotence of whiteness. African American characters were heavily shaded with black ink, purposefully positing a singular, standardized notion of Blackness. Images of African Americans with awkwardly enlarged lips and simian attributes advanced ideas of stalled evolution while implicitly heralding whiteness as supreme.[113] Children were often displayed as primates, or more typically as pickaninnies—an offensive derivative of *pequenino*, a Portuguese term for "little child."[114] Donning platted hair and happy dispositions, the children were featured in a variety of denigrating poses, from consuming watermelon through smiling lips amid a scattering of rinds to strumming a banjo barefoot in a field of cotton. Postcards that depicted Black male children sitting on the banks of a lake or swamp while alligators approached them with open jaws were also common. At times, the images featured violent portrayals of children's heads and upper extremities suspended from alligators' mouths as they were devoured.[115]

Black misrepresentations captured in this form of iconography merged and reproduced dual conceptions of racial othering. Featured as purveyors of hilarity at one extreme to deserving of a violent death at the other, from the dissolutely humorous to the categorically morbid, mailable images that sought to denigrate Black intelligence or banalize the death of African Americans allowed a white audience to view the images as clear evidence of their distance from and superiority to African Americans. The images thus helped to create and reproduce rigid, immeasurably harmful depictions of Blackness that could infect both the minds and engagements of those who encountered them, effectively rendering Black lives cheap and dispensable. Postcards of Black lynching victims were no exception. On August 2, 1920, a crowd numbering over one thousand hanged sixteen-year-old Lige Daniels in Center, Texas. Accused of beating to death a white woman, the wife of a local farmer, Daniels reportedly confessed the crime to a grand jury. Upon hearing of the confession, a mob stormed the jail and destroyed a steel cell to gain access to Daniels. He was then dragged outside and hanged from an oak tree on the courthouse lawn. A woman familiar with the alleged victim mailed a postcard that featured members of the crowd standing just below Daniels's hanging corpse. Her inscription on the reverse read as follows: "This was made in the court yard in Center, Texas. He is a 16 year old Black boy. He killed Earl's grandma. She was Florence's mother. Give this to Bud. From Aunt Myrtle."[116]

Postcards assist in decoding the personal choices and belief systems of senders, and frequently, by extension, receivers. Inscriptions and other markings enable insight into how people perceive of what they witness and how they situate themselves in the related narrative. Postcards of lynchings in particular reveal something about the view of the people, not simply through the images captured and disseminated, but, perhaps more tellingly, through inscriptions included. By purchasing a postcard of a lynching, individuals were arresting the memorial attributes into a souvenir. By mailing the cards to others, individuals distributed the experience commemorated by the image and thus widened the audience and sphere of influence. But by including written communication of the experience associated with the memorialized scene, the sender was allowing others to discern something about his or her interpretation of the pictured event. After a Dallas woman witnessed the lynching of Allen Brooks on March 3, 1910, she purchased a postcard of the hanging and forwarded it to her friend, Dr. John W. T. Williams in Lafayette, Kentucky, the following week. The inscription read: "Well John—This is a token of a great day we had in Dallas, March 3, a negro was hung for an assault on a three year old girl. I saw this on my noon hour."[117] The woman went on to situate herself in the lynching narrative; "I was very much in the bunch. You can see the negro hanging on a telephone pole."[118] She witnessed Brooks hanging in the city's downtown streets during her *noon hour*, likely a reference to lunchtime. She chose to venerate the event through a pictorial item of reminiscence that heralded mob death as worthy of commemoration. The sepia-toned image, featuring a lifeless, tethered body hovering above the gawking crowd, rendered almost benign the violent death due to the inscription that ran along the front border: "all is OK and would like to get a post from you," the sender nudged in closing.[119] The postcard captured a grotesque, murderous scene that certainly appalls most audiences today, and that also caused many during the time to squirm with repulsion, yet the image was used as a salutation and, in this case, a friendly jolt for a reciprocal jester.

Thousands of postcards featuring Brooks's lynching were printed within days of the event, clear evidence that this form of entertainment medium

left: Image of Lige Daniels, lynched on August 2, 1920, in Center, Texas. *Wiki Commons.*

below: Postcard of Lige Daniels's lynching. The inscription on postcard reads: "This was made in the court yard in Center Texas he is a 16 year old Black boy. He killed Earl's grandma. She was Florence's mother. Give this to Bud. From Aunt Myrtle." *Lynching in Texas Staff,* "Lynching of Lige Daniels," Lynching in Texas, accessed July 30, 2021, *http:// www.lynchingintexas.org/items/ show/96.*

This was made in the court yard in Center Texas
POST a 16 year old Black boy CARD
STAMP HERE
CORRESPONDENCE   ADDRESS
He Killed Earl's Grandma
She was Florence Mother.
Give this to Bud
Frome
aunt myrtle

Postcard of Allen Brooks's lynching with inscription. The inscription reads as follows: "Taken March 3, 1910: two hours after the lynching of the negro "Brown" He was drug through the street from the court house [sic] and hanged to the south west corner of the arch The crowd seen in the picture is nothing to be compared with the mob, at the time this picture was taken the mob had allready [sic] left scene and was on their way to the jail after [illegible] another negro victim." The writer incorrectly calls Brooks "Brown." *Image from "Downtown Dallas Two Hours After the Lynching of Allen Brooks," courtesy DeGolyer Library, Southern Methodist University*

had broad interest. A local man appealed to United States District Attorney William H. Atwell for assistance in stopping the dissemination of the post-cards by mail. Atwell replied that no law had been broken except "the law of common decency and love of the city in which one lives," which, the district attorney continued, "should be law enough to make a man think a second time before sending such pictures out through the mail."[120] In this instance, it seems "the law of common decency" fell palpably short as a regulatory agent.

Will Stanley was affixed to a chain and placed atop a fire in Temple, Texas, on July 30, 1915. As many as ten thousand people participated

Postcard of lynching of Allen Brooks with inscription, 1910, in Dallas, Texas. Inscription reads as follows: "Well John—This is a token of a great day we had in Dallas, March 3, a negro was hung for an assault on a three year old girl. I saw this on my noon hour all is OK and would like to get a post from you." *Image courtesy Dallas Historical Society, Dallas, Texas.*

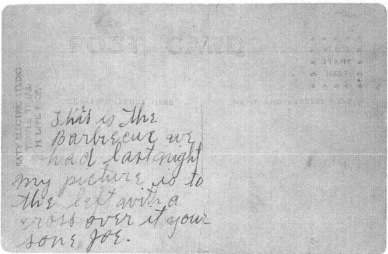

Postcard of Will Stanley's burned corpse. Many studies have erroneously published this as an image of Jesse Washington. H. Lippe. Katy Electric Studio. Temple, Texas, 1915. *Wiki Commons.*

in Stanley's lynching. Local photographers approached the lynching as an opportunity to profit from individuals' interests in memorializing the event they had witnessed. Katy Electric Studio in Temple captured multiple images of Stanley's tortuous death and sold them for ten cents apiece. The studio converted at least one of the images of the lynching into a postcard. It features Stanley's shriveled and charred remains dangling from a chain, surrounded by multiple adults and children unabashedly facing the camera. Stanley's outer extremities are disturbingly absent, having succumb entirely to the flames. There is a cloth around his midriff to conceal his genitalia. One of the postcards found its way into the hands of Waco resident Joe Meyers, an oiler in Bellmead, four miles from Waco. An inscription written by Meyers, who found himself pictured in the background of a postcard that displayed the burned remains of Will Stanley, reveals much about the relationship between racialized mob violence and leisure. He mailed the postcard, on which he identified his position in the crowd with a mark that is barely visible on the surviving artifact, to a parent with his hauntingly cavalier interpretation of his experience in the inscription: "This is the barbeque we had last night[.] my picture is to the left with a cross over it[.] your son Joe."[121] Invoked perhaps at least partially in jest, the use of the term *barbeque* is nonetheless suggestive of the cavalier attitude that typified racialized mob violence in Texas. Joe's message captures, with nearly unspoiled precision, how presence at a torturous mob death of a Black person was considered leisure.[122]

CHAPTER 5

"To See for Themselves"

Technology, Tourism, and
the Experiential Lynching

"Thousands Visit Sherman Sunday," the headline read in the *Sherman Daily Democrat* on May 11, 1930, days following the lynching of George Hughes.[1] "Thrilled by the lurid newspaper accounts, radio accounts which were given ever over national hook-ups, and no end of hearsay, thousands of people from the surrounding counties and state were in Sherman Sunday to see for themselves," the article read.[2] The "roads leading to Sherman were filled with a constant stream of automobiles," the journalist further penned, "and the streets on which cars were allowed to travel were congested."[3] Visitors spent their Sunday holiday in Sherman, away from work and other duties, to tour the courthouse where Hughes spent his last moments before he succumbed to the flames that engrossed him. The previous Friday, Hughes fell victim to the ostensibly insatiable appetite of a white mob resentful over both the presence and prosperity of the growing African American town in and around Sherman (see chapter 3). As described earlier, after law enforcement agents placed Hughes in a courthouse vault to buffer him from the murderous intent of the mob, a firebombing intended to thwart the agents' protective efforts likely killed Hughes. Once the premises cooled, a group entered the building and broke down the door of the vault to retrieve Hughes. "When the men who went into the vault shoved the body through the hole and dumped it to the ground two stories below," a commentator observed, "women screamed and clapped their hands and great cheer went up."[4] Those gathered outside the building seemed jubilant, a mood temporarily disrupted by national guardsmen who surrounded the building and fired perhaps fifty shots above the crest of the mob in a failed effort to disperse it. In response, mob members peppered the militia with bricks, wood, and other debris. A girl at a soda stand handed empty bottles to men and boys as they walked past her, to be used as missiles against law enforcement. As the volley of makeshift munitions continued, Hughes was fastened to the back of an automobile and dragged to the Black section of town where he was burned. Several of his lynchers sang and cheered along the way. By the Sunday holiday, any signs of the mob's actions downtown existed as rubble strewn across a lot where the courthouse once stood. Local African Americans continued to seek refuge where they could in the aftermath of the white violence that destroyed large portions of the local Black community. While some residents began to clear the wreckage of the mayhem and destruction that had consumed much of the weekend, an aural backdrop of automobile engines filled the air in and around Sherman. The constant tide of tourists that Sunday who arrived in the area, hailing from around the county and far beyond to somehow partake in what they perceived as events worthy of their leisure time, existed as a disturbing, yet perennial, reminder that scenes of racialized lynching were tourist attractions in Texas.

By the late nineteenth century, lynching in Texas converted ordinary landscapes into sites of identity reification and cultural construction both produced and reproduced by changes in racial interface as well as the expanding tourism industry. Technological advances during the period—including the expansion of railroad systems, more comfortable travel options, increased investment in resorts and other venues for vacation, and the invention and eventual proliferation of the automobile—rendered travel for leisure a transformative element of the nation's cultural and physical landscapes. Americans increasingly began to venture outside of their everyday environs in search of ways to spend their leisure time while, in turn, transforming the manner in which many reified their own identities. Some historians have argued that starting in the late nineteenth century, tourism increasingly provided an avenue to take advantage of modern technology to, in an utterly ironic fashion, assuage anxieties ushered in by industrial capitalism. Cultural historian John Sears, for instance, argues that the disenchantment with the industrializing urban landscapes many Americans felt by the second half of the nineteenth century encouraged a search for the sublime, a longing for the peaceful enjoyment of both natural phenomena and manmade attractions. I argue that, in Texas, industrial capitalism did not simply create anxieties associated with modern technology, it engendered racial animosity and threats to the racial hierarchy. Black migration and racialized labor competition produced by the growth of industrial capitalism during the late nineteenth century, together with the attendant issues related to Black residential encroachment into historically white spaces, upset the normative order of race relations. The anxiety many white Texans harbored over such changes could be quelled by centering the perceived antagonist at the center of a tourism experience. Texas lynching sites thus became critical spaces of identity reinforcement for whites during a time when disenchantment with Black migration and the attendant contestation over labor competition, Black prosperity, residential space, and increased social visibility heightened extant racial tensions and altered how white Texans thought about and engaged in racialized forms of social control.

How one chooses to engage leisure time is often influenced by societal guidelines that reflect the provinciality and social norms of one's society. To use one's spare time to tour a lynching site hours or days following a mob murder (or even moments before the murder) underscores the socially normalized nature of the lynching act itself. Tourism played a metamorphic role in the creation and promotion of culture in Texas by the late nineteenth and early twentieth centuries; the touring of spaces where lynchings of African Americans were slated to or had occurred became part of the cultural identity of the state. Acceptable cultural expressions are validated by acts of remembrance that embrace the visiting of spaces as worthwhile of leisure time expenditure. Thus, the relationship of tourism to the culture produced and reproduced by a new lynching narrative is symbiotic. As Sears argues, "America's cultural identity was not given by tradition . . . it had to be created." Tourism, he further contends, "played a powerful role in America's invention of itself as a culture." Texas was no exception. Late nineteenth century tourists in Texas began to carve a new cultural identity during the era, one marked in large measure not only by racialized mob violence but by the visiting of sites that firmly established a constitutive dynamism of us versus them.

Railroads and the Business of Lynching

As America approached the end of the nineteenth century, railroad companies positioned themselves to take full advantage of, and further transform, the emerging commercial space carved by both the shifting culture of lynching in Texas and by the increase in the American appetite for leisure travel. By adding additional train run times to and from the sites of lynchings, or by simply carrying lynchers or lynching-site tourists on extant runs, varied railroad companies helped produce and reproduce the tourist experience, and by extension, expanded both the experiential and idiomatic renderings of racialized violence. An early-twentieth-century observer astutely noted, in reference to these excursion trains, that the railroad companies were utilizing a previously "neglected feature of railroading"—the utilization of trains for the touring of lynching sites. Trains delivered spectators to the site of an impending lynching within hours after telegrams, local circulars, signs, newspaper advertisements, or word-of-mouth delivered notice of impending activities to potential participants, enabling them to arrive in time to witness or partake in the gruesome acts. Other times, visitors boarded trains hours or days after the lynching occurred to tour these landscapes of racialized violence. Disgorged from the passenger cars, the curious, the crude, the vengeful, the thrill-seekers joined local townsfolk at the sites where the ritual of mob death would occur (or had occurred), thus extending the experience of lynching—from the hunt to the ritualistic execution—to people from across the state while further concretizing white supremacy.[5]

Railroad tracks were laid with increasing intensity in Texas following the close of Reconstruction in 1874. Approximately 2,440 miles of track traversed the state in 1879. Over the next decade, an additional six thousand miles would be laid in varied portions of the state. At the dawn of the twentieth century, railroad companies greatly expanded their trails in the state, placing Texas as the state with the greatest mileage of railroad track in the nation—a status that remains unshaken. By 1932, the total mileage exceeded seventeen thousand, dismantling the previous difficulty in traveling and greatly expanding the leisure options of residents across the state.[6]

When Henry Smith disembarked the train at Paris, Texas, on February 1, 1893, the sea of heads visible from the depot's platform revealed the fate that awaited him. Captured in Arkansas on February 1, Smith was transported to Paris, Texas, to be tortured and burned to death by a mob (see chapter 2).[7] An observation by one of Smith's eventual lynchers takes on additional meaning through the lens of the railroad's role in lynching tourism. He emphasized, "Every train that arrived from any direction was crowded to suffocation by the aroused people of neighboring towns at even considerable distances from us."[8] The railroads in northeastern Texas had posted bulletins notifying local residents that anyone who helped search for Henry Smith, an African American man accused in the murder of a three-year-old white girl, would receive free transportation. Some boarded those trains to find the alleged assailant. Others filled the railcars simply to witness the excitement that the day surely promised once Smith was found. "All the railroads tendered their roads for the transportation of men back and forth," a commentator revealed, "and there has been no lack of means to meet expenses."⁹ "People were here from every part of this section," the observer continued.¹⁰ "When the news reached here yesterday," that Smith was captured, "it spread through the country like wildfire. At every country town, anvils boomed forth the announcement of Smith's capture, and people poured in here in a constant stream all night and day on horseback," he reported.¹¹ The firing of anvils, should the observer's commentary be taken as literal, reveals the celebratory nature of the impending event. Even if meant metaphorically, the reference still bespeaks the festive air surrounding Smith's fate. The trains would do their part to fill the town with visitors who wished to partake in the day's events: "They came from Dallas, Fort Worth, Sherman, Denison, Bonham, Texarkana, Fort Smith, Ark., and a party of fifteen from Hempstead County, Arkansas, where he was captured. Every train that came in was loaded to its utmost capacity."¹² Residents from around the state requested that the railroad companies run "special trains to bring people here to see the un-paralleled punishment of a fiend for an unparalleled crime."¹³

A hallmark of modernity, trains considerably enhanced people's ability to engage in lynching if they so pleased, as evidenced by the use of trains in the narrative of Smith's capture and death. In an industrializing era, trains were a modern form of transportation that could deliver far more people to sites of lynching, and in a timelier manner, than would a horse and carriage. Locomotion and the attendant freedom of travel rendered lynchings more accessible, and, by extension, more acceptable. Increased numbers of individuals could tour the sites of torturous mob murders during their leisure time, which thus conceivably changed their perception of what constituted leisure by presenting and reinforcing an acceptance of this type of social violence.

Recall the story of twenty-two-year-old John Henderson who, in 1901, found himself occupying the same cramped spaces of a railroad car as those who would use their leisure time to watch him die. Accused of killing Valle Younger—a white woman from Corsicana, Texas—Henderson remained in a McLennan County jail until Corsicana citizens pressured the governor to return Henderson to the city, promising to provide the accused man a fair trial and protection from mob violence. After some prodding by local law enforcement agents, the governor relented, and Henderson found himself aboard a train en route to Corsicana. "The first train this morning on the Cotton Belt from Hillsboro was so crowded it could carry no more. Runners were sent over the county announcing the arrival of Henderson here and all the morning people have been swarming into the city to take part in or witness the execution of the penalty to be inflicted on the negro. After his confession it was decided to burn him at the stake at 2 o'clock."[14] The promises of local residents clearly fell disturbingly short as Henderson met his fate atop a burning pyre as thousands of area residents watched him slowly die. Some trains arrived too late for passengers to witness the events: "The northbound Central train, arriving here at 12 o'clock, was crowded with people from the southern part of the county, who expressed disappointment at being too late."[15]

Similar to Henderson, Dudley Morgan was transported to the site of his death by burning in the same railcar as passengers whose final destination was the point where Morgan disembarked. They, too, were there for a lynching. It had become normalized for railways to be part and parcel to racialized lynching in Texas, from the delivery of the victim to transport of the spectators and tourists. In the case of Robert Henson Hilliard's lynching in Tyler, railroads were used both to transport individuals to the site of lynching and to assist in efforts to apprehend Hilliard. Railroads, it seemed, helped lynching become a modern form of racial terror.

By the time of Hilliard's lynching on October 30, 1895, three railroad lines traversed Tyler, which had more than eight thousand inhabitants and served as the seat of Smith County. An article printed at the time of the lynching noted that the city boasted "a library with 15,000 volumes, a substantial court-house, a banking house, the public educational institution known as the Charnwood Institute, one daily and three weekly newspapers, seven churches, and several manufacturing interests."[16] It was a modern city, by most measures. Thousands would witness Hilliard burn to death while chained to a stake in Tyler, Texas. Leaders of the lynch mob had voted unanimously that he should die by burning. The International and Great Northern Railroad (I&GN) carried hundreds of strangely curious witnesses from nearby towns to the scene of Hilliard's burning just before the flames were ignited. One observer recalled that "care was given to regulate the burning so he would not die too soon and thus escape part of the awful suffering which had been prepared for him."[17] A superintendent of the Cotton Belt railway commanded that an engine be sent forty-five miles to Rusk Penitentiary to collect bloodhounds for the chase.

The Automobile and Racialized Lynchings

By the early twentieth century, automobiles diverted business from railroad companies that had profited from transporting people to sites of lynching. The railroads, however, continued to serve an important function in the ability of individuals across the state to engage their free time in the witnessing and partaking of lynchings, or the touring of lynching sites after the acts occurred. But automobiles were so readily used as modes of transportation to lynching sites after the turn of the century that a commentator insisted they infringed on the railroads' "lynching carnival" industry.[18] The pronouncement is a poignant yet muddled reminder that industrialization transformed how people thought about and engaged in tourism and experienced racial terror. Despite the increasing popularity of automobiles, trains aided in maintaining the "lynching carnival" business well into the twentieth century. An observer commented in 1938 that "modern trainmen schooled in the doctrine of service" delivered word of impending lynchings by informing railroad travelers and others along the tracks. Nonetheless, automobiles were increasingly becoming part of the new lynching culture in Texas.

On May 16, 1930, a shootout between George Johnson, an African American tenant farmer, and local whites galvanized people from around the state. Hours before violence erupted near Honey Grove, Johnson had announced that he planned to leave the employ of E. F. Fortenberry, a white landowner. Hughes shot and killed Johnson after the two engaged in a heated argument. Some reports indicate that the dispute ensued because Johnson owed Fortenberry money. Others suggest that Fortenberry became upset over Johnson's desire to terminate his employment. It is possible that both issues led to the argument. Despite the cause, what remains consist in the accounts is that just hours after Fortenberry's death, a mob comprised of about four hundred white men and led by the local sheriff sought Johnson at his cabin, where he had barricaded himself. News of the ensuing standoff "spread by radio and nearby Paris [Texas] put out an 'extra,'" a local newspaper reported.[19] Visitors hailed from Fannin and surrounding East Texas counties, arriving by car, to fill the streets and partake in the lynching episode. They were a part of the mob, traveling to the site of a pending lynching during their leisure hours to somehow partake in the events of the day. A crowd of white men, women, and children lined the road in eyeshot of the cabin where the shootout was taking place. After surveying the populated landscape, one observer contended that it seemed "the scene of the battle was laid for the advantage of the thousand or more spectators who quickly gathered on the highway, and who were just out of firing range, but yet close enough to see every move of the armed posse. . . ."[20] While people gathered to witness the day's events unfold, shots were fired into Johnson's cabin. He promptly fired back. The battle lasted nearly two hours. As the parties exchanged gunfire, news of the violent engagement was announced by radio and drew additional residents from around the area to the streets adjacent to the cabin. Paris, Texas, located approximately twenty-two miles from Honey Grove, issued an "extra," which encouraged an even more people to the site of the fray.[21] When Johnson's return-fire ceased, a local farmer volunteered to enter the cabin and survey the results of the shooting. When he saw Johnson's lifeless body slumping against a door, several individuals rushed the cabin and dragged his corpse to the highway. A chain was affixed to Johnson's neck, and the other end was then secured to a truck, which "led the procession back to town," according to a local journalist, before arriving in the Black portion of Honey Grove.[22] Johnson's remains were hanged from a tree in the yard of a Black church. Members of the mob then doused him in gasoline and set him on fire.[23]

Access to automobiles and the associated freedom of movement enabled individuals to participate in lynching far from home if they so wished. The purchase of the first automobile in Texas occurred in 1899, and automobiles quickly became a common means of transportation for residents of the state. Interested tourists could travel to the scenes of lynchings several hours or even days following the acts through the simple ease of getting into their cars whenever their schedules permitted. "A throng of the curious, . . . mounted steadily during the day until thousands of people and hundreds of motor cars lined the streets" in Kirvin, Texas, during May of 1922. Each was anxious to visit the site where three Black men were burned by a mob numbering near five hundred.[24]

By the early twentieth century, lynch mobs regularly integrated the car into the lynching narrative. Typically, the dragging took place after the body had been hanged or burned. As evidenced by the use of the automobile to drag George Hughes's corpse to the local African American community near Sherman, Texas, the existence and proliferation of cars added a modern, ritualistic sequence to both the lynching of African Americans in Texas and the touring of the sites of lynching. Mobs would drape a chain or rope over the neck of the victim's remains, affix the loose end to the bumper of a car or truck, and drive the streets of the town or city. A mob of two hundred fastened thirty-year-old John Griggs to the back of an automobile near Newton, Texas, after shooting him seventeen times and hanging him from a tree. It was common for the driver to head for the nearest Black community.[25] In 1920, a Black journalist lamented how brothers Herman and Irving Arthur's "charred and smoking bodies were . . . chained to an automobile and dragged for hours through the streets [of Paris, Texas], particularly in sections inhabited by our Race."[26] Members of the lynch mob generally fol-

George Johnson hid in the edifice pictured here during the shootout in Honey Grove, Texas. *"Mob Violence Near Sherman,"* Sweetwater Sunday Reporter, *May 18, 1930.*

lowed the pseudo-hearse and frequently burned or vandalized Black-owned establishments along the way, as they did in Sherman.[27] Through the use of cars in the mob murder of African Americans, the discourse of lynching became especially resonate with the descriptions of varied recreational activities. Reporters often used the word "parade" to describe the ritualistic dragging of a burned body and the "procession" that followed. Automobiles also served to illuminate the scenes of lynchings, casting light on gruesome affairs that were conducted after sunset. When a mob of seven hundred hanged fifteen-year-old Earnest Collins and sixteen-year-old Benny Mitchell in Columbus, Texas, in 1935, the headlights of a car assisted the mob in tying the youths to a tree at night. At times, members of Texas lynch mobs used a car as a hanging platform which, when pulled away, sent victims plunging to their death. A mob of approximately thirty-five took Bert Moore and Dooley Morton from a sheriff near Columbus, Texas. The mob placed nooses around their necks as they stood atop one of the six automobiles that had driven Moore, Morton and their lynchers to a church near the area. "Beneath the swinging bodies where heavy marks of an automobile," reported a journalist, "which indicated how the hanging was carried out."[28]

Sunday Sightseeing

When McLennan County Sheriff Dan Ford and Judge Jack Harrison arrived in Robinson, Texas, on Sunday July 14, 1889, they found the lifeless remains of Henry Davis swaying from a tree and marked by multiple gunshot wounds. There was no sign of who murdered Davis, except for a cryptic notice pinned to his chest. It read as follows: "Take Warning: Executed by 150 for seven attempts to rape white women."[29] Davis was detained by three white men after allegedly entering the home of an affluent, local rancher who had left to purchase supplies. The rancher's wife charged that Davis entered the home in her husband's absence and sexually assaulted her. As they were transporting Davis to a jail in Waco that Saturday, a mob of men on horseback, partially donning red handkerchiefs over their faces, apprehended Davis and transported him to the post oak tree where he would face his final moments. The following Sunday, throngs of tourists from "all over," according to a commentator, visited the "scene of the hanging," likely arriving by foot, carriage, or perhaps by train.[30] Many tourists arrived before the sheriff and judge in time to witness Davis dangling from the tree. By Monday, in an apparent display of their determination to thwart any additional lynchings and quell the eerie curiosity that had befallen white visitors, approximately thirty armed Black men mounted horses and rode about the town. As they rode, they ordered all remaining visitors to leave the area; each obliged.[31]

The tourists who arrived in Robinson that Sunday in July to visit the site of Davis's murder represented a cultural phenomenon that would become a recurrent aspect of lynching in Texas. The touring of lynching sites became an option for leisure among whites in Texas, one shaped by changes in lynching culture. Race was central to the idea that sites of lynching could serve as viable options for touring on Sundays as spaces of racialized violence became critical sites for identity reification among white Texans. During the early twentieth century, as travel by carriage or train began to give way to travel by automobile, technological advances in transportation would impact travel in general and on Sundays in particular. The automobile, however, would provide tourists with an unprecedented ease of travel, one that coalesced with nationwide changes regarding work, leisure, and travel on what many considered the Sabbath Day. Sundays transformed during the period from a day of rest under Christian doctrine, to a day of tourism. The Sunday drive would be filled with moments of aimless cruising or entertaining stops not too far from home. In Texas, the touring of sites of lynching would be added to the proverbial list of attractions suitable for family outings.

The Sunday holiday in the United States existed as a common but contested idea by the late nineteenth century. Sunday had traditionally functioned in the country as a Sabbath that marked a clear division between respite and recreation. During the first half of the nineteenth century, most Americans avoided travel on Sundays, with the exception of attending church. Increasingly, the Sabbath for Americans, most of whom remained Christian throughout the southern region, gave way to leisure travel on Sundays. Whether "by carriage or wagon," by foot, excursion trains, or later by car, Americans "began to take pleasure excursions on Sundays," argues historian Alexis McCrossen.[32] "While some Americans believed that such 'Sabbath pleasuring' threatened the sanctity of the day, others looked forward each week to going on Sunday excursions," she contends.[33] The Sunday holiday was being altered across the nation from a day of rest to one of leisure outings. In Texas, these outings were increased shaped by the racial tensions that transformed lynching to a racialized spectacle of violence.

On Sunday, November 12, 1905, three African American men were hanged in Henderson, Texas, for the alleged murder of a white man named Henry Howell the previous week. John Reese, Robert Askew, and Henry Sherrow sat in a jail that morning while any potential or naïve hope for a court trial gave way to doom imposed by the boisterous clanging of chisels and hammers used by a mob of white men to destroy the doors of the cell. The mob then placed ropes around the necks of the three Black men and took them to the courthouse yard, where they secured them to a sycamore tree and hanged them. One commentator observed that "crowds of people from the country" arrived in Henderson that day "to see the results of the work of the mob."[34]

The visitors to Robinson that Sunday in 1889, to Henderson on that Sunday in November 1905, or any number of visitors on other Sundays during the heyday of racialized terror in the state were among those white Texans who would use their Sunday holiday to engage in leisure outings. Their leisure experiences on those specific days, however, did not likely include sites typical of the era's most popular tourist attractions, such as amusement parks, resorts, or parks. Instead, the leisure experience of tourists in Texas who visited the sites of lynching relied upon the hanging, shooting, or burning deaths of African Americans in the state to help satiate their desire for weekend pleasure.

CHAPTER 6

"Lynchings, Not Bull Fights, Are Allowed in Texas"

The African American Press, Lynching, and the Discourse of Leisure

*Manuel showed her his open hand: "Look at this fin-
ger, how meager it seems, and this one even weaker,
and this other one no stronger, and this one all by
himself and on his own." Then he made a fist: "But
now, is it strong enough, big enough, solid enough? It
seems so doesn't it?"*

—JACQUES ROUMAIN, *Masters of the Dew*

As Jesse Washington's limp but living body neared the public square of Waco on that unforgettable day in May of 1916, a member of the gathered crowd lassoed the teenager with a chain that others in attendance tossed over the limb of an oak tree. Serving as a torturous prologue to their victim's fiery fate, the mob "ripped the boy's clothes off," severed Washington's ear and then "unsexed him," according to the National Association for the Advancement of Colored People (NAACP) agent sent to Texas to gather facts related to the case. Several men then yanked the dangling end of the chain in concert and hoisted Washington into the air. The agent reported that "fingers, ears, pieces of clothing, toes and other parts of the Negro's body were cut off by members of the mob." Thousands cheered as his blood-soaked body ascended. Some in attendance busily collected combustible material and constructed a funeral pyre beneath the swaying boy while others doused him in oil. As members of the mob lowered his mutilated

213

body closer to the hodgepodge of wooden and cardboard debris, a little boy received the peculiar honor of lighting the fire. Recall how crowds of people on ground level shouted in "delight" as "the negro's body commenced to burn," according to a witness.[1] Several women "laugh[ed] and chat[ted]" while the youth was reduced to a charred mass.[2] "Everybody pressed closer to get souvenirs of the affairs," the agent reported.[3] Boys yanked the teeth from the burnt corpse and "sold them to some men for five dollars apiece."[4] Each link of the chain affixed to Washington's body sold for twenty-five cents.[5]

News of Washington's brutal murder and the attendant fanfare alarmed NAACP officials in New York. The heinousness of his death stood as an ardent indicator of how southern society heralded lynching as socially acceptable and even entertaining. But the manner in which Washington's lynching was carried out and enjoyed also provided the organization with an opportunity to place the recreational attributes of the act at the forefront of public consciousness, and thereby solicit support and funds from a horrified public for its antilynching cause. When readers picked up the supplemental issue in the NAACP's the *Crisis* the July following the lynching, they were exposed to eight pages of scandalous details about the murder of a teenager in a "typical southern town."[6] Edited by W. E. B. Du Bois and dubbed the "Waco Horror," the issue was disseminated to forty-two thousand subscribers, seven hundred and fifty newspapers, and every member of the United States Congress.[7] "This is an account of one lynching," Du Bois grieved in closing: "It is horrible, but it is matched in horror by scores of others in the last thirty years."[8] The issue then quantified the number of Black men lynched during the previous three decades, a list followed by a pointed call to action: "What are we going to do about this record? The civilization of America is at stake. The sincerity of Christianity is challenged. The National Association for the Advancement of Colored People proposes immediately to raise a fund of at least $10,000 to start a crusade against this modern barbarism."[9] For several months following the incident, the *Crisis* revisited the "Waco Horror" when appealing to readers for funds; the appeals typically emphasized the size of the crowd, the cheering heard during the burning, and the souvenirs purchased and collected.

In what would become a familiar occurrence during the early twentieth century, journalists for many newsprints, such as the *Crisis*, seized upon the character of lynchings in Texas as opportunities to affect change. The lynch mobs would unwittingly provide the fodder upon which the Black press would capitalize to reach the conscience of the nation. With their meticulously detailed narratives of lynching as a form of recreation, progressive journalists sought to shock their reading public out of its apparent apathy. The language and imagery of leisure filled their articles, editorials, and published satirical commentary, revealing in riveting detail how lynching was so often trivialized as "a bit of fun." By stressing that frivolous entertainment was characteristic of lynching, they recognized the powerful impact of exposing the callousness of this form of social violence: a contagion of recreational murder would beckon more immediate public action than would a sober, isolated, punitive act. Furthermore, by presenting and authenticating the interconnectedness of leisure and lynching, they worked to demonstrate that the relationship between murder and recreation was not just hyperbolic rhetoric but was instead part of a now-normative culture of racialized social violence—an epidemic of barbarism, shorn of guilt or horror, that must be eradicated. To use language as an illustrative medium for the reporting of torture and pain as sport, to expose an ethos of amusement that assaulted readers' moral conventions, was to harness, in measures small or large, widespread derision and disgust that could possibly work to produce change. Public opinion, Du Bois insisted, "irresistible when aroused, should be enlisted against this barbarism in our midst."[10]

When readers picked up the *Cleveland Advocate*'s Saturday broadsheet on September 4, 1915, the bold characterization of murder as a lighthearted form of entertainment in one of the featured editorials was clearly intended to jolt the readers' conventional notions of normality, civility, and leisure. Appearing among editorials that explored partisan politics in Cleveland, accusations of graft in Chicago, and the xenophobic expressions of a southern United States Senator who bragged of his mission to repeal the fifteenth amendment, stood the obliquely related article that described the lynching of two Black men in Texas and the crowd that seemed to consume the murderous antics as recreation. "Here is the latest 'Texas Diversion,'" the article proclaimed as it began to report on a set of heinous yet cavalier killings in the state. Part of a larger series dubbed "A Texas Diversion," the critique included a detailed description of a scene in which a mob awaited the delivery of victims to the town square for a public burning.[11] A reporter described the setting through prose that conveyed a deliberate impression: "When the posse returned with the two trophies of the chase a large crowd awaited the train of automobiles. Word of the hunt had gone over the telephone lines and the district gathered eagerly for a Texas Sunday afternoon diversion."[12] The Ohio-based African American circular ran the story on the front page to increase the visibility and credibility of their long-standing allegations concerning this type of activity. The editorial added a jeering commentary that further reflected, condemned, and ridiculed the lynching's recreational atmosphere: "The smell of burning flesh—the groans of the victim—the cheering, howling, swearing of a crowd [were] the necessary attributes of a 'Texas Sunday afternoon diversion,'" one that entailed "burning 'two trophies of the chase.'"[13] Preemptively refuting claims that the mob acted to punish a capital crime, the journalist added "Let the metropolitan journals of the country take note. This is not the hanging of a 'life-sentenced prisoner.' It is the burning at the stake of TWO NEGROES."[14]

Rhetorical in nature, the closing portion of the article featured a series of questions and statements that begged an exploration of the course and nature of lynching in Texas at the time. "Where is the clarion voice of civilization?" beseeched the journalist, "What condemnation is heaped on the heads of the Texas gang?"[15] The article ended by asking Texas: "QUO VADIS," which, translated from Latin, means *whither goest thou?*[16] The scoffing nature of the inquiries implicitly probed the honor, moral direction, and civil nature of a society that not only permitted but gaily fostered an environment in which Black bodies could be destroyed to the ovation of a gleeful crowd—one haughtily enjoying a "Sunday afternoon diversion." The reporter explicitly conflates leisure and lynching through his repetitive use and deliberate placement of the term diversion. The term *diversion* itself relies on an interdependency of task, toil or some difficulty, and a retreat from that context. The measured pairing of diversion with Sunday further illustrates the journalist's construction of an algorithm that linked mob murder and leisure. By the early twentieth century, Sunday had become firmly recognized as a recurring holiday—a day free of labor in an increasingly industrializing society. The exhibition of death as diversion on a Sunday further reified the journalist's careful parceling of lynching as leisure.

The lexicon of recreational social violence editorialized by the *Cleveland Advocate, Crisis,* and other periodicals revealed a new, progressive approach to the journalistic recounting of lynching. This was not the first time journalists for African American periodicals had used the medium of the written word to address and dismantle racial injustice.[17] During the antebellum era, for instance, the limited number of Black newspapers at the time often railed against slavery. Following the Civil War, the Black press frequently heralded the accomplishments of newly freed African Americans and encouraged them to create economic self-sufficiency to counter the economic strongholds of white supremacy. At times, members of the Black press encouraged emigration as a form of resistance to racial terror and oppression. This chapter builds on previous studies by examining what has until now been absent from the historiography: an analysis of journalists who prudently exploited the imagery of leisure and lynching in an effort to expose and attack the lynching of Black people. These journalists hinged their critiques on the flippant attitudes of southern whites toward the torture and death of African Americans in the South. Intending to shock audiences and subsequently prompt them to action, this type of antilynching literature appealed to readers' understanding that such acts were at odds with both a normal sense of justice and of traditional modes of entertainment. Commenting on the NAACP's extensive work to expose the crime of lynching and gain support for antilynching legislation, Walter White specified early in the twentieth century that "the methods of the N.A.A.C.P. have not been gentle, for it was realized that a century-old public indifference to mob murders would not be penetrated by blandishments or by sugar-coating the facts."[18] The effectiveness of the journalists' work required forthrightness in the use of details and language that would move their audiences to a useful level of heartrending discomfort, thereby breaking through public complacency that could hinder change. The content of their articles and editorials exposed how contemporaries interpreted and consumed lynching while the prose reveals how journalists sought to configure those perceptions in an effort to incite social and political action.[19]

Descriptions of hangings, burnings, draggings, or other modes of lynching Black bodies in the state—and all of the related fanfare, including the purchasing of souvenirs and postcards, the viewing of photographic displays, the touring of lynching sites, the taking of excursion trains chartered specifically for transport to lynchings—were framed in a language of leisure by journalists. When an African American journalist for an Austin-based paper detailed the lynching of William Sullivan in Plantersville, Texas, in 1892, he reported that, while Sullivan was chained to a joist inside a local building awaiting his death and preventing him from escaping, Deputy Sheriff James Augus "went around and notified all the best white people in the town that they could engage in the pastime of killing a 'Nigger' that day if they wished."[20] The use of the word *pastime* is significant here. "This young nigger is smart and talks back to white people," the officer announced, "and now is a good chance to remove him."[21] Augus's pronouncements, replete with anticipation and seeming excitement, revealed much about the acceptability and interpretation of lynching by the local community. To ensure that the act of murdering African Americans continued with a level of precision, Augus beseeched that S. B. Baker, a local citizen, "be sure and tell all those German imigrants [sic] to be there because we want to teach them how to lynch a Nigger before we do any thing [sic] else."[22] It should be noted that typically, dragging took place after the body had been hanged or burned. Members of the lynch mob generally followed the pseudo-hearse and often burned or vandalized Black-owned establishments along the way.[23] In Sullivan's case, however, the dragging took place before he was murdered. When Augus arrived with Sullivan on horseback to the eventual site of the lynching, one of the individuals gathered to assist in the murderous act struck the young Black man in the back of his head with a Winchester rifle. He fell from the horse unconscious and was then dragged approximately five hundred yards, his head hitting rocks and other objects along the way. Once his body was hoisted into the air, he "did not flinch because he was already dead," a witnessed insisted.[24]

Journalists exposing lynching as a *pastime, sport, bullfight, hunt,* or any other signifier of leisure in which Black bodies were burned, hanged, or dragged in a kind of parade for enjoyment, rendered an already grisly form of racialized social control particularly heinous and wholly deplorable to audiences targeted by antilynching writings.[25] This, in turn, produced a negative impression of the region that assailed the guarded civility of the readership. Then, to further beleaguer the self-assured, urbane character that their audiences considered themselves to possess—a civil disposition validated by the journalists' juxtaposition of an uncivilized, southern white culture—the writers added the unsavory element of pleasure to the narrative of mob murder. Any given evening post or weekend circular of the time revealed, in lexis or photographs, quotidian options for spending leisure time: baseball, afternoon teas, book clubs, nickelodeons, visits to local parks—these were socially acceptable leisure activities, typically benign and civil entertainment mediums beneficial to the formation of moral and ethical character. Watching a teenager slowly burn atop a funeral pyre during one's free time, then sifting through his ashes for corporal souvenirs hardly fit into that paradigm. The writers' prose therefore implored readers to reflect on the meaning of leisure, on their own constructs of what qualified as entertainment, and then to do the ostensibly impossible—imagine torture and death as pleasurable.

These journalists should be understood as acting within a matrix of Progressivism in their efforts to fight lynching and counter the detrimental effects of racialized violence (see chapter 3 for additional information on Progressivism in Texas). The relationship between Progressive reform and African Americans has been explored extensively and effectively by historians and other scholars for decades. C. Vann Woodward and August Meier, for example, exposed the racially prohibitive agendas of white Progressives in the South. By the 1970s, historians, perhaps most notably Jack Temple Kirby, argued that progress for white southerners unfolded in the social and political encumbrance of African Americans. John Dittmer further explored this thesis by examining how African American Progressives responded to the segregationist schemes of local white people as they implemented changes that addressed the economic, political, and social ailments of their communities. Scholars have since produced an abundance of studies that focus on the reformist efforts of Black Progressives and how they assumed responsibility for the Black masses in urban centers and rural communities across the nation. From magisterial studies on Black club women who organized temperance groups or protested for the right to vote, to Black church workers who established kindergartens and preschools, to organizations such as the Urban League that endeavored to ease the transition for southern migrants who ventured North, Black Progressives have been investigated and chronicled in works by a host of scholars during the twentieth and twenty-first centuries. What has remained largely lacking from the broad scholarship on Black Progressives is how Black journalists used their writings to agitate against lynching; furthermore, an exploration of their efforts to use the language and imagery of leisure to draw attention to the iniquity of lynching has been absent from the scholarship until now.[26]

The ephemeral nature of newspaper articles in the public mind required that the journalists' work displayed and reflected the egregious nature of the leisure element in Texas lynching in a grand manner. If the articles and editorials were going to serve as impetuses to action, then they had to deliver an impactful and memorable narrative. Accordingly, the task of the journalists was somewhat uncomplicated: Texans who partook in lynching directly provided the arsenal to be used against them. Typically extracting unaltered language and actions from actual events, these journalists were most often simply exposing, analyzing, and recounting participants' own descriptions or timing of events. For instance, participants' perfunctory use of words and phrases such as *barbeque, neck-tie party,* and *carnival* to describe lynching supplied writers with verbatim artillery in their offensive against mob violence.[27] Such ammunition was provided by Joe, who found himself pictured in the background of one postcard featuring the remains of Will Stanley, referring to the event as a *barbeque*.[28] Similarly, recall the response of one minister's wife to another during the burning of George Johnson in Honey Grove, Texas—"Come, I never did see a nigger burned and I mustn't miss the chance." These and other similar statements further underscored the arguments journalists and other observers made in seeking to rally support against lynching.[29] In explaining a continuing conflict between Texas colonels, one journalist insisted, "It is common in all countries for men to resent being omitted from the entertainments given by their friends. But it is only in Texas that a lynching is a social function the withholding of an invitation to which is a matter of lifelong resentment, and it was the omission of such an invitation that one of the Colonels had cherished for years as a cause of offense against the other."[30]

Mob violence on Armistice Day in Texas provided journalists with additional ammunition necessary for the vivid disclosure of murderous recreation in the state. The cessation of fire between Germany and the Allied nations on November 11, 1918, was celebrated eight years later "in thousands of communities" with "processions and patriotic speeches," an article in the Black-owned *Pittsburgh Courier* announced.[31] "Throughout the United States, vociferously admitted by its spokesmen to the cradle and saviour [sic] of liberty, the conventional forms of celebration held sway," the reporter continued, adding that "the one exception was Texas," On November 11, 1926, in a town outside Houston, Robert and Silvia Brown, an African American married couple, were burned inside their cabin by a mob of local whites.[32] Tanner Evans, an associate of the couple, also met his death in that incident—he was shot before the mob bludgeoned his head. "Armistice Day had been appropriately celebrated in Texas," the reporter proclaimed.[33] The *Chicago Defender* referred to the triple lynching as "a warming up exercise" for the day's festivities.[34]

Prejudicial Reporting and the Demonization of Blackness

Journalists often influence the sociopolitical posture of audiences; targeted audiences interpret events and circumstances according to the biased parameters established by news mediums. Prejudicial publicity distributed through white southern—and some northern—newspapers affected the public fervor that condoned and frequently endorsed lynching.[35] Many prolynching or seemingly neutral newspapers and other print media served to produce, promote, and reproduce the prejudicial misconduct that denied the accused a fair and impartial trial by creating a symbiotic relationship between Blackness and misconduct. Sank Majors, an African American resident of McClellan County, repeatedly vocalized his innocence from an Austin jail cell, where he awaited trial, to a reporter for the *Waco Times*

Herald who visited him. Local newspaper accounts acknowledged Majors's protests, but nonetheless included condemning passages in their reports such as, "Sank Majors, who assaulted Mrs. Ben Robert near Waco. . . ."[36] Mainstream news outlets following emancipation typically sensationalized any transgression involving African Americans by playing to the fears many of their readers harbored regarding the assumed innately criminal character of the group, particularly of African American men. In her transformative study of lynching in the South, entitled *On Lynchings*, the valiant Ida B. Wells quotes a Memphis newspaper as an example of the destructive charges waged against African Americans: "Nothing but the most prompt, speedy and extreme punishment can hold in check the horrible and bestial propensities of the Negro race."[37] Writer James Weldon Johnson, in his famed *The Autobiography of an Ex-Coloured Man*, similarly explores the intersectionality of race, gender, social perceptions, and the media. He argues that white southerners classified African Americans into three distinct groups, the most menacing of which, typically comprised of "ex-convicts" and "barroom loafers," purportedly hated "everything covered with a white skin, and in return . . . are loathed by the whites."[38] Southern white people, in turn, "regard[ed] them just about as a man would a vicious mule, a thing to be worked, driven, and beaten, and killed for kicking."[39] NAACP executive secretary Walter White charged that whites became most familiar with this illusory class of African Americans through white newspapers. Such depictions were so common, White contended, that Blacks "learned to read with considerable caution accounts in the white press of events involving white and coloured individuals," and often sought news from "their own press" to avoid such racist biases.[40] While mainstream newspapers of the period frequently cast Blacks as dishonest, distrustful, and inclined to thievery, they often, and perhaps most detrimentally, advanced the idea that Black men sought to somehow annihilate the supposed and socially constructed virtue of white women through rape or other acts of sexual misconduct. Though it has been well documented that the majority of lynching victims were not accused of rape or other types of sexual transgressions against white women, the dialectic of the sex-crazed Black brute and chaste white woman nonetheless factored significantly into the public's image of Black men as debased.[41]

The pretrial publication of inflammatory prose related to alleged crimes often successfully convicted African Americans in the public mind. Prejudice produced or reproduced by mainstream newspapers typically overshadowed the probative value of legal due process. Accusatory headlines offer a glimpse into how newspapers authenticated and propagated a criminal image of African Americans that enabled their conviction in the court of public opinion. As White stressed in 1922, countless southern papers, as well as some in the North, featured "[Blacks] in flaming headlines whenever a crime was charged to a Negro."[42] Much to White's point, the opinion mainstream news media succeeded in molding was one that routinely found the lynched individual guilty of a crime without due process. Richard M. Perloff contends, "the news media are important in the history of lynching because they helped to uphold the social order and molded public opinion on this issue."[43] Perloff found that even before a reader delved into the article, the headlines convicted the accused and subsequently worked to forge an image of Black men as rapists or murderers. A *New York Times* headline, for instance, announced in 1900: "NEGRO MURDERS A CITIZEN. POSSEES ARE LOOKING FOR HIM AND HE WILL BE LYNCHED."[44] Newspapers in Texas were no exception. Comparable findings in Texas mainstream newspapers demonstrate that publication of inflammatory headlines often asserted guilt and condoned summary justice in a single printed line. Headlines such as "ASSAULTED BY A NEGRO," or "BAD NEGRO LYNCHED" did this with precision. A 1903 article that appeared on the front page of the *Houston Chronicle and Herald* announced "Black Brutes' Awful Deeds: Would Be Criminal Assaulter Shot to Death Near Henderson."[45] A 1910 *Dallas Times Herald* headline, "Brute's Crime; A Mob's Vengeance," used language that at once convicted the accused and justified mob violence.[46] The article went on to condone the lynching of Allen Brooks, who was taken by a mob from a courtroom and hanged.

If the conclusive improbability of judicial conviction safeguarded whites' involvement in lynching, then newspapers' reverence for summary justice further absolved any related wrongdoing. Local journalists not only often failed to criminalize lynching but often cast lynch mobs into a heralded social position.[47] Following the burning of Will Stanley, "some women picked up what appeared to be bones from the negro's ashes" for souvenirs, according to the *Austin Statesman*.[48] Concerned about how the state would be characterized in the national press for killing and mutilating Stanley, the *El Paso Morning News* bemoaned:

> The vultures of the press that will seek to traduce the fair name and fame of the state will present the tragedy in its most awful details and there will be severe criticism of this outbreak of lawlessness in the home city of the governor of Texas. All Texas will be reviled and held up to scorn as a state where the majesty of the law is delib-

erately trampled under foot [sic], and where crime is so rampant that thousands can find enjoyment in the incineration of a helpless negro upon the public square.[49]

The reporter then praised the actions of the lynchers and insisted that it was acceptable for a community to take the law into its own hands, adding that the brutality of the murders committed would not be discussed, and that this brutality is what warranted the manner in which Stanley was lynched. But the reporter's brusque use of the word *enjoyment* reveals the scorn aimed at journalists who sought to authenticate the link between pleasure and lynching, and the sneer in the phrase *helpless negro* seeks to undermine the validity of that cause.[50]

Appropriating Prejudicial Reporting: The Black Press and the Shame of Civilization

Journalists who sought to persuade public opinion about the exacting of justice that lynching allegedly achieved presented a particular challenge for the Black press. Lynching victims accused of crimes were cast as undeserving of empathy due to their purported transgressions against white society. Black journalists had to work earnestly to shift the public's focus from questions about the lynched person's guilt or innocence to the culpability of the perpetrators of lynching. Drawing from the same prejudicial atmosphere that created a pretext for denial of due process of lynching victims, the Black press that produced editorials, articles, and cartoons illuminating the recreational aspects of lynching sought to prejudice their readers against a southern culture that engaged in public displays of unlawful execution. Black journalists who frequently presented lynchers as enjoying the violence and spectacle of lynching attempted to expose and reproduce an image of southern society that rendered it despoiled and in utter need of reform. They reappropriated and redeployed the culture of prejudicial influence that those who supported lynching strove to create and maintain. In this case, the accused was the whole of southern white society and the prejudicial character cast upon it was one that presented it as frighteningly malevolent and wholly uncivilized.

Exposing Texans' sordid culture of racial violence in print had a profound prejudicial influence on the readership for Black publications. Walter White observed that a "considerable number" of Black newspapers and magazines were "of immense importance in helping to shape both white and Negro public opinion" on various topics, particularly lynching, during the early years of the twentieth century.[51] Ranging from "inferior, cheaply printed local sheets of four pages to great national weeklies," these broadsheets repeatedly took a stand against lynching.[52] Black newspapers, White insisted, successfully "create[d] a stupendous racial consciousness on the question of lynching which has added mightily to the grim determination of Negroes to fight against mob-law."[53] White's assessment of the moral imperative imposed by the Black press underscores the authority exercised by journalists who sought collective activism through prose. The challenge, then, was to firmly establish lynching as a savage culture by stressing how it embraced certain protocols of recreation and amusement. A 1920 article printed by a Black newspaper underscores journalists' attempts. Entitled "Lynchings, Not Bull Fights, Are Allowed in Texas," the article reads as follows:

> El Paso, Tex., Feb. 24.—A number of Mexicans [individuals] made the mistake here Sunday of attempting to stage a bull fight, in the corral of a local packing plant here, with matadors, picadors . . . and all the traditional appurtenances [apparatus] of the Spanish national sport, instead of staging a lynching. As a result, the police authorities swarmed down on them, broke up the bull fight, and arrested the promoters. Had it been just an ordinary lynching of a Colored man the sport would have been allowed to proceed, and the coroner would have brought in the usual verdict of 'died from unknown hands.'[54]

By presenting white Texans as an ostensibly uncivilized ensemble of recreational murderers, journalists could at once bolster the refined image their readers had of themselves while establishing Texas as a space where racialized violence was woven into the very performance of an everyday life that they claimed was civilized. Given that mass-attended burnings and hangings of African Americans occurred with deliberate impunity, it is hardly surprising that many early-twentieth-century antilynching editorials hurled indictments against white Texans who harbored vainglorious notions of civilization. In August 1915, a journalist for the Ohio-based *Cleveland Advocate* wrote about the burning alive of Will Stanley in Temple, Texas. With unreserved candor, the journalist announced that Stanley had been lynched by "white men—they who claim the title of builders of civilization."[55] The reporter then prefaced his retelling of the events with this challenge: "Read the following news item, and guess if you can from what benighted part of the universe it comes, and whether it is a word-picture describing an orgy of cannibals in the darkest days of the past."[56] In the presence of "boys and girls of tender years," a mob "yelled and cheered as they shoved the Colored man into the flames."[57] As described in a previous chapter of this book, Stanley's murder offered a gruesome example of the conventions of lynching. Recall that he made six attempts to remove himself from the flames, each time hampered by the chains affixed to his body. Thousands watched as Stanley burned shortly after midnight, and once the fire consumed him, his charred remains were hanged to a telegraph pole to serve as a warning to others, while members of the crowd sifted through the ashes for souvenirs.[58] Comparing Stanley's lynching to "an orgy of cannibals in the darkest days of the past," the journalist insisted "It matters not whether [he] was guilty. . . . He was a human being and was entitled to a fair trial in a court of law."[59] Charging that "the veneer of civilization which is so sparingly glued on upon the savage fabric of the low-bred white man, has 'worn off thin' in Texas," the reporter entreated the following:

> Let the American people recoil in horror at the tales of atrocities from the battle fields of war-ridden Europe; let them rise in indignation at the slaughter of the innocents on the steamship Lusitania; let them with dignified scorn point the finger of derision at the barbarism of black Hayti [sic], but let them now hide their faces with shame over the cannibalistic orgy of the Texas whites.[60]

The reporter's shrewd questioning of white Texans' civilized nature relied upon certain suppositions harbored by American society. One need only peruse the exhibits at the 1893 World's Columbian Exposition, held in Chicago, Illinois, to garner how Americans carefully constructed a portrait of American nationalism that underscored the dialectics of white and other, civilized and savage—an organizational dyad that mirrored the self-aggrandized renderings of the nation's identity. Fair promoters sought to create within the provisional confines of the grandiose "White City" a pageantry that touted whiteness and modernity as the earmarks of a civilized nation. The fair itself bolstered white achievement by juxtaposing western technological, agricultural and architectural advancements with primordial exhibits of the darker races.[61] As historian Thomas Holt noted:

> the fair's spatial dualism was rendered visually and literally by the neoclassical stylings of the "White City" at its center and the darkly raucous, vaguely chaotic Midway on its periphery. In the first site were formal official exhibits of nation states and civil societies; in the second, one found ethnographic spectacles of ostensibly primitive peoples and a carnivalesque atmosphere.[62]

Any fair visitor could venture through the Texas building, for instance—a grand edifice adorned by colonnades and artistic glass skylights, housing such modern technological advancements as the telephone—then stroll to the Dahomean African village on the Midway to view Black men swathed in grass skirts sitting amid nearly naked Black women.[63]

Journalists who criticized lynching grouped all those present at a lynching into the category of *murderer, lynching party*, or some other signifier of collective responsibility. Thus, when antilynching publications underscored the recreational attributes of lynching as indicators of an uncivilized society, they typically implicated all those in attendance, consequently ensuring that any scorn hurled at the lynchers would encompass the thousands of local townsfolks who participated in the lynching and consumed it as entertainment, whether through gawking, cheering, touring, or the collecting of body parts. It would also include members of the local community who were not present, but who condoned the act. As a result, the act could be viewed by readers as a cultural epidemic rather than as isolated incidents involving a few rabblerousers. The moniker of *uncivilized* could thereby be applied to the society as a whole and not simply to those who had an immediate hand in a lynching, which consequently enabled the reviling of the entire society as a culture that condoned and enjoyed lynching. Indeed, the leisure atmosphere of the lynching was produced and energized just as much by the spectators as by those who lit the pyre or hoisted the rope. The spectacle forged relied on mass attendance; it was through the highly visible, conspicuous character of the lynching that much of the tenable leisure element was created.

The *Dallas Express*, an African American Texas newspaper, launched a campaign against mob violence in 1919 that accentuated the hypocrisy of a culture that boasted about its civilization yet merrily hanged Black people or burned them alive. In a column entitled "The Mirror," the paper frequently reprinted editorials about lynching from other African American circulars, including the *Chicago Defender, Baltimore Afro-American*, and *Pittsburgh Courier*, in an effort to urge its readers "to use every power at [their] command to see that members of mobs are apprehended and punished to the full extent of the law."[64] The paper picked up the majority of its articles about lynching from one of two sources, however: the Associated Negro Press (ANP) or the NAACP. Each reprinted article included the following introduction:

> . . . in order that we may receive added strength and determination to continue the fight against the acknowledged disgrace of

Christian civilization, lynching. As these men are thinking and gaining the courage to speak out in defense of Civilization and Justice others will be constrained to speak out and do if we continue as we are doing to make public the need of a Public Opinion which stands for strict Justice.[65]

The "disgrace of Christian civilization" discussed in the *Dallas Express*'s preamble illustrates how the ability of cultures that condoned lynching and yet proclaimed themselves Christian often provided the third prong in a tripartite formulation for a critique of civilization. The interrelatedness of modernity, race, and religion served as a particularly useful scheme for advancement that could be heralded by the nation at-large and lampooned by its critics. In his famed 1895 speech "Why Is the Negro Lynched?," Frederick Douglass acknowledged the progress made by a modern nation, but mocked southerners portentous self-image by charging "there is nothing in the history of savages to surpass the blood-chilling horrors and fiendish excesses perpetrated against the coloured people of this country, by the so-called enlightened and Christian people of the South."[66] To further advance his point, Douglass declared, "It is commonly thought that only the lowest and most disgusting birds and beasts, such as buzzards, vultures and hyenas, will gloat over and prey upon dead bodies; but the Southern mob, in its rage, feeds it vengeance by shooting, stabbing and burning their victims, when they are dead."[67] Booker T. Washington also questioned the veracity of the supposed contrast between a civilized Christian society and the purportedly uncivilized, non-Christian nations of darker hued peoples. "Worst of all," Washington contended, "these outrages take place in communities where there are Christian churches; in the midst of people who have their Sunday schools, their Christian Endeavor Societies and Young Men's Christian Associations where collections are taken up for sending missionaries to . . . the so-called heathen world."[68] The *Chicago Defender*, in an article entitled "Civilized Savages," went as far as to chastise "white churches of America" for their failure to admonish or even address the uncivilized behavior of white southerners who engaged in lynching: "The sending of missionaries to so-called heathen peoples by the church in America is one colossal joke."[69] Continuing the contemptuous reprimand, the journalist queried if the "savage" people that missionaries were attempting to convert were "any worse than the half savage human monsters of the South."[70] The journalist then insisted, "the moral depravity that will make grown-ups lead little children to the scene of the burning of a human being needs missionary work of the highest order. . . . The Southern white, not to be outdone, cuts off the fingers and toes of his Black victim and gives them to his children as souvenirs."[71] Then, as if to deliver a final blow to any lingering perception of civility, the journalist swore that his charges "are matters of common knowledge" and "the press makes almost daily mention of these things."[72] As late as 1934, the *Chicago Defender* continued this line of assault. It described the lynching of John Griggs near Newton, Texas, as having "all the earmarks of such Christian culture and refinement as would be expected from the hill-billies of Texas."[73] Accused of "associating with a white woman," Griggs was "dragged through the streets" by a mob comprised of local citizens, sheriffs, and "leaders in the church" whose "vicious and barbarous temperament . . . took on the form of a Roman holiday."[74]

Parody and the Authentication of Leisure

On December 2, 1905, the African American *Cleveland Journal* printed "Texas Man and Maiden," a poem that mocked, through its parodistic prose, the illusory concept of civilization in the state. The poem also admonished the cavalier attitude of Texas lynchers as it derided the relationship between leisure and lynching.

> Oh, where are you going, my pretty maid?
> I'm going a lynching, sir, she said.
> And what is the noose, my pretty maid?
> There's nothing but hemp and a struggling wretch
> And many hands willing to carry and fetch.
>
> May I go with you, my pretty maid?
> If you carry the oil, kind sir, she said;
> If you carry the oil and a match or two
> For there will be good and plenty to do
> So come right along, it hasn't begun,
> And be sure you're in time not to miss the fun. . . .[75]

The Texas lynchers depicted in the poem are not wild-eyed barbarians acting within a storm of fury that ignites a lapse in lucidity. Much the opposite, they are urbane, composed. They are civil in their exchange, evidenced largely by their use of deferential salutations. The man and woman are logical, coherent, and demure. The poet thus demonstrates that the sensibilities of Texas lynchers are not only cruel, but utterly dismissive of humanity. Indeed, their composed disposition renders the act of which they

"A Larger Crowd Than . . . the Circus." This is an image of the crowd that lynched Joe Winters on May 20, 1922, in Conroe, Texas. *Image from the NAACP's "The Looking Glass,"* The Crisis: A Record of the Darker Races *25, no. 1 (November 1922), 37.*

speak particularly ghastly. The inclusion of "Texas Man and Maiden" in the *Cleveland Journal* reveals in microcosm how Black journalists, writers, and publishers worked to structure an impression of southern society situated in unadulterated contrast to the established, civil, and largely predictable notions of leisure harbored by its readership. By mocking those who were so cavalier about murder, those who treated Black lives with such dismissiveness and disdain, they were promoting and reproducing a particular image of Texas society. African American journalists cast lynching as normalized, acceptable behavior for refined men and women. The journalists' depictions at once exposed the relationship between leisure and lynching and firmly established it as endemic to Texas culture.

The poem also reflects a larger and broader understanding of the implications of the act. The cynical nature of the piece reveals something about the readers' familiarity with the relationship between recreational murder and Texas society. "Texas Man and Maiden" is parody, and thereby reflective of authentic occurrences. Cultural historian Lawrence Levine argues that the ability to understand parody requires a knowledge of, or familiarity with, a particular act: "It is difficult to take familiarities with that which is not already familiar; one cannot parody that which is not well known."[76] The expectation that the sardonic tone of the commentary would be understood, then, required a widespread understanding of lynching—the link between leisure and lynching can thereby be gauged through the satirical tenor of the prose. While the facetious spirit of the poem's commentary relied upon a *familiarity* with the parodied act, it did not necessarily require a definitive perception of it. Parody procures its ideas and meaning from actual events, and subsequently infuses the events with a larger significance.[77] That significance can be infused with a specific meaning or importance by the manner in which the event is presented. If an audience has a certain perception of an event or series of events, the parodist can work to enhance and then shape that perception. Parody can thus reflect the mocking of actual events commingled with an attempt to authenticate occurrences. African American journalists had faith in their readership's prior understanding that lynching was frequently interpreted as a form of leisure by local communities, but they needed to raise the level of that potential understanding to move past any boundaries of complacency that could interfere with efforts to prevent lynching. Parody offered a suitable option for dismantling harmful indifference. Journalists could at once rely upon readers' reasonable familiarity with the nexus between leisure and lynching as they worked to mold the trajectory of any elicited anger.

Editorial cartoons served as a particularly useful means of parodying the relationship between lynching and leisure. Cartoons that featured controversial, political, or highly troubling matters provide polemical commentary through their images and language. Certain lynching cartoons reflected and reproduced a complex duality. While numerous editorial cartoons tackled mob violence as a theme for illustration, some satirized lynching participants' language and practices as they publicized the recreational features of lynching. In 1916, the *Chicago Defender* published a cartoon that sardonically queried in its title: "Since Lynching Must Go On In America, Why Not—."[78] The cartoon equated lynching with a seasonal sport, such as hunting, that required a license and mandated that a set of regulations be followed by those who engaged in it. This was a form of journalism that found safe expression in the pages of the *Chicago Defender*, an African American circular established by Georgia native Robert S. Abbott in 1905 after he became dejected by repeated incidents of discrimination in the North (on one occasion, for instance, he was told to step out of a breadline at a white church to make room for a white man). By the end of World War I, Abbott's *Chicago Defender* enjoyed a circulation of nearly a quarter million nationwide, which does not account for those who read an issue found in a local business or at the home of a friend or neighbor. The paper's dissemination often took the form of being tossed from speeding trains by Black railroad porters, thereby ensuring that the issues found their way to communities across the country. While the *Chicago Defender* highlighted Black achievement and worked to lure southern African Americans to northern urban centers, it also regularly featured articles, editorials, and cartoons on varied forms of legal and extralegal racial intolerance that targeted African Americans in the South. Lynching and other forms of racial terror were particularly disturbing to Abbott, who subscribed to his stepfather's routine declaration that a useful newspaper could serve as a powerful tool in the plight of African Americans to achieve social justice. It is no wonder, then, that all of Abbott's circulars—the *Chicago Defender,* the *Whip*, and the *Searchlight*—would pay particular attention to racial terror in their crusade to expose and eradicate racial discrimination and social violence.[79]

The NAACP and the Imagery of Lynching as Leisure

For decades, the NAACP worked to draw the nation's attention to the atrocity of lynching. Walter White vaunted, "the outstanding accomplishment of the work of the N.A.A.C.P. . . . has been against lynching." Through detectives and investigators employed by the organization, the details of numerous atrocities were uncovered and exposed.[80] Indeed, a central focus of the organization during the early decades of the twentieth century was the eradication of lynching first through exposure, then through the passage of federal antilynching law legislation. The *Crisis* was a major part of the success that the NAACP achieved in disseminating information about lynching. As White described it:

> The N.A.A.C.P. has made the facts about lynching familiar to the entire United States and to foreign countries through more than four thousand meetings; through the distribution of millions of pieces of literature, a number of them facsimile reproductions of stories of lynchings first printed in newspapers in the very communities in which they occurred; through *The Crisis* . . . and through an efficient press service, which goes weekly to each of the two hundred and fifty Negro newspapers and, when there is news of special interest to them, to white newspapers and news-distributing organizations throughout the world.[81]

As the circular lambasted the act of lynching, writers continuously sought to emphasize the devaluation of Black lives in America. To that end, the *Crisis* printed speeches, stories, and letters that served to reveal in small

As the Lynching Record Mounts

In this editorial cartoon, the *Chicago Defender* mocks the heralding of Christianity, civility, and their attendant morality in the United States. Circa early twentieth century.

or large measure the cheapened nature of African American existence across the South. In 1911, a Florida man wrote a letter to the *Crisis* in which he claimed to represent white disdain for African Americans: "If you look in the bible [sic] it will tell you that [the negro] first originated from an animal. . . . We Southern people don't care to equal ourselves with animals."[82]

"Since Lynching Must Go On In America—," *Chicago Defender*, December 11, 1916.

NAACP officials worked to entice northerners and southerners, regardless of color, to act in opposition to lynching and remain attentive to the economic impact that lynching could have on local industry. In an internal memo outlining how to most effectively apply funds to a campaign aimed at preventing lynching, the national office suggested that "a capable white man of tact and personal force, could be employed" to appeal to local chambers of commerce, farmer's alliances, boards of trade, and other economic associations. Continued mob violence, the memo cautioned, could negatively affect "trade and business" by "increasing scarcity of labor brought about by emigration of the Negro common laborer."[83]

More important than its counsel on the potential financial backlash of lynching was the NAACP's continued efforts to alert the nation to the character of mob violence in the South. The organization's journalists stood at the forefront of progressive journalists who exposed and employed the imagery of leisure connected with lynching incidents by mounting a dialectical arsenal against that particular form of racial terror. To this end, writers for the NAACP's the *Crisis* regularly characterized lynching as an act in which many of the individuals who participated did so in pursuit of amusement. In 1914, for instance, the organ reported that "a party of drunken hoodlums, seeking 'sport,' accost[ed] an inoffensive Negro and one of them [shot] him dead—'just for fun.'"[84] Another column characterized a lynching party as "often made up of a mob bent upon diversion, and proceeding in a mood of rather frolicsome ferocity, to have a thoroughly good time."[85] In a 1916 *Crisis* column entitled "Our Lynching Culture," one correspondent declared that Americans outside of the South "have to blush with shame to think that there are men holding American citizenship whose nervous systems need the occasional 'thrill' of a fellow-creature's agony."[86] On other occasions, *Crisis* writers equated the lynch mobs' cheers to those heard at events such as bullfights.[87]

Journalists for the NAACP who exposed and mocked a culture of social violence and leisure revealed the debased nature of Black lives in the South as they tapped the indignation stirred in their readership. Their actions yielded the alarm necessary to redress the type of racialized social violence that plagued Texas and the South at-large. *Crisis* writers frequently followed macabre descriptions of mobs murdering Black men "for sport" with pleas that readers donate to the NAACP's antilynching fund. Certain Texas lynchings, such as that of Jesse Washington, provided opportunities for the NAACP to promote such a cause and energize its crusade against lynching. It was the manner in which his lynching was carried out and enjoyed that provided the organization with an opportunity to place the recreational attributes of the act at the forefront of public consciousness, and thereby solicit funds and support for its cause from a horrified public. The heinousness of his death stood as a grisly indicator of how southern societies heralded lynching as acceptable and even pleasurable. Once again, the lynchers and their supporters provided the fodder while the press capitalized on the social implications of the consumption of torture and death as leisure. The supplemental edition discussed how the massive crowd of men, women, and children, which numbered in the thousands, celebrated as Washington commenced to burn. It exposed how those in attendance vied for souvenirs taken from Washington's charred corpse and the devices of his murder. In closing, the issue emphasized that the account chronicled was merely one representative instance in a southern narrative of racial murder. The report was an urgent call for the realization of American liberalism, an appeal that commingled concepts of civilization and religion as it contextualized proper and humane behavior in a society that accepted and even heralded unpunished murder. "The civilization of America is at stake. The sincerity of Christianity is challenged," Du Bois avowed.[88]

In addition to the forty-two thousand *Crisis* subscribers, seven hundred and fifty newspapers and every member of the United States Congress given a copy of "The Waco Horror," twelve thousand copies were distributed to the public to solicit additional funds for the NAACP's antilynching campaign.[89] Readers responded to the printed depictions of Washington's lynching with clear distress. In July, 1916, Sara E. Parsons wrote to the national office in New York about the "cruel, barbarous and unjust treatment of suspected Negroes."[90] Parsons enclosed a check for the NAACP's antilynching fund, which she increased to twenty-five dollars from ten dollars after she "read about the Waco horror for the first time" the night before mailing her letter.[91] "The response has been splendid," boasted Du Bois.[92] By October 7, over $11,000 had been raised at a cost of $1,203.73, leaving nearly $10,000 to be deposited into the NAACP's antilynching fund. The organization commented that the total amount raised was particularly noteworthy considering that "both races [white and Black] contributed in about equal measure."[93] The funds would be used to bring national attention to the horrors of lynching and to encourage the passage of antilynching legislation. A one-page ad that appeared in later issues of the *Crisis* used Washington's death as a reason for people to contribute to the antilynching fund. J. E. Spingarn, Chairman of the NAACP Board of Directors, wrote a brief commentary reminding readers of the story of the "Waco Horror." By entreating readers to revisit Du Bois's detailed description of Washington's death, Spingarn appealed to readers' sense of outrage over the lynching in which the boy's "teeth brought $5 apiece and the chain that had bound him 25 cents a link."[94] By entreating readers to remember the detailed chronicling of Washington's death Spingarn appealed to their sense of outrage over a lynching that could be engaged in with seeming amusement and casualty.[95]

For several months following the incident, the *Crisis* revisited the "Waco Horror" when appealing to readers for funds, emphasizing the size of the crowd, the cheering heard during the burning, and the souvenirs purchased and collected. A one-page ad that appeared in later issues of the *Crisis* discussed Washington's death to urge readers to contribute to the antilynching fund.

In 1917, the NAACP organized an antilynching conference in New York in an effort to "wake to the need for action."[96] Du Bois characterized the conference as "a step toward civilization comparable only to the abolition conventions."[97] In a memorandum calling for support, the group charged, "the story of the years of lynching shows many courageous and determined efforts on the part of public officials to secure indictments against mob leaders, but without success."[98] It was clear, he continued, "that the force of public opinion throughout the country should be brought to bear upon this question and that methods of remedy should be discussed and passed upon."[99] James Weldon Johnson, together with other members of the organization, planned a mass march to take place during the conference. As Robert L. Zangrando contends in his study on the NAACP's campaign against lynching, "because the [East St. Louis riot] drew national attention, the NAACP thought it timely to dramatize its own campaign against racist brutality."[100] The "Negro Silent Protest Parade," organized largely to protest racial violence in the aftermath of the East St. Louis riot, used Washington's murder to bring national attention to the dreadful epidemic of lynching.[101] Marchers carried placards that encouraged onlookers to question if Waco represented a "Center of American Culture."[102] Other placards queried, "MOTHER, DO LYNCHERS GO TO HEAVEN?" and implored "GIVE ME A CHANCE TO LIVE."[103] Between nine thousand and ten thousand men, women, and children marched down Fifth Avenue in New York City on a Saturday at the end of July. As they marched, boys disseminated pamphlets that outlined the NAACP's mission to end racial terror. The material read in part:

> We march because by the Grace of God and the force of truth, the dangerous, hampering walls of prejudice and inhuman injustices must fall. We march because we want to make impossible a repetition of Waco, Memphis, East St. Louis, by arousing the conscience of the country and bringing the murders of our brothers, sisters, and innocent children to justice. . . . We march because we want our children to live in a better land and enjoy fairer conditions than have fallen to our lot.[104]

The soft beating of drums served as an aural backdrop for the largely African American and entirely silent group of protesters. Their silence created a visual commentary on the uncivilized, savage nature of collective racial violence; the hush in the crowd of thousands of Black protestors stood in stark contrast to the vicious chaos of rioters in Missouri and lynch mobs in Texas. Here, once again, the civility of white southerners was challenged. It was a challenge designed to shape public opinion against a culture that could find entertainment and pleasure in the mob murder of Black people.

EPILOGUE

Lynching, Then and Now

The moment haunts me. It resides in my consciousness as a harbinger of stalled progress. It grasps my existence with the tension of every maddening expression of racial othering and inhumanity I have witnessed, studied, experienced. It was the moment when I saw the slender, round face of a young Black man, gleaming with the innocence of an unsuspecting altruist—the moment I read his last words, filled with the clemency seemingly reserved for an ethereal being. "You are all phenomenal. You are beautiful and I love you," he said to police officers as they wrestled him to the ground before he lost consciousness. It was the moment I realized that Elijah McClain was lynched. I fell back into my chair, crestfallen. As a professor of African American history and scholar of lynching during the late nineteenth and early twentieth centuries, I teach this as a part of the nation's sordid past, including the destabilizing impact it has on the African American community. In recent years, I had largely shied away from making such historical comparisons out of respect for the unique circumstances that helped define and contribute to the countless lynchings that swept the United States throughout the first half of the twentieth century. As I complete this monograph during 2020, however, the comparison became more prescient as the world has seemingly collapsed into its own wretched history.

The events that occurred or became visible in 2020 have allowed us all to bear witness to a disturbing and unavoidable reality: lynching is not a relic of a Jim Crow past; it is in fact a modern form of racial terror. The spectacular brutality once preserved and disseminated through photography and corporeal souvenirs is now captured by cell phones and body cameras, allowing society to witness racial terror in all of its modern forms. The recent asphyxiating tide of murders—the aural and visual replaying of death—has left us all gasping for breath. Still writhing from the suffocating reality of Ahmaud Arbery's murder in Georgia, we were forced to confront the indescribable pain of witnessing George Floyd's murder in Minnesota.

And yet the term *murder* somehow fails to convey the extraordinary cruelty of their killings. Elijah McClain, Ahmaud Arbery, and George Floyd were all lynched.

Each case presents a set of facts comparable to the history of lynching in the US as defined by the Tuskegee Institute: a killing that occurs without due process, committed by "three or more persons, done under the pretext of service to justice, race, or tradition." Lynching victims in the first decades following the Civil War were often white. Their alleged crimes typically involved horse theft, cattle theft, or murder. Furthermore, their bodies were frequently found hanging from trees in the hours or days following their deaths, and the parties that lynched them, if seen, were often masked. By stark contrast, after Reconstruction, the lynching of Black bodies was done with a visibility, impunity, and fanfare that would come to define a new culture of lynching discussed in this study.

The white patrolling of Black people's place has too often served as the superlative entity in an algorithm for what renders a crime a crime; expressions of freedom, sovereignty, and advancement by Black people continue to function as crime in the same manner as violent misconduct. What appear as seemingly benign activities continue to gain potency when the perceived aggressor is Black and the racial hierarchy is ostensibly threatened.

Over the last few years, we have seen increasingly that freedom expressions of Black people are still surveilled and criminalized. White citizens who believe they are patrolling their local environments are in fact patrolling racial boundaries. They have in recent months called the police on Black people who are, for instance, giving a dog a treat, hosting a lemonade stand, having a barbeque, attempting to use the gym in their own residential building, picking up trash in their front yard, or simply jogging. Crime, then, is still something defined by historically specific phenomena, by the nuances of an everyday existence, by social interactions, and ideas about race and identity, by sheer racism. At times, the outcome is death.

McClain was returning from the store in Aurora, Colorado, after purchasing iced tea for his brother. Donning a ski mask—a choice his sister said he often made because "he had anemia and would sometimes get cold"—McClain was approached by several police officers who ordered him to stop. The person who called the police reported that McClain seemed suspicious but did not pose a threat. Moments later, officers wrestled McClain, who was autistic, to the ground. His last words should be repeated in their entirety to convey a full picture of his humanity:

I can't breathe. I have my ID right here. My name is Elijah McClain. That's my house. I was just going home. I'm an introvert. I'm just different. That's all. I'm so sorry. I have no gun. I don't do that stuff. I don't do any fighting. Why are you attacking me? I don't even kill flies! I don't eat meat! But I don't judge people, I don't judge people who do eat meat. Forgive me. All I was trying to do was become better. I will do it. I will do anything. Sacrifice my identity, I'll do it. You are all phenomenal. You are beautiful and I love you. Try to forgive me. I'm a mood Gemini. I'm sorry. I'm so sorry. Ow, that really hurt. You are all very strong. Teamwork makes the dream work. Oh, I'm sorry I wasn't trying to do that. I just can't breathe correctly.

Officers placed McClain in a carotid hold. First responders administered an injection of ketamine to McClain in an alleged effort to sedate him. McClain suffered a heart attack en route to the hospital and passed away days later on August 30, 2019.

The outcomes for Arbery and Floyd were similar. When Gregory McMichael contacted 911 after seeing Arbery jogging down the street, the operator inquired of McMichael the nature of the crime being committed. He replied in part, "There's a black male running down the street." We can imagine that in the minds of the men who killed Arbery, he was not a young man innocently jogging down a neighborhood street on a sunny day. He was the conflation of Blackness and criminality that has pervaded an American consciousness and has been produced and reproduced across time and space. Two months following the death of Arbery, four officers apprehended and killed Floyd for allegedly attempting to use a counterfeit twenty-dollar bill to purchase cigarettes. Each death points to an undeniable conclusion: The extraordinary violence exacted upon McClain, Arbery, and Floyd was done so to punish the criminal act of Black existence, to demonstrate and enact the triumph of white over Black.

During the heyday of lynching, local citizens and law enforcement agents could (and did) act without—although at times with—sanction from the court and public administrators because they assumed their ultimate authority to be judge, juror, and executioner of last resort. Lynchers settled into a knowledge, a comfort that their actions would not be disrupted, and they would not be prosecuted. The men who killed McClain, Arbery, and Floyd similarly acted as judge, jury, and executioners. None of the three victims were afforded due process nor the opportunity to demonstrate their innocence, and each of the killers seemed confident that they would not be prosecuted for their actions.

Indeed, the police killings of Floyd and McClain sit squarely on a historical continuum of lynchings committed by police officers, a reality that runs counter to many people's notion that lynchers often acted in opposition to law enforcement. Before William Sullivan was hanged by a mob in Plantersville, Texas, led by Deputy Sheriff James Augus, Sullivan claimed he was married to a white woman. Augus chained Sullivan to a ceiling column then traveled around the area inviting local residents to witness Sullivan's death: "This young nigger is smart and talks back to white people, and now is a good chance to remove him," he shouted.

The state failed, in the killings of McClain, Arbery, and Floyd, to exact justice initially or at all, and instead validated racial vigilantism as a viable form of justice. Mike Freeman, the county attorney for Hennepin County, Minnesota, who first investigated the death of Floyd, said during a press conference that his job "is to prove that [officer Derek Chauvin] violated criminal statute—but there is other evidence that doesn't support a criminal charge." Similarly, when Travis McMichael, Gregory McMichael, and William Bryan murdered Arbery on February 23, 2020, District Attorney George E. Barnhill, who early on investigated the case, penned a letter that sought to exonerate Arbery's murderers. "It is my professional belief the autopsy confirms what we had already viewed as shown in the videotape, with the photographs and from the witness statements taken immediately at the scene," Barnhill stated, insisting that, "we do not see grounds for an arrest of any of the three parties." He added that they were in "hot pursuit" of a criminal due to the baseless claim that break-ins had recently occurred in the neighborhood. Charges were brought against those involved in the deaths of Floyd and Arbery within days and months of their murders, respectively. It was two years until charges were brought against any of the individuals responsible for the death of McClain.

An autopsy conducted by the Adams County coroner declared that the cause of McClain's death was inconclusive. His death, the coroner argued, could have been caused by the carotid hold or natural causes. As a result, District Attorney Dave Young cleared the officers involved in McClain's death of any wrongdoing. "The forensic evidence revealed that the cause of death was undetermined," Young argued. "Specifically, the pathologist who conducted the autopsy stated that he was unable to conclude that the actions of any law enforcement officer caused Mr. McClain's death. . . . Based on the facts and evidence of this investigation I cannot prove beyond a reasonable doubt that the officers involved in this incident were not justified in their actions."

In the cases of Arbery and Floyd, the initial, state-sanctioned autopsies similarly failed to provide clear culpability for the men who murdered them. This conclusion is reminiscent of lynchings from the past when coroners' reports worked to absolve lynchers of any wrongdoing. After completing a formal inquest into John Henderson's mob death by burning in 1901, for instance, Justice of the Peace and Coroner H. G. Roberts presented his ruling: "I find that the deceased came to his death at the hands of the incensed and outraged feelings of the best people in the United States, the citizens of Navarro and adjoining counties. . . . His death was fully merited and commendable." Frighteningly glaring complexities and historical continuums are nearly impossible to ignore. In addition to the vigilantism and state-sanctioned violence, there is a common thread that further weaves together the narratives of their deaths. These episodes of modern, racialized social violence serve as a reminder that the concept of crime is not static. Crime is mutable, informed by historical processes of racial othering, by the clear reality that Blackness in this country remains a threat. It is as if time has buckled under the weight of lingering, lethal notions of Blackness. We can imagine that in the minds of the men who murdered Arbery, for instance, he was not a young man innocently jogging down a neighborhood street on a sunny day. He was the conflation of Blackness and criminality that has pervaded an American consciousness and has been produced and reproduced across time and space.

The murderers' arguments that they believed each of their victims to be a threat are laden with many of the elements of racial othering and perceived menace that have plagued African Americans for decades. We have witnessed the passage of civil rights legislation, the election of a Black president, the slow establishment of new social and moral paradigms that have rendered such things as murdering a person for attempting to vote a relic of an iniquitous past. None of these has resulted in systemic change to prevent the type of violence and brutality that attended the murders of McClain, Arbery, and Floyd, largely because some realities remain as unfalteringly timeless as the magnetic pull that drags the ocean's waves to the shores. The Black body has historically been seen as less than—at times good only for profit, at other times as a source of terror. What these modern lynchings reveal is that for some white people in America, a challenge to the supposed racial hierarchy continues to be a criminal act.

Recognizing with an aching swiftness the racial alterity that had diminished his humanity, as I have written earlier in this work, Frantz Fanon gave voice to the conscious renderings of converging ideologies, abhorrence, iniquities:

> The Negro is an animal, the Negro is bad, the Negro is mean, the Negro is ugly; look, a nigger, it's cold, the nigger is shivering, the nigger is shivering because he is cold, the little boy is trembling because he is afraid of the nigger, the nigger is shivering with cold, that cold that goes through your bones, the handsome little boy is trembling because he thinks that the nigger is quivering with rage, the little white boy throws himself into his mother's arms: Mama, the nigger's going to eat me up.

The murderers of McClain, Arbery, and Floyd cast the same fraudulent and cruel judgement upon their Black bodies: "The Negro is an animal. The Negro is bad. The Negro is mean." As Arbery lay in the middle of the street dying from a gunshot wound, Travis McMichael reportedly stood over him and exclaimed, "fucking nigger."

Some things have changed, however. These brutal deaths have engendered an unprecedented call for reform. We have witnessed in the past months people come together across racial, ethnic, generational, and religious boundaries, flooding streets around the world, taking to social media and calling on corporations to demand change. What a beautiful reality, one that renders the past distinct. They demonstrate the veracity of the words spoken by the late John Lewis: "When you see something that is not right, not fair, not just, you have a moral obligation to continue to speak up, to speak out."

The Last Known Lynching in Texas

There was not a steady decline in lynchings in Texas until the latter half of the 1940s. Other states experienced a marked reduction in the number of lynchings during the previous decade. In Texas, by contrast, nearly twenty Black men met their death by lynching during the 1930s. Some of the most heinous and public lynchings in the state occurred during the period. By the time America entered World War II, lynching in Texas declined exponentially. There are only two documented murders by mob violence in the state during the 1940s. Multiple, intersecting factors led to the act's decline in the state. In part, negative exposure for the state related to racialized violence just as the state was attempting to court business from around the country. Continuous national exposure of the state's failure to mitigate lynching during the period prompted governors and local officials to work more diligently to stymie the violence. Additionally, the focus of the state and the country had shifted to involvement in World War II, which not only took many into military service, but also led to the outward migration of thousands of Black Texans to northern and western states where they sought to take advantage of industrial work related to the war, as well as the lessening of racialized social violence. Such migration worked to deplete extant cheap labor forces for the state. The abhorrent nature of James Byrd Jr.'s 1989 lynching reminds us, however, much like the murders of McClain, Arbery, and Floyd, that racialized violence in Texas and America at-large is not simply a relic of a Jim Crow past.[1]

On the morning of June 7, 1998, Byrd—a forty-nine-year-old African American—left his parents' residence and began walking home alone along Huff Creek Road in Jasper, Texas. He was approached by three white men, John William King, Lawrence Russell Brewer, and Shawn Allen Berry, who offered him a ride home. Byrd accepted their offer. The men then drove their unsuspecting passenger to a remote area, beat him, and urinated on him. King, Russell, and Berry tied Byrd by his ankles to the back of a pickup truck using log chains and dragged him until he died and his body was dismembered. Byrd's injuries demonstrate that he attempted to continuously reposition himself while being dragged as to somehow avoid horrific injury. His efforts were sadly in vain. Portions of his corpse were found dispersed in seventy-five different areas along the three-mile stretch of country road that the men traveled. Byrd's torso was located approximately one mile from his head. The murderous trio left what body parts remained affixed to the truck at a Black cemetery before heading to eat at a local restaurant. Byrd's body was so dismembered and destroyed that law enforcement agents used his driver's license, found on a portion of his body, to identify Byrd and contact his family.[2]

Born on May 2, 1949, in Beaumont, Texas, to Stella and James Byrd Sr., Byrd was one of eight children. He was raised in Jasper, an East Texas town with a sobering history of racial strife. The Greater New Bethel Baptist Church was a central part of the family's life. James Sr. was a deacon of the church, and Stella taught Sunday school. James Jr., whom his parents endearingly called "Son," excelled in school. Shortly after graduating from high school, he married and had three children.

Hundreds of grievers gathered in and outside the funeral home on the day Byrd's family laid him to rest. Among the mourners were Kweisi

Mfume, the president of the National Association for the Advancement of Colored People (NAACP); basketball legend Dennis Rodman, who covered the cost of Byrd's funeral and made a donation to the family; and boxing promoter Don King, who provided $100,000 to Byrd's family for living expenses.

John William King, Lawrence Russel Brewer, and Shawn Allen Berry were suspected of the crime by local law enforcement agents. Jasper residents knew that King was a Klansman who donned a tattoo of a Black man being lynched. Brewer was a member of a white supremacist gang. All three men were indicted on charges of capital murder. King and Brewer were sentenced to death. In 1999, a judge sentenced Berry to life in prison. Their sentences would mark the first time there had been a conviction that resulted in prison time for any individual who aided in the lynching of a Black person in the state of Texas. King was executed by lethal injection in 2011, Berry in 2019.

Byrd's death focused the nation's attention on the continued prevalence of racial violence in modern America. In 2001, Texas then-Governor Rick Perry signed the James Byrd Hate Crime Act into law. Byrd's mother, Stella, was instrumental in ensuring the passage of the legislation. In 2009, the United States Congress passed the Matthew Shepard and James Byrd Jr. Hate Crimes Prevention Act, which President Barack Obama signed into law. Shepard, a twenty-one-year-old white man from Wyoming, was abducted by Aaron McKinney and Russell Henderson in 1998. The men drove Shepard to an isolated area, tied him to a fence, brutally beat him, and left him to die because he was queer. The new law extended the reach of the 1969 hate crime law by classifying crimes committed against people due to gender identity, disability, and sexual orientation as hate crimes. It also strengthened extant laws related to hate crimes based on race, religion, or national origin.

One year following Byrd's death, the City of Jasper erected the James Byrd Jr. Memorial Park in his honor. The park, a local space where children from various racial backgrounds are often seen playing with one another, now represents momentous change in the face of abject racism. It serves as a reminder of progress and an augury of possibility. We can all pause for a moment to appreciate and uplift the harmony and humanity represented by this park, and then we are reminded—with the prodigious swiftness of an avalanche as we learn about the deaths of George Floyd, Elijah McClain, Ahmaud Arbery, Freddie Gray, Ronald Greene, Eric Garner, and others— that there is much work to be done.

APPENDIX

List of Lynching Victims
in Texas, 1866–1942

The alleged victim of crimes in the "Alleged Crime" column is likely white unless otherwise noted. If the number of individuals in the mob is indicated, mob members were likely unmasked unless otherwise indicated. If it reads "Mob of unknown size," the mob could have been masked or unmasked. By the end of the nineteenth century and beyond however, most mobs were unmasked.

DATE	NAME	RACE	GENDER	CITY	COUNTY	ALLEGED CRIME	MODE OF DEATH	SIZE OF MOB
1866	Unnamed	Black	Unknown	Unknown	Bell	Unknown	Unknown	Mob of unknown size
1866	Unnamed	Black	Unknown	Unknown	Bell	Unknown	Unknown	Mob of unknown size
1866	Unnamed	Black	Unknown	Unknown	Bell	Unknown	Unknown	Mob of unknown size
1866	Unnamed	Black	Unknown	Unknown	Bell	Unknown	Unknown	Mob of unknown size
1866	Unnamed	Black	Unknown	Unknown	Bell	Unknown	Unknown	Mob of unknown size
1866	Unnamed	Black	Unknown	Unknown	Bell	Unknown	Unknown	Mob of unknown size
1866	Unnamed	Black	Unknown	Unknown	Bell	Unknown	Unknown	Mob of unknown size
January 2, 1868	D. McKinney	White	Male	Navasota	Grimes	Shot man and killed him	Shot	Masked men in crowd of unknown size; speaking "broken" English and Dutch
November, 1868	George Smith	Black	Male	Jefferson	Marion	Unknown	Unknown	Mob of unknown size
April 6, 1869	Unnamed	Black	Male	Henderson	Rusk	Murder	Hanged	Unknown
April 6, 1869	Unnamed	Black	Male	Henderson	Rusk	Murder	Hanged	Unknown
April 6, 1869	Unnamed	Black	Male	Henderson	Rusk	Murder	Hanged	Unknown
April 6, 1869	Unnamed	Black	Male	Henderson	Rusk	Murder	Hanged	Unknown
April 6, 1869	Unnamed	Black	Male	Henderson	Rusk	Murder	Hanged	Unknown
June, 1873	Unnamed	Black	Male	Pilot Point	Denton	Attempted rape	Hanged	Unknown
June 29, 1873	Mat. Wallace	White	Male	Waco	McLennan	Cattle theft	Hanged	Thirty

March 12, 1874	Unnamed	Unknown	Unknown	Denison	Grayson	Horse theft	Unknown	Unknown
March, 1874	Unnamed	Black	Male	Bryan	Brazos	Unknown	Unknown	Mob of unknown size
March, 1874	Unnamed	Black	Male	Bryan	Brazos	Unknown	Unknown	Mob of unknown size
March, 1874	Unnamed	Black	Male	Bryan	Brazos	Unknown	Unknown	Mob of unknown size
March, 1874	Unnamed	Black	Male	Bryan	Brazos	Unknown	Unknown	Mob of unknown size
March, 1874	Unnamed	Black	Male	Bryan	Brazos	Unknown	Unknown	Mob of unknown size
March, 1874	Unnamed	Black	Male	Bryan	Brazos	Unknown	Unknown	Mob of unknown size
April 8, 1874	Turner Ardazal	White	Male	Near Orange	Orange	Murder of woman and two children	Shot	Mob of unknown size
May 26, 1874	W. L. Coleman	White	Male	East of Belton	Bell	Murder of wife	Shot	103, masked
May 26, 1874	Crow	White	Male	East of Belton	Bell	Horse theft	Shot	103, masked
May 26, 1874	Windfield Becknell	White	Male	East of Belton	Bell	Robbery	Shot	103, masked
May 26, 1874	Marion McDonald	White	Male	East of Belton	Bell	Horse theft	Shot	103, masked
May 26, 1874	J. T. McDonald	White	Male	East of Belton	Bell	Assault	Shot	103, masked
May 26, 1874	W. T. Smith	White	Male	East of Belton	Bell	Unknown	Shot	103, masked

DATE	NAME	RACE	GENDER	CITY	COUNTY	ALLEGED CRIME	MODE OF DEATH	SIZE OF MOB
May 26, 1874	William Cowan	White	Male	East of Belton	Bell	Horse theft	Shot	103, masked
May 26, 1874	John Daily	White	Male	East of Belton	Bell	Robbery	Shot	103, masked
May 26, 1874	Henry Grumbler	White	Male	East of Belton	Bell	Murder and horse theft	Shot	103, masked
June 5, 1874	McIntyre	White	Male	Austin	Travis	Unknown	Unknown	Masked mob of unknown size
June 5, 1874	Walker	White	Male	Austin	Travis	Unknown	Unknown	Masked mob of unknown size
June, 1874	Tom Summerville	Black	Male	Bryan	Brazos	Theft	Hanged	Mob of unknown size
June 22, 1874	Unnamed	Mexican	Male	Refugio	Refugio	Murder	Hanged	Mob of unknown size
June 22, 1874	Unnamed	Mexican	Male	Refugio	Refugio	Murder	Hanged	Mob of unknown size
June 22, 1874	Unnamed	Mexican	Male	Refugio	Refugio	Murder	Hanged	Mob of unknown size
August, 1875	Unnamed	Black	Male	Unknown	Bosque	Attempted murder	Hanged	Mob of unknown size
August, 1875	Unnamed	Black	Male	Unknown	Bosque	Attempted murder	Hanged	Mob of unknown size
August, 1875	Unnamed	White	Male	Unknown	Bosque	Attempted murder	Hanged	Mob of unknown size
August, 1875	Unnamed	White	Male	Unknown	Bosque	Attempted murder	Hanged	Mob of unknown size

April, 1875	Unnamed	Mexican	Male	Corpus Christi	Nueces	Raiding	Unknown	Mob of unknown size
November, 1875	Sam Thomas	Black	Male	Clinton	DeWitt	Unknown	Hanged	500
February, 1876	Unnamed	Black	Unknown	Unknown	Bell	Horse theft	Shot	Masked mob of unknown size
February, 1876	Unnamed	Black	Unknown	Unknown	Bell	Horse theft	Shot	Masked mob of unknown size
February, 1876	Unnamed	Black	Unknown	Unknown	Bell	Horse theft	Shot	Masked mob of unknown size
February, 1876	Unnamed	Black	Unknown	Unknown	Bell	Horse theft	Shot	Masked mob of unknown size
February, 1876	Unnamed	Black	Unknown	Unknown	Bell	Horse theft	Shot	Masked mob of unknown size
February, 1876	Unnamed	Black	Unknown	Unknown	Bell	Horse theft	Shot	Masked mob of unknown size
January 20, 1876	Anthony Smith	Black	Male	Cameron	Milam	Murder of a white man	Burned and shot	40 to 50
February 29, 1876	Jim Irvin	White	Male	Giddings	Lee	Horse theft	Hanged	Masked mob of unknown size
February 29, 1876	Tom Irvin	White	Male	Giddings	Lee	Horse theft	Hanged	Masked mob of unknown size
February 29, 1876	Pete Shaw	White	Male	Giddings	Lee	Horse theft	Shot	Masked mob of unknown size

DATE	NAME	RACE	GENDER	CITY	COUNTY	ALLEGED CRIME	MODE OF DEATH	SIZE OF MOB
Circa June 1, 1876	Unnamed	White	Male	Unknown	Unknown	Horse theft	Unknown	Mob of unknown size
Circa June 1, 1876	Unnamed	White	Male	Unknown	Unknown	Horse theft	Unknown	Mob of unknown size
Circa June 1, 1876	Unnamed	White	Male	Unknown	Unknown	Horse theft	Unknown	Mob of unknown size
Circa June 1, 1876	Unnamed	White	Male	Unknown	Unknown	Horse theft	Unknown	Mob of unknown size
Circa June 1, 1876	Unnamed	White	Male	Unknown	Unknown	Horse theft	Unknown	Mob of unknown size
Circa June 1, 1876	Unnamed	White	Male	Unknown	Unknown	Horse theft	Unknown	Mob of unknown size
Circa June 1, 1876	Unnamed	White	Male	Unknown	Unknown	Horse theft	Unknown	Mob of unknown size
Circa June 1, 1876	Unnamed	White	Male	Unknown	Unknown	Horse theft	Unknown	Mob of unknown size
Circa June 1, 1876	Unnamed	White	Male	Unknown	Unknown	Horse theft	Unknown	Mob of unknown size
Circa June 1, 1876	Unnamed	White	Male	Unknown	Unknown	Horse theft	Unknown	Mob of unknown size
Circa June 1, 1876	Unnamed	White	Male	Unknown	Unknown	Horse theft	Unknown	Mob of unknown size

Date	Name	Race	Sex	Location	County	Offense	Method	Mob size
Circa June 1, 1876	Unnamed	White	Male	Unknown	Unknown	Horse theft	Unknown	Mob of unknown size
Circa June 1, 1876	Unnamed	White	Male	Unknown	Unknown	Horse theft	Unknown	Mob of unknown size
Circa June 1, 1876	Unnamed	White	Male	Unknown	Unknown	Horse theft	Unknown	Mob of unknown size
Circa June 1, 1876	Unnamed	White	Male	Unknown	Unknown	Horse theft	Unknown	Mob of unknown size
Circa June 1, 1876	Unnamed	White	Male	Unknown	Unknown	Horse theft	Unknown	Mob of unknown size
Circa June 1, 1876	Unnamed	White	Male	Unknown	Unknown	Horse theft	Unknown	Mob of unknown size
June 9, 1876	Henderson	White	Male	Near Albany	Shackelford	Horse theft	Hanged	60 or 70
June 9, 1876	Floyd	White	Male	Near Albany	Shackelford	Horse theft	Hanged	60 or 70
July, 1876	W. M. McElroy	White	Male	Near Gonzales	Gonzales	Unknown	Hanged	Mob of unknown size
July, 1876	Stuart Campbell	White	Male	Near Gonzales	Gonzales	Unknown	Hanged	Mob of unknown size
July, 1876	Tucker Campbell	White	Male	Near Gonzales	Gonzales	Unknown	Hanged	Mob of unknown size
September, 1876	Al Beene	Black	Male	Mexia	Limestone	Incendiarism	Hanged	Mob of unknown size

DATE	NAME	RACE	GENDER	CITY	COUNTY	ALLEGED CRIME	MODE OF DEATH	SIZE OF MOB
September, 1876	Unnamed	White	Male	Unknown	Basque	Rumor spread by jealous man who was courting the same girl as the lynching victim; rumor indicated that man spoke ill of the girl; girl's father gathered a party and lynched the man	Hanged	Mob of unknown size
September 22, 1877	Jim Green	White	Male	Station Creek	Coryell	Cattle theft	Shot while leaving burning home	50 to 100
September 22, 1877	Bill Green	White	Male	Station Creek	Coryell	Cattle theft	Shot while leaving burning home	50 to 100
October 31, 1877	Dudley Hansford	White	Male	Near Perry	Fallas	Cattle theft	Hanged	40
November, 1877	Unnamed	Black	Male	Unknown	Walker	Murder of a deputy	Hanged	Mob of unknown size

Date	Name	Race	Sex	Place	County	Alleged Offense	Method	Mob Size
May 31, 1878	Fred Robinson	Black	Male	Groesbeck	Limestone	Rape	Hanged	Mob of unknown size
June, 1878	Bill Johnson	Black	Male	Near Helena	Karnes	Attempted rape	Unknown	Mob of unknown size
September, 1878	Unnamed	Black	Unknown	Near Richmond	Fort Bend	Cattle theft	Unknown	Mob of unknown size
July 4, 1878	Unnamed	Black	Male	Near Lindale	Smith	Assault of a white woman	Hacked to pieces	Mob of unknown size
Late April, 1879	Collier	White	Male	Unknown	Lampasas	Harboring a desperado	Unknown	Mob of unknown size
June 1, 1879	Jesse Allison	Black	Male	Unknown	County near McLennan	Unknown	Unknown	Mob of unknown size
June 1, 1879	George	Black	Male	Unknown	County near McLennan	Unknown	Shot and hanged	Mob of unknown size
June 1, 1879	Tom Fair	Black	Male	Unknown	County near McLennan	Unknown	Shot	Mob of unknown size
July 18, 1879	Marcellus Floyd	Black	Male	Richmond	Fort Bend	Attempted rape	Hanged	Mob of unknown size
July 25, 1879	Bill Statworth	White	Male	Unknown	County adjacent to Galveston	Threatening life of local resident	Shot	30
February 22, 1880	Unnamed	Unknown	Male	Near Linden	Cass	Rape	Mutilated and burned	Mob of unknown size

DATE	NAME	RACE	GENDER	CITY	COUNTY	ALLEGED CRIME	MODE OF DEATH	SIZE OF MOB
March 25, 1880	Bob Curley	White	Male	Valley Plains	Cass	Attempted rape	Hanged	Masked mob of unknown size
May, 1880	Matt Henderson	White	Male	Unknown	Denton	Horse theft	Hanged	Mob of unknown size
May, 1880	Charles Gray	White	Male	Unknown	Denton	Horse theft	Hanged	Mob of unknown size
June 11, 1880	Henry Quarles	Black	Male	Houston	Harris	Murder	Hanged	Mob of unknown size
August 18, 1880	Reuben Caruthers	Black	Male	Near Brenham	Washington	Cattle theft	Unknown	40 masked men
Approx. September 7, 1880	Taliaferro	Black	Male	Millican	Brazos	Robbery and murder	Hanged	Masked mob of unknown size
January / February 1881	California Joe	White	Male	Dennison	Grayson	Murder	Unknown	Mob of unknown size
January / February 1881	Barrana	White	Male	Dennison	Grayson	Murder	Unknown	Mob of unknown size
February 3, 1881	Albert Williams	Black	Male	Columbus	Colorado	Horse theft	Unknown	Masked mob of unknown size
April, 1881	Unnamed	Unknown	Unknown	Unknown	Hill	Horse theft	Unknown	Mob of unknown size
April, 1881	Unnamed	Unknown	Unknown	Unknown	Hill	Horse theft	Unknown	Mob of unknown size
April, 1881	Unnamed	Unknown	Unknown	Unknown	Hill	Horse theft	Unknown	Mob of unknown size
End of August, 1881	Unnamed	Black	Male	Orange	Orange	Attempting to kill sheriff	Unknown	Mob of unknown size

Date	Name	Race	Gender	County 1	County 2	Alleged crime	Method	Mob size
End of August, 1881	Unnamed	Black	Male	Orange	Orange	Attempting to kill sheriff	Unknown	Mob of unknown size
End of August, 1881	Unnamed	Black	Male	Orange	Orange	Attempting to kill sheriff	Unknown	Mob of unknown size
End of August, 1881	Unnamed	Black	Male	Orange	Orange	Attempting to kill sheriff	Unknown	Mob of unknown size
End of August, 1881	Unnamed	Black	Male	Orange	Orange	Attempting to kill sheriff	Unknown	Mob of unknown size
End of August, 1881	Unnamed	Black	Male	Orange	Orange	Attempting to kill sheriff	Unknown	Mob of unknown size
End of August, 1881	Unnamed	Black	Male	Orange	Orange	Attempting to kill sheriff	Unknown	Mob of unknown size
End of August, 1881	Unnamed	Black	Male	Orange	Orange	Attempting to kill sheriff	Unknown	Mob of unknown size
End of August, 1881	Unnamed	Unknown	Unknown	Dolores	Webb	Horse theft	Unknown	Mob of unknown size
End of August, 1881	Unnamed	Unknown	Unknown	Dolores	Webb	Horse theft	Unknown	Mob of unknown size
End of August, 1881	Unnamed	Unknown	Unknown	Dolores	Webb	Horse theft	Unknown	Mob of unknown size
End of August, 1881	Unnamed	Unknown	Unknown	Dolores	Webb	Horse theft	Unknown	Mob of unknown size
August 21, 1881	Sam Saxton	Black	Male	Orange	Orange	Desperado	Shot	150
August 21, 1881	Unnamed	Black	Male	Orange	Orange	Desperado	Hanged	150

DATE	NAME	RACE	GENDER	CITY	COUNTY	ALLEGED CRIME	MODE OF DEATH	SIZE OF MOB
October, 1881	Unnamed	Black	Unknown	Near Longview	Gregg / Harrison	Murder of white girl	Unknown	Mob of unknown size
October, 1881	Unnamed	Black	Unknown	Near Longview	Gregg / Harrison	Murder of white girl	Unknown	Mob of unknown size
October, 1881	Unnamed	Black	Unknown	Near Longview	Gregg / Harrison	Murder of white girl	Unknown	Mob of unknown size
1881	Unnamed	Unknown	Male	Unknown	Unknown	Riding another man's mule	Unknown	Mob of unknown size
January 2, 1882	Peter Nicholas	White	Male	Graham	Young	Escaped convict	Shot when trying to escape	200
January 2, 1882	D. McDonald	White	Male	Graham	Young	Escaped convict	Shot when trying to escape	200
January 2, 1882	McDonald	White	Male	Graham	Young	Escaped convict	Shot when trying to escape	200
January 2, 1882	McDonald	White	Male	Graham	Young	Escaped convict	Shot when trying to escape	200
February 25, 1882	D. B. Deering	White	Male	Gainesville	Cooke	Horse theft	Hanged	100
June 22, 1882	Unnamed	White	Male	Elm Bottom	Denton	Horse theft	Hanged	Mob of unknown size; found in the morning

Date	Name	Race	Gender	Location	County	Alleged Crime	Method	Mob
June 22, 1882	Unnamed	White	Male	Elm Bottom	Denton	Horse theft	Hanged	Mob of unknown size; found in the morning
June 22, 1882	Unnamed	White	Male	Elm Bottom	Denton	Horse theft	Shot	Mob of unknown size; found in the morning
June 22, 1882	Unnamed	White	Male	Elm Bottom	Denton	Horse theft	Shot	Mob of unknown size; found in the morning
July 8, 1882	Ed Sayles	Black	Male	Meriden	Iredell	Rape	Hanged	Masked men, unknown number
July 28, 1882	Pablo Aguilar	Mexican	Male	Laredo	Webb	Protesting a lynching	Shot	Mob of unknown size
July 28, 1882	Frank	"Mulatto"/ Mexican	Male	Near Tascosa	Oldham	Murder of deputy sheriff	Unknown	Mob of unknown size
July 28, 1882	Pedro Gomez	Mexican	Male	Laredo	Webb	Unknown	Shot	Mob of unknown size
August 2, 1882	George Porter	Unknown	Male	Lampasas	Lampasas	Horse theft	Shot	25 men
August 8, 1882	Augustine Agirer	Mexican	Male	Oatmanville	Travis	Filed a complaint in court against a white man	Shot	Mob of unknown size
September 9, 1882	Unnamed	Black	Male	Comanche	Comanche	Rape of white girl	Unknown	Mob of unknown size
November 26, 1882	George W. Fraley	White	Male	Hazel Dell	Comanche	Stealing cotton	Hanged	12 men
November 26, 1882	James Fraley	White	Male	Hazel Dell	Comanche	Stealing cotton	Hanged	12 men

DATE	NAME	RACE	GENDER	CITY	COUNTY	ALLEGED CRIME	MODE OF DEATH	SIZE OF MOB
End of November, 1882	Unnamed	Unknown	Unknown	Near Coleman	Coleman	Cattle theft	Hanged	Mob of unknown size
November 30, 1882	Unnamed	Mexican	Male	George West	Live Oak	Murder	Shot	3
December 2, 1882	Terry (surname)	White	Male	Hazel Dell	Comanche	Cattle theft	Hanged	Mob of unknown size
December 2, 1882	Terry (surname)	White	Male	Hazel Dell	Comanche	Cattle theft	Hanged	Mob of unknown size
December 29, 1882	S. W. Stidham	White	Male	Columbus	Colorado	Murder	Hanged	Mob of unknown size
April 15, 1883	Chaney	White	Male	Gatesville	Coryell	Unknown	Shot	Mob of unknown size
April 23, 1883	Julian Campes	Mexican	Male	Collins	Nueces	Horse theft	Hanged	Mob of unknown size
April 23, 1883	Herman Robles	Mexican	Male	Collins	Nueces	Horse theft	Hanged	Mob of unknown size
June 14, 1883	Joseph Anderson	Black	Male	Cotulla	LaSalle	Stealing	Hanged (head and legs missing)	Mob of unknown size
June 14, 1883	Unnamed	Mexican	Unknown	Cotulla	LaSalle	Unknown	Hanged	Mob of unknown size

Date	Name	Race	Gender	Location	County	Alleged Crime	Method	Mob Size
June 26, 1883	Alexander Lacy	Black	Male	Jefferson	Marion	Rape of a white woman	Crowd intended to burn him, but decided to hang him from a bridge	500
June 27, 1883	Jasper Douglas	Black	Male	Jefferson	Marion	Rape of a white woman	Hanged and shot	150
August 17, 1883	Martin Bradley	Black	Male	Terrell	Kaufman	Entering the room of a white woman	Hanged from a tree	50 masked men
October 18, 1883	Louis Foster	Black	Male	Near South Union Church	Lavaca	Helped an escaped convict	Hanged from a tree and shot in the head	Mob of unknown size
November 14, 1883	David Bailey	White	Male	Comanche	Comanche	Murder	Hanged	Mob of unknown size
December 7, 1883	Unnamed	Mexican	Male	Near Fort Davis	Jeff Davis	Murder	Hanged	Mob of unknown size
December 7, 1883	Unnamed	Mexican	Male	Near Fort Davis	Jeff Davis	Murder	Hanged	Mob of unknown size
December 7, 1883	Unnamed	Mexican	Male	Near Fort Davis	Jeff Davis	Murder	Hanged	Mob of unknown size
December 7, 1883	Unnamed	Mexican	Male	Near Fort Davis	Jeff Davis	Murder	Hanged	Mob of unknown size

DATE	NAME	RACE	GENDER	CITY	COUNTY	ALLEGED CRIME	MODE OF DEATH	SIZE OF MOB
December 24, 1883	Henry Pfeiffer	White	Male	McDade	Bastrop	Horse theft	Hanged	50 masked men
December 24, 1883	Wright McLemore	White	Male	McDade	Bastrop	Burglary	Hanged	50 masked men
December 24, 1884	Thad McLemore	White	Male	McDade	Bastrop	Burglary	Hanged	50 masked men
March 25, 1884	Bill Burleson	Black	Male	Gonzales	Gonzales	Attempted rape of a white woman	Hanged	150
April 13, 1884	Gibbs	Black	Male	Lyons	Burleson	Murder of a white woman	Burned	Newspaper reported: "the whole community"
April 14, 1884	Charles Michand	Black	Male	Palestine	Anderson	Attempted rape	Hanged	Mob of unknown size
July 25, 1884	William Smith	Black	Male	Milano	Milam	Rape and theft	Hanged	Mob of unknown size
August 6, 1884	Ben Dick	White	Male	Lone Oak Bayou	Chambers	Cattle theft	Shot and hanged	Mob of unknown size
August 13, 1884	Green McCullough	White	Male	Cotulla	La Salle	Murder	Hanged	100
August 19, 1884	Richard Flechsig	White	Male	Galveston	Galveston	Attempted rape of white woman	Hanged	Mob of unknown size

August 23, 1884	John Howard	White	Male	Langford's Cove (modern day Evant)	Coryell	Burning a thresher and wheat	Shot	Mob of unknown size
August 24, 1884	Robert Riley	Black	Male	Refugio	Refugio	Assault	Shot	Mob of unknown size
August 24, 1884	George Hawes	Black	Male	Refugio	Refugio	Attempting to stop a lynching; attempting to stop mob at jail	Shot	Mob of unknown size
September 12, 1884	William A. Taylor	Black	Male	Dallas	Dallas	Rape	Hanged	500 masked men
November 30, 1884	Unnamed	Mexican	Male	George West	Live Oak	Murder	Shot	Mob of unknown size
November 30, 1884	Unnamed	Mexican	Male	George West	Live Oak	Murder	Shot	Mob of unknown size
December 2, 1884	Perry Reilly	Black	Male	Sulphur Springs	Hopkins	Murder and robbery	Hanged	100
January 11, 1885	Thomas Peddy	Black	Male	Greenville	Hunt	Rape	Hanged	100 masked men
January 19, 1885	Daniel Sutton	Black	Male	Tyler	Smith	Unknown	Unknown	Masked mob of unknown size
February 5, 1885	Benjamin Hawkins (under seventeen years old)	Black	Male	Franklin	Robertson	Murder	Hanged	200

DATE	NAME	RACE	GENDER	CITY	COUNTY	ALLEGED CRIME	MODE OF DEATH	SIZE OF MOB
February 7, 1885	James Gazziers	Black	Male	Benchley	Brazos	Unknown	Shot and hanged	Mob of unknown size
February 7, 1885	Thomas Morris	Black	Male	Schulenburg	Fayette	Rape of white girl	Hanged	Masked mob of unknown size
February, 1885	Unnamed	Black	Male	Uvalde	Uvalde	Rape	Unknown	Mob of unknown size
February 28, 1885	Manuel Flores	Mexican	Male	David Lovel's sheep farm	Dimmit	Cattle theft	Hanged	Mob of unknown size
February 28, 1885	Unnamed	Mexican	Male	David Lovel's sheep farm	Dimmit	Cattle theft	Hanged	Mob of unknown size
February 28, 1885	Unnamed	Mexican	Male	David Lovel's sheep farm	Dimmit	Cattle theft	Hanged	Mob of unknown size
March 4, 1885	Unnamed	Black	Male	Batesville	Zavala	Rape	Shot	Mob of unknown size
May 23, 1885	William Deal	White	Male	Coyote Peek	Eastland	Unknown	Hanged	Mob of unknown size
May 23, 1885	Andrew Cade	White	Male	Coyote Peek	Eastland	Unknown	Hanged	Mob of unknown size
June 5, 1885	Henry Lumpkins	Black	Male	Hearne	Robertson	Murder of a Black man	Hanged	Mob of African Americans and whites, unknown size
June 8, 1885	Samuel Dyer	White	Male	Bonham	Fannin	Murder	Hanged	More than 100 masked men

June 8, 1885	Eli Dyer	White	Male	Bonham	Fannin	Murder	Hanged	More than 100 masked men
Jun 21, 1885	Andrew Jackson	Black	Male	Elkhart	Anderson	Murder of a white woman	Hanged	Several hundred people
Jun 21, 1885	Lizzie Jackson	Black	Female	Elkhart	Anderson	Murder of a white woman	Hanged	Several hundred people
June 21, 1885	Frank Hayes	Black	Male	Elkhart	Anderson	Murder of a white woman	Hanged	Several hundred people
June 21, 1885	Joseph Norman	Black	Male	Elkhart	Anderson	Murder of a white woman	Hanged	Several hundred people
June 21, 1885	William Rogers	Black	Male	Elkhart	Anderson	Murder of a white woman	Hanged	Several hundred people
June 22, 1885	Unnamed	White	Unknown	Gainesville	Cooke	Horse theft	Unknown	Mob of unknown size
June 22, 1885	Unnamed	White	Unknown	Gainesville	Cooke	Horse theft	Unknown	Mob of unknown size
June 22, 1885	Unnamed	White	Unknown	Gainesville	Cooke	Horse theft	Unknown	Mob of unknown size
June 22, 1885	Unnamed	White	Unknown	Gainesville	Cooke	Horse theft	Unknown	Mob of unknown size
June 22, 1885	Unnamed	White	Unknown	Gainesville	Cooke	Horse theft	Unknown	Mob of unknown size
June 22, 1885	Unnamed	White	Unknown	Gainesville	Cooke	Horse theft	Unknown	Mob of unknown size
June 22, 1885	Unnamed	White	Unknown	Gainesville	Cooke	Horse theft	Unknown	Mob of unknown size
June 22, 1885	Unnamed	White	Unknown	Gainesville	Cooke	Horse theft	Unknown	Mob of unknown size
June 22, 1885	Unnamed	White	Unknown	Gainesville	Cooke	Horse theft	Unknown	Mob of unknown size
June 22, 1885	Unnamed	White	Unknown	Gainesville	Cooke	Horse theft	Unknown	Mob of unknown size
June 22, 1885	Unnamed	White	Unknown	Gainesville	Cooke	Horse theft	Unknown	Mob of unknown size

DATE	NAME	RACE	GENDER	CITY	COUNTY	ALLEGED CRIME	MODE OF DEATH	SIZE OF MOB
June 22, 1885	Unnamed	White	Unknown	Gainesville	Cooke	Horse theft	Unknown	Mob of unknown size
June 11, 1885	Bill Williams	White	Male	Gainesville	Cooke	Horse theft	Hanged	Unknown size
June 11, 1885	Frank Morgan	White	Male	Gainesville	Cooke	Horse theft	Hanged	Unknown size
June 11, 1885	James Moore	White	Male	Gainesville	Cooke	Horse theft	Hanged	Unknown size
June 21, 1885	Andy Jackson	Black	Male	Elkhart	Anderson	Murder	Hanged	400 to 500
June 25 or 26, 1885	John Martin	Black	Male	Bells	Grayson	Rape and murder	Hanged	Mob of unknown size
July 5, 1885	James Hathorne	Black	Male	Trinity	Trinity	Attempted rape of white child	Hanged	Unknown size
July 7, 1885	John Lawrence	Black	Male	Baxter Springs	Cherokee	Attempted rape of white teenager	"Hanged from a rafter of an unfinished house"	More than 20
August 26, 1885	Albert Lackey / Lockie	White	Male	Blanco	Blanco	Murdered five people	Hanged	50 to 80
September 25, 1885	David Anderson	Black	Male	Orange	Orange	Murder	Hanged	100
September 28, 1885	Squire Carter	Black	Male	McDade	Bastrop	Unknown	Shot	3 or 4 masked people
October 9, 1885	Benjamin Little	Black	Male	Mt. Pleasant	Titus	Slander of white family	Hanged	60 to 80

Date	Name	Race	Sex	Place	County	Alleged Crime	Method	Mob
January 21, 1886	Sidney Brown	Black	Male	Rockdale	Milam	Attempted Murder	Hanged	Mob of unknown size
February 8, 1886	R. T. Garrett	White	Male	Paris	Lamar	Murder	Hanged	75 to 100 masked men
March 15, 1886	Thomas Oscar Polk	White	Male	Copperas Cove	Coryell	Horse theft	Hanged	7 or 8 masked men
Apr 17, 1886	M. C. Christian	White	Male	McDade	Bastrop	Burning a church	Shot	Mob of unknown size
April 19, 1886	Andres Martinez	Mexican	Male	Collins	Nueces	Horse theft and shooting two men	Shot	50 masked men
April 19, 1886	Jose Maria Cadena	Mexican	Male	Collins	Nueces	Horse theft and shooting two men	Shot	50 masked men
April 24, 1886	Unnamed	Black	Unknown	Washington	Washington	Unknown	Unknown	Unknown
April 25, 1886	Juan Salles	Mexican	Male	Big Springs	Howard	Murder	Burned in a storehouse	Mob of unknown size
April 28, 1886	Mateo Cadena	Mexican	Male	Los Indios Ranch	Duval	Horse theft	Hanged	Mob of unknown size
June 29, 1886	Ed Williams	Black	Male	Gainesville	Cooke	Attempted rape	Unknown	Mob of unknown size
July 14, 1886	W. P. Pruitt	White	Male	Sipe Springs	Comanche	Attempted murder	Hanged and shot	5
July 10, 1886	Sidney Davis	Black	Male	Morgan	Bosque	Rape	Hanged	500
July 20, 1886	Porter Sorell	Black	Male	Luling	Caldwell	Rape	Shot	15 masked men

DATE	NAME	RACE	GENDER	CITY	COUNTY	ALLEGED CRIME	MODE OF DEATH	SIZE OF MOB
July 26, 1886	Unnamed	Black	Male	De Leon	Comanche	Murder	Hanged; father of deceased woman wanted the accused burned	750
August 3, 1886	Bill Harris	Black	Male	Whitehall	McLennan	Rape	Hanged	30
September 1, 1886	John Smith	Black	Male	Greenville	Hunt	Murder	Hanged	40 masked men
October 3, 1886	Thomas Farrar	Black	Male	Throckmorton	Throckmorton	Rape and murder	Hanged	32 masked men
October 11, 1886	Alexander Washington	Black	Male	Somerset	Bexar	Attempted rape	Hanged	Masked mob of unknown size
October 29, 1886	Jim Petland	Black	Male	Kildare	Cass	Assault	Hanged	Mob of unknown size
November 1, 1886	William Hewey	"Mulatto"	Male	Shepherd	San Jacinto	Murder of employer's son	Hanged from tree	Mob of unknown size
November 29, 1886	Factor Jones	Black	Male	DeKalb	Bowie	Murder	Shot	Mob of unknown size
November 29, 1886	Dick Butler	Black	Male	DeKalb	Bowie	Murder	Shot	Mob of unknown size
December 2, 1886	Ephraim Jones	Black	Male	Brenham	Washington	Murder	Hanged	Masked mob of 20 to 60

Date	Name	Race	Sex	City	County	Reason	Method	Mob
December 2, 1886	Alfred Jones	Black	Male	Brenham	Washington	Murder	Hanged	Masked mob of 20 to 60
December 2, 1886	Shad Felder	Black	Male	Brenham	Washington	Murder	Hanged	Masked mob of 20 to 60
December 16, 1886	James Howard	White	Male	Texarkana	Bowie	Cruelty to his wife	Hanged from bridge and shot	30 masked people
February 3, 1887	Coly Thompson	Black	Male	Sequin	Guadalupe	Murder	Hanged	35 masked men
February 3, 1887	Andy Williams	Black	Male	Sequin	Guadalupe	Murder	Hanged	35 masked men
February 3, 1887	Warren Wilson	Black	Male	Sequin	Guadalupe	Murder	Hanged	35 masked men
February 16, 1887	James Richards	Black	Male	Anderson	Anderson	Shooting and killing a white man (a deputy sheriff)	Hanged	75 masked people
May 15, 1887	Andrew McGehee	Black	Male	Willis	Montgomery	Attempted murder	Shot in jail cell by mob	Mob of unknown size
October 12, 1887	Unnamed	Mexican	Unknown	Rio Grande City	Starr	Kidnapping	Unknown	Mob of unknown size
October 12, 1887	Unnamed	Mexican	Unknown	Rio Grande City	Starr	Kidnapping	Unknown	Mob of unknown size
October 12, 1887	Unnamed	Mexican	Unknown	Rio Grande City	Starr	Kidnapping	Unknown	Mob of unknown size

DATE	NAME	RACE	GENDER	CITY	COUNTY	ALLEGED CRIME	MODE OF DEATH	SIZE OF MOB
October 12, 1887	Unnamed	Mexican	Unknown	Rio Grande City	Starr	Kidnapping	Unknown	Mob of unknown size
October 12, 1887	Unnamed	Mexican	Unknown	Rio Grande City	Starr	Kidnapping	Unknown	Mob of unknown size
December 9, 1887	Cecilio Barrea	White	Male	Rio Grande City	Starr	Kidnapping	Hanged	20
December 9, 1887	Vivian Diaz	Mexican	Male	Rio Grande City	Starr	Kidnapping	Hanged	20
January 3, 1888	William Bolo	White	Male	Madisonville	Madison	Murder and theft	Shot	200 to 300
February 28, 1888	William Battle	Black	Male	Spanish Camp	Wharton	Dispute over land	Hanged	Mob of unknown size
February 28, 1888	Unnamed	Black	Unknown	Spanish Camp	Wharton	Dispute over land	Shot	Mob of unknown size
February 28, 1888	Unnamed	Black	Unknown	Spanish Camp	Wharton	Dispute over land	Shot	Mob of unknown size
February 28, 1888	Unnamed	Black	Unknown	Spanish Camp	Wharton	Dispute over land	Shot	Mob of unknown size
February 28, 1888	Unnamed	Black	Unknown	Spanish Camp	Wharton	Dispute over land	Shot	Mob of unknown size
February 28, 1888	Unnamed	Black	Unknown	Spanish Camp	Wharton	Dispute over land	Shot	Mob of unknown size

Date	Name	Race	Gender	Location	County	Reason	Method	Mob Size
February 28, 1888	Unnamed	Black	Unknown	Spanish Camp	Wharton	Dispute over land	Burned in cabin	Mob of unknown size
February 28, 1888	Unnamed	Black	Unknown	Spanish Camp	Wharton	Dispute over land	Burned in cabin	Mob of unknown size
August 27, 1888	Unnamed	Unknown	Male	Near Palo Duro Canyon	Armstrong	Outlaw	Shot	17
August 27, 1888	Unnamed	Unknown	Male	Near Palo Duro Canyon	Armstrong	Outlaw	Shot	17
August 27, 1888	Unnamed	Unknown	Male	Near Palo Duro Canyon	Armstrong	Outlaw	Shot	17
August 27, 1888	Unnamed	Unknown	Male	Near Palo Duro Canyon	Armstrong	Outlaw	Shot	17
August 27, 1888	Unnamed	Unknown	Male	Near Palo Duro Canyon	Armstrong	Outlaw	Shot	17
August 27, 1888	Unnamed	Unknown	Male	Near Palo Duro Canyon	Armstrong	Outlaw	Shot	17
August 27, 1888	Unnamed	Unknown	Male	Near Palo Duro Canyon	Armstrong	Outlaw	Shot	17

DATE	NAME	RACE	GENDER	CITY	COUNTY	ALLEGED CRIME	MODE OF DEATH	SIZE OF MOB
August 27, 1888	Unnamed	Unknown	Male	Near Palo Duro Canyon	Armstrong	Outlaw	Shot	17
August 27, 1888	Unnamed	Unknown	Male	Near Palo Duro Canyon	Armstrong	Outlaw	Shot	17
August 27, 1888	Unnamed	Unknown	Male	Near Palo Duro Canyon	Armstrong	Outlaw	Shot	17
August 27, 1888	Unnamed	Unknown	Male	Near Palo Duro Canyon	Armstrong	Outlaw	Shot	17
August 27, 1888	Unnamed	Unknown	Male	Near Palo Duro Canyon	Armstrong	Outlaw	Shot	17
August 27, 1888	Unnamed	Unknown	Male	Near Palo Duro Canyon	Armstrong	Outlaw	Shot	17
August 27, 1888	Unnamed	Unknown	Male	Near Palo Duro Canyon	Armstrong	Outlaw	Shot	17
August 27, 1888	Unnamed	Unknown	Male	Near Palo Duro Canyon	Armstrong	Outlaw	Shot	17

Date	Name	Race	Gender	Location	County	Alleged Offense	Method	Mob
August 27, 1888	Unnamed	Unknown	Male	Near Palo Duro Canyon	Armstrong	Outlaw	Shot	17
August 27, 1888	Harrison Spencer	Black	Male	Longview	Gregg	Political dispute	Hanged	Masked Ku Klux Klan mob of unknown size
October 3, 1888	Aaron Bean	Black	Male	Jasper	Jasper	Attempted assault	Shot	Mob of unknown of size
October 15, 1888	Joseph Joiner	Black	Male	Hutto	Williamson	Attempted assault of white girl	Hanged	Masked mob of unknown size
October 17, 1888	Nat Nathaniel	Black	Male	Brazoria	Brazoria	Murder of a white man	Hanged	Masked mob of unknown size
January 19, 1889	Alfred Marlow	White	Male	Graham	Young	Murder	Shot	30 masked men
February 7, 1889	Nick Adkins	Black	Male	Kilgore	Gregg	Mistaken identity	Shot	Masked mob of 5 or 6
February 15, 1889	William C. Smith	White	Male	San Saba	San Saba	Unknown	Hanged	Mob of unknown size
February 15, 1889	Asa Brown	White	Male	San Saba	San Saba	Unknown	Hanged	Mob of unknown size
February 19, 1889	Unnamed	Black	Unknown	Liberty	Liberty	Murder	Unknown	Unknown
February 19, 1889	Unnamed	Black	Unknown	Liberty	Liberty	Murder	Unknown	Unknown

DATE	NAME	RACE	GENDER	CITY	COUNTY	ALLEGED CRIME	MODE OF DEATH	SIZE OF MOB
April 14, 1889	George Driggs	Black	Male	Hempstead	Waller	Attempted rape of a white woman	Hanged	Masked mob of unknown size
May 17, 1889	Unnamed	Black	Unknown	Millican	Brazos	Rape	Unknown	Unknown
July 13, 1889	Henry Davis	Black	Male	Robinson	McLennan	Attempted rape of white women	Hanged and shot	150
July 23, 1889	George Lewis	Black	Male	Linden	Cass	Poisoning well	Hanged	Masked mob of unknown size
July 28, 1889	Roma Newton, twelve years old	Likely White	Female	Bonhams	Fannin	Unknown	Hanged	Mob of unknown size
July 26, 1889	George Lindley	Black	Male	Wolfe City	Hunt	Unknown	Shot	Mob of unknown size
August 14, 1889	James Brooks	Black	Male	Orange	Orange	Rape	Hanged	500
August, 1889	Unnamed	Unknown	Male	Pleasanton	Atascosa	Unknown	Hanged	Mob of unknown size
December 14, 1889	Unnamed	White	Male	White Rock	Dallas	Theft	Hanged	6
December 14, 1889	Unnamed	White	Male	White Rock	Dallas	Theft	Hanged	6
January 4, 1890	Bedford Cade	Black	Male	New Salem	Rusk	Unknown	Hanged	Mob of unknown size

Date	Name	Race	Sex	Location	County	Cause	Method	Mob
March 26, 1890	Bill Clark	Black	Male	Headsville	Robertson	Rape and murder	Hanged and shot	Mob of unknown size
April 3, 1890	William Williams	Black	Male	Kosse	Limestone	Rape	Hanged and shot	200
April 24, 1890	Simon Garrette	Black	Male	San Augustine	San Augustine	Attempted murder by poisoning	Hanged	Mob of unknown size
April 24, 1890	Jerry Teel, fifteen years old	Black	Male	San Augustine	San Augustine	Attempted murder by poisoning	Hanged	Mob of unknown size
April 24, 1890	Unnamed	Black	Unknown	Cameron Station	Milam	Rape	Unknown	Unknown
May 12, 1890	Edward Bennett	Black	Male	Hearne	Robertson	Attempted rape of a white woman	Hanged	Mob of unknown size
June 1, 1890	Thomas Brown	Black	Male	Hooks Ferry	Red River	Nuisance	Shot	Mob of unknown size
June 4, 1890	Bill Jones	Black	Male	Chester	Polk	Murder of a white man	Hanged	Masked mob of unknown size
June 12, 1890	Unnamed	Mexican	Male	Taylor	Williamson	Rape	Shot and hanged	20
June 28, 1890	Jack Bailey	Black	Male	Near Paris	Lamar	Cause unknown	Hanged	Mob of unknown size
July 3, 1890	Patrick Henry	Black	Male	Neches	Anderson	Gambling	Hanged and head hit with ax	Mob of unknown size

DATE	NAME	RACE	GENDER	CITY	COUNTY	ALLEGED CRIME	MODE OF DEATH	SIZE OF MOB
July 21, 1890	Melena (surname), five years old	Mexican	Female	Hutto	Williamson	Unknown	Shot	Mob of unknown size
July 21, 1890	Vitolo Melena	Mexican	Male	Hutto	Williamson	Unknown	Shot	Mob of unknown size
July 21, 1890	Melena (surname) (wife of Vitolo Melena)	Mexican	Female	Hutto	Williamson	Unknown	Shot	Mob of unknown size
July 22, 1890	Andy Young	Black	Male	Near Deport	Red River	Race prejudice; "difficulty with some white boys"	Shot	4 to 7 men
July 30, 1890	John Walton	Black	Male	Cypress	Harris	Theft	Shot	Mob of unknown size
August 4, 1890	John Brown	Black	Male	Anderson	Grimes	Rape of white woman	Hanged and shot	500
August 14, 1890	Unnamed	Black	Male	Near Mart	Limestone	Rape	Unknown	Mob of unknown size
December 13, 1890	Charles Gillard	Black	Male	Bastrop	Bastrop	Possibly due to Gillard defeating J. S. Shooner, a white opponent, in an election	Shot	Mob of unknown size
December 1, 1890	Andrew Taylor Baugh	White	Male	Rio Grande border	Unknown	Horse and cattle theft	Hanged	Mob of unknown size

Date	Name	Race	Gender	Location	County	Alleged offense	Method	Mob size
January 1, 1891	Charles Beale	Black	Male	Chilton	Falls	Rape and murder	Hanged	Mob of unknown size
February 4, 1891	Jesus Salceda	Mexican	Male	Knicherbocker	Tom Green	Seducing a rancher's daughter; mistaken identity	Hanged	3
February 23, 1891	Thomas Rowland	Black	Male	Douglass	Cherokee	Robbery	Hanged	Mob of unknown size
March 29, 1891	William Fields	White	Male	Mineola	Wood	Attempted rape	Hanged	Mob of unknown size
May 27, 1891	Williams Hartsfield	Black	Male	Near Belden	Cass	Being troublesome	Shot	Mob of unknown size
June 8, 1891	Monroe Sheppard	Black	Male	Near Belden	Cass	Being troublesome	Shot	Mob of unknown size
June 3, 1891	Evan Shelby	White	Male	Wickliffe		Murder	Unknown	Unknown
June 8, 1891	William Hartfield	Black	Male	Near Belden	Cass	Being troublesome	Shot	Mob of unknown size
May 27, 1891	Munn Sheppard	Black	Male	Near Belden	Cass	Being troublesome	Shot	Mob of unknown size
July 22, 1891	William Johnson, seventeen years old	Black	Male	Henderson	Rusk	Attempted rape	Hanged	Mob of unknown size

DATE	NAME	RACE	GENDER	CITY	COUNTY	ALLEGED CRIME	MODE OF DEATH	SIZE OF MOB
October 26, 1891	Lee Green	Black	Male	Seven miles west of Queen City	Cass	Murder of a white woman and child Robbery	Burned	500 to 1,000
November 9, 1891	Unnamed	Black	Unknown	Gay Hill	Washington	Argument	Hanged	Mob of unknown size
November 9, 1891	Unnamed	Black	Unknown	Gay Hill	Washington	Argument	Hanged	Mob of unknown size
November 22, 1891	William Black	Black	Male	Moscow	Polk	Insults	Hanged	Mob of unknown size
January 28, 1892	Joseph Shields	White	Male	Timpson	Shelby	Unknown	Hanged	4
May 18, 1892	Arthur Burrows	White	Male	Midway	Madison	Rape or attempted rape of young girl	Shot	Mob of unknown size
June 25, 1892	Prince Wood	Black	Male	Spurger	Tyler	Rape of white women	Shot	50 masked men
June 25, 1892	Thomas Smith	Black	Male	Spurger	Tyler	Rape of white women	Shot	50 masked men
June 25, 1892	Henry Gaines	Black	Male	Spurger	Tyler	Rape of white women	Shot	50 masked men
September 6, 1892	John Walker	Black	Male	Paris	Lamar	Rioting	Hanged	Mob of unknown size

Date	Name	Race	Sex	Location	County	Alleged Offense	Method	Mob Size
September 6, 1892	William Armor	Black	Male	Paris	Lamar	Rioting	Hanged	Mob of unknown size
September 6, 1892	John Ransom	Black	Male	Paris	Lamar	Rioting	Hanged	Mob of unknown size
September 17, 1892	William Sullivan	Black	Male	Plantersville	Grimes	Claimed that a white woman was his wife; woman allegedly encouraged to accuse him of rape	Dragged by rope and then hanged	Mob of unknown size
September 19, 1892	Unnamed	Black	Male	Paris	Lamar	Rape	Unknown	Mob of unknown size
February 1, 1893	Henry Smith	Black	Male	Paris	Lamar	Murder of four-year-old white girl	Burned	10,000
February 7, 1893	William Butler	Black	Male	Hickory Creek, five miles East of Paris	Lamar	Race prejudice relative of Henry Smith; accused of knowing the location of Henry Smith and not revealing it	Shot and hanged	Mob of unknown size

DATE	NAME	RACE	GENDER	CITY	COUNTY	ALLEGED CRIME	MODE OF DEATH	SIZE OF MOB
February 7, 1893	Perry Bratcher	Black	Male	New Boston	Bowie	Rape	Unknown	Mob of unknown size
July 12, 1893	Robert Larkin	Black	Male	Unknown	Osceola	Unknown	Unknown	Mob of unknown size
July 15, 1893	M. Jazo	Mexican	Male	Near El Paso	El Paso	Murder	Hanged	Mob of unknown size
July 28, 1893	Alexander Brown	Black	Male	Bastrop	Bastrop	Murder	Unknown	Mob of unknown size
August 1, 1893	Henry Reynolds	Black	Male	Post Mill	Montgomery	Rape of a woman and murder of a man	Hanged	Mob of unknown size
August 31, 1893	Unnamed	Black	Male	Yarborough	Grimes	No offense	Unknown	Mob of unknown size
September 30, 1893	Unnamed	Black	Male	Houston	Harris	No offense	Unknown	Mob of unknown size
December 31, 1893	Edward Murcher (father)	Black	Male	Waco	McLennan	Unknown	Unknown	5 men with masks
December 31, 1893	Jesse Murcher (son)	Black	Male	Waco	McLennan	Unknown	Unknown	5 men with masks
December 31, 1893	Albert Murcher (son)	Black	Male	Waco	McLennan	Unknown	Unknown	5 men with masks
December 31, 1893	George Murcher (son)	Black	Male	Waco	McLennan	Unknown	Unknown	5 men with masks

Date	Name	Race	Sex	Location	County	Alleged Offense	Method	Mob
January 7, 1894	Judas Miller	White	Male	Fort Ringgold	Starr	Unknown	Hanged	Mob of unknown size
April 8, 1894	Edward B. Cash	White	Male	Gatesville	Coryell	Unknown	Hanged and shot	Mob of unknown size
April 14, 1894	Unnamed	Black	Female	Unknown	Travis	Murder	Shot	Mob of unknown size
April 14, 1894	Unnamed	Black	Male	Unknown	Travis	Murder	Shot	Mob of unknown size
April 14, 1894	Unnamed	Black	Male	Unknown	Travis	Murder	Shot	Mob of unknown size
April 14, 1894	Alfred Bren	Black	Male	Gatesville	Coryell	Unknown	Unknown	Mob of unknown size
May 8, 1894	Unnamed	Black	Male	West	McLennan	Writing a letter to a white woman	Mob attempted to hang him, but when he ran, the mob shot him	
May 16, 1894	Henry Scott	Black	Male	Jefferson	Marion	Murder	Hanged	100
June 13, 1894	Lon Hall	Black	Male	Sweet Home	Lavaca	Murder	Hanged	Mob of unknown size
June 13, 1894	Bascom Cook	Black	Male	Sweet Home	Lavaca	Murder	Hanged	Mob of unknown size
June 28, 1894	John Williams	Black	Male	Sulphur Springs	Hopkins	Murder	Hanged and shot	Mob of unknown size
July 14, 1894	William Griffith, seventeen years old	Black	Male	Woodville	Tyler	Rape	Hanged	30 masked men

DATE	NAME	RACE	GENDER	CITY	COUNTY	ALLEGED CRIME	MODE OF DEATH	SIZE OF MOB
August 14, 1894	Unnamed	Black	Female	Thirty miles from Austin	Travis	Murder of a child	Taken from jail and shot	Mob of unknown size
August 14, 1894	Unnamed	Black	Male	Thirty miles from Austin	Travis	Murder of a child	Taken from jail and shot	Mob of unknown size
August 14, 1894	Unnamed	Black	Male	Thirty miles from Austin	Travis	Murder of a child	Taken from jail and shot	Mob of unknown size
October 5, 1894	Henry Gibson	Black	Male	Fairfield	Freestone	Attempted rape	Shot	Mob of unknown size
December 20, 1894	James Allen	Black	Male	Brownsville	Cameron	Burning a barn	Shot	Mob of unknown size
March 7, 1895	Ike Manion	Black	Male	Athens	Henderson	Murder	Shot	5
April 12, 1895	Nelson Calhoun	Black	Male	Corsicana	Navarro	Rape of a white woman	Escaped from mob and was shot	Mob of unknown size
April 30, 1895	George Jones	Native American	Male	Devers	Liberty	Assault	Shot	Mob of unknown size
May 25, 1895	John Crocker	White	Male	Wharton	Wharton	Murder	Shot	Mob of unknown size
May 25, 1895	Mrs. John Crocker	White	Female	Wharton	Wharton	Murder	Shot	Mob of unknown size
May 25, 1895	John Crocker's son	White	Male	Wharton	Wharton	Child of murderers	Shot	Mob of unknown size
June 11, 1895	Walter Johnson	Black	Male	Lufkin	Angelina	Rape	Hanged	Hundreds

June 11, 1895	Alexander White	Black	Male	Keno	Liberty	Murder of a man	Hanged	Mob of unknown size
July 20, 1895	John Cherry	Black	Male	Keno	Liberty	Murder of a man	Hanged	Mob of unknown size
July 20, 1895	Mary Phillips	Black	Female	Near Mart	Falls	Phil Arnold (white) killed Abe Phillips, senior; Abe Phillips junior killed Arnold; family killed for that murder	Dynamite thrown into home	Mob of unknown size
July 20, 1895	Willie Phillips	Black	Male	Near Mart	Falls	Phil Arnold (white) killed Abe Phillips, senior; Abe Phillips junior killed Arnold; family killed for that murder	Dynamite thrown into home	Mob of unknown size
July 20, 1895	Hannah Phillips, twelve years old	Black	Female	Near Mart	Falls	Phil Arnold (white) killed Abe Phillips, senior; Abe Phillips junior killed Arnold; family killed for that murder	Dynamite thrown into home	Mob of unknown size

DATE	NAME	RACE	GENDER	CITY	COUNTY	ALLEGED CRIME	MODE OF DEATH	SIZE OF MOB
July 20, 1895	Abe Phillips Jr., seventeen years old	Black	Male	Near Mart	Falls	Phil Arnold (white) killed Abe Phillips senior; Abe Phillip junior killed Arnold; family killed for that murder	Dynamite thrown into home	Mob of unknown size
July 20, 1895	Edward Phillips, thirteen years old	Black	Male	Near Mart	Falls	Phil Arnold (white) killed Abe Phillips senior; Abe Phillips junior killed Arnold; family killed for that murder	Dynamite thrown into home	Mob of unknown size
July 20, 1895	Benjamin Johnson	Black	Male	Near Mart	Falls	Phil Arnold (white) killed Abe Phillips senior; Abe Phillips junior killed Arnold; family killed for that murder	Dynamite thrown into home	Mob of unknown size

Date	Name	Race	Gender	Town	County	Reason	Method	Mob
July 20, 1895	Abe Phillips Senior	Black	Male	Near Mart	Falls	Phil Arnold (white) killed Abe Phillips senior; Abe Phillip junior. killed Arnold; family killed for that murder	Dynamite thrown into home	Mob of unknown size
July 20, 1895	K. D. Taylor	Black	Male	Near Mart	Falls	Phil Arnold (white) killed Abe Phillips senior; Abe Phillips junior killed Arnold; family killed for that murder	Dynamite thrown into home	Mob of unknown size
July 23, 1895	Unnamed	Black	Female	Brenham	Washington	Race prejudice		Mob of unknown size
July 24, 1895	Squire Loftin	Black	Male	Lexington	Lee	Rape	Hanged	Mob of unknown size
August 2, 1895	James Mason	Black	Male	Daingerfield	Morris	Unknown	Shot	7 men
August 2, 1895	Mrs. James Mason	Black	Female	Daingerfield	Morris	Unknown	Shot	7 men
August 12, 1895	William Stephens	Black	Male	Pacio	Delta	Race prejudice/ refusing to leave land	Shot	Mob of unknown size (Whitecappers)
August 21, 1895	Jefferson Cole	Black	Male	Paris	Lamar	Race prejudice/ refusing to leave land	Shot	Mob of unknown size

DATE	NAME	RACE	GENDER	CITY	COUNTY	ALLEGED CRIME	MODE OF DEATH	SIZE OF MOB
August 22, 1895	Unnamed	Black		Wharton	Wharton	Murder	Unknown	Mob of unknown size
October 11, 1895	Floantina Suitta	Mexican	Male	Cotula	La Salle	Murder	Shot and hanged	10 masked men
October 29, 1895	Robert Henson Hilliard	Black	Male	Tyler	Smith	Murder of a white woman	Burned	5,000
November 21, 1895	Unnamed	Black	Unknown	Unknown	Madison	Mistaken identity; accused of riding horse over a little girl and inflicting serious injuries on her	Unknown	Mob of unknown size
March 23, 1896	Ike Pizer	Black	Male	Near Emporia	Angelina	Insulting white women	Hanged	Mob of unknown size
May 3, 1896	Will Bendy	Black	Male	Beaumont	Jefferson	Murder	Shot and hanged	Mob of unknown size
August 19, 1896	Anderson Vaughn	Black	Male	Hillside	McLennan	Race prejudice	Beaten and shot	25
February 29, 1896	Younger Lewis / Elmer Lewis / "Kid" Lewis	White	Male	Wichita Fall	Wichita	Bank robbery and murder	Hanged	Several thousand

Date	Name	Race	Gender	City	County	Alleged crime	Method	Mob size
February 29, 1896	Foster Crawford	White	Male	Wichita Fall	Wichita	Bank robbery and murder	Hanged	Several thousand
May 3, 1896	William Benby	Black	Male	Beaumont	Jefferson	Murder	Hanged and shot	Mob of unknown size
June 10, 1896	Louis Whitehead	Black	Male	Bryan	Brazos	Attempted rape of a white girl	Hanged May have later been burned	300
June 10, 1896	George L. Johnson	Black	Male	Bryan	Brazos	Attempted rape of a white girl	Hanged May have later been burned	300
June 10, 1896	James Reddick	Black	Male	Bryan	Brazos	Attempted rape of white woman	Hanged May have later been burned	300
January 25, 1897	Eugene Washington	Black	Male	Bryan	Brazos	Rape	Hanged	Mob of unknown size
March 4, 1897	Will Hughes	Black	Male	Elgin	Bastrop	Burglary	Shot	Masked mob of unknown size
April 27, 1897	Hal Wright	Black	Male	Harleton	Harrison	Robbery and arson	Shot	Masked mob of unknown size
April 27, 1897	Russell Wright	Black	Male	Harleton	Harrison	Robbery and arson	Shot	Masked mob of unknown size

DATE	NAME	RACE	GENDER	CITY	COUNTY	ALLEGED CRIME	MODE OF DEATH	SIZE OF MOB
April 30, 1897	Fayette Rhone	Black	Male	Sunnyside	Waller	Murder of a Black man, child, and woman	Hanged	Mob of white and Black people
April 30, 1897	William Gates	Black	Male	Sunnyside	Waller	Murder of a Black man, child, and woman	Hanged	Mob of white and Black people
April 30, 1897	Louis Thomas	Black	Male	Sunnyside	Waller	Murder of a Black man, child, and woman	Hanged	Mob of white and Black people
April 30, 1897	James Thomas, fourteen years old	Black	Male	Sunnyside	Waller	Murder of a Black man, child, and woman	Hanged	Mob of white and Black people
April 30, 1897	Benjamin Thomas, fifteen years old	Black	Male	Sunnyside	Waller	Murder of a Black man, child, and woman	Hanged	Mob of white and Black people
April 30, 1897	Aaron Thomas, thirteen years old	Black	Male	Sunnyside	Waller	Murder of a Black man, child, and woman	Hanged	Mob of white and Black people

Date	Name	Race	Sex	City	County	Alleged crime	Method	Mob size
May 13, 1897	David Cotton	Black	Male	Rosebud	Falls	Attempted assault of a white woman	Hanged	1,000 masked people
May 13, 1897	Henry Williams	Black	Male	Rosebud	Falls	Attempted assault of a white woman	Hanged	1,000 masked people
May 13, 1897	Sabe Stewart	Black	Male	Rosebud	Falls	Attempted assault of a white woman	Hanged	1,000 masked people
May 18, 1897	William White	Black	Male	San Augustine	San Augustine	Murder	Shot	Masked mob of unknown size
May 23, 1897	William Jones	White	Male	Tyler	Smith	Murder	Shot	500
August 7, 1897	Benjamin Gay	Black	Male	Sulphur Bluff	Hopkins	Arson	Hanged	Mob of unknown size
August 8, 1897	Esseck White	Black	Male	Nacogdoches	Nacogdoches	Attempted rape of white women	Hanged (newspaper noted that "a threat to fire had been made, but if it had been carried out, a very bloody conflict would have ensued."	500

DATE	NAME	RACE	GENDER	CITY	COUNTY	ALLEGED CRIME	MODE OF DEATH	SIZE OF MOB
August 10, 1897	Rev. Captain Jones	White	Male	Monkstown	Fannin	Elopement	Shot	Mob of unknown size
August 26, 1897	William Bembry / William Bonner	Black	Male	Bellville	Austin	Rape	Hanged	200
August 26, 1897	Wesley Johnson	White	Male	Mooreville	Falls	Attempted rape	Hanged	Mob of unknown size
October 11, 1897	Robert Carter	Black	Male	Brenham	Washington	Murder	Shot	Mob of unknown size
November 18, 1897	Thomas Sweat	Black	Male	Allenfarm	Brazos	Murder	Shot and hanged	Mob of unknown size
April 5, 1898	Carlos Guillen	Black	Male	Brownsville	Cameron	Murder	Shot	300
June 6, 1898	George Washington	Black	Male	Weimar	Colorado	Murder	Hanged	500
June 9, 1898	Dee Watkins	Black	Male	Nacogdoches	Nacogdoches	Race prejudice	Shot	Mob of Whitecappers
June 14, 1898	Laura Cebron (Mrs. Jake Cebrose)	Black	Female	Plano	Collin	Race prejudice / "nothing"	Shot	50 to 20 Whitecappers
August 8, 1898	Dan Ogg	Black	Male	Palestine	Anderson	Entering the room of a white couple	Hanged and shot	200

Date	Name	Race	Gender	Location	County	Reason	Method	Mob Size
May 24, 1899	James Humphrey (father)	White	Male	Aley	Henderson	Helping murderer to escape	Hanged	30
May 24, 1899	Humphrey (son)	White	Male	Aley	Henderson	Helping murderer to escape	Hanged	30
May 24, 1899	Humphrey (son)	White	Male	Aley	Henderson	Helping murderer to escape	Hanged	30
June 28, 1899	Allie Thompson	Black	Male	Waskom	Harrison	Rape	Shot	Mob of unknown size
July 14, 1899	Abe Brown	Black	Male	Near Gilead	Upshur	Rape and murder	Shot	Mob of unknown size
July 14, 1899	Ed Magee	Black	Male	Near Iola	Grimes	Murder	Hanged	Mob of unknown size
July 25, 1899	Henry Hamilton	Black	Male	Near Navasota	Grimes	Burned a white church in retaliation for a lynching	Hanged	Several hundred people
February 11, 1900	James Sweeney	White	Male	Port Arthur	Jefferson	Murder of white person	Hanged from electric light pole	8
November 15, 1900	Jim Shaw	Black	Male	Jefferson	Marion	Attempted murder; assaulting a white man	Taken from jail and hanged from a railroad bridge	1,000

DATE	NAME	RACE	GENDER	CITY	COUNTY	ALLEGED CRIME	MODE OF DEATH	SIZE OF MOB
November 15, 1900	Freeman Perhune	Black	Male	Jefferson	Marion	Attempted murder; assaulting a white man	Taken from jail and hanged from a rail-road bridge	1,000
November 15, 1900	Elijah Wortham	Black	Male	Jefferson	Marion	Attempted murder; assaulting a white man	Taken from jail and hanged from a rail-road bridge	1,000
March 13, 1901	John Henderson	Black	Male	Corsicana	Navarro	Rape of a white woman	Burned	5,000
June 15, 1901	Unnamed	Mexican	Male	Ottine	Gonzales	Outlawry	Hanged	1,000
June 16, 1901	Unnamed	Mexican	Male	Belmont	Gonzales	Outlawry	Shot	Mob of unknown size
August 2, 1901	Abe Wilder	Black	Male	Near Dexter	Cooke	Murdering a white woman	Burned	1,500
August 25, 1901	Felix Martinez	Mexican	Male	Kennedy	Karnes	Unknown	Shot	Mob of unknown size
September 30, 1901	George Muckelroy	Black	Male	Hallsville	Harrison	Dispute with white land-owner over cotton crop	Hanged	Mob of unknown size

Date	Name	Race	Gender	Location	County	Reason	Method	Mob size
September 30, 1901	Ras Muckelroy	Black	Male	Hallsville	Harrison	Dispute with white land-owner over cotton crop	Hanged	Mob of unknown size
September 30, 1901	Unnamed	Black	Unknown	Hallsville	Harrison	Dispute with white land-owner over cotton crop	Hanged	Mob of unknown size
September 30, 1901	Unnamed	Black	Unknown	Hallsville	Harrison	Dispute with white land-owner over cotton crop	Hanged	Mob of unknown size
September 30, 1901	Unnamed	Black	Unknown	Hallsville	Harrison	Dispute with white land-owner over cotton crop	Hanged	Mob of unknown size
September 30, 1901	Thomas Walker	Black	Male	Hallsville	Harrison	Dispute with white land-owner over cotton crop	Beaten and hanged	Mob of unknown size
October 25, 1901	Gaines Gordon	Black	Male	Quitman	Wood	Murder of a white man	Hanged	200
December 25, 1901	J. H. McClinton	Black	Male	Near Deport	Lamar	Reported someone for violating laws	Shot	Mob of unknown size
March 11, 1902	Nathan Bird	Black	Male	Luling	Caldwell	Protecting son from a mob	Shot	Mob of unknown size

DATE	NAME	RACE	GENDER	CITY	COUNTY	ALLEGED CRIME	MODE OF DEATH	SIZE OF MOB
March 11, 1902	Carlbert Bird	Black	Male	Luling	Caldwell	Fighting with a white boy	Possibly hanged	Mob of unknown size
May 22, 1902	Dudley Morgan	Black	Male	Lansing	Harrison	Assaulting a white woman	Burned	4,000
September 4, 1902	Jesse Walker	Black	Male	Hempstead	Waller	Rape; assaulting a white woman	Hanged	400 to 500 people
September 9, 1902	William E. Robuck	White	Male	Brownsville	Cameron	Murder	Shot	Mob of unknown size
October 4, 1902	Utt Duncan	Black	Male	Columbus	Colorado	Attempted rape / attempted assault on a white woman	Hanged	100
October 21, 1902	Jim Wesley	Black	Male	Hempstead	Waller	Assault and murder	Hanged	2,000
October 21, 1902	Reddick Barton	Black	Male	Hempstead	Waller	Assault and murder	Hanged	2,000
January 14, 1903	Charles Tunstall	Black	Male	Angleton	Brazoria	Murder	Shot and burned in cell	Mob of unknown size
January 14, 1903	Ransom O'Neal	Black	Male	Angleton	Brazoria	Murder	Shot and burned in cell	Mob of unknown size
April 26, 1903	Hensley Johnson	Black	Male	Carthage	Panola	Attempted rape	Hanged	Mob of unknown size

Date	Name	Race	Sex	Location	County	Reason	Method	Mob
July 23, 1903	Mooney Allen	Black	Male	Beaumont	Jefferson	Murder	Shot and hanged	Mob of unknown size
July 31, 1903	Unnamed	Black	Male	Alto	Cherokee	Insulting white women and shooting into home	Hanged	Mob of unknown size
October 1, 1903	Walter Davis	Black	Male	Marshall	Harrison	Murder of white constable	Hanged and shot	Several hundred
October 14, 1903	Joseph Durfee	Black	Male	Angelton	Brazoria	Murder of a white woman	Hanged	Mob of unknown size
March 21, 1904	John Maynard	Black	Male	Mont-gomery	Mont-gomery	Murder of a white man	Hanged	Mob of unknown size
July 30, 1904	John Larremore	Black	Male	Lockhart	Caldwell	Made an offen-sive remark	Hanged	Masked mob of 8
August 29, 1904	Oscar Tucker	Black	Male	Weimer	Colorado	Attempted rape	Hanged	Mob of unknown size
February 16, 1905	Carlos Munoz	Mexican	Male	Near Lockhart	Caldwell	Rape	Shot and hanged	100
February 17, 1905	William Johnson	Black	Male	Smithville	Bastrop	Rape	Shot	Mob of unknown size
March 14, 1905	Julius Stevens	Black	Male	Longview	Gregg	Assaulting a white man	Shot in jail	Mob of unknown size
June 20, 1905	Ford Simon	Black	Male	Riverside	Walker	Rape	Hanged	Mob of unknown size

DATE	NAME	RACE	GENDER	CITY	COUNTY	ALLEGED CRIME	MODE OF DEATH	SIZE OF MOB
July 20, 1905	Sam Green, sixteen years old	Black	Male	New Braunfels	Comal	Attack of child	Shot in jail by mob	Mob of unknown size
July 29, 1905	Andres Humphrey	Black	Male	Near Avery	Red River	Attempted rape	Hanged	300
August 8, 1905	Sank Majors	Black	Male	Waco	McLennan	Attempted rape	Hanged Crowd was going to burn him but woman whom he allegedly raped (farmer's wife) asked that he be hanged and not burned	2,000
August 11, 1905	Thomas Williams	Black	Male	Sulphur Springs	Hopkins	Attempted rape	Burned	3,000 to 6,000
September 7, 1905	Steve Davis	Black	Male	Howard	Ellis	Assaulting a white woman	Burned	2,000 to 3,000
November 12, 1905	John Reese	Black	Male	Henderson	Rusk	Knowledge of a murder / murder	Hanged	Mob of unknown size

Date	Name	Race	Sex	Town	County	Reason	Method	Mob size
November 12, 1905	Robert Askew	Black	Male	Henderson	Rusk	Knowledge of a murder / murder	Hanged	Mob of unknown size
November 12, 1905	Henry Sherrow	Black	Male	Henderson	Rusk	Knowledge of a murder / murder	Hanged	Mob of unknown size
January 10, 1906	Benjamin Harris	Black	Male	Moscow	Polk	Murder of a white man	Hanged	50 to 70 men
April 24, 1906	Lincoln Porter	Black	Male	Groesbeck	Limestone	Rape / entering room of a white woman	Shot	Mob of unknown size
April 25, 1906	George (fifteen or seventeen years old)	Black	Male	Oakwood	Leon	Entering the home of a white widow	Hanged	7 men
September 15, 1906	Mitchell Frazier	Black	Male	Rosebud	Falls	Assaulting a white man	Hanged	Mob of unknown size
October 26, 1906	"Slab" Pitts	Black	Male	Toyah	Reeves	Living with a white woman	Dragged and hanged	Mob of unknown size
July 14, 1907	Fred Wilson	Black	Male	Del Rio	Val Verde	Murder	Shot	Mob of unknown size
August 5, 1907	Thomas Hall	Black	Male	Runge	Karnes	Attempted assault on a white woman	Hanged	Mob of unknown size
November 4, 1907	Alex Johnson	Black	Male	Cameron	Milam	Attempted rape	Hanged	500

DATE	NAME	RACE	GENDER	CITY	COUNTY	ALLEGED CRIME	MODE OF DEATH	SIZE OF MOB
December 26, 1907	Anderson Calloway	Black	Male	Marquez	Leon	Attempted rape / entering room of a white woman	Hanged	Mob of unknown size
February 28, 1908	Charley Scott	Black	Male	Conroe	Montgomery	Attempted rape	Hanged	Mob of unknown size
March 7, 1908	John Campbell	Black	Male	Navasota	Grimes	Attempted murder	Hanged	Mob of unknown size
March 16, 1908	James Kinder	Black	Male	Magnolia	Montgomery	Attempted rape	Shot	Mob of unknown size
March 16, 1908	Alf Riley	Black	Male	Magnolia	Montgomery	Attempted rape	Shot	Mob of unknown size
April 9, 1908	Albert Fields	Black	Male	Longview	Gregg	Rape	Hanged	Several hundred people
April 19, 1908	Jasper Douglas	Black	Male	Atlanta	Cass	Rape of his stepsister	Hanged	Mob of unknown size
May 7, 1908	John Williams	Black	Male	Naples	Morris	Murder; conspiracy to murder two white men	Hanged	Mob of unknown size
June 21, 1908	Jerry Evans	Black	Male	Hemphill	Sabine	Murder of a white man	Hanged from tree	150
June 21, 1908	William Johnson	Black	Male	Hemphill	Sabine	Murder of a white man	Hanged from tree	150

Date	Name	Race	Sex	City	County	Reason	Method	Mob size
June 21, 1908	Hardi Evans	Black	Male	Hemphill	Sabine	Murder of a white man	Hanged from tree	150
June 21, 1908	William Manuel	Black	Male	Hemphill	Sabine	Murder of a white man	Hanged from tree	150
June 21, 1908	Moses Spellman	Black	Male	Hemphill	Sabine	Murder of a white man	Hanged from tree	150
June 21, 1908	Frank Williams	Black	Male	Hemphill	Sabine	Murder of a white man	Hanged from tree	150
June 21, 1908	Burgha Singleton	Black	Male	Hemphill	Sabine	Murder	Shot	150
June 21, 1908	Cleveland Williams	Black	Male	Hemphill	Sabine	Murder	Hanged	150
June 21, 1908	Ned Williams	Black	Male	Hemphill	Sabine	Murder	Hanged	150
June 21, 1908	Henry Thomas	Black	Male	Hemphill	Sabine	Murder	Shot	150
July 15, 1908	Unnamed	Black	Male	Beaumont	Jefferson	Mistaken identity	Shot	1,000
July 28, 1908	Ted Smith	Black	Male	Greenville	Hunt	Rape and assault	Burned	1,000
August 14, 1908	Mose Jackson	Black	Male	Bellville	Austin	Unknown reason	Hanged	Mob of unknown size
September 12, 1908	Daniel Newton	Black	Male	Brookshire	Waller	Murder of a white man	Hanged	Mob of unknown size

DATE	NAME	RACE	GENDER	CITY	COUNTY	ALLEGED CRIME	MODE OF DEATH	SIZE OF MOB
March 7, 1909	Will Clark	Black	Male	Rockwall	Rockwall	Father refused to allow a posse to search premises for Anderson Ellis	Shot	Mob of unknown size
March 7, 1909	Anderson Ellis	Black	Male	Rockwall	Rockwall	Attempted rape	Burned	1,000
March 29, 1909	Joe Redden	Black	Male	Dawson	Navarro	Insulting a white woman	Hanged	200
April 30, 1909	"Creole" Mose	Black	Male	Marshall	Harrison	Murder of a deputy sheriff and injuring a constable	Hanged	Mob of unknown size
April 30, 1909	"Pie" Hill	Black	Male	Marshall	Harrison	Murder of a deputy sheriff and injuring a constable	Hanged	Mob of unknown size
April 30, 1909	Matt Chase	Black	Male	Marshall	Harrison	Murder of a deputy sheriff and injuring a constable	Hanged	Mob of unknown size
May 1, 1909	James Hodges	Black	Male	Tyler	Smith	Assaulting a white girl; mistaken identity	Hanged	Mob of unknown size
May 28, 1909	Thomas Barnett	White	Male	Abilene	Taylor	Murder	Shot	50 masked people

Date	Name	Race	Gender	Location	County	Alleged Crime	Method	Mob Size
September 16, 1909	Jake Keyes	Black	Male	Sandy Point	Brazoria	Aiding a fugitive	Shot	80
September 16, 1909	Steve Hayes	Black	Male	Sandy Point	Brazoria	Murder	Shot and hanged	200
September 18, 1909	Sylvester Volbaum	Black	Male	Anchor	Brazoria	Unknfown	Shot	Mob of unknown size
September 18, 1909	Peter Vann	Black	Male	Anchor	Brazoria	Unknown	Shot	Mob of unknown size
December 20, 1909	Louis "Coke" Mills	Black	Male	Rosebud	Falls	Murder	Hanged	50
March 3, 1910	Allen Brooks	Black	Male	Dallas	Dallas	Molesting a white female child	Hanged	Thousands
April 5, 1910	Frank Bates	Black	Male	Centerville	Leon	Murder; jail-breaking and shooting white men	Hanged	Mob of unknown Size
June 5, 1910	Douglas Lemon	Black	Male	Orange	Orange	Unknown	Shot	Mob of unknown size
June 5, 1910	Rankin Moore	Black	Male	Orange	Orange	Unknown	Shot	Mob of unknown size
June 20, 1910	Leonard Johnson	Black	Male	Rusk	Cherokee	Murder of a white woman	Burned	Mob of unknown size
July 5, 1910	Unnamed	Black	Male	Rodney	Navarro	Attempted rape	Hanged	Mob of unknown size
July 5, 1910	Bob Cannon	Black	Male	Dawson	Navarro	Attempted rape	Hanged	Mob of unknown size

DATE	NAME	RACE	GENDER	CITY	COUNTY	ALLEGED CRIME	MODE OF DEATH	SIZE OF MOB
July 22, 1910	Henry Gentry	Black	Male	Belton	Bell	Attempted break in of home of white woman, a widow; murder of a white man	Shot and burned	1,000
July 29, 1910	Jeff Wilson	Black	Male	Near Slocum	Anderson	Argument over a promissory note	Shot	200 to 300
July 29, 1910	Alex Holly	Black	Male	Near Slocum	Anderson	Argument over a promissory note	Shot	200 to 300
July 29, 1910	Cleve Larkin	Black	Male	Near Slocum	Anderson	Argument over a promissory note	Shot	200 to 300
July 29, 1910	John Hays	Black	Male	Near Slocum	Anderson	Argument over a promissory note	Shot	200 to 300
July 29, 1910	William Forman	Black	Male	Near Slocum	Anderson	Argument over a promissory note	Shot	200 to 300
July 29, 1910	Abe Wilson	Black	Male	Near Slocum	Anderson	Argument over a promissory note	Shot	200 to 300

July 29, 1910	Ned Larkin	Black	Male	Near Slocum	Anderson	Argument over a promissory note	Shot	200 to 300
July 29, 1910	Sam Baker	Black	Male	Near Slocum	Anderson	Argument over a promissory note	Shot	200 to 300
July 29, 1910	Dick Wilson	Black	Male	Near Slocum	Anderson	Argument over a promissory note	Shot	200 to 300
July 29, 1910	Ben Dancer	Black	Male	Near Slocum	Anderson	Argument over a promissory note	Shot	200 to 300
July 29, 1910	Will Burley	Black	Male	Near Slocum	Anderson	Argument over a promissory note	Shot	200 to 300
July 29, 1910	Unnamed	Black	Male	Near Slocum	Anderson	Argument over a promissory note	Unknown	200 to 300
July 29, 1910	Unnamed	Black	Male	Near Slocum	Anderson	Argument over a promissory note	Unknown	200 to 300
July 29, 1910	Unnamed	Black	Male	Near Slocum	Anderson	Argument over a promissory note	Burned	200 to 300
July 29, 1910	Unnamed	Black	Male	Near Slocum	Anderson	Argument over a promissory note	Shot	200 to 300

DATE	NAME	RACE	GENDER	CITY	COUNTY	ALLEGED CRIME	MODE OF DEATH	SIZE OF MOB
November 3, 1910	Antonio Rodriguez	Mexican	Male	Rock Springs	Edwards	Murder	Burned	Mob of unknown size
June 19, 1911	Antonio Gomez, four-teen years old	Mexican	Male	Thorndale	Milan	Murder	Hanged	Mob of unknown size
August 11, 1911	"Commo-dore" Jones	Black	Male	Farmersville	Collin	Insulting a white woman	Hanged	75
October 29, 1911	Will Ollie	Black	Male	Marshall	Harrison	Assault	Hanged and shot	500
November 6, 1911	Riley Johnson	Black	Male	Clarksville	Red River	Attempted rape / assault	Shot	Mob of unknown size
February 13, 1912	George Saunders	Black	Male	Marshall	Panola	Providing gun to man accused of murder	Hanged	Mob of unknown size
February 13, 1912	Mary Jackson	Black	Female	Marshall	Panola	Providing gun to man accused of murder	Hanged	Mob of unknown size
May 25, 1912	Dan Davis	Black	Male	Near Tyler	Smith	Attempted rape / assault	Burned	2,000
January 17, 1913	Henry Mouzon	Black	Male	Cooper	Delta	Murder of a white girl	Hanged then shot and burned	200

Date	Name	Race	Sex	Location	County	Alleged crime	Method	Mob size
January 23, 1913	Dick Stanley, sixteen years old	Black	Male	Fulbright	Red River	Attempted rape / assault	Hanged	150 to 200
February 24, 1913	Robert Perry	Black	Male	Near Karnack	Harrison	Horse theft	Shot	Mob of unknown size
February 25, 1913	Anderson	Black	Male	Elysian Fields	Harrison	Murder	Hanged	Mob of unknown size
May 13, 1913	Gus Finley	Black	Male	Daingerfield	Morris	Murder	Hanged	Mob of unknown size
June 5, 1913	Richard Galloway	Black	Male	Near Newton	Newton	Argument at a picnic	Found on railroad tracks with bullets in head	Mob of unknown size
September 21, 1913	William Davis	Black	Male	Franklin	Robertson	Murder of white man	Hanged and burned	1,000
January 2, 1914	David Lee	Black	Male	Jefferson	Marion	Wounding a white constable; assault	Hanged	12 or 15
February 28, 1914	Jesse Morgan	Black	Male	Alpine	Brewster	Assault and highway robbery	Shot	Mob of unknown size
March 13, 1914	William Williams	Black	Male	Hearne	Robertson	Attempted murder	Hanged	Mob of unknown size
June 5, 1914	William Robertson	Black	Male	Navasota	Grimes	Murder of white man	Shot	Mob of unknown size

DATE	NAME	RACE	GENDER	CITY	COUNTY	ALLEGED CRIME	MODE OF DEATH	SIZE OF MOB
October 14, 1914	Joseph Durfee	Black	Male	Angleton	Brazoria	Murder of white woman	Hanged	Mob of unknown size
May 9, 1915	Alex Kinley	Black	Male	Big Sandy	Upshur	Murder	Hanged	Mob of unknown size
Jul 29, 1915	Adolfo Munz	Mexican	Male	Brownsville	Cameron	Murder	Hanged	7 or 8 men
July 30, 1915	Will Stanley	Black	Male	Temple	Bell	Murder of three white children	Burned	5,000
August 8, 1915	Eusebio Hernandez	Mexican	Male	Norias	Kenedy	Outlawry	Shot	Mob of unknown size
August 8, 1915	Abraham Salinas	Mexican	Male	Norias	Kenedy	Outlawry	Shot	Mob of unknown size
August 8, 1915	Juan Tobar	Mexican	Male	Norias	Kenedy	Outlawry	Shot	Mob of unknown size
August 16, 1915	Unnamed	Mexican	Male	San Benito	Cameron	Murder	Shot	Mob of unknown size
August 16, 1915	Unnamed	Mexican	Male	San Benito	Cameron	Murder	Shot	Mob of unknown size
August 16, 1915	Unnamed	Mexican	Male	San Benito	Cameron	Murder	Shot	Mob of unknown size
August 16, 1915	Unnamed	Mexican	Male	San Benito	Cameron	Murder	Shot	Mob of unknown size
August 16, 1915	Unnamed	Mexican	Male	San Benito	Cameron	Murder	Shot	Mob of unknown size
August 16, 1915	Unnamed	Mexican	Male	San Benito	Cameron	Murder	Shot	Mob of unknown size
August 24, 1915	John Slovak	White	Male	Shiner	Lavaca	Pillage and murder	Shot	8 to 10
August 29, 1915	King Richmond	Black	Male	Sulphur Springs	Hopkins	Murder of a white deputy sheriff	Burned	6,000

August 29, 1915	Joe Richmond	Black	Male	Sulphur Springs	Hopkins	Murder of a white deputy sheriff	Shot and then burned	6,000
August 30, 1915	Pascual Orozco	Mexican	Male	High Lonesome Peak	Culberson	Horse theft	Shot	Mob of unknown size
August 30, 1915	Unnamed	Mexican	Male	High Lonesome Peak	Culberson	Horse theft	Shot	Mob of unknown size
August 30, 1915	Unnamed	Mexican	Male	High Lonesome Peak	Culberson	Horse theft	Shot	Mob of unknown size
August 30, 1915	Unnamed	Mexican	Male	High Lonesome Peak	Culberson	Horse theft	Shot	Mob of unknown size
August 30, 1915	Unnamed	Mexican	Male	High Lonesome Peak	Culberson	Horse theft	Drowned in Rio Grande River	Mob of unknown size
September 2, 1915	Earl Donaldson	White	Male	Near Brownsville	likely Cameron	No crime; kidnapped	Shot	30 to 40
September 2, 1915	Smith	White	Male	Near Brownsville	likely Cameron	No crime; kidnapped	Shot	30 to 40
September 2, 1915	Unnamed	Mexican	Male	Los Cuates	Cameron	Murder of two white men	Shot	Mob of unknown size
September 2, 1915	Unnamed	Mexican	Male	Los Cuates	Cameron	Murder of two white men	Shot	Mob of unknown size
September 2, 1915	Unnamed	Mexican	Male	Los Cuates	Cameron	Murder of two white men	Shot	Mob of unknown size

DATE	NAME	RACE	GENDER	CITY	COUNTY	ALLEGED CRIME	MODE OF DEATH	SIZE OF MOB
September 10, 1915	Alejos Vela	Mexican	Male	Harlingen	Cameron	Murder	Shot	Mob of unknown size
September 10, 1915	Angel Rincenes	Mexican	Male	Harlingen	Cameron	Murder	Shot	Mob of unknown size
September 10, 1915	Ignacio Rivera	Mexican	Male	Harlingen	Cameron	Murder	Shot	Mob of unknown size
September 14, 1915	Unnamed	Mexican	Unknown	San Benito	Cameron	Banditry	Shot	Mob of unknown size
September 14, 1915	Unnamed	Mexican	Unknown	San Benito	Cameron	Banditry	Shot	Mob of unknown size
September 14, 1915	Unnamed	Mexican	Unknown	San Benito	Cameron	Banditry	Shot	Mob of unknown size
September 14, 1915	Unnamed	Mexican	Unknown	San Benito	Cameron	Banditry	Shot	Mob of unknown size
September 14, 1915	Unnamed	Mexican	Unknown	San Benito	Cameron	Banditry	Shot	Mob of unknown size
September 14, 1915	Unnamed	Mexican	Unknown	San Benito	Cameron	Banditry	Found in water / drowned	Mob of unknown size
September 27, 1915	Antonio Longoria	Mexican	Male	Bazan Ranch Cemetery	Hidalgo	Unknown	Shot	Mob of unknown size

Date	Name	Ethnicity	Gender	Location	County	Reason	Method	Mob size
September 27, 1915	Jesus Bazan	Mexican	Male	Bazan Ranch Cemetery	Hidalgo	Unknown	Shot	Mob of unknown size
September 28, 1915	Unnamed	Mexican	Male	Ebenezer (modern day Alamo)	Hidalgo	Outlawry	Hanged and shot	Mob of unknown size
October 19, 1915	Unnamed	Mexican	Male	Near Brownsville	Cameron	Train-wrecking and murder	Hanged	Possibly hundreds
October 19, 1915	Unnamed	Mexican	Male	Near Brownsville	Cameron	Train-wrecking and murder	Hanged	Possibly hundreds
October 19, 1915	Unnamed	Mexican	Male	Near Brownsville	Cameron	Train-wrecking and murder	Hanged	Possibly hundreds
October 19, 1915	Unnamed	Mexican	Male	Near Brownsville	Cameron	Train-wrecking and murder	Hanged	Possibly hundreds
October 19, 1915	Unnamed	Mexican	Male	Near Brownsville	Cameron	Train-wrecking and murder	Hanged	Possibly hundreds
October 19, 1915	Unnamed	Mexican	Male	Near Brownsville	Cameron	Train-wrecking and murder	Hanged	Possibly hundreds
October 19, 1915	Unnamed	Mexican	Male	Near Brownsville	Cameron	Train-wrecking and murder	Hanged	Possibly hundreds
October 19, 1915	Jesus Ybarra	Mexican	Male	Near Brownsville	Cameron	Train-wrecking and murder	Shot and hanged	Possibly hundreds
October 19, 1915	Santiago Selis	Mexican	Male	Near Brownsville	Cameron	Train-wrecking and murder	Shot and hanged	Possibly hundreds
October 19, 1915	Trinity Ybarra	Mexican	Male	Near Brownsville	Cameron	Train-wrecking and murder	Shot	Possibly hundreds
October 19, 1915	Severo Garcia	Mexican	Male	Near Brownsville	Cameron	Train-wrecking and murder	Shot	Possibly hundreds

DATE	NAME	RACE	GENDER	CITY	COUNTY	ALLEGED CRIME	MODE OF DEATH	SIZE OF MOB
November 1, 1915	Juan Tevar	Mexican	Male	Norias	Kenedy	Outlawry	Shot	Mob of unknown size
January 24, 1916	W. J. Mayfield	White	Male	New Boston	Bowie	Murder	Hanged	25 masked men
May 5, 1916	Tom Dickson	Black	Male	Hempstead	Waller	Attacking a white girl	Hanged	Mob of unknown size
May 15, 1916	Jesse Washington	Black	Male	Waco	McLennan	Rape and murder	Burned	10,000 to 15,000
June 20, 1916	Geronimo Lerma	Mexican	Male	Near Brownwood	Brown	Murder	Shot	400
August 6, 1916	Stephen Brown	Black	Male	Seymour	Baylor	Murder of white man	Shot	Mob of unknown size
August 19, 1916	Ed Lang	Black	Male	Rice	Navarro	Attempted assault on white woman	Hanged	200
October 4, 1916	Will Spencer	Black	Male	Graceton	Upshur	Fired shots at a constable	Shot and hanged	Mob of unknown size
November 5, 1916	Joe Johnson	Black	Male	Bay City	Matagorda	Murder of white man	Hanged	50
November 28, 1916	Buck Thomas	Black	Male	Clarksville	Red River	Assault on white man and woman	Hanged	Mob of unknown size
June 22, 1917	Benjamin Harper	Black	Male	Courtney	Grimes	Drove car that killed white girl	Hanged	Mob of unknown size

Date	Name	Race	Sex	City	County	Cause	Method	Mob size
June 23, 1917	Elijah Hays	Black	Male	Reisel	McLennan	Argument with white man	Beaten with stick of stovewood	15
June 25, 1917	Chester (Henry) Sawyer	Black	Male	Galveston	Galveston	Attempted rape of white woman	Shot, stabbed, and hanged	A few men
July 3, 1917	Gilbert Guidry	Black	Male	Orange	Orange	Attempted assault	Shot	200
August 22, 1917	Charles Jones	Black	Male	Elysian Fields	Harrison	Entering the room of a white woman; attempted rape	Hanged	5
September 3, 1917	Charles Jennings	Black	Male	Beaumont	Jefferson	Cause unknown	Hanged	500
September 21, 1917	Burl Smith	Black	Male	Goose Creek (Baytown)	Harris	Attacking a white woman	Hanged	300 to 400
January 28, 1918	Longino Flores	Mexican	Male	Porvenir	Presidio	Raiding	Shot	Mob of unknown size
January 28, 1918	Alberto Garcia	Mexican	Male	Porvenir	Presidio	Raiding	Shot	Mob of unknown size
January 28, 1918	Eutimio Gonzales	Mexican	Male	Porvenir	Presidio	Raiding	Shot	Mob of unknown size
January 28, 1918	Ambrosio Hernandez	Mexican	Male	Porvenir	Presidio	Raiding	Shot	Mob of unknown size
January 28, 1918	Pedro Herrera	Mexican	Male	Porvenir	Presidio	Raiding	Shot	Mob of unknown size

DATE	NAME	RACE	GENDER	CITY	COUNTY	ALLEGED CRIME	MODE OF DEATH	SIZE OF MOB
January 28, 1918	Severiano Herrera	Mexican	Male	Porvenir	Presidio	Raiding	Shot	Mob of unknown size
January 28, 1918	Manuel Morales	Mexican	Male	Porvenir	Presidio	Raiding	Shot	Mob of unknown size
January 28, 1918	Serapio Jimenez	Mexican	Male	Porvenir	Presidio	Raiding	Shot	Mob of unknown size
January 28, 1918	Vivian Herrera	Mexican	Male	Porvenir	Presidio	Raiding	Shot	Mob of unknown size
January 28, 1918	Roman Nieves	Mexican	Male	Porvenir	Presidio	Raiding	Shot	Mob of unknown size
January 28, 1918	Juan Jimenez	Mexican	Male	Porvenir	Presidio	Raiding	Shot	Mob of unknown size
January 28, 1918	Tiburcio Jimenez	Mexican	Male	Porvenir	Presidio	Raiding	Shot	Mob of unknown Size
January 28, 1918	Macedonio Huerta	Mexican	Male	Porvenir	Presidio	Raiding	Shot	Mob of unknown size
January 28, 1918	Pedro Jimenez	Mexican	Male	Porvenir	Presidio	Raiding	Shot	Mob of unknown size
January 28, 1918	Antonio Castaneda	Mexican	Male	Porvenir	Presidio	Raiding	Shot	Mob of unknown size
May 27, 1918	Kirby Goolsbee	Black	Male	Woodville	Tyler	Attacking white girl	Likely hanged	Mob of unknown size

June 1, 1918	Sarah Cabiness (mother)	Black	Female	Phelps	Walker	Conspiracy to avenge killing of a family member by police	Shot in home and then home set on fire	Mob of unknown size
June 1, 1918	Peter Cabiness (son)	Black	Male	Phelps	Walker	Conspiracy to avenge killing of a family member by police	Shot in home and then home set on fire	Mob of unknown size
June 1, 1918	George Cabiness (son)	Black	Male	Phelps	Walker	Resisting arrest	Shot in home and then home set on fire	Mob of unknown size
June 1, 1918	Cute Cabiness (son)	Black	Male	Phelps	Walker	Conspiracy to avenge killing of a family member by police	Shot in home and then home set on fire	Mob of unknown size
June 1, 1918	Lena Cabiness (daughter)	Black	Female	Phelps	Walker	Conspiracy to avenge killing of a family member by police	Shot in home and then home set on fire	Mob of unknown size
June 1, 1918	Thomas Cabiness (son)	Black	Male	Phelps	Walker	Conspiracy to avenge killing of a family member by police	Shot in home and then home set on fire	Mob of unknown size

DATE	NAME	RACE	GENDER	CITY	COUNTY	ALLEGED CRIME	MODE OF DEATH	SIZE OF MOB
June 1, 1918	Tenola Cabiness (son)	Black	Male	Phelps	Walker	Conspiracy to avenge killing of a family member by police	Shot in home and then home set on fire	Mob of unknown size
June 4, 1918	Edward Valentine, seventeen years old	White	Male	Sanderson	Pecos	Murder	Shot	Mob of unknown size
July 27, 1918	Jim Brown	Black	Male	Ben Hur	Limestone	Entering room of white woman and burning her	Hanged	Mob of unknown size
September 18, 1918	Abe O'Neal	Black	Male	Bluff Lake	Terrell	Shooting a white man	Unknown	Unknown
November 14, 1918	Charles Shipman	Black	Male	Unknown	Fort Bend	Disagreement with white plantation owner	Unknown	Unknown
January 20, 1919	Bragg Williams	Black	Male	Hillsboro	Hill	Murder of white woman and child	Burned	Between 300 and 400 people. One estimate places the number at 7,000
May 1, 1919	Shag	Black	Male	Kilgore	Gregg	Unknown	Unknown	Mob of unknown size

Date	Name	Race	Sex	Location	County	Accusation	Method	Mob Size
June 17, 1919	Lemuel Walters	Black	Male	Longview	Gregg	White woman said she loved him and wanted to marry him; miscegenation	Shot	12 to 15
July 24, 1919	Chilton Jennings	Black	Male	Gilmer	Upshur	Attacking a white woman	Taken from jail and hanged in courthouse yard	500 people
October 21, 1919	John White	Black	Male	Crosby	Harris	Stealing a watch	Burned	Mob of unknown size
May 8, 1920	Charles Arline	Black	Male	Woodville	Tyler	Threatened to kill a white man	Flogged	40 masked men
June 30, 1920	Washington Giles	Black	Male	Damon Mound	Brazoria	Murdering deputy sheriff	Shot	250
June 30, 1920	Ezra Giles	Black	Male	Damon Mound	Brazoria	Murdering deputy sheriff	Shot	250
June 30, 1920	Jodie Gordon	Black	Male	Damon Mound	Brazoria	Aiding in escape of Giles brothers	Hanged	250
June 30, 1920	Elijah Anderson	Black	Male	Damon Mound	Brazoria	Aiding in escape of Giles brothers	Hanged	250

DATE	NAME	RACE	GENDER	CITY	COUNTY	ALLEGED CRIME	MODE OF DEATH	SIZE OF MOB
July 6, 1920	Herman Arthur	Black	Male	Paris	Lamar	Murder of two white men	Burned, tied to automobile, and dragged for hours through town, including Black portion of town	3,000
July 6, 1920	Irving Arthur	Black	Male	Paris	Lamar	Murder of two white men	Burned, tied to automobile, and dragged for hours though town, including Black portion of town	3,000
August 2, 1920	Lige Daniels	Black	Male	Center	Shelby	Killing a white woman	Hanged	1,000
September 16, 1920	Oscar Beasley	Black	Male	Angleton	Brazoria	Murder of Brazoria county sheriff	Hanged	300

Date	Name	Race	Sex	City	County	Alleged crime	Manner of death	Size of mob
December 23, 1920	Thomas W. Vickery	White	Male	Fort Worth	Tarrant	Murder of a white policeman	Hanged and then shot	Mob of unknown size
August 15, 1921	Alex Winn	Black	Male	Datura	Limestone	Assaulting a white girl	Hanged and then burned	Mob of unknown size
October 11, 1921	Wylie McNeely	Black	Male	Leesburg	Camp	Assaulting a white girl	Burned	1,000
November 20, 1921	Henry Cade	Black	Male	Sour Lake	Hardin	Assault	Hanged	300
November 30, 1921	Robert Murtore, fifteen years old	Black	Male	Ballinger	Runnels	Attacking a nine-year-old white girl	Shot	Mob of unknown size
December 11, 1921	Fred Rouse	Black	Male	Fort Worth	Tarrant	Attempted murder of two white men	Hanged	40 men
December 11, 1921	Lonnie Newsome	Black	Male	Near Gladewater	Upshur	Unknown	Hanged	Mob of unknown size
December 13, 1921	"Curly" Hackney	White	Male	Waco	McLennan	Raping a white child	Hanged	300
February 2, 1922	Manual Duarte	Mexican	Male	Brownsville	Cameron	Refused to leave	Shot	Mob of unknown size
February 10 or 11, 1922	P. Norman	Black	Male	Texarkana	Bowie	Attacking a white woman or murder of elderly person / mistaken identity	Shot	4 masked men

DATE	NAME	RACE	GENDER	CITY	COUNTY	ALLEGED CRIME	MODE OF DEATH	SIZE OF MOB
May 6, 1922	John Cornish	Black	Male	Kirvin	Freestone	Murder of white girl	Burned	500
May 6, 1922	Snap Curry	Black	Male	Kirvin	Freestone	Murder of white girl	Burned	500
May 6, 1922	Mose Jones	Black	Male	Kirvin	Freestone	Murder of white girl	Burned	500
May 6, 1922	J. H. Varney -	Black	Male	Kirvin	Freestone	Murder of a white girl	Burned	500
May 8, 1922	Tom Cornish	Black	Male	Kirvin	Freestone	Implicated in murder of white girl	Hanged	Mob of unknown size
May 8, 1922	Shattucks Green	Black	Male	Kirvin	Freestone	Implicated in murder of white girl	Hanged	Mob of unknown size
May 17, 1922	Jim Early	Black	Male	Plantersville	Grimes	Attacking a white woman	Hanged	Mob of unknown size
May 19, 1922	Hullen Owens	Black	Male	Texarkana	Bowie	Murder of white man	Shot, dragged, and burned	Mob of unknown size
May 20, 1922	Mose Brozier	Black	Male	Alleyton	Colorado	Assault on white girl	Hanged	300
May 20, 1922	Joe Winters	Black	Male	Conroe	Montgomery	Assault on white girl	Burned	Thousands

Date	Name	Race	Sex	City	County	Alleged crime	Method	Mob size
May 23, 1922	Colbert Wilson	Black	Male	Bryan	Brazos	Shooting cattle and arson	Beaten	5 or 6
May 26, 1922	Jesse Thomas	Black	Male	Waco	McLennan	Attacking a white woman	Shot and burned	Several hundred
June 23, 1922	Warren Lewis, eighteen years old	Black	Male	Near Dacus	Montgomery	Attacking a white woman	Hanged	300
September 7, 1922	O. J. Johnson	Black	Male	Newton	Newton	Murder	Hanged and shot	Mob of unknown size
September 9, 1922	Grover C. Everett	Black	Male	Abilene	Taylor	The mob robbed him	Shot	Masked mob of unknown size
November 9, 1922	Elias Villareal Zarate	Mexican	Male	Weslaco	Hidalgo	Assault	Shot	8
December 11, 1922	George Gay	Black	Male	Streetman	Freestone	Uncle of man accused of assaulting a white woman	Chained to a tree and shot multiple times	1,000
December 14, 1922	Unnamed	Black	Male	Pilot Point	Denton	Unemployment and horse theft	Unknown	Mob of unknown size
December 14, 1922	Unnamed	Black	Male	Pilot Point	Denton	Unemployment and horse theft	Unknown	Mob of unknown size
July 3, 1923	Jesse Bullock	Black	Male	Schulenburg	Fayette	Assaulting white girl	Hanged	300
June 7, 1924	William B. Smith	Black	Male	Grapeland	Houston	Attempted rape	Shot	Mob of unknown size

DATE	NAME	RACE	GENDER	CITY	COUNTY	ALLEGED CRIME	MODE OF DEATH	SIZE OF MOB
March 1926	Unnamed	White	Unknown	Unknown	Unknown	Shot	Unknown	Mob of unknown size
September 7, 1926	Matt Zaller	White	Male	Raymond-ville	Willacy	Murder	Shot	Mob of unknown size
September 7, 1926	Jose Nunez	Mexican	Male	Raymond-ville	Willacy	Murder	Shot	Mob of unknown size
September 7, 1926	Delancio Nunez	Mexican	Male	Raymond-ville	Willacy	Murder	Shot	Mob of unknown size
September 7, 1926	Cinco Gonzales	Mexican	Male	Raymond-ville	Willacy	Murder	Shot	Mob of unknown size
September 7, 1926	Tomas Nunez	Mexican	Male	Raymond-ville	Willacy	Murder	Shot	Mob of unknown size
November 10, 1926	Scott Evans	Black	Male	Katy	Fort Bend	Death for revenge of mur-der of white man	Shot and burned	5
November 10, 1926	Robert Brown	Black	Male	Katy	Fort Bend	Death for revenge of mur-der of white man	Shot and burned	5
November 10, 1926	Sally Brown	Black	Female	Katy	Fort Bend	Death for revenge of mur-der of white man	Shot and burned	5
February 1, 1927	Tom Payne	Black	Male	Willis	Van Zandt	Attempted murder of a white man	Hanged	40

Date	Name	Race	Gender	Town	County	Alleged crime	Method	Mob size
May 21, 1928	Eolis "Buddy" Evans (also appears as "Evins" in some sources)	Black	Male	Center	Shelby	Murder of a white man	Hanged	200 to 300
June 20, 1928	Robert Powell	Black	Male	Houston	Harris	Killing a detective	Taken from Jefferson Davis Hospital to bridge eight miles from Houston and hanged	8
September 16, 1928	Jose Hernandez	Mexican	Male	Malakoff	Henderson	Murder	Shot	5
September 1, 1929	Cleve Williams	Black	Male	Calvert	Robertson	Writing several notes to a white woman	Shot	Mob of unknown size
November 19, 1929	Marshall Ratliff	White	Male	Eastland	Eastland	Robbery	Hanged	1,000
May 9, 1930	George Hughes	Black	Male	Sherman	Grayson	Assaulting a white woman	Burned	Thousands
May 16, 1930	George Johnson	Black	Male	Honey Grove	Fannin	Assaulting a white woman	Hanged, shot, and burned	Several thousand
June 18, 1930	Bill Roan	Black	Male	Bryan	Brazos	Attempted assault of white woman	Shot	Mob of unknown size

DATE	NAME	RACE	GENDER	CITY	COUNTY	ALLEGED CRIME	MODE OF DEATH	SIZE OF MOB
June 28, 1930	Jack Robertson	Black	Male	Round Rock	Williamson	Shooting and seriously wounding a white man and his wife after argument over payment for work	Shot	150
December 29, 1931	Higinio Mendiola	Mexican	Male	Edinburg	Hidalgo	Murder	Hanged	7
April 1, 1932	Dave Tillis	Black	Male	Crockett	Houston	Attempted to attack a white woman	Hanged at night from a tree	4
June 10, 1933	Caldwell Washington	Black	Male	Taylor	Williamson	Assault	Hanged	Mob of unknown size
May 23, 1933	W. C. Lovell, seventeen years old	Black	Male	Four miles East of Carthage	Panola	Attacking a white woman	Shot	25
December 7, 1933	David Gregory	Black	Male	Kountze	Hardin	Murdering a white woman	Shot, then body was dragged and burned	300 to 400
June 29, 1934	John Griggs	Black	Male	Newton	Newton	Attacking a white girl	Hanged, shot, then dragged by car	200

Date	Name	Race	Gender	City	County	Accusation	Method	Mob size
November 12, 1935	Benny Mitchell, sixteen years old	Black	Male	Columbus	Colorado	Accused of killing a white nineteen-year-old girl	Hanged	700
November 12, 1935	Ernest Collins, fifteen years old	Black	Male	Columbus	Colorado	Accused of killing a white nineteen-year-old girl	Hanged	700
January 10, 1936	Gordon Walton Harris	White	Male	Bethany	Panola	Evicting Black tenants	Beaten with axes	8 African Americans
January 16, 1936	Mace Gray	Black	Male	Carthage	Panola	Running down two white girls with his car	Shot	Mob of unknown size
1937	Ernest McGowan	Black	Male	Unknown	Waller	Reporting a group of white men who had attacked him	Unknown	Mob of unknown size
July 13, 1942	William Vinson	Black	Male	Texarkana	Bowie	Assault	Hanged	15

NOTES

Introduction

1. Lauretta Holman Goodman, "Question to a Mob," in *Heralding Dawn: An Anthology of Verse by Texas Negroes*, ed. J. Mason Brewer (Dallas: Superior Typesetting Co., 1934). Lauretta Holman Goodman, an African American woman, was born in Sulphur Springs, Texas, sometime during the end of the nineteenth century. She lived there for much of her young life. Goodman and her parents moved to Texarkana, Texas, during her adolescence. By adulthood, Goodman had relocated to Dallas, Texas.

2. "Mob Takes Negro from Court House, Burns Him At Stake," *Waco Times*, May 16, 1916; Standard Certificate of Death, Texas State Board of Health, Jesse Washington, McLennan County, May 26, 1916, Vital Records, Genealogy, Dallas Public Library, Dallas, Texas.

3. "Mob Takes Negro from Court House," *Waco Times*.

4. "Mob Takes Negro from Court House," *Waco Times*; Philip Dray, *At the Hands of Persons Unknown: The Lynching of Black America* (New York: The Modern Library, 2002), 217.

5. "Mob Takes Negro From Court House," *Waco Times*; W. E. B. Du Bois, "The Waco Horror," supplement, *Crisis* 12 (July 1916), 3

6. "White Man for Crime Which Boy Was Lynched: Police Jail Husband of Dead Woman; the Soul of Jesse Washington Still Cries Out 'I Never Did It'"; "Will They Convict and Hang the Guilty Man Now That an Innocent Boy Has Been Murdered?" *Chicago Defender*, June 9, 1910.

7. Patricia Bernstein, "An 'Exciting Occurrence': The Lynching" in *Anti-Black Violence in Twentieth-Century Texas*, ed. Bruce A. Glasrud (College Station: Texas A&M Press, 2015); James M. SoRelle, "Jesse Washington Lynching," Handbook of Texas Online, http://www.tshaonline.org/handbook/online/articles/jcj01.

8. Report of Elisabeth Freeman, Papers of the NAACP, Box C-370, Manuscript Division, Library of Congress, 8; see Bernstein, "An 'Exciting Occurrence.'"

9. Report of Elisabeth Freeman, 8; see Bernstein, "An 'Exciting Occurrence.'"

10. Du Bois, "The Waco Horror," 3; Dray, *At the Hands of Persons Unknown*, 217.

11. Du Bois, "The Waco Horror," 3.

12. The terms *crowd* and *mob* underlie the concept of participation examined in this study. They are used frequently and interchangeably throughout the following pages and are specifically intended to describe and implicate those who directly or indirectly participated in lynching—from those who hoisted the dangling end of a noose; to those who lighted the funeral pyre; to the spectators who cheered or spewed lethal directives, or simply witnessed ritualized murder without making any effort to stop it.

13. Du Bois, "The Waco Horror," 3.

14. Du Bois, "The Waco Horror," 3.

15. Du Bois, "The Waco Horror," 3–4.

16. "Mob Takes Negro From Court House," *Waco Times*.

17. Report of Elisabeth Freeman, 14.

18. Du Bois, "The Waco Horror," 4.

19. Du Bois, "The Waco Horror," 4.

20. "British Suffragist Here in War on Lynching Due to Burning of Boy at Waco," *Detroit Journal*, July 21, 1916, www.elizabethfreeman.org.

21. In this study, *lynch mob* is used to describe individuals gathered at a lynching. It will be used throughout this study as a collective reference to those who directly partook in an individual's lynching as well as to spectators—those who witnessed the lynching first-hand.

22. "Mob Takes Negro From Court House," *Waco Times*.

23. National Association for the Advancement of Colored People (NAACP) Files, Administrative File, box C-370, folder—Waco. Library of Congress, Manuscript Division.

24. NAACP Files, Administrative File—Waco.

25. NAACP Files, Administrative File—Waco; "15,000 Witness Burning of Negro in Public Square," *New York World*, May 16, 1916, reprinted in Ginzburg, Ralph, *100 Years of Lynchings* (Baltimore: Black Classic Press, 1962), 103.

26. *Waco Morning News*, May 16, 1916, as quoted in SoRelle, James M., "The 'Waco Horror': The Lynching of Jesse Washington," *Southwestern Historical Quarterly* 86, no. 4 (April 1983); Hale, Grace Elizabeth, *Making Whiteness: The Culture of Segregation in the South, 1890–1940* (New York: Pantheon Books, 1998), 218; "British Suffragist Here in War on Lynching Due to Burning of Boy at Waco," *Detroit Journal*, July 21, 1916; NAACP Files, Administrative File—Waco.

27. "Mob Takes Negro From Court House," *Waco Times*; Hale, *Making Whiteness*, 218; SoRelle "The 'Waco Horror,'" 527; Dray, *At the Hands of Persons Unknown*, 217; Du Bois, "The Waco Horror," 4.

28. Report of Elisabeth Freeman, 14; NAACP Files, Administrative File, box C-370, folder—Waco.

29. "Mob Takes Negro From Court House, Burns Him At Stake," *Waco Times* 16 May 1916; "15,000 Witness Burning of Negro in Public Square," *New York World*, May 16, 1916, reprinted in Ginzburg, Ralph, *100 Years of Lynchings* (Baltimore: Black Classic Press, 1962), 103; Du Bois, "Waco Horror," 6; Agnus Warre Barnes, *Waco, Texas: A Postcard Journey* (Charleston, SC: Arcadia Publishing, 1999), 8; Wood, 77; Dora Apel, *Imagery of Lynching: Black Men, White Women, and the Mob* (New Brunswick, NJ: Rutgers University Press, 2004), 31.

30. "A Lynching and Its Sequel. Six Men Killed in the Most Approved Texas Fashion," *New York Times*, December 26, 1883; "The Trouble at McDade," *New York Times*, December 27, 1883; Elliot, Claude, "Ireland, John," *Handbook of Texas Online* (http://www.tshaonline.org/handbook/online/articles/fir01). Published by the Texas State Historical Association.

31. In his 1894 study *Southern Outrages: A Statistical Record of Lawless Doings*, R. C. O. Benjamin defined lynching as "the summary infliction of punishment by private and unauthorized citizens." The Tuskegee Institute, one of the primary

entities that documented lynchings, emphasized the violence attendant to the act; "any such violence by a mob which results in the death or maiming of the victim or victims." Writers of the Federal Anti-Lynching Bill regarded Tuskegee's definition of lynching as adequate and used it in early antilynching bills. Two components of lynching delineate it from other forms of violence: the act is pursued bereft of judicial mandates, and the act is committed by a group of persons. Cutler, James E., *Judge Lynch: An Investigation Into The History of Lynching in The United States* (London and Bombay: Longmans, Green, and Co., 1905), 10; R. C. O. Benjamin, *Southern Outrages: A Statistical Record of Lawless Doings* (Colored Lawyers National Bar Association, 1894), 14; Goldbeck, J. Helen, ed., *A Survey of the Black's Response to Lynching* (New Mexico Highlands University Medial Materials Center, 1973), 1.

32. Samuel Burdett, *A Test of Lynch Law: An Exposé of Mob Violence and the Courts of Hell*, 1901.

33. Burdett, *A Test of Lynch Law.*

34. Equal Justice Initiative, *Lynching in America: Confronting the Legacy of Racial Terror: Third Edition* (Montgomery, AL), https://lynchinginamerica.eji.org /report/. The EJI determined that 335 African Americans lost their lives to lynching in Texas between 1877 and 1950.

35. See appendix. Some lynchings doubtless remain absent from the written record due to a lack of media coverage, the secrecy of the act, and the logistical difficulty of perusing all sources that potentially contain information on lynchings in Texas. For studies that use the NAACP numbers, see Marquart et al., *The Rope, The Needle, and The Chair*; James M. SoRelle, "The 'Waco Horror': The Lynching of Jesse Washington," *Southwestern Historical Quarterly* 86, no. 4 (April 1983); Neil R. McMillen, *Dark Journey: Black Mississippians in the Age of Jim Crow* (Urbana: University of Illinois Press, 1990), 229; Mary Elizabeth Estes, *An Historical Survey of Lynchings in Oklahoma and Texas* (Master's Thesis, University of Oklahoma, 1942), 125; "Lynching, By State," Papers of the NAACP, Series A, Part 7, reel 20.

36. Untitled article, *Wheeling Daily Register* (Wheeling, WV), January 21, 1868.

37. "Spirit of the Press," *Evening Telegraph* (Philadelphia, PA), January 23, 1869.

38. "General News Items," *The Morning Star and Catholic Messenger* (New Orleans, LA), June 11, 1876; untitled article, *Fayetteville Observer* (Fayetteville, TN), June 29, 1876; untitled article, *Fairfield Herald* (Winnsboro, SC), July 5, 1876; "Miscellany," *Spirit of Democracy* (Woodsfield, OH), June 13, 1876.

39. Untitled article, *Cincinnati Daily Star*, April 22, 1878.

40. W. Fitzhugh Brundage, *Lynching in the New South: Georgia and Virginia, 1880–1930* (Urbana: University of Illinois Press, 1993), 5.

41. Brundage, *Lynching in the New South*, 5.

42. For information on the lynching of whites in Texas during the nineteenth century, see W. C. Holdes, "Law and Lawlessness on the Texas Frontier, 1875–1890," *Southwestern Historical Quarterly 44* (July 1940–April 1941), 188–203; J. L. Wilkinson, *The Trans-Cedar Lynching and the Texas Penitentiary* (New York: Carlton Press, 1974).

43. Amy Louise Wood, *Lynching and Spectacle: Witnessing Racial violence in America, 1890–1940* (Chapel Hill: University of North Carolina Press, 2009), 5.

44. Grace Elizabeth Hale, *Making Whiteness: The Culture of Segregation in the South, 1890–1940* (New York: Vintage Books, 1999); Litwack, Leon, *Without Sanctuary: Lynching Photography in America* (Santa Fe, NM: Twin Palms, 2000).
45. Brundage, *Lynching in the New South*, 13.
46. Michael J. Pfeifer, "At the Hands of Persons Unknown? The State of the Field of Lynching Scholarship," *The Journal of American History* (December 2014), 832–60.
47. Michel Foucault, *Discipline and Punish: The Birth of the Prison* 2nd ed. (New York: Vintage Books, 1995), 34–35.
48. Foucault, *Discipline and Punish: The Birth of the Prison*, 34–35.
49. Edgar Gardner Murphy, *The Basis of Ascendancy* (New York, 1909), 29–30.
50. C. Vann Woodard, *Origins of the New South, 1877–1913* (Baton Rouge: Louisiana State University Press, 1951), 155.
51. W. J. Cash, *The Mind of the South* (New York: Vintage Books, 1941), 124.
52. White, *Rope and Faggot: A Biography of Judge Lynch*, 102.
53. Woodward, *Origins of the New South, 1817–1913*, 354.
54. "The New Negro," *The Herald*, Austin, Texas, October 17, 1895.
55. See Gilmore, Glenda, *Gender and Jim Crow*; see also Williamson, Joel, *A Rage for Order*.
56. "Little Letters from the South," Wm. Cowart to Mr. Villard, Newberry, Florida, April 1, 1911, in the *Crisis* 5, 1911, 32.
57. Steven M. Gelber, *Hobbies: Leisure and The Culture of Work in America* (New York: Columbia University Press, 1999), 11.
58. Henry Louis Mencken, *Prejudices: Fourth Series* (1924), 266–67.
59. Mencken, *Prejudices*, 266–67.
60. James H. Dormon, "Shaping the Popular Images of Post-Reconstruction American Blacks: The 'Coon Song' Phenomenon of the Gilded Age," *American Quarterly 40*, no. 4 (December 1988), 450–71; J. Stanley Lemons, "Black Stereotypes as Reflected in Popular Culture, 1880–1920," *American Quarterly* 29, no. 1 (Spring 1977), 102–16; William J. Mahar, *Behind The Burnt Cork Mask: Early Blackface Minstrelsy and Antebellum American Popular Culture* (Urbana: University of Illinois Press, 1999). The depiction of Blacks in minstrelsy had undergone a shift by the late nineteenth century. Blacks were pictured as grossly disfigured beings as the popularity of minstrelsy increased. Prior to the 1880s, illustrations depicted Blacks as humans. Whereas by the end of the nineteenth century, monstrous caricatures started to dominate. Minstrel cartoons with "ugly, animal-like features" were displayed more frequently. Thus, popular culture's perception of Blacks grew less egalitarian by the late nineteenth century.
61. E. L. Godkin, "Judge Lynch As An Educator," *The Nation* 57 (1893), 222–23.
62. "Birth of Jim Crow," *Ebony*, August 1962, 110.
63. Mencken, *Prejudices*, 266–67.
64. Estes, "An Historical Survey of Lynchings in Oklahoma and Texas," 56.
65. Robert Stebbins, *Amateurs, Professionals, and Serious Leisure* (Montreal: McGill-Queen's University Press, 1992), 5.
66. In this study, *recreation* is used in reference to an activity pursued during leisure time. It will be used interchangeably at times with *leisure* when referencing an

activity pursued during nonwork hours. *Leisure* will be used both as an adjective in reference to an activity and as a noun in reference to non-work hours. The *Dictionary of Social Sciences* defines *recreation* as "any activity pursued during leisure, either individual or collective, that is free and pleasureful." For information on the interrelatedness and interchangeability of leisure and recreation, see Kaplan, 19–20; Perkins and Cushman, 71–73; Larrabee, 234–35; Owens, 61; Martin H. Neumeyer and Esther R. Neumeyer, *Leisure and Recreation: A Study of Leisure and Recreation In Their Sociological Aspects* (New York: The Ronald Press Company, 1958), 16. Neumeyer and Neumeyer note that "in an early *Oxford English Dictionary*, *leisure* is defined as 'freedom or opportunity to do something specific or implied.'"

67. Robert A. Steppins, "Choice and Experiential Definitions of Leisure," *Leisure Sciences 27* (2005), 349–52.

68. W. J. Cash, *The Mind of the South* (Vintage, 1991, first published 1941), 122; see Joel Williamson, *The Crucible of Race: Black-White Relations in the American South Since Emancipation* (New York: Oxford University Press, 1984).

69. Cash, *The Mind of the South*, 122.

70. Frantz Fanon, *Black Skins, White Masks* trans. Charles Lam Markman (New York: Grove Press, 1968), 117.

71. Fanon, *Black Skins*, 117.

72. Grace Elizabeth Hale, *Making Whiteness: The Culture of Segregation in the South, 1890–1940* (New York: Vintage Books, 1998).

73. Christopher Waldrep, "Wars of the World: The Controversy over the Definition of Lynching, 1899–1940," *The Journal of Southern History* 66, no. 1 (February 2000), 75.

74. Waldrep, "Wars of the World," 75.

75. Emmett Till Antilynching Act, Report from Committee on the Judiciary, October 31, 2019, 2; Michael A. Bellesiles, ed., *Lethal Imagination: Violence and Brutality in American History* (New York: New York University Press, 1999), 238; Christopher Waldrep, *African Americans Confront Lynching: Strategies of Resistance from the Civil War to the Civil Rights Era* (Lanham: Rowan and Littlefield, 2009), 169. For an expanded discussion of how the definition of lynching has been subject to historical variances, see Christopher Waldrep, "Wars of the World: The Controversy over the Definition of Lynching, 1899–1940," *The Journal of Southern History* 66, no. 1 (February 2000).

76. Postcard to Captain J. J. Sanders, Aldrich Collection, [AR 83-10-253B]; "Five Men Hanged at Tombstone," *Frontier Times* 5, no. 10, July 1923. For "neck-tie parties," see multiple newspaper articles, including untitled article, *Ouachita Telegraph* (Monroe, LA), January 31, 1879.

77. Postcard to Captain J. J. Sanders, Aldrich Collection, [AR 83-10-253B]; "Five Men Hanged at Tombstone," *Frontier Times* 5, no. 10, July 1923; Raper, Arthur, *Tragedy of Lynching* (Chapel Hill: University of North Carolina Press, 1933). Some Black Texans were dragged by a rope until death. For instance, Hullen Owens was dragged to death on May 19, 1922, Texarkana, Texas. "Lynchings May, 1922," Papers of the NAACP, Series A, Part 7, reel 20.

78. E. L. Godkin, "Judge Lynch As An Educator," *The Nation* (1899), 222–23.

Chapter 1

1. W. E. B. Du Bois, "The Waco Horror: A Report on Lynching," *Crisis Supplement* 12 (July 1916), 5.

2. Du Bois, "The Waco Horror," 5; SoRelle, James M., "The 'Waco Horror': The Lynching Of Jesse Washington," *Southwestern Historical Quarterly* 87, no. 4, April 1983, 527.

3. Du Bois, "The Waco Horror," 5.

4. Roy Nash to Elizabeth Freeman, Correspondence, May 16, 1916, http://www.elizabethfreeman.org/PDF/naacp/naccptltr1_3big.pdf.

5. Peg Johnson, "London 1905–1911: The Making of a Militant Suffragette," http://www.elizabethfreeman.org/london.php.

6. Roy Nash to Elizabeth Freeman, May 16, 1916.

7. Roy Nash to Elizabeth Freeman, May 16, 1916.

8. Elizabeth Freeman to her mother, January 23, 1916. Aptheker, Herbert, ed., *The Correspondence of W. E. B. Du Bois: Volume 1, Selections, 1877–1934* (Amherst: University of Massachusetts Press, 1973), 219.

9. Patricia Bernstein, *The First Waco Horror: The Lynching of Jesse Washington and the Rise of the NAACP* (College Station: Texas A&M University Press, 2005); Amanda Freudensprung, "New Life for Hamilton House: 120-year-old building becomes home for business," *Waco Tribune-Herald,* April 25, 2013.

10. Du Bois, "The Waco Horror," 7–8; *Travelers' Official Guide of the Railway and Steam Navigation Lines in the United States and Canada* (New York: National Railway Publication Co.), 579.

11. "Hanged and Burned," News release, August 11, 1905, http://www.lynchingintexas.org/items/show/66#&gid=1&pid=4.

12. "Further Details of Graceton Lynching: Squire Jones Gave Accurate Details of Affair," *Upshur Echo*, October 12, 1916, East Texas Research Center, Ralph W. Steen Library, Stephen F. Austin State University, Nacogdoches, Texas.

13. The origins of mob violence in the greater United States date back to the eighteenth-century colonial period. See W. Fitzhugh Brundage, *Lynching in the New South: Georgia and Virginia, 1880–1930* (Urbana: University of Illinois Press, 1993), introduction.

14. US Work Projects Administration, Federal Writers' Project, Library of Congress, Interview with Edward W. Riley, Sheldon F. Gauthier (interviewer), Tarrant County, Texas, Folklore Project, Life Histories, 1936–39 MSS55715: BOX A734.

15. James E. Cutler, *Judge Lynch: An Investigation into the History of Lynching in the United States* (London and Bombay: Longmans, Green, and Co), 97–98; Cora Montgomery, *Eagle Pass, Or, Life on the Border* 18 (New York: G.P. Putnam and Company, 1852), 165.

16. Cutler, *Judge Lynch,* 165; McMillen, 240.

17. Frederick Douglass, "Lynching Black People Because They Are Black," *The Christian Educator* 5, no. 3 (April 1894).

18. Robert P. Ingalls, "Lynching and Establishment Violence in Tampa, 1858–1935," *Journal of Southern History* 53, no. 4 (November 1987), 613–44, 616; Edward L. Ayers, *Vengeance and Justice: Crime and Punishment in the 19th-Century American South* (New York, 1984), 155.

19. "On Negro Ravishers," *Austin Herald*, December 8, 1894, University of Texas, Texas History Manuscript Division, Austin, Texas.

20. "On Negro Ravishers," *Austin Herald*.

21. "On Negro Ravishers," *Austin Herald*.

22. "Article 1," *Baltimore Afro-American*, October 14, 1895.

23. "Article 1," *Baltimore Afro-American*.

24. Bolton Smith, *A Philosophy of Race Relations* (Memphis: March, 1919), 11.

25. For a discussion on southerners' interpretation of law and criminal justice, see O. F. Hershey, "Lynch Law," *The Green Bag*, September 1900 (12:466).

26. Senechal de la Roche argues that "those lynched by 'mass mobs' (from fifty to several thousand people) typically were blacks of lower status accused of assaulting or killing their employers or police officers—prominent victims with close ties to many citizens. Lynchings with fewer participants might occur as well, such as those committed covertly by 'private mobs' of four or five partisans of the victim," she continues. "In these cases, the alleged offender again typically was a low-status black with few ties, but the victim was usually a low-status white who drew partisans only from a small circle of his or her relatives, friends, and neighbors." Roberta Senechal de la Roche, "Why Is Collective Violence Collective?" *Sociological Theory* 19, no. 2 (July 2001), 126–44, 131.

27. Frederick Douglass, "Lynching Black People Because They Are Black," *Christian Recorder* 5, no. 3, April 3.

28. "Lynch Law & Mob Violence," *Herald*, July 18, 1896; Bacote, Samuel William, "Who's Who Among the Colored Baptists of the United States" (Kansas City, MO: Franklin Hudson Publishing Co., 1913), 247.

29. "Special Dispatch to N.Y. Tribune," Papers of the NAACP, Series A, Part 7, Reel 20. For examples of offenses that caused one to be lynched, see Wells, Ida B., *Red Record*; White, *Rope and Faggot*, 98–99; NAACP, *Thirty Years of Lynching*, 96; untitled article, *Muskogee Cimeter* (Muskogee, Indian Territory, OK), August 17, 1905. For a complete list of accusations in Texas, see appendix. There are multiple instances of lynchings in Texas of individuals accused of race prejudice.

30. Lynching in Texas Staff, "Lynching of Charley Scott," *Lynching in Texas*, https://www.lynchingintexas.org/items/show/87.

31. Lynching in Texas Staff, "Lynching of Unknown," *Lynching in Texas*, https://www.lynchingintexas.org/items/show/862.

32. "Mob Lynch Texas Negro," *Spokane Press* (Spokane, WA), April 26, 1905.

33. "High-Minded Texans," *New York Times*, October 12, 1885.

34. "High-Minded Texans," *New York Times*.

35. "High-Minded Texans," *New York Times*.

36. "Texas - A Sheriff Led the Mob: A Hundred Germans Made to Witness a Lynching," *The Herald*, January 7, 1892.

37. "Texas - A Sheriff Led the Mob: A Hundred Germans Made to Witness a Lynching," *The Herald*; Lynching in Texas Staff, "Lynching of John White," *Lynching in Texas*, http://www.lynchingintexas.org/items/show/996.

38. Introduction, James Allen and John Littlefield, *Without Sanctuary: Photographs and Postcards of Lynching in America* (Santa Fe, NM: Twin Palms, 2000); Glenda, *Gender and Jim Crow: Women and the Politics of White Supremacy in North Carolina, 1896–1920* (Chapel Hill: University of North Carolina Press, 1995).

39. "The Dogwood Tree," postcard published by Harkrider Drug Co., Center, Texas, in Papers of the NAACP, Series A, Part 7, Reel 1; National Humanities Center, http://nationalhumanitiescenter.org/pds/maai2/politics/text5/dogwood tree.pdf.

40. "The Dogwood Tree"; "Eleven Killed in Race War: Rangers and Militia Are Called Out in Texas. Lynchings Avenge Murder," *Baltimore Afro-American,* June 27, 1908, University of Washington, Proquest Historical Newspapers.

41. *Constitution of the Republic of Texas,* General Provisions, Section 9.

42. When the legal slave trade to the United States from Africa ended in 1808, the illegal importation of slaves from the continent continued. There is evidence that an extensive importation of human cargo continued well into the antebellum era through ports situated on the Gulf of Mexico such as Galveston. The slaves were frequently sold to people in bordering areas that were a part of the United States. When discussing the importation of African slaves to the area, one smuggler noted: "I soon learned how readily, and at what profits, the Florida negroes were sold into the neighboring American States. The [coffle] . . . [would] cross the boundary into Georgia, where some of our wild Africans were mixed with various squads of native blacks, and driven inland, till sold off, singly or by couples, on the road." W. E. B. Du Bois, *The Suppression of the African Slave-trade to the United States of America, 1638–1870* (New York: Longmans, Green, and Co., 1904), 111.

43. Dale Baum, *Counterfeit Justice: The Judicial Odyssey of Texas Freedwoman Azeline Harris* (Baton Rouge: Louisiana State University Press, 2009), 38; Dwonna Goldstone, *Integrating the 40 Acres: The 50-Year Struggle for Racial Equality at the University of Texas* (Athens: University of Georgia Press, 2006), 2.

44. Walter White, *Rope and Faggot: A Biography of Judge Lynch* (Notre Dame, IN: University of Notre Dame, 2001), original publication date, 1929, 93.

45. Michael J. Pfeifer, , *The Roots of Rough Justice: Origins of American Lynching* (Urbana: University of Illinois Press, 2011), 34.

46. Pfeifer, *The Roots of Rough Justice*, 32.

47. Pfeifer, *Roots,* 33.

48. Susanna Delfino, Michele Gillespie, and Louis M Kyriakoudes, eds., *Southern Society and Its Transformations 1790–1860* (Columbia: University of Missouri Press, 2011), 59; Pfeifer, *Roots,* 20–22, 32, appendix. For information on the 1860 hangings of enslaved people, see Donald E. Reynolds, *Texas Terror: The Slave Insurrection Panic of 1860 and the Secession of the Lower South* (Baton Rouge: Louisiana State University Press, 2007).

49. Ralph A. Wooster, *Civil War Texas: a History and a Guide* (Austin: Texas State Historical Association, 1999), 1; Teresa Palomo Acosta, "Juneteenth," *Texas State Historical Association,* https://tshaonline.org/handbook/online/articles/lkj01.

50. Robert C. Conner, *General Gordon Granger: The Savior of Chickamauga and the Man Behind "Juneteenth"* (Havertown, PA: Casemate Publishers, 2013), 177; "From Texas; Important Orders by General Granger. Surrender of Senator Johnson of Arkansas. A Soattering of Rebel Forces," *New York Times,* July 7, 1865.

51. "Texas Cotton Crop, 1869," *The Texas Almanac for 1870, and Emigrant's Guide to Texas* (January 1870), 96.

52. "Texas Cotton Crop, 1869," *The Texas Almanac for 1870, and Emigrant's Guide to Texas*, 96.

53. David A. Williams, *Bricks without Straw: A Comprehensive History of African Americans in Texas* (Austin, TX: Eakin Press, 1997), chapter 3.

54. Ida B. Wells, "The Case Stated, 1895," in Waldrep, Christopher, ed., *Lynching in America: A History in Documents* (New York: New York University Press, 2006), 4.

55. Letter from Hopkins County, Records of the Assistant Commissioner for the State of Texas Bureau of Refugees, Freedmen and Abandoned Lands, 1865 – 1869 (Washington, DC: National Archives Microfilm Publication), M821, Roll 32, as quoted in Equal Justice Initiative, "Reconstruction in America: Racial Violence after the Civil War, 1865–1876" (2020).

56. Letter from Hopkins County, M821, Roll 32.

57. James W. Marquart, Sheldon Ekland-Olson, and Jonathan R. Sorensen, *The Rope, The Chair, and the Needle: Capital Punishment in Texas, 1923–1990* (Austin: University of Texas Press, 1994), 3; "Slavery," *The Handbook of Texas*, Texas State Historical Association: A Digital Gateway to Texas History, https://www.tsha online.org/handbook/online/articles/yps01; "Lynching," *The Handbook of Texas*, Texas State Historical Association: A Digital Gateway to Texas History, http://www.tshaonline.org/handbook/online/articles/jgl01.

58. "Burning of Texas Negro," *El Paso Morning News*, August 4, 1915, in NAACP Papers, Series A, Part 7, Reel 1.

59. Lynching in Texas Staff, "Lynching of James Hodges," *Lynching in Texas*, http://www.lynchingintexas.org/items/show/274.

60. White, *Rope and Faggot: A Biography of Judge Lynch*, 89.

61. See appendix for a chronological list of lynchings and crimes of the accused in Texas.

62. "Young Negro Lynched by Big Mob in Texas: Man Accused of Attacking Girl Is Taken From Sheriff, Tied to Tree and Shot Dead," *New York Times,* December 12, 1922; NAACP, "Lynching Record for 1922," Papers of the NAACP, Series A, Part 7, reel 20; Marquart, Ekland-Olson, and Sorensen, *The Rope, The Chair, and the Needle*, 3; "Texas Citizens Burn Negro After He Writes Confession," *Birmingham Age-Herald*, May 26, 1912.

63. The Grangers often encouraged Blacks to stay with their former masters.

64. See Records of Subassistant Commissioner of the 40th District, Bureau of Refugees, Freedman, and Abandoned Lands *United States Bureaus of Refugees, Freedmen, and Abandoned Lands,* reels 6–7, on file at Dallas Public Library, Dallas, Texas; see Marsha Prior and Terry Anne Schulte, "Where Dignity Lives: Freedman's Town/North Dallas," in Peter, Duane E., et al., *Freedman's Cemetery: A Legacy of A Pioneer Black Community in Dallas, Texas* (Austin: Texas Department of Transportation, Environmental Affairs Division, Archeology Studies Program, Report No. 21, 2000); "The Freedman's Bureau," The Freedman's Bureau Online: Records of the Bureau of Refugees, Freedmen and Abandoned Lands.

65. "Report to Bureau from W. H. Horton," December 6, 1867, United States Bureau of Refugees, Freedmen, and Abandoned Lands, Texas/Dallas History and Archives Division, Dallas Public Library; Prior and Schulte, "Where Dignity Lives: Freedman's Town/North Dallas," 65.

66. Prior and Schulte, "Where Dignity Lives: Freedman's Town/North Dallas," 65.

67. "Letter from W. H. Horton to Lieutenant Kirkman, Acting Assistant Adjutant General," August 26, 1867, M821, Reel 21. United States Bureau of Refugees, Freedmen, and Abandoned Lands; Prior and Schulte, "Where Dignity Lives: Freedman's Town/North Dallas," 66.

68. Prior and Schulte, "Where Dignity Lives: Freedman's Town/North Dallas," 66.

69. Prior and Schulte, "Where Dignity Lives: Freedman's Town/North Dallas," 66.

70. Prior and Schulte, "Where Dignity Lives: Freedman's Town/North Dallas," 66; Report of the Special Committee on Lawlessness and Violence in Texas, 7, http://babel.hathitrust.org/cgi/pt?id=mdp.35112105037875;view=1up;seq=7 made available in electronic form by the University of Michigan Law School.

71. Texas, Constitutional Convention, *Report of the Special Committee on Lawlessness and Violence in Texas* (Austin: Printed at the office of the Daily Republican, 1868), 7; Kenneth W. Howell, *Still the Arena of Civil War: Violence and Turmoil in Reconstruction Texas, 1865–1874* (Denton, TX: University of North Texas Press, 2012), 2.

72. *Report of the Special Committee on Lawlessness and Violence in Texas*, 5.

73. *Report of the Special Committee on Lawlessness and Violence in Texas*, 5.

74. *Report of the Special Committee on Lawlessness and Violence in Texas*, 5.

75. "Lynching," *The New Handbook of Texas* 4 (Austin: Texas Historical Association, 1996), 346–47.

76. *Report of the Special Committee on Lawlessness and Violence in Texas*, 5.

77. *Report of the Special Committee on Lawlessness and Violence in Texas*, 5, 9.

78. *Report of the Special Committee on Lawlessness and Violence in Texas*, 5, 9; "How He Escaped Lynching," *New York Times*, December 5, 1885.

79. *Report on the Special Committee of on Lawlessness and Violence in Texas*, 9.

80. *Report on the Special Committee of on Lawlessness and Violence in Texas*, 9.

81. *Report on the Special Committee of on Lawlessness and Violence in Texas*, 9.

82. *Report on the Special Committee of on Lawlessness and Violence in Texas*, 10.

83. *Report on the Special Committee of on Lawlessness and Violence in Texas*, 10.

84. "Slayer of White Woman Dies in Auto," *Santa Cruz Sentinel* (Santa Cruz, CA), December 7, 1933, from Lynching in Texas Staff, "Lynching of David Gregory," *Lynching in Texas*, http://www.lynchingintexas.org/items/show/510.

85. News clipping attached to letter addressed to Franklin D. Roosevelt, December 25, 1933, Department of Justice Central Files, Straight Numerical Files, RG 60, Box 1278.

86. W. E. King, owner of the *Dallas Express*, proudly displayed his partisan affiliation by printing "The Republican Party Is The Ship, All Else Is The Sea—Frederick Douglas," across the front page of issues of his newspaper by 1900; "Col. W. E. King Passes," August 22, 1919; Margot, 17; Hall, Josie Briggs, *Hall's Moral and Mental Capsule* (Dallas: Reverend R. S. Jenkins, Publisher, 1905), 198.

87. Mark Odintz, "Brazos County," *Handbook of Texas Online*, http://www.tsha online.org/handbook/online/articles/hcb13.

88. Cynthia Skove Nevels, *Lynching to Belong: Claiming Whiteness Through Racial Violence* (College Station: Texas A&M University Press, 2009), 17–19; Dale Baum, "A Statute on the Texas A&M University Campus to a Former Slave?", originally published in *The Touchstone: Alternative Views for Brazos River Valley*,

summer 1994, http://www.tamu.edu/faculty/gaines/sb276.html, http://www
.tshaonline.org/handbook/online/articles/hcb13

89. Barry A. Crouch, *The Freedman's Bureau and Black Texans* (Austin: University of Texas Press, 1999), 107; Nevels, *Lynching to Belong*, 19.

90. Nevels, *Lynching to Belong*, 19–21; Crouch, *The Freedman's Bureau*, 103.

91. Joel Williamson, *The Crucible of Race: Black-White Relations in the South Since Emancipation* (New York: Oxford University Press, 1984), 44.

92. White, *Rope and Faggot: A Biography of Judge Lynch*, 96.

93. "Brute's Crime; A Mob's Vengeance: Judge Lynch Takes Possession of the Court House and Deals Out Justice to Allen Brooks," *Dallas Daily Times Herald*, March 3, 1910.

94. "Brute's Crime; A Mob's Vengeance: Judge Lynch Takes Possession of the Court House and Deals Out Justice to Allen Brooks," *Dallas Daily Times Herald*.

95. "Brute's Crime; A Mob's Vengeance: Judge Lynch Takes Possession of the Court House and Deals Out Justice to Allen Brooks," *Dallas Daily Times Herald*; "Dallas Mob Hangs Negro From Pole At Elks' Arch: Fights Way Into Court Room and Takes Allen Brooks from Armed Officers," *Dallas Morning News*, March 4, 1910, http://photographyblog.dallasnews.com/2013/03/today-in -dallas-photo-history-1910-allen-brooks-lynched-in-downtown-dallas-by -angry-mob.html/; "Brute's Crime: A Mob's Vengeance," *Dallas Times Herald*, March 3, 1910.

96. "Brute's Crime; A Mob's Vengeance: Judge Lynch Takes Possession of the Court House and Deals Out Justice to Allen Brooks," *Dallas Daily Times Herald*; "Dallas Mob Hangs Negro From Pole At Elks' Arch: Fights Way Into Court Room and Takes Allen Brooks from Armed Officers," *Dallas Morning News*.

97. "Brute's Crime; A Mob's Vengeance: Judge Lynch Takes Possession of the Court House and Deals Out Justice to Allen Brooks," *Dallas Daily Times Herald*; "Dallas Mob Hangs Negro From Pole At Elks' Arch: Fights Way Into Court Room and Takes Allen Brooks from Armed Officers," *Dallas Morning News*; "Dallas Mob Hangs Negro From Pole At Elks' Arch: Fights Way Into Court Room and Takes Allen Brooks from Armed Officers," *Dallas Morning News*, March 4, 1910. http://photographyblog.dallasnews.com/2013/03/today-in -dallas-photo-history-1910-allen-brooks-lynched-in-downtown-dallas-by -angry-mob.html/.

98. "The Texas Vigilantes: A Later Account of the Orange Excitement—Outrages By the 'Hoodlums,'" *New York Times*, September 3, 1881; "Three Negroes Lynched in Texas," *New York Times*, November 18, 1900.

99. "Judge Lynch Holds Court," *Dallas Daily Times Herald*, March 3, 1910.

100. "Judge Lynch Holds Court," *Dallas Daily Times Herald*.

101. "Judge Lynch Holds Court," *Dallas Daily Times Herald*.

102. "Condemn the Law—Not the Courts, By E. G. Senter," *Daily Times*.

103. "Condemn the Law—Not the Courts, By E. G. Senter," *Daily Times*.

104. "Condemn the Law—Not the Courts, By E. G. Senter," *Daily Times*.

105. "Mob Probe Has Started: Grand Jury at Work on Lynching Case," *Dallas Daily Times Herald*, March 10, 1910.

106. "Negro Is Lynched By Parties Unknown," *Galveston Daily*, June 26, 1917, Southern Methodist University, Dallas, Texas.

107. "Texans Lynch A White Man: Had Been Tried for Murder and Acquitted—Was Hanged to a Pole in Port Arthur," *New York Times*, February 12, 1900; "White Men Lynched in Texas: Mob in Henderson County Kills Three Farmers Accused of Having Aided a Murderer to Escape," *New York Times*, May 26, 1899; *Thirty Years of Lynching*, 97.

108. Bureau of Vital Statistics, Standard Death Certificate, July 24, 1919. Texas State Board of Health.

109. Chronological List of Lynchings, NAACP papers Series A, Part 7, reel 18 (*The Poledo Pioneer*, May 3, 1920); Allen Turner, "Hate Crime Killer Executed," *Houston Chronicle*, September 21, 2011.

110. "The Negro Calhoun Lynched," *Austin Weekly Statesman*, April 18, 1895.

111. "Texas Prosecutor Condones Lynching: Callas Hanging of Two Negroes at Columbus 'Expression of People's Will,'" *New York Times*, 1935. Papers of the NAACP, Reel 18, Series A.

112. "Texas Prosecutor Condones Lynching: Callas Hanging of Two Negroes at Columbus 'Expression of People's Will,'" *New York Times*.

113. "Texas Prosecutor Condones Lynching: Callas Hanging of Two Negroes at Columbus 'Expression of People's Will,'" *New York Times*.

114. "Mob Burns Negro At Temple in View of 10,000 People," *Waco Morning News*, July 31, 1915, from Lynching in Texas Staff, "Lynching of Will Stanley," *Lynching in Texas*.

115. "The Burden," *Crisis* 11, no. 3 (January 1916), 145.

116. "Burned at the Stake," *The Marshall Messenger*, August 3, 1915, from Lynching in Texas Staff, "Lynching of Will Stanley," *Lynching in Texas*.

117. "Burned at the Stake," *The Marshall Messenger*.

118. "Mob Burns Negro at Temple in View of 10,000 People," *Waco Morning News*, July 31, 1915, from Lynching in Texas Staff, "Lynching of Will Stanley," *Lynching in Texas*. http://www.lynchingintexas.org/items/show/736.

119. "The Burden," *Crisis* 11, no. 3 (January 1916), 145; "Negro Will Stanley Burned At Stake By Frenzied Bell County Mob—Negro Confesses As Accessory," *The Daily Courier Gazette,* July 31, 1915, from Lynching in Texas Staff, "Lynching of Will Stanley," *Lynching in Texas*. http://www.lynchingin texas.org/items/show/736.

120. "Tragedy of Temple Now Old History: General Verdict Is Guilty Negro Met His Fate—Three Funeral Held," *Dallas Daily Times Herald*, August 1, 1915, Dallas, Texas.

121. "Tragedy of Temple Now Old History: General Verdict Is Guilty Negro Met His Fate—Three Funeral Held," *Dallas Daily Times Herald*.

122. "Is A Closed Incident," *The Cameron Herald*, August 12, 1915, from Lynching in Texas Staff, "Lynching of Will Stanley," *Lynching in Texas*. http://www .lynchingintexas.org/items/show/736.

123. "Is A Closed Incident," *The Cameron Herald*, August 12, 1915, from Lynching in Texas Staff, "Lynching of Will Stanley," *Lynching in Texas*.

124. For examples of white reporters in Texas who condemned lynchers, see "Go the Whole Way of Law Against The Lyncher," *San Antonio Express,* 24 January 1919. The *San Antonio Express* regularly printed articles that condemned the act of lynching; "Lynchers Must Go," *San Antonio Inquirer,* August 18, 1918; untitled newspaper article, *Goliad Guard,* February 3, 1893. No instances were found in

which a local newspaper reporter criticized a lynching that occurred in his or her town.

125. News Release, "N.A.A.C.P. Writes U. S. Senators On Kirvin [sic], Texas, Burning At Stake," May 12, 1922, Papers of the NAACP, Series A, Part 7, reel 20; News Release, "Ask Federal Troops In Texas Race Riots," 5 June 1922, Papers of the NAACP, Series A, Part 7, reel 20; "Finds Triple-Lynching Victims Were Probably Innocent," *New York World*, January 2, 1923, article reprinted in Ginzburg, Ralph, *100 Years of Lynching* (Baltimore: Black Classic Press, 1962), 164.

126. "A. W. Hodde to Warren G. Harding, August 20, 1921, Department of Justice Files, Box 3605, National Archives, College Park, Maryland; "Freestone Mob Takes Vengeance for Girl's Life," *Austin Statesmen*, 22 May 1922, University of Texas; "2 Lynched As Warning To All Nigger Loafers," *Pittsburg American*, December 29, 1922, article reprinted in Ginzburg, *100 Years of Lynching*, 167–68.

127. "2 Lynched As Warning To All Nigger Loafers," *Pittsburg American*, December 29, 1922, article reprinted in Ginzburg, *100 Years of Lynching*, 164, 167–68; Monte Akers, *Flames After Midnight: Murder, Vengeance, and the Desolation of a Texas Community, Revised Edition* (Austin: University of Texas Press, 1999), 112; News Release, "N.A.A.C.P. Writes U. S. Senators On Kirvin [sic], Texas, Burning At Stake," May 12, 1922, Papers of the NAACP, Series A, Part 7, reel 20; "Mob Burns Three Negroes at Dawn of Day Kirvin," *Dallas Morning News*, May 7, 1922; "Finds Triple-Lynching Victims Were Probably Innocent," *New York World*, January 2, 1923, article reprinted in Ginzburg, *100 Years of Lynching*, 164. For a comprehensive examination of the 1922 Kirvin lynchings, see Akers, *Flames After Midnight: Murder, Vengeance, and the Desolation of a Texas Community, Revised Edition* (Austin: University of Texas Press, 1999).

Chapter 2

1. Morrison & Fourmy, Morrison & Fourmy's General Directory of the City of Galveston: 1895–1896, book, 1895/1896, Houston, Texas, texashistory.unt.edu /ark:/67531/metapth894034/, University of North Texas Libraries, The Portal to Texas History, texashistory.unt.edu, crediting Rosenberg Library, 174; "The Week's Weather: Meteorological Conditions Which Obtained Throughout the State of Texas," *The Galveston Daily News*, November 23, 1895.

2. "5 O'Clock Extra in Public Square: A Texas Negro Burned," *Lowell Daily Sun* (Massachusetts), October 30, 1895; "A Negro Burned at the Stake," *London Standard*, October 31, 1895.

3. NAACP, *Thirty Years of Lynching in the United States, 1889–1918* (New York: Negro Universities Press, 1919), 12; "Lynchings," Papers of the NAACP, Series A, Part 7, reel 18.

4. NAACP, *Thirty Years of Lynching in the United States, 1889–1918*, 12.

5. "The Subject of a Mass Meeting Last Night," *The Herald*, November 23, 1895; "General News," *Afro-American*, November 2, 1895.

6. "The Subject of a Mass Meeting Last Night," *The Herald*; "Twelfth Census of the United States," Schedule No. 1—Population, Galveston County, Texas, 1900: 186; Boudreaux, Tommie D., and Alice M. Gatson, *African Americans of*

Galveston (Charleston, SC: Arcadia Publishing, 2013), 7; "Bad Negro Lynched," *Galveston Daily News*, April 13, 1895; "Breckenridge & Scruggs," Stereographs, Call No.: Lot 11782, Prints and Photographs Division, Library of Congress, Washington DC; Lynching in Texas Staff, "Lynching of Robert Henson Hilliard," *Lynching in Texas*, http://www.lynchingintexas.org/items/show/355.

7. "Assassinated," *Temple Times,* August 9, 1895; "Twelfth Census of the United States," Schedule No. 1—Population, Galveston County, Texas, 1900, 186; see appendix for additional information on the lynching of Black women.

8. "The Subject of a Mass Meeting Last Night," *The Herald*, 1895.

9. "The Subject of a Mass Meeting Last Night," *The Herald*.

10. "The Subject of a Mass Meeting Last Night," *The Herald*.

11. "The Subject of a Mass Meeting Last Night," *The Herald*.

12. Travis L. Summerlin, "Cranfill, James Britton Buchanan Boone," Handbook of Texas Online, http://www.tshaonline.org/handbook/online/articles/fcr07.

13. Stephen J. Leonard, *Lynching in Colorado, 1859–1919* (Boulder: University Press of Colorado, 2002), 138

14. Untitled article, *State Republican* (Jefferson City, MO), April 27, 1893.

15. Untitled article, *Chariton Courier* (Keytesville, MO), June 22, 1894.

16. "The Texas Method," *The Record-Union* (Sacramento, CA), May 7, 1899.

17. "The Texas Method," *The Record-Union*.

18. According to research done for this project, there were not incidents of the burning of a white person by mob.

19. Randolph B. Campbell, *The Laws of Slavery in Texas: Historical Documents* (Austin: University of Texas Press, 2010), 63.

20. Untitled article, *Fort Worth Democrat* (Fort Worth, TX), March 4, 1876.

21. "On Negro Ravishers," *The Austin Herald* (Austin, TX), December 8, 1894, University of Texas, History Manuscript Division.

22. "On Negro Ravishers," *The Austin Herald*.

23. "On Negro Ravishers," *The Austin Herald*.

24. Newspaper clipping from anonymous sender, Jessie Daniel Ames, 1866–1972, Folder 15: Newspaper clippings, 1926–1954, Louis Round Wilson Special Collections Library, University of North Carolina.

25. Newspaper clipping from anonymous sender, Jessie Daniel Ames, 1866–1972, Folder 15.

26. "The Subject of a Mass Meeting Last Night," *Herald*.

27. "Young Negro Lynched by Big Mob in Texas," *New York Times*, December 12, 1922.

28. Burdett, *A Test of Lynch Law*, 33.

29. Burdett, *A Test of Lynch Law*, 33.

30. Frederick Douglass, "Lynching Black People Because They Are Black," *Christian Educator*, April 1894, 105.

31. Frederick Douglass, "Lynching Black People Because They Are Black," 105.

32. Frederick Douglass, "Lynching Black People Because They Are Black," 105.

33. "The Monster Lynched: Hanging of Mrs. Heitmiller's Negro Ravisher," *Austin American Statesman*, August 5, 1886, from Lynching in Texas Staff, "Lynching of Bill Harris," *Lynching in Texas*, http://www.lynchingintexas.org/items/show/587.

34. "The Monster Lynched: Hanging of Mrs. Heitmiller's Negro Ravisher," *Austin*

American Statesman, August 5, 1886, from Lynching in Texas Staff, "Lynching of Bill Harris," *Lynching in Texas*, http://www.lynchingintexas.org/items/show/587.

35. Lynching in Texas Staff, "Lynching of Alex Winn," *Lynching in Texas*, http://www.lynchingintexas.org/items/show/441.

36. "Special to the News," *Galveston Daily News*, May 23, 1902.

37. Papers of the NAACP as quoted in *St. Louis Post-Dispatch*, 1912.

38. Papers of the NAACP as quoted in *St. Louis Post-Dispatch*, 1912.

39. Papers of the NAACP as quoted in *St. Louis Post-Dispatch*, 1912; "Negro Burned by Tyler Mob," *The Daily Advocate* (Victoria), May 27, 1912; "2,000 Aid in Burning Negro at the Stake," *New York Times*, May 26, 1912; "Tyler Citizens Burn a Negro," *The Crosbyton Review* (Crosbyton, TX), May 30, 1912.

40. "Our Ellis County Citizens Protect Their Homes," *The Waxahachie Daily Light* (Waxahachie, TX), September 8, 1905.

41. "Negro is Burned at the Stake," *Evening-Times Republican* (Marshalltown, IA), September 8, 1905.

42. "Texas Negro Burned at Stake—Usual Crime," *The Pensacola Journal* (Pensacola, FL), September 8, 1905; "Men, Women, and Children Burn Negro Fiend," *Trenton Times*, September 8, 1905.

43. "Men, Women, Children Burn Negro Fiend," *Trenton Times*, September 8, 1905; "Dead Negro's Boy Burned at Belton," *Galveston Daily News*, July 23, 1910.

44. See appendix for a comprehensive list of how the victims of lynch mobs were killed in Texas.

45. Foucault, Michel, *Discipline and Punish: The Birth of the Prison* (Vintage Books: 2nd edition, 1995), 34.

46. "Negro Murderer Burned: The Fiend Who Outraged and Murdered a Young Woman Caught, and His Captors Burn Him. He Dies Like a Stoic," *Bonham News* (Bonham, TX), August 23, 1901.

47. "Negro Murderer Burned: The Fiend Who Outraged and Murdered a Young Woman Caught, and His Captors Burn Him. He Dies Like a Stoic," *Bonham News*, August 23, 1901.

48. "Abe Wilder Caught, Confessed and Burned," *The Schulenburg Sticker* (Schulenburg, TX), August 29, 1901.

49. "Abe Wilder Caught, Confessed and Burned," *The Schulenburg Sticker*, August 29, 1901.

50. "Abe Wilder Caught, Confessed and Burned," *The Schulenburg Sticker*, August 29, 1901; "Black Brute Pays Awful Penalty for Dastardly Assault," *Abilene Semi-Weekly Farm Reporter*, July 29, 1908, Lynching in Texas Staff, "Lynching of Ted Smith," *Lynching in Texas*, https://www.lynchingintexas.org/items/show/548; News Release, "N.A.A.C.P. Writes U. S. Senators On Kirvin [sic], Texas, Burning At Stake," 12 May 1922, Papers of the NAACP, Series A, Part 7, reel 20; "Record of Bloody May," *Austin American Statesman*, June 1922; "Vengeance," May 6, 1922. W. E. B. Du Bois Papers (MS 312). Special Collections and University Archives, University of Massachusetts Amherst Libraries. For a comprehensive examination of the 1922 Kirvin lynchings, see Akers, *Flames After Midnight*.

51. "Signs Announce Texas Burning: Lynching Advertised Hours Before Victims Arrived With Sheriff," *Chicago Defender*, July 17, 1920.

52. "How Arthur Boys Were Lynched and Three Young Sisters Raped," *New York Age*, September 4, 1920.

53. "Sisters Raped by Twenty White Men: Inside Facts About Lynching in Paris, Texas, Told by a Letter to National Association. BROTHERS LYNCHED Bodies Burned and Dragged Through Streets of Colored Section," *Baltimore Afro American*, September 10, 1920; Foucault, 38–39, 164; "Signs Announce Texas Burning: Lynching Advertised Hours Before Victims Arrived with Sheriff," *Chicago Defender*, July 17, 1920; "How Arthur Boys Were Lynched and Three Young Sisters Raped," *New York Age*, September 4, 1920; "Armed Men Patrol Paris, Texas," *Austin American Statesman*, July 7, 1920.

54. Linda O. McMurray, *To Keep the Waters Troubled: The Life of Ida B. Wells* (Oxford: Oxford University Press, 1998), 201; Dan Monroe and Bruce Tap, *Shapers of the Great Debate on the Civil War: A Biographical Dictionary* (Westport, CT: Greenwood Press, 2005), 91.

55. McMurray, *To Keep the Waters Troubled*, 201.

56. Ruth A. Rouff, *Ida B. Wells: A Woman of Courage* (West Berlin, NJ: Townsend Press, 2010), 52.

57. Rouff, *Ida B. Wells*, 52.

58. Ida B. Wells, *The Red Record: Tabulated Statistics and Alleged Causes of Lynching in the United States* (Chicago: Donohue & Menneberry, 1895).

59. According to research done for this project, there were not incidents of the burning of a white person by mob.

60. "Robinson Found Alive," *Mineola Monitor*, March 30, 1889; Winegarten, *Black Texas Women: A Source Book* (Austin: University of Texas Press, 1996), 68; Ida B. Wells, "Lynch Law in All Its Phases," Speech, Tremont Temple, Boston, February 13, 1893; Shechter, Patricia, *Ida B. Wells-Barnett: An American Reform, 1880–1930*.

61. Wells, *The Red Record*, chapter 3.

62. "The Fearful Retribution," *Taylor County News* (Abilene, TX), February 10, 1893.

63. Wells, *The Red Record*, chapter 3.

64. "The Fearful Retribution," *Taylor County News*.

65. "The Great American Mania and Its Cause," *Galveston Daily News*, April 1, 1893; Blum, Edward J. and W. Scott Poole, eds., *Vale of Tears: New Essays on Religion and Reconstruction* (Macon: Mercer University Press, 2005), 50; Dray, *At the Hands of Persons Unknown*, 77.

66. Atticus Haygood, "The Burning of Negroes," *Public Opinion* 14, nos. 1, 2.

67. Haygood, "The Burning of Negroes," 2; Some secondary sources written about the Henry Smith lynching indicate that Myrtle Vance was four years old at the time of her death. This is incorrect. Her headstone indicates that she was three years old.

68. White, *Rope and Faggot: A Biography of Judge Lynch*, 89.

69. Rosie Cuison Villazor and Kevin Noble Malliard, *Loving v. Virginia in a Post-Racial World: Rethinking Race, Sex, and Marriage* (Cambridge: Cambridge University Press, 2012), 39.

70. Wells, *The Red Record: Tabulated Statistics and Alleged Causes of Lynching in the United States* (Chicago: Donohue & Menneberry, 1895); "Burned At the Stake: A Black Man Pays for a Town's Outrage," *New York Sun*, 2 February 1893.

Reprinted in Gilbert Osofsky, *The Burden of Race: A Documentary History of Negro-White Relations in America* (New York: Harper and Row, 1967), 181–84, http://historymatters.gmu.edu/d/5487/.

71. Wells, *The Red Record*, 29; Dray, *At the Hands of Persons Unknown*, 77; see E. R. Bills, *Black Holocaust: The Paris Horror and a Legacy of Texas Terror* (Fort Worth: Eakin Press, 2015).

72. Wells, *The Red Record*, 31.

73. Osofsky, *The Burden of Race*, 181–84.

74. Vance, *The Facts in the Case*, 58.

75. Vance, *The Facts in the Case*, 22.

76. Osofsky, *The Burden of Race*, 181–84; Vance, *The Facts in the Case*, 15, 19, 74.

77. Vance, *The Facts in the Case*, 23–24.

78. Osofsky, *The Burden of Race*, 181–84.

79. B. O. Flower, "The Burning of Negroes in the South: A Protest and a Warning," *The Arena* 7, no. 41 (April 1893), 634.

80. Wells, *The Red Record*, 35.

81. Wells, *The Red Record*, 35.

82. Wells, *The Red Record*, 35.

83. Vance, *The Facts in the Case*, 60.

84. Editorial, "The Texas Holocaust," *Christian Recorder*, February 16, 1893, African American Newspapers Collection.

85. Flower, "The Burning of Negroes in the South," 637.

86. Flower, "The Burning of Negroes in the South," 637.

87. "Gov. Hogg Aroused," *New York Times*, February 3, 1893; Vance, *The Facts in the Case*, 75.

88. "Gov. Hogg Aroused," *New York Times*.

89. "Gov. Hogg Aroused," *New York Times*.

90. "Gov. Hogg Aroused," *New York Times*.

91. "Gov. Hogg Aroused," *New York Times*.

92. Vance, *The Facts in the Case*, 68.

93. Wells, *The Red Record*, 17.

94. Dray, *At the Hands of Persons Unknown*, 79; NAACP, *Thirty Years of Lynching*.

95. Telegram from Sheriff W. D. Robinson to Governor Joseph D. Sayers, March 8, 1901, Papers of Governor J. D. Sayers, 1901, Texas State Archives, Austin, Texas.

96. Telegram from Sheriff W. D. Robinson to Governor Joseph D. Sayers, March 8, 1901, Papers of Governor J. D. Sayers, 1901, Texas State Archives, Austin, Texas.

97. Telegram from Governor Joseph D. Sayers to Sheriff W. D. Robinson, March 8, 1901, Papers of Governor J. D. Sayers, 1901, Texas State Archives, Austin, Texas.

98. Telegram from Governor Joseph D. Sayers to Sheriff W. D. Robinson, March 8, 1901.

99. Telegram from County Attorney Luther W. Johnson to Governor Joseph D. Sayers, March 9, 1901, Papers of Governor J. D. Sayers, Texas State Archives, Austin, Texas.

100. Telegram from County Attorney Luther W. Johnson and Sheriff W. D. Robinson to Governor Joseph D. Sayers, March 9, 1901, Papers of Governor J. D. Sayers, 1901.

101. Letter from citizens of Corsicana to Sheriff W. D. Robinson, March 8, 1901, Papers of Governor J. D. Sayers, 1901.

102. Telegram from Sheriff W. D. Robinson to Governor Joseph D. Sayers, March 11, 1901, Papers of Governor J. D. Sayers, 1901.

103. Telegram from Governor Joseph D. Sayers to Sheriff W. D. Robinson, March 11, 1901, Papers of Governor J. D. Sayers, 1901.

104. Telegram from Governor Joseph D. Sayers to Sheriff W. D. Robinson, March 11, 1901.

105. Telegram from Sheriff W. D. Robinson and County Attorney Luther A. Johnson to Governor Joseph D. Sayers, March 11, 1901, Papers of Governor J. D. Sayers, 1901.

106. Telegram from S. W. Johnson, Mayor, S. A. Peace, A. Fergesson, M. Kenner, G. W. Hardy to Governor Joseph D. Sayers, March 11, 1901, Papers of Governor J. D. Sayers, 1901.

107. Telegram from S. W. Johnson, Mayor, S. A. Peace, A. Fergesson, M. Kenner, G. W. Hardy to Governor Joseph D. Sayers, March 11, 1901.

108. Telegram from Governor Joseph Sayers to S. W. Johnson, S. A. Peace, et al., March 11, 1901.

109. Telegram from S. W. Johnson, S. A. Peace, et al. to Governor Joseph Sayers, March 11, 1901.

110. Telegram from District Attorney O. C. Kirvin to Governor Joseph Sayers, March 12, 1901.

111. Telegram from Governor Joseph Sayers to District Attorney O. C. Kirvin, March 12, 1901; telegram from District Attorney O. C. Kirvin to Governor Joseph Sayers, March 12, 1901; "Mob Got Him," *Daily Times Herald*, March 13, 1901.

112. C. C. Weaver, Mayor of Itasca, to J. D. Sayers, Governor of Texas, March 13, 1901, Papers of Governor J. D. Sayers, 301–189, March 10–15, 1901, Texas State Archives, Austin, Texas.

113. C. C. Weaver, Mayor of Itasca, to J. D. Sayers, Governor of Texas, March 13, 1901.

114. C. C. Weaver, Mayor of Itasca, to J. D. Sayers, Governor of Texas, March 13, 1901; "Texas Lynchers Defiant: No Effort to Punish Men Who Burned the Negro Henderson, Although Governor Has Full Power," *New York Times*, March 15, 1901; Photograph of John Henderson's lynching, Texas/Dallas History and Archives Division, Dallas Public Library; "The Corsicana Negro Burned at the Stake," *Daily Times Herald* (Dallas, TX), March 13, 1901; "Burned at the Stake," *Bonham News*, March 15, 1901; "The Corsicana Negro Burned at the Stake," *Daily Times Herald* (Dallas, TX), March 13, 1901; "Fate Of Negro Brute At Hands Of A Mob: Further Details of the Death of John Henderson at Corsicana, Texas," *Bay Press Gazette* (Green Bay, WI), March 14, 1901 and "Died at the Stake: Such Was the Terrible Fate of a Texas Fiend, *The Times and Democrat* (Orangeburg, SC), March 20, 1901, Lynching in Texas Staff, "Lynching of John Henderson," *Lynching in Texas*, https://www.lynchingintexas.org/items/show/210.

115. C. C. Weaver, Mayor of Itasca, to J. D. Sayers, Governor of Texas, March 13, 1901; "Texas Lynchers Defiant: No Effort to Punish Men Who Burned the Negro Henderson, Although Governor Has Full Power," *New York Times*, March 15, 1901; Photograph of John Henderson's lynching, Texas/Dallas History and Archives Division, Dallas Public Library; "The Corsicana Negro

Burned at the Stake," *Daily Times Herald* (Dallas, TX), March 13, 1901; "Burned at the Stake," *Bonham News*, March 15, 1901; "The Corsicana Negro Burned at the Stake," *Daily Times Herald* (Dallas, TX), March 13, 1901; "Fate Of Negro Brute At Hands Of A Mob: Further Details of the Death of John Henderson at Corsicana, Texas," *Bay Press Gazette* (Green Bay, WI), March 14, 1901 and "Died at the Stake: Such Was the Terrible Fate of a Texas Fiend, *The Times and Democrat* (Orangeburg, SC), March 20, 1901, Lynching in Texas Staff, "Lynching of John Henderson," *Lynching in Texas*, https://www.lynching intexas.org/items/show/210.

116. Telegram from G. W. Hardy to General Thomas Scurry, The Western Union Telegram Company, March 13, 1901, 11:34 a.m., Texas. Governor (1899–1903: Sayers), Box 301–189, Texas State Archives.

117. Telegram from G. W. Hardy to General Thomas Scurry, The Western Union Telegram Company, March 13, 1901, 11:44 a.m.

118. Telegram from Adjunct General Thomas Scurry to Col. G. W. Hardy, The Western Union Telegram Company, March 13, 1901.

119. Telegram from Sheriff W. D. Robinson to Governor Joseph D. Sayers, The Western Union Telegram Company, March 13, 1901, 2:53 p.m.

120. Telegram, Corsicana District Attorney O. C. Kirvin to Governor Joe D. Sayers, 1:05 p.m., March 13, 1901; The confession, posted in newspapers, read as follows: "I, John Henderson, colored, 22 years old, murdered an unknown white lady three miles north of Corsicana the 6th of March, 1901. There was no one present but myself, the woman and two little children. I murdered her and left her in the house without any intention of robbing her. I don't know why I did it. (Signed) 'JOHN HENDERSON'"; "Fate Of Negro Brute At Hands Of A Mob: Further Details of the Death of John Henderson at Corsicana, Texas," *Bay Press Gazette* (Green Bay, WI), March 14, 1901, Lynching in Texas Staff, "Lynching of John Henderson," *Lynching in Texas*, https://www.lynchingintexas.org/items/show/210.

121. "Fate Of Negro Brute At Hands Of A Mob: Further Details of the Death of John Henderson at Corsicana, Texas," *Bay Press Gazette* (Green Bay, WI), March 14, 1901, Lynching in Texas Staff, "Lynching of John Henderson," *Lynching in Texas*, https://www.lynchingintexas.org/items/show/210.

122. "Texas Lynchers Defiant: No Effort to Punish Men Who Burned the Negro Henderson, Although Governor Has Full Power," *New York Times*, March 15, 1901.

123. "Texas Lynchers Defiant: No Effort to Punish Men Who Burned the Negro Henderson, Although Governor Has Full Power," *New York Times*.

124. "Joseph Draper Sayers," Texas State Historical Society: A Digital Gateway to Texas History, *Handbook of Texas*, http://www.tshaonline.org/handbook/online /articles/fsa41; "Lynching," Texas State Historical Society: A Digital Gateway to Texas History, *Handbook of Texas*, http://www.tshaonline.org/handbook/online /articles/jgl01; "Texas Lynchers Defiant: No Effort to Punish Men Who Burned the Negro Henderson, Although Governor Has Full Power," *New York Times*, March 15, 1901.

125. "Topics of the Times," *New York Times*, March 15, 1901; unnamed article, *Austin Tribune*, March 13, 1901.

126. "Topics of the Times," *New York Times*; "The Week," *Nation* 72, March 21,

1901; newspaper clipping, *Austin Tribune*, March 13, 1901; Sayers, March 7, 1901, Texas State Library and Archives Commission. Governor (1899–1903: Sayers).

127. "Burned at the Stake: Negro Pays a Fearful Penalty for Murder and Assault—Crime is Confessed," *The Weekly Herald* (Weatherford), August 22, 1901.

128. "Retributive Justice: Abe Wilder, the Murderer of Mrs. Caldwell, Burned at the Stake," *Sunday Gazetteer* (Dennison, TX), August 25, 1901.

129. "Retributive Justice: Abe Wilder, the Murderer of Mrs. Caldwell, Burned at the Stake," *Sunday Gazetteer*.

130. "Retributive Justice: Abe Wilder, the Murderer of Mrs. Caldwell, Burned at the Stake," *Sunday Gazetteer*.

131. "Retributive Justice: Abe Wilder, the Murderer of Mrs. Caldwell, Burned at the Stake," *Sunday Gazetteer*.

132. Jacqueline Dowd Hall, *Revolt Against Chivalry: Jessie Daniel Ames and the Women's Campaign Against Chivalry* (New York: Columbia University Press, 1993), 150.

133. "Negro Rapist Lynched In Texas: His Companion In Crime Will Be Lynched As Soon As Caught," *The Wichita Daily Eagle* (Wichita, KS), August 8, 1897.

134. Frederick Douglass, "Lynching Black People Because They Are Black," *The Christian Recorder* 5, no. 3, April 3.

135. "Texas - A Sheriff Led the Mob: A Hundred Germans Made to Witness a Lynching," *The Herald*, January 7, 1892.

136. Francis James Grimke, "The Lynching of Negroes in the South" (Washington, 1899), 43–44.

137. "Wrong Negro under Arrest. Was Persuaded by a Colored Detective to Make a Confession," *Fort Worth Star-Telegram*, July 8, 1903.

138. "Wrong Negro under Arrest. Was Persuaded by a Colored Detective to Make a Confession," *Fort Worth Star-Telegram*; Charles Frank Robinson II, *Dangerous Liaisons: Sex and Love in the Segregated South* (Fayetteville: University of Arkansas Press, 2003), 21.

139. Robinson, *Dangerous Liaisons*, 21.

140. Twelfth Census of the United States, Schedule No. 1 – Population, 1900, 28; Thirteenth Census of the United States: 1910—Population, McLennan County.

141. Report of Elisabeth Freeman, 4, Papers of the NAACP, Box C-370, Manuscript Division, Library of Congress.

142. W. E. B. Du Bois, *The Waco Horror*, as printed in Anne P. Rice, *Witnessing Lynching: American Writers Respond* (New Brunswick, NJ: Rutgers University Press, 2003), 143.

143. "Negro Taken to Dallas for Safe Keeping," *The Daily Herald*, May 10, 1916; Patricia Bernstein, "An 'Exciting Occurrence,' in Glasrud and Smallwood, *Anti-Black Violence in Twentieth-Century Texas*; James M. SoRelle, "Jesse Washington Lynching," Handbook of Texas Online, http://www.tshaonline.org/handbook /online/articles/jcj01; James M. SoRelle, "The 'Waco Horror': The Lynching of Jesse Washington," in Glasrud and Smallwood, *Anti-Black Violence in Twentieth-Century Texas*, 186.

144. Some historical records list Lucy Fryer's last name as "Fryar."

145. "Sworn Confession by Jesse Washington," *Waco Daily Times-Herald*, May 10,

1916; "Murderer of Mrs. Lucy Fryer to be Tried Next Monday," *Waco Semi-Weekly*, May 13, 1916.

146. The original confession included graphic details of sexual assault that were changed or eliminated in the version newspapers published. For instance, the *Waco Daily-Times Herald* included the cryptic "and then I assaulted her" in place of the following: "and then I pulled up her clothes and crawled on her and screwed her. By screwing her I mean that I stuck my male organ into her female organ, and while I was doing this she was trying to push me off. When I got through screwing her I got off of her." See Bernstein, *The Waco Horror: The Lynching of Jesse Washington and the Rise of the NAACP*, 95–96.

147. Bernstein, *The Waco Horror: The Lynching of Jesse Washington and the Rise of the NAACP*, 96.

148. Bernstein, *The Waco Horror: The Lynching of Jesse Washington and the Rise of the NAACP*, 96.

149. "White Man for Crime Which Boy Was Lynched: Police Jail Husband of Dead Woman; the Soul of Jesse Washington Still Cries Out 'I Never Did It'"; Will They Convict and Hang the Guilty Man Now That an Innocent Boy Has Been Murdered?" *Chicago Defender*, June 9, 1916; Du Bois, "The Waco Horror," 2; Patricia Bernstein, *The Waco Horror: The Lynching of Jesse Washington and the Rise of the NAACP* (College Station: Texas A&M University, 2005), 94–96.

150. "EXTRA IN PUBLIC SQUARE: A Texas Negro Was Burned Alive," *Lowell Daily Sun* (Massachusetts), October 30, 1895; "BURNED TO DEATH: A Negro Fiend Swiftly and Terribly Punished," *The Daily Hesperian*, October 31, 1895.

151. Letter from M. W. D. Norman et al. to President William Howard Taft, August 13, 1910.

152. Letter to Attorney General Wickersham, December 21, 1911, Records of the Department of Justice, Central Files.

153. Letter from Max Eastman to President Woodrow Wilson, Records of the Department of Justice, Central Files, 158260.

154. Letter from Max Eastman to President Woodrow Wilson, Records of the Department of Justice, Central Files, 158260.

155. Letter from Max Eastman to President Woodrow Wilson, Records of the Department of Justice, Central Files, 158260.

156. Letter from Max Eastman to President Woodrow Wilson, Records of the Department of Justice, Central Files, 158260.

157. "Lynchers Emulating Germans," *Official Bulletin*, Records of the Department of Justice, Central Files, Box 276-1.

158. President Woodrow Wilson, Proclamation condemning lynching, July 26, 1918.

159. "Negro Murderer Burned to Death at Hillsboro," *The Daily Herald* (Weatherford, TX), January 21, 1919; "Negro Murderer Pays the Penalty," *The West Weekly News and Times* (West, TX), January 24, 1919; "Bragg Williams in Dallas County Jail for Safe Keeping," *The Dallas Express*, January 11, 1919; "Negro Burned by a Great Mob at Hillsboro," *The Hopkins County Echo*, January 24, 1919.

160. Annie Wells death certificate, Bureau of Vital Statistics, December 2, 1918, Itasca, Hill County, Texas; Curtis Wells death certificate, Bureau of Vital

Statistics, December 2, 1918, Itasca, Hill County, Texas, http://www.findagrave
.com/cgi-bin/fg.cgi?page=gr&GRid=48816057&ref=acom, and death certificate; "Lynching Case Submitted to High Court," *San Antonio Evening News*,
February 27, 1919; "Hillsboro Steps in the Limelight and Bragg Williams is
Burned at the Stake," *The Dallas Express*, January 25, 1919; National Association
for the Advancement of Colored People, *Burning at the Stake in the United States*,
June 1919, 9.

161. National Association for the Advancement of Colored People, *Burning at the
Stake in the United States*, June 1919, 10.

162. "Negro Murderer Burned to Death at Hillsboro," *The Daily Herald*; "Negro
Burners in Texas Held for Court Contempt," *The Daily Ardmoreite* (Ardmore,
OK), February 12, 1919, http://www.lynchingintexas.org/items/show
/28#&gid=1&pid=2; "Hillsboro Lynching Inquiry," *The Temple Daily Telegram*,
January 30, 1919.

163. "Mob Violence Must Be Ended: Get Lynchers Hobby Orders; Probe Begun,"
San Antonio Express, 1919.

164. "Mob Violence Must Be Ended: Get Lynchers Hobby Orders; Probe Begun,"
San Antonio Express.

165. "Mob Violence Must Be Ended: Get Lynchers Hobby Orders; Probe Begun,"
San Antonio Express.

166. Letter from Walter W. Paris, William King, and J. W. Dobbs, Atlanta, Georgia,
to President Woodrow Wilson, Paris, France, Department of Justice Files,
Straight Numerical Files, Box 3814.

167. Letter from Walter W. Paris, William King, and J. W. Dobbs, Atlanta, Georgia,
to President Woodrow Wilson, Paris, France.

168. Letter from Walter W. Paris, William King, and J. W. Dobbs, Atlanta, Georgia,
to President Woodrow Wilson, Paris, France.

169. Letter from Walter W. Paris, William King, and J. W. Dobbs, Atlanta, Georgia,
to President Woodrow Wilson, Paris, France.

170. Letter from Walter W. Paris, William King, and J. W. Dobbs, Atlanta, Georgia,
to President Woodrow Wilson, Paris, France; "Negro Murderer Burned to
Death at Hillsboro," *The Daily Herald* (Weatherford, TX), January 21, 1919;
"Negro Murderer Pays the Penalty," *The West Weekly News and Times* (West, TX),
January 24, 1919; "Bragg Williams in Dallas County Jail for Safe Keeping," *The
Dallas Express*, January 11, 1919; "Negro Burned by a Great Mob at Hillsboro,"
The Hopkins County Echo, January 24, 1919.

171. Letter from Walter W. Paris, William King, and J. W. Dobbs, Atlanta, Georgia,
to President Woodrow Wilson, Paris, France.

172. Letter from Walter W. Paris, William King, and J. W. Dobbs, Atlanta, Georgia,
to President Woodrow Wilson, Paris, France.

173. National Association for the Advancement of Colored People. Telegram released
to the morning papers of June 4, June 3, 1918. W. E. B. Du Bois Papers (MS
312). Special Collections and University Archives, University of Massachusetts
Amherst Libraries.

174. National Association for the Advancement of Colored People. Telegram released
to the morning papers of June 4, June 3, 1918.

175. Letter to Franklin D. Roosevelt, December 25, 1933, Department of Justice
Central Files, Straight Numerical Files, RG 60, Box 1278.

176. See appendix.
177. Letter to Franklin D. Roosevelt from Willie C. Brown, April 27, 1935, Department of Justice Central Files, Straight Numerical Files, RG 60, Box 1278, File 41.
178. Letter to Franklin D. Roosevelt from Willie C. Brown.
179. Letter to Franklin D. Roosevelt from Willie C. Brown; Sean Dennis Cashman, *America Ascendant: From Theodore Roosevelt to FDR in the Century of American Power, 1901–1945* (New York: New York University Press, 1998), 337.
180. Telegram, "Ask Federal Troops In Texas Race Riots," May 12, 1922, Papers of the NAACP.
181. Press Release, "N.A.A.C.P. Writes U. S. Senators on Kirvin, Texas, Burning at Stake," May 12, 1922, Papers of the NAACP.
182. Letter from M. F. Cyrus, Corsicana, Texas, to President Warren G. Harding, Washington, DC, May 19, 1922, Department of Justice Files, Central Files, Box 1276-1.
183. Letter from M. F. Cyrus, Corsicana, Texas, to President Warren G. Harding, Washington, DC.
184. Letter from M. F. Cyrus, Corsicana, Texas, to President Warren G. Harding, Washington, DC.
185. Dyer Anti-Lynching Bill:
APRIL 20 (calendar day, JULY 28), 1922.

AN ACT To assure to persons within the jurisdiction of every State the equal protection of the laws, and to punish the crime of lynching.

Be it enacted by the Senate and House of Representatives of the United States of America in Congress assembled, That the phrase "mob or riotous assemblage," when used in this act, shall mean an assemblage composed of three or more persons acting in concert for the purpose of depriving any person of his life without authority of law as a punishment for or to prevent the commission of some actual or supposed public offense.

SEC. 2. That if any State or governmental subdivision thereof fails, neglects, or refuses to provide and maintain protection to the life of any person within its jurisdiction against a mob or riotous assemblage, such State shall by reason of such failure, neglect, or refusal be deemed to have denied to such person the equal protection of the laws of the State, and to the end that such protection as is guaranteed to the citizens of the United States by its Constitution may be secured it is provided:

SEC. 3. That any State or municipal officer charged with the duty or who possesses the power or authority as such officer to protect the life of any person that may be put to death by any mob or riotous assemblage, or who has any such person in his charge as a prisoner, who fails, neglects, or refuses to make all reasonable efforts to prevent such person from being so put to death, or any State or municipal officer charged with the duty of apprehending or prosecuting any person participating in such mob or riotous assemblage who fails, neglects, or refuses to make all reasonable efforts to perform his duty in apprehending or prosecuting to final judgment under the laws of such State all persons so participating except such, if any, as are to have been held to answer for such participation in any district court of the United States, as herein provided, shall be guilty of a felony, and upon conviction thereof shall be punished by imprisonment not exceeding five years or by a fine of not exceeding $5,000, or by both such fine and imprisonment.

Any State or municipal officer, acting as such officer under authority of State law, having in his custody or control a prisoner, who shall conspire, combine, or confederate with any person to put such prisoner to death without authority of law as a punishment for some alleged public offense, or who shall conspire, combine, or confederate with any person to suffer such prisoner to be taken or obtained from his custody or control for the purpose of being put to death without authority of law as a punishment for an alleged public offense, shall be guilty of a felony, and those who so conspire, combine, or confederate with such officer shall likewise be guilty of a felony. On conviction the parties participating therein shall be punished by imprisonment for life or not less than five years.

SEC. 4. That the district court of the judicial district wherein a person is put to death by a mob or riotous assemblage shall have jurisdiction to try and punish, in accordance with the laws of the State where the homicide is committed, those who participate therein: Provided, That it shall be charged in the indictment that by reason of the failure, neglect, or refusal of the officers of the State charged with the duty of prosecuting such offense under the laws of the State to proceed with due diligence to apprehend and prosecute such participants the State has denied to its citizens the equal protection of the laws. It shall not be necessary that the jurisdictional allegations herein required shall be proven beyond a reasonable doubt, and it shall be sufficient if such allegations are sustained by a preponderance of the evidence.

SEC. 5. That any county in which a person is put to death by a mob or riotous assemblage shall, if it is alleged and proven that the officers of the State charged with the duty of prosecuting criminally such offense under the laws of the State have failed, neglected, or refused to proceed with due diligence to apprehend and prosecute the participants in the mob or riotous assemblage, forfeit $10,000, which sum may be recovered by an action therefor [sic] in the name of the United States against any such county for the use of the family, if any, of the person so put to death; if he had no family, then to his dependent parents, if any; otherwise for the use of the United States. Such action shall be brought and prosecuted by the district attorney of the United States of the district in which such county is situated in any court of the United States having jurisdiction therein. If such forfeiture is not paid upon recovery of a judgment therefor [sic], such court shall have jurisdiction to enforce payment thereof by levy of execution upon any property of the county, or may compel the levy and collection of a tax, therefor [sic], or may otherwise compel payment thereof by mandamus or other appropriate process; and any officer of such county or other person who disobeys or fails to comply with any lawful order of the court in the premises shall be liable to punishment as for contempt and to any other penalty provided by law therefor [sic].

SEC. 6. That in the event that any person so put to death shall have been transported by such mob or riotous assemblage from one county to another county during the time intervening between his capture and putting to death, the county in which he is seized and the county in which he is put to death shall be jointly and severally liable to pay the forfeiture herein provided.

SEC. 7. That any act committed in any State or Territory of the United States in violation of the rights of a citizen or subject of a foreign country secured to such citizen or subject by treaty between the United States and such foreign country, which act constitutes a crime under the laws of such State or Territory, shall constitute a like crime against the peace and dignity of the United States, punishable in like manner as in the courts of said State or Territory, and within the period limited by the laws of such State or Territory, and may be prosecuted in the courts of the United States, and upon conviction the sentence executed in like manner as sentences upon convictions for crimes under the laws of the United States.

SEC. 8. That in construing and applying this act the District of Columbia shall be deemed a county, as shall also each of the parishes of the State of Louisiana.

That if any section or provision of this acts shall be held by any court to be invalid, the balance of the act shall not for that reason be held invalid.

186. Tom Connally, "The Anti-Lynching Bill: Speech of Tom Connally of Texas in the House of Representatives," January 25, 1922, 28, Sam Houston State University.
187. Connally, Tom, "The Anti-Lynching Bill: Speech of Tom Connally of Texas in the House of Representatives"; Handbook of Texas Online, George N. Green, "Connally, Thomas Terry," http://www.tshaonline.org/handbook/online/articles/fco36.; Cashman, *America Ascendant,* 337.
188. "A Senate Apology for History on Lynching," *Washington Post,* June 14, 2005.
189. Sandra E. Garcia, "3 Black U.S. Senators Introduce Bill to Make Lynching a Federal Hate Crime," *New York Times,* July 29, 2018.

Chapter 3

1. Letter from Richard Turner, Waco, Texas, To Attorney General and Department of Justice, Washington, DC, August 10, 1905, Department of Justice Files, Straight Numerical File, Box 213, File 62503, National Archives, College Park, Maryland.
2. Letter from Richard Turner, Waco, Texas, To Attorney General and Department of Justice.
3. Letter from Richard Turner, Waco, Texas, To Attorney General and Department of Justice.

4. The National Association for the Advancement of Colored People, *Thirty Years of Lynching*, 98.

5. James M. SoRelle, "The 'Waco Horror': The Lynching of Jesse Washington." *The Southwestern Historical Quarterly* 86, no. 4 (1983), 517–36, 519, http://www .jstor.org/stable/30236945.

6. SoRelle, The 'Waco Horror,'" 519; Vivian Elizabeth Smyrl, "Mclennan County," *Handbook of Texas Online* (http://www.tshaonline.org/handbook/online/articles /hcm08); Roger N. Conger, "WACO, TX," *Handbook of Texas Online*, http:// www.tshaonline.org/handbook/online/articles/hdw01.

7. Waco History Timeline, *Waco Messenger*, www.wacomessenger.com.

8. Letter from Richard Turner, Waco, Texas, to Attorney General and Department of Justice, Washington, DC, August 10, 1905.

9. Letter from Richard Turner, Waco, Texas, to Attorney General and Department of Justice.

10. Letter from United States Attorney, Department of Justice, Western District of Texas, San Antonio, Texas, Attorney General, Department of Justice, Washington, DC, August 24, 1905, Department of Justice Files, Straight Numerical File, Box 213, File 62503.

11. Letter from United States Attorney, Department of Justice, Western District of Texas, San Antonio, Texas, Attorney General.

12. For detailed information on the number of mills and extent of various industries in eastern Texas towns and counties, see the *Texas Almanac* and Ruth Allen, *East Texas Lumber Workers: An Economic and Social Picture, 1870–1950* (Austin: University of Texas Press, 1961); *Dallas City Directory, 1891–1892* (Dallas: Morrison & Fourmy, 1891), 4.

13. Department of the Interior, *Compendium of the Eleventh Census: Part I, Population* (Washington, DC: Government Printing Office, 1892), 576.

14. "Negroes Cling to Places of Birth," *Dallas Morning News*, 18 December 1921; Department of Commerce, *Thirteenth Census of the United States Taken in the Year 1910* (Washington, DC: Government Printing Office, 1913), 852; J. C. Smith and C. P. Horton, *Historical Statistics of Black American: Media to Vital Statistics* (New York: Gale Research Inc., 1995), 1469; Bernadette Pruitt, *The Other Great Migration: The Movement of Rural African Americans to Houston, 1900–1941*, 214.

15. Ruth A. Allen, *East Texas Lumber Workers: An Economic and Social Picture, 1870–1950* (Austin: University of Texas Press, 1961), 55.

16. A. Barr, *Black Texans: A History of African Americans in Texas, 1528–1995* (Norman: University of Oklahoma Press, 1996), 137.

17. William F. Ogburn, *The Social Effects of Aviation* (Boston: Houghton Mifflin Co., 1946), 402.

18. Clara H. Lewis and John R. Stockton, "MANUFACTURING INDUSTRIES," *Handbook of Texas Online*.

19. H. L. Mencken, "'Prejudices'—Fourth Series," Elmer Scott Collection, Radio 30-31, Box 3, Folder 27; Neumeyer and Neumeyer, 7.

20. "The New Negro," *Herald* (Austin, TX), October 17, 1895.

21. White, *Rope and Faggot: A Biography of Judge Lynch*, 102.

22. "The Real Black Menace," *100% American*, January 5, 1923.

23. "The Real Black Menace," *100% American*.

24. "The Real Black Menace," *100% American*.

25. "The Real Black Menace," *100% American.*

26. Edward Dean Martin, *The Behavior of Crowds* (New York: Harper and Brothers, 1920), 122.

27. Martin, *The Behavior of Crowds*, 123.

28. Martin, *The Behavior of Crowds*, 123.

29. March Church Terrell, "Lynching from a Negro's Point of View," *The North American Review*, 178, no. 571 (June 1904), 853–68, 856.

30. "Objected to Negro's 'Airs,'" *The Madison Daily Leader*, December 6, 1906.

31. Edgar Gardner Murphy, *The Basis of Ascendancy* (New York, 1909), 29–30.

32. White, *Rope and Faggot*, 11.

33. Frederick Douglass, "Lynch Law in the South," in Phillip, S. Foner, ed., *Frederick Douglass: Selected Speeches and Writings* (Chicago: Lawrence Hill Books, 1999), 746–50.

34. As quoted in "The Looking Glass," *Crisis* 11, no. 5 (March 1916).

35. "Texas Mob Burns Human Being in Public Square," *Chicago Defender*, August 7, 1915.

36. *Texas Almanac* (1904), 140.

37. "Thirteenth Census of the United States Taken in the Year 1910: Manufacturers, 1909," 8, Department of Commerce, Bureau of the Census, 122.

38. *Texas Almanac* (1904), 153, 160, 217–18.

39. Allen, *East Texas Lumber Workers*, 23.

40. Bruce A. Glasrud and James Smallwood, ed., *The African American Experience in Texas: An Anthology* (Lubbock: Texas Tech University Press, 2007), 206–7.

41. Glasrud and Smallwood, *The African American Experience in Texas,* 206–7.

42. Phillip Luke Sinitiere, "'Outline of Report on Economic Condition of Negroes In the State of Texas': W. E. B. Du Bois's 1935 Speech At Prairie View State College," *Phylon* (1960–) 54, no. 1 (Summer 2017), 4.

43. Sinitiere, "Outline," 4.

44. Sinitiere, "Outline," 4.

45. W. E. B. Du Bois (William Edward Burghardt), 1868–1963. Letter from W. E. B. Du Bois to Rachel Davis Du Bois, April 5, 1935. W. E. B. Du Bois Papers (MS 312), Special Collections and University Archives, University of Massachusetts Amherst Libraries.

46. Sinitiere, "Outline," 19.

47. Sinitiere, "Outline," 19.

48. W. T. Block, "Milltowns and Ghost Towns: East Texas Before the Great Sawmilling and Logging Era," East Texas Research Center, Ralph W. Steen Library, Stephen F. Austin State University.

49. Block, "Milltowns and Ghost Towns."

50. Thad Sitton and James H. Conrad, *Nameless Towns: Texas Sawmill Communities, 1880–1942*, 10.

51. Sitton and Conrad, *Nameless Towns*, 11.

52. Allen, *East Texas Lumber Workers*, 22–30.

53. *Texas Almanac* (1904), 205, 243–44.

54. Allen, *East Texas Lumber Workers*, 100; Robert S. Maxwell, "Lumber Industry," *Handbook of Texas Online* (http://www.tshaonline.org/handbook/online/articles /drl02).

55. Maxwell, "Lumber Industry."; Allen, *East Texas Lumber Workers*, 27, 35.

56. As quoted in Allen, *East Texas Lumber Workers*, 27.

57. The average number of days that the lumber mills operated was 260.3, five fewer than the national average. On average, wage earners in the lumber and sawmills worked fewer than seven hours per day.

58. Allen, *East Texas Lumber Workers*, 100; William Powell Jones, *The Tribe of Black Ulysses: African American Lumber Workers in the Jim Crow South* (Urbana: University of Illinois Press, 2005), 1; Maxwell, "Lumber Industry"; James R. Green, "The Brotherhood of Timber Workers 1910–1913: A Radical Response to Industrial Capitalism in the Southern U. S. A.," *Past & Present*, no. 60 (August 1973), 161–200.

59. Sitton and Conrad, *Nameless Towns*, 105.

60. Sitton and Conrad, *Nameless Towns*, 105.

61. Sitton and Conrad, *Nameless Towns*, 105; "Aldridge Sawmill: Logging in the Pineywoods," Texas Beyond History, The University of Texas, http://www.texas beyondhistory.net/aldridge/logging.html.

62. Sitton and Conrad, *Nameless Towns*, 109–10.

63. Sitton and Conrad, *Nameless Towns*, 108.

64. Sitton and Conrad, *Nameless Towns*, 108–9.

65. Sitton and Conrad, *Nameless Towns*, 109; Bowles, "The History of Trinity County, Texas," 111.

66. Sitton and Conrad, *Nameless Towns*, 109.

67. *Sanborn Insurance Maps, Dallas County, 1892*, Dallas/Texas History and Archives Division, Dallas Public Library, Dallas, Texas; *Sanborn Insurance Maps, Chicago*, University of Illinois at Chicago, Chicago, Illinois.

68. "Dallas City Council," *Dallas Morning News*, March 6, 1890.

69. "City Politics," *Dallas Express*, January 13, 1900.

70. "City Politics," *Dallas Express*.

71. Some of the businesses owned by Blacks included grocery stores, meat markets, saloons, barber shops, and clothing stores. For detailed information on the number and location of Black-owned business in Dallas before the turn-of-the-century, see Marsha Prior and Terry Anne Schulte, "Freedman's Town/ North Dallas: The Convergence and Development of an African American Community," in Duane Peter et al., *Freedman's Cemetery: A Legacy of a Pioneer Black Community* (Austin: Department of Transportation, 2000).

72. Carter, Evelyn, personal communication with author, Dallas, Texas, 1998.

73. Carter, personal communication.

74. Carter, personal communication.

75. Carter, personal communication.

76. Carter, personal communication; *Dallas City Directory, 1924*; "Segregation and Bomb Throwing," *Dallas Express*, 26 February 1927; "The Second Attempt at Bombing a Negro Home," *Dallas Express*, 5 March 1927; "Caddo Street Home Bombed," *Dallas Express*, 12 March 1927.

77. Carter, personal communication; "Segregation and Bomb Throwing," *Dallas Express*, 26 February 1927; "The Second Attempt At Bombing A Negro Home," *Dallas Express*, 5 March 1927; "Caddo Street Home Bombed," *Dallas Express*, 12 March 1927.

78. An agreement made between white residents on Thomas Avenue in North Dallas in 1927 stipulated that their properties would not be sold to African Americans pursuant to a local ordinance that allowed for such an agreement. In

City of Dallas v. Garner W. Brice et al., the City attempted to enforce the terms of the agreement after property owners on Thomas alleged depreciation of their property value due to integration. Courts found the ordinance unconstitutional in 1929. Defeated, the remaining whites sold their Thomas Avenue homes to Blacks. See *Brice et al. v. City of Dallas et al.*, 300 S.W. 970, November 19, 1929, Decided; "Segregation of Races to Be Litigated," *Dallas Morning News*, January 10, 1929. Local African Americans recognized these residential distinctions, often alluding to the "rich" who lived in State-Thomas, or to the "nice-homes" on North Central Avenue. Dallas City Directories, 1905, 1910, 1918; Sanborn map, 1905; L. P. Fuller, ed., *The American Institute of Architects: Guide to Dallas Architecture* (Dallas: McGraw-Hill Construction Information Group, 1999).

79. The location of several of the Black enclaves within the corporate limits of Dallas was determined through the use of city directories. Information about location and expansion of Freedman's Town and North Dallas was in large part determined by plotting residences of Black and white people in the area on a map. Several other African American communities existed outside of the city limits including Elm Thicket (near Love Field Airport), Upper White Rock (in the area surrounding Preston and Alpha Roads), Lower White Rock (in vicinity of Forest Avenue and Central Expressway), Thomas Hill Community (in Oak Cliff), Little Egypt (Northwest Highway and Abrams Road). All of these enclaves were eventually incorporated into the city limits of Dallas as landowners sold tracts of land to the city. *Dallas City Directory, 1873* (Dallas: Lawson & Edmondson, 1873; *Dallas City Directory, 1875* (Dallas: Butterfield and Rundlett, 1875); Information on the location of other Black enclaves outside of the city limits was taken from W. L. McDonald, *Dallas Remembered: A Photographic Chronicle of Urban expansion, 1870–1925* (Dallas: Dallas Historical Society, 1978), 17, 118, 179; Mamie McKnight, *African American Families and Settlements of Dallas: On the Inside Looking Out. Exhibition, Family Memoirs, Personality Profiles and Community Essays* 2 (Dallas: Black Dallas Remembered, 1990); Robert Prince, *A History of Dallas: From a Different Perspective* (Nortex Press, 1993), 31–32.

80. *Dallas City Council Minutes* vol. 9:456, April 3, 1889; 15, no. 86, April 9, 1891; *Dallas City Directory, 1891–1892* (Morrison & Fourmy, 1891); *Dallas County Deed Records* 95, no. 619 (1889); 95, no. 474–76 (1889); 106, no. 567 (1889); Department of the Interior, *Compendium of the Eleventh Census: Part I, Population* (Washington, DC: Government Printing Office, 1892), 576; *Murphy and Bolanz Addition Book I*; Committee on Codification, *The Code of the City of Dallas, Texas* (Dallas: Press of John F. Worley, 1898), 11; *Dallas County Deed Record* 25, July 1887, vol. 85:426; *Murphy and Bolanz Addition Book I* (Dallas, n.d.), on file Dallas/Texas History, Dallas Public Library, Dallas, Texas.

81. *Dallas County Deed Records* 181, no. 534 (February 25, 1895); 181, no. 534 (June 22, 1896); 248, no. 42 (April 10, 1900).

82. Committee on Codification, *The Code of the City of Dallas, Texas* (Dallas: Press of John F. Worley, 1898), 11; see *Dallas City Council Minutes* 1 (21 November 1872), 50; "Fourteenth Census of the United States Taken in the Year 1920, Volume II, Population, 1920," Department of Commerce, Bureau of the Census (Washington, DC: Government Printing Office, 1922), 51.

83. See Gilbert Osofsky, *Harlem: The Making of a Ghetto: Negro New York, 1890–1930* (New York: Harper & Row, 1963); Several editorials in the *Dallas Express*, during the postwar years discuss the scheming practices of local real estate agents and land brokers who catered to Black customers and incited fear in white property owners.

84. "Negro's House In Dallas Is Blown Up, Ordered Out," news clipping, Papers of the NAACP, part 12, reel 19.

85. Terry Anne Schulte, "'Negro Districts': The Municipal Struggle for Racial Homogeneity in Dallas' White Neighborhoods," Master's thesis, Southern Methodist University, 2002; Several studies examine Black encroachment into white neighborhoods. See Boyle, Kevin, *Arc of Justice: A Saga of Race, Civil Rights, and Murder in the Jazz Age* (Holt Paperbacks: 2005); Arnold R. Hirsch, *Making the Second Ghetto: Race and Housing in Chicago, 1940–1960* (Chicago: University of Chicago Press, 1998); Sugrue, Thomas, *The Origins of the Urban Crisis: Race and Inequality in Postwar Detroit* (Princeton: Princeton University Press, 1996).

86. City of Dallas Ordinance 195, sec. 1.

87. City of Dallas Ordinance 195, sec. 1.

88. City of Dallas Ordinance 195, sec. 4.

89. *Buchanan v. Warley*, 245 U. S. 60.

90. *Buchanan v. Warley*, 245 U. S. 60.

91. See *Minutes of the City Council, Petitions*, 1917–1926. Dallas City Hall, Dallas, Texas.

92. See Terry Anne Schulte, "'Negro Districts': The Municipal Struggle for Racial Homogeneity in Dallas's White Neighborhoods," Master's Thesis. Southern Methodist University, 2002.

93. *City of Dallas et al. v. Liberty Annex Corporation*, 19 S.W.2d 845.

94. "Our New Segregation Case," *Dallas Express*, June 26, 1926.

95. "Our New Segregation Case," *Dallas Express*.

96. *City of Dallas et al. v. Liberty Annex Corporation*, 19 S.W.2d 845; News clipping, "High Court Hits Texas Segregation," *The St. Louis Argus*, Papers of the NAACP, Part 5, reel 1; "Our New Segregation Case," *Dallas Express*, June 26, 1926.

97. News clipping, "The Segregation Problem," *The Dallas Times Herald*, Papers of the NAACP, Part 5, reel 1.

98. News clipping, "The Segregation Problem," *The Dallas Times Herald*.

99. News clipping, "Here is the New 'Court Proof Segregation Measure' Which May Soon Become a Texas Law," *Dallas Express*, 29 January 1927, Papers of the NAACP, Part 5, reel 1.

100. News clipping, "Here is the New 'Court Proof Segregation Measure' Which May Soon Become a Texas Law," *Dallas Express*.

101. News clipping, "Here is the New 'Court Proof Segregation Measure' Which May Soon Become a Texas Law," *Dallas Express*.

102. "All Measures Have Opposition But the Segregation Law," *Dallas Express*, September 1927.

103. "All Measures Have Opposition But the Segregation Law," *Dallas Express*.

104. "All Measures Have Opposition But the Segregation Law," *Dallas Express*.

105. Walter White, New York, to John W. Rice, Dallas, March 31, 1927, Papers of the NAACP, Part 5, reel 1.

106. News clipping, "On Segregation in Dallas," *Dallas Express*, December 18, 1926, Papers of the NAACP, Part 5, reel 1. Upon receiving word of the new law, the NAACP national office contacted Texas branches of the organization. The group reported that the "so-called segregation law appears to be clearly unconstitutional and we have got to knock it out through the courts." Most Texas branches were defunct by that time. Further research needs to be done to determine whether or not the NAACP attempted to challenge the law in court. Walter White, New York, to John W. Rice, Dallas, 31 March 1927, Papers of the NAACP, Part 5, reel 1.

107. "C. E. Ulrickson Headed Committee on City Planning," *Dallas Morning News*, October 1, 1935.

108. *A Program of Public Improvement*, Report of the Ulrickson Committee for the city of Dallas, 1927, Texas/Dallas History and Archives Division, Dallas Public Library.

109. *A Program of Public Improvement*, Report of the Ulrickson Committee for the city of Dallas, 1927, Texas/Dallas History and Archives Division, Dallas Public Library.

110. Elmer Scott, Dallas, to Major E. A. Wood, Dallas, June 13, 1928, Elmer Scott Collection, Dallas Historical Society, Dallas, Texas; "Chamber Urges Voters to Defeat City Segregation Measure. Supports Ulrickson Plan," *Dallas Express*, 17 December 1927.

111. *Dallas County Deed Records* 512, no. 583 (1911), on file at the Dallas County Recorder's Office, Dallas, Texas.

112. See *Dallas County Deed Records* for the years 1911–30.

113. *Dallas County Deed Records* 585, no. 146 (1913).

114. *Dallas County Deed Records* 585, no. 146 (1913).

115. John Dittmer, *Black Georgia in the Progressive Era: 1900–1920* (Urbana: University of Illinois Press, 1977); Arthur Link and R. McCormick, *Progressivism* (Wheeling: Harlan Davidson, 1983), 2.

116. For a listing of Texas segregation legislation, see *Complete Texas Statutes* (Kansas City, MO: Vernon Law Book Company, 1920).

117. See Jack Temple Kirby, *Darkness at the Dawning: Race and Reform in the Progressive South* (Philadelphia: J. B. Lippincott, 1972); also see C. Vann Woodward, *Origins of the New South, 1817–1913* (Baton Rouge: Louisiana State University Press, 1951).

118. "Colored Teachers Protest," *Dallas Morning News*, June 29, 1901.

119. A. Barr, *Black Texans*, 51, 140; John Hope Franklin, *From Slavery to Freedom: A History of African Americans,* 7th ed. (New York: McGraw-Hill, 1994), 262.

120. For information on how African American churches assumed the agendas of settlement houses, and were for all intents and purposes settlement houses, see Elizabeth Lasch-Quinn, *Black Neighbors: Race and the Limits of Reform in the American Settlement House Movement* (Chapel Hill: University of North Carolina Press, 1993); see also Milton Sernett, *Bound For the Promised Land: African American Religion and the Great Migration* (Durham: Duke University Press, 1997).

121. Barr, *Black Texans*, 56, 82; "Vagrants," *Dallas Weekly Herald*, December 7, 1865; Franklin, *From Slavery to Freedom*, 225–26; C. H. Moneyhon, "Black Codes," in *Handbook of Texas Online.* http://www.tsha.utexas.edu/handbook/online/articles

/view/HH/fhafw.html; *Complete Texas Statutes*, Title 1, art. 8; see also Complete Texas Statutes for various statutes related to segregation.

122. *Complete Texas Statutes*, 1, 59, 715, 1045, 1164, 1175.

123. "White Republicans," *Fort Worth Weekly Gazette*, September 18, 1890.

124. Marvin W. Dulaney, "AFRICAN AMERICANS," *Handbook of Texas Online*, http://www.tshaonline.org/handbook/online/articles/pkaan. Uploaded on June 9, 2010.

125. P. D. Casdorph, *Republicans, Negroes, and Progressives in the South, 1912–1916* (Tuscaloosa: University of Alabama Press, 1981), 90–91; J. O. Chisum, "Dallas Negro History," Papers of John and Ethelyn M. Chisum, Box 2, Folder 1, Texas/Dallas History and Archives Division, Dallas Public Library; Rice, *Witnessing Lynching*, 34–35; W. E. King, owner of the *Dallas Express*, proudly displayed his partisan affiliation by printing "The Republican Party Is The Ship, All Else Is The Sea—Frederick Douglas," across the front page of issues of his newspaper as early as 1900. African American Dallasite and attorney Ammon S. Wells served as a Texas delegate to the National Republican Convention in 1904. "Col. W. E. King Passes," 22 August 1919; Margot, 17; Josie Briggs Hall, *Hall's Moral and Mental Capsule* (Dallas: Reverend R. S. Jenkins, Publisher, 1905), 198.

126. J. Mason Brewer, *Negro Legislatures of Texas and Their Descendent* (Dallas: Friends of the Dallas Public Library, 1938 reprinted in 1991), 62; Darlene Clark Hine, *Black Victory: The Rise of Fall of the White Primary in Texas* (Millwood: KTO Press, 1979), 33; J. M. Kousser, *The Shaping of Southern Politics Suffrage, Restriction and the Establishment of the One-Party South, 1880–1910* (New Haven: Yale University Press, 1974), 205–6.

127. Brewer, *Negro Legislatures*, 62; Hine, *Black Victory*, 33; Kousser, *The Shaping of Southern Politics Suffrage*, 205–6. Davidson's bill was not the first of its kind to be presented before the Texas legislature. An earlier bill, presented during the 1875 constitutional convention in Texas, also called for a poll tax as a prerequisite for voting. Republicans and Grangers (a comparatively liberal faction of the Democratic Party), however, defeated the bill out of concern that several for their white and Black constituents would be politically incapacitated by the poll tax, consequently weakening the parties' power. Although it was presented under the auspices of attempting to limit the bartering of votes of both Black and white people, not aimed at disfranchising one more than the other, the undergirding racism inherent in the proposed tax was given voice in several contemporary newspaper editorials addressing the defeat of the poll tax. A particularly egregious editorial favoring the poll tax appeared in the *Waco Examiner*. Commenting on the exclusion of the poll tax in the revised state constitution, the 1875 article insisted "the most obnoxious feature of the new Constitution is the injustice done to all of the counties that have the misfortune to be peopled by a majority of negroes" (Kousser, 35); Rice, *Witnessing Lynching*, 24.

128. Terrell Election Law 1903: Title 36, Sec. 9.

129. Hine, *Black Victory*, 37–38.

130. Kousser, *The Shaping of Southern Politics Suffrage*, 202.

131. Rice, Lawrence, *Negro in Texas: 1874–1900* (Baton Rouge: Louisiana State University Press, 1971), 136; Kousser, *The Shaping of Southern Politics Suffrage*, 201–3; D. Casdorph, *Republicans, Negroes, and Progressives in the South, 1912–1916* (Tuscaloosa: University of Alabama Press, 1981), 90–91; J. O. Chisum,

"Dallas Negro History," Papers of John and Ethelyn M. Chisum, Box 2, Folder 1, Texas/Dallas History and Archives Division, Dallas Public Library; Rice, *Witnessing Lynching*, 34–35.

132. Rice, *Witnessing Lynching*, 136.

133. Barr, *Black Texans*, 80; Brewer, 110–11; Hine, 40; Ogden, F., *The Poll Tax in the South* (Tuscaloosa: University of Alabama Press, 1958), 121; Kousser, 201–2.

134. Durward Pruden, "A Sociological Study of a Texas Lynching," *Studies in Sociology* 1, no. 1 (Dallas: The Department of Sociology, Southern Methodist University, 1936), 9. In an effort to protect the identity of those discussed in his study, Pruden referred to Sherman as "Leeville."

135. Pruden, "A Sociological Study of a Texas Lynching," 9.

136. Pruden, "A Sociological Study of a Texas Lynching," 5.

137. Information about the establishment of Black settlements along railway lines in the Dallas area and Dallas County, for instance, was in large part determined by plotting residences of Black and white people in the area on a map. See Prior and Schulte; *Dallas City Directory, 1873* (Dallas: Lawson & Edmondson, 1873; *Dallas City Directory, 1875* (Dallas: Butterfield and Rundlett, 1875); W. L. McDonald, *Dallas Remembered: A Photographic Chronicle of Urban expansion, 1870–1925* (Dallas: Dallas Historical Society, 1978), 17; Mamie McKnight, *African American Families and Settlements of Dallas: On the Inside Looking Out. Exhibition, Family Memoirs, Personality Profiles and Community Essays* II (Dallas: Black Dallas Remembered, 1990); Prince, Robert, *A History of Dallas: From a Different Perspective* (Nortex Press, 1993), 31–32.

138. Pruden, "A Sociological Study of a Texas Lynching," 5.

139. Pruden, "A Sociological Study of a Texas Lynching," 5.

140. Pruden, "A Sociological Study of a Texas Lynching," 7; Brian Hart, "Sherman, TX," *Handbook of Texas Online* (http://www.tshaonline.org/handbook/online/articles/hds03); Handbook of Texas Online, Donna J. Kumler, "Grayson County," http://www.tshaonline.org/handbook/online/articles/hcg09.

141. "Body of Assaulter Dragged Through Streets by Mob," *Morning Avalanche* (Lubbock, TX), May 10, 1930; "Officers Unable to Save Sherman Negro," *The Daily News-Telegram* (Sulphur Springs, TX) May 11, 1930; Statement from Frank Hamer, May 13, 1930, in Texas Governor Dan Moody Records, box 2007/170-53, Archives and Information Services Division, Texas State Library and Archives Commission.

142. Durward Pruden, "A Sociological Study of a Texas Lynching," *Studies in Sociology* 1, no. 1 (Dallas: The Department of Sociology, Southern Methodist University, 1936) as reprinted in *Crisis*, January 1937, 4.

143. "Mob," *Sherman Daily Democrat*, May 29, 1930, University of Texas, History Manuscript Division, Austin, Texas; Pruden, "A Sociological Study of a Texas Lynching," 3.

144. "Body of Assaulter Dragged Through Streets by Mob," *Morning Avalanche* (Lubbock, TX), May 10, 1930.

145. Pruden, "A Sociological Study of a Texas Lynching," 4.

146. NAACP Files, Administrative File, box C-369, folder – Sherman, Library of Congress.

147. NAACP Files, Administrative File, box C-369, folder – Sherman.

148. NAACP Files, Administrative File, box C-369, folder – Sherman.

149. Pruden, "A Sociological Study of a Texas Lynching," 3–5; Lynching in Texas

Staff, "Lynching of George Hughes," *Lynching in Texas*, http://www.lynching intexas.org/items/show/39.

150. Pruden, "A Sociological Study of a Texas Lynching," 5; "Negroes are Warned to Quit Sherman, Tex.," *World*, May 14, in Papers of the NAACP, box C-370, Manuscript Division, Library of Congress.

Chapter 4

1. P. L. Prattis, "Horizon: The Beam and the Mote" *Pittsburgh Courier*, December 12, 1964, quoting the *Chicago Record-Herald*, May 23, 1902; "Atrocity in Texas: Negro Burned to Death by Pitiless Executioners," *Washington Post*, May 23, 1902.

2. Primary sources use both McKee and McKay.

3. "NEGRO TORTURED TO DEATH BY MOB of 4,000," *Chicago Record-Herald*, May 23, 1902, as quoted in Ralph Ginzburg, *100 Years of Lynchings* (Baltimore: Black Classic Press, 1962), 45–46; "EYES BURNED OUT WITH HOT COALS," *Los Angeles Herald* 24, no. 234, May 23, 1902, California Digital Newspaper Collection; "Countdown," *Baltimore Afro-American*, July 14, 1962; Prattis, "Horizon: The Beam and the Mote" *Pittsburgh Courier*, December 12, 1964, quoting the *Chicago Record-Herald*, May 23, 1902; "ATROCITY IN TEXAS: Negro Burned to Death by Pitiless Executioners," *Washington Post*, May 23, 1902.

4. "NEGRO TORTURED TO DEATH BY MOB of 4,000," *Chicago Record-Herald*, May 23, 1902, as quoted in Ginzburg, Ralph, *100 Years of Lynchings* (Baltimore: Black Classic Press, 1962), 45–46; "EYES BURNED OUT WITH HOT COALS," *Los Angeles Herald* 24, no. 234, May 23, 1902, California Digital Newspaper Collection; "ATROCITY IN TEXAS: Negro Burned to Death by Pitiless Executioners," *Washington Post*, May 23, 1902.

5. "5 O'Clock Extra in Public Square: A Texas Negro Was Burned," *Lowell Daily Sun* (Massachusetts), October 30, 1895; "Unbridled License," *Leavenworth Times* (Leavenworth, KS), October 31, 1895.

6. "BURNED TO DEATH: A Negro Fiend Swiftly and Terribly Punished," *The Daily Hesperian* (Gainesville, TX), October 31, 1895.

7. "Series of fifteen stereographs relating to the murder of a woman in Tyler, Texas," photographs by C. A. Davis, published by Breckenridge and Scruggs company, LOT 11782 (F) [P&P], Prints and Photographs Division, Library of Congress (series hereafter referred to as "Breckenridge & Scruggs"), stereographs, "9. Building the Scaffold," "12. The Torch Applied"; NAACP, *Thirty Years of Lynching*, 12; George C. Werner, "International-Great Northern Railroad," Handbook of Texas Online, http://www.tshaonline.org/handbook/online /articles/eqi04; Lynching in Texas Staff, "Lynching of Robert Henson Hilliard," *Lynching in Texas*, http://www.lynchingintexas.org/items/show/355.

8. "Breckenridge & Scruggs," stereographs.

9. "Breckenridge & Scruggs," Stereographs, "9. Building the Scaffold," "12. The Torch Applied"; NAACP, *Thirty Years of Lynching*, 12; Handbook of Texas Online, George C. Werner, "International-Great Northern Railroad," http:// www.tshaonline.org/handbook/online/articles/eqi04.

10. *Fort Worth Morning Register* 4, 289, 3, September 11, 1900; "City Marshal to

take Boy to Calaboose," *The San Marcos Times*, January 13, 1919; "The Nigger Shooter is Causing Trouble," *Daily Courier-Light* (Corsicana, TX), February 2, 1905.

11. "'Nigger-Shooter' Good as Rifle for Cecil Alexander," *The Abilene Reporter News*, October 1, 1939.

12. "'Nigger-Shooter' Good as Rifle for Cecil Alexander," *The Abilene Reporter News*.

13. Marion Butts Collection, 1946, PA2005-4/445, Photographic Archives, Dallas Public Library; "Boys Slay 1,379 Rats With Old-Time, 'Nigger-Shooter,'" *The San Antonio Evening News*, August 26, 1920.

14. As quoted in Kenneth W. Goings, *Mammy and Uncle Moses: Black Collectibles and American Stereotyping* (Bloomington: Indiana University Press, 1994), xiii and xiv.

15. Robert Weems, *Desegregating the Dollar: African American Consumers in the Twentieth Century* (New York: New York University Press, 1998), 41.

16. Weems, *Desegregating the Dollar*, 41.

17. "Eye-Witness Describes Rioting in E. St. Louis: Brutality Worse Than the Massacre of the French Huguenots," *The Baltimore Afro-American*, July 7, 1917.

18. W. E. B. Du Bois, *Dark Waters: Voices from Within the Veil* (New York: Harcourt, Brace and Howe, 1920), 84.

19. Thomas Holt, "Marking: Race, Race-making, and the Writing of History," AHA Presidential Address, *American Historical Review* 100, no. 1 (February 1995), 1–20.

20. Holt, "Marking," 1–20.

21. Ralph Ellison, *Invisible Man*, Second Vintage International Edition (New York: Random House, 1995, 1947), prologue.

22. Ellison, *Invisible Man*, prologue.

23. Thomas Holt, AHA Presidential Address, 1995.

24. Ellison, *Invisible Man*, 196.

25. Ellison, *Invisible Man*, 201–2.

26. Ellison, *Invisible Man*, 201–2.

27. Vance, *The Facts in the Case of the Horrible Murder of Little Myrtle Vance and its Fearful Expiation in Paris, Texas* (Paris: P. L. James, 1893), 15.

28. Vance, *The Facts in the Case*, 17.

29. Vance, *The Facts in the Case*, 44.

30. Vance, *The Facts in the Case*, 44, 35; *New York Sun*, 2 February 1893. Reprinted in Gilbert Osofsky, *The Burden of Race: A Documentary History of Negro-White Relations in America* (New York: Harper and Row, 1967), 181–84; Daisy Harvill, "PARIS, TX," *Handbook of Texas Online* (http://www.tshaonline.org/handbook/online/articles/hdp01), published by the Texas State Historical Association.

31. Ida B. Wells, *The Red Record: Tabulated Statistics and Alleged Causes of Lynching in the United States* (Chicago: Donohue & Menneberry, 1895.

32. Vance, *The Facts in the Case*, 60.

33. Vance, *The Facts in the Case*, 19.

34. Robert Wilson Shufeldt, *The Negro: A Menace to American Civilization* (Boston, The Gorham Press: 1907), 138; Wood, *Lynching and Spectacle*, 72; J. L. Mertins Photographs, Prints & Photographs, Library of Congress; "Torture for 50 minutes with hot irons [lynching of Henry Smith, Paris, Texas], Prints &

Photographs Collection, CN 08222, Center for American History, University of Texas, Austin.

35. Vance, *The Facts in the Case,* 69.

36. Wells, *The Red Record,* 28.

37. *The Facts in the Case,* 74; *An Historical Survey of Lynchings in Oklahoma and Texas,* 99 from the *New York World Telegram,* December 8, 1933, cited in Supplement 15 to *Thirty Years of Lynching;* Wells-Barnett, Ida. B., *Crusade for Justice,* 85.

38. James H. Dormon, "Shaping the Popular Images of Post-Reconstruction American Blacks: The 'Coon Song' Phenomenon of the Gilded Age," *American Quarterly* 40, no. 4 (December 1988), 450–71; Lemons, J. Stanley, "Black Stereotypes as Reflected in Popular Culture, 1880–1920," *American Quarterly* 29, no. 1 (Spring 1977), 102–16; William J. Mahar, *Behind The Burnt Cork Mask: Early Blackface Minstrelsy and Antebellum American Popular Culture* (Urbana: University of Illinois Press, 1999); Steven C. Dubin, "Symbolic Slavery: Black Representations in Popular Culture," *Social Problems* 34, no. 2 (April 1987), 122–40.

39. William R. Leach, *Land of Desire: Merchants, Power, and the Rise of a New American Culture* (New York: Vintage Books, 1993), xiii.

40. As quoted in Donald O. Case, "Serial Collecting as Leisure, and Coin Collecting in Particular," *Library Trends,* 57(4) Spring 2009, 729–52.

41. W. J. Cash, *The Mind of the South* (Vintage Books: New York, 1941), 124.

42. White, *Rope and Faggot: A Biography of Judge Lynch,* 102.

43. "The Black Menace," *100% America,* January 25, 1923.

44. Woodward, *Origins of the New South, 1817–1913,* 354.

45. "New Negro Society," *Austin Weekly Statesman,* April 18, 1907.

46. Unnamed article, *Hallettsville New Era* (Hallettsville, TX), April 19, 1907.

47. Unnamed article, *Hallettsville New Era.*

48. NAACP, *Report of the National Association of the Advancement of Colored People for the Years 1917 and 1918: Eighth and Ninth Annual Reports, A Summary of Work and an Accounting,* 11.

49. "The Effects of Radical Teachings," *The Texas Republican,* July 24, 1868.

50. For example, see "The Black Devil's Just Reward," *The Orange Daily Tribune,* October 16, 1902; Front page, *The Sticker* (Fayette County, TX), May 11, 1899.

51. Leon Litwack, *Trouble in Mind: Black Southerners in the Age of Jim Crow* (New York: Vintage Books, 2010), 184.

52. See Kenneth Goings, *Black Collectibles and American Stereotyping* (Bloomington: Indiana University Press, 1994).

53. "Sam and the Cooter," *Honey Grove Signal,* August 24, 1894.

54. "Sam and the Cooter," *Honey Grove Signal.*

55. "Sam and the Cooter," *Honey Grove Signal.*

56. "Inherent Talent," *Dallas Daily Times Herald,* December 9, 1901.

57. "First Sight of the Melons," *Southern Mercury,* June 27, 1895; see also "'Nigger' Votes," *Southern Mercury,* January 5, 1893; "A Negro Wedding 1868," *Southern Mercury,* January 5, 1898.

58. Kimberly Wallace-Sanders, *Mammy: A Century of Race, Gender, and Southern Memory* (Ann Arbor: University of Michigan Press, 2008), 3.

59. Wallace-Sanders, *Mammy*, 3.

60. Wallace-Sanders, *Mammy*, 3.

61. *The Montgomery Advertiser*, May 23, 1902, quoted in Louis R. Harlan, Raymond W. Smock, and Barbara S. Kraft, eds., *The Booker T. Washington Papers 6*, 1901–2 (Urbana: University of Illinois Press), 480.

62. "Negro Tortured to Death by Mob of 4,000," *Chicago Record-Herald*, May 23, 1902.

63. "Mob of 5000 Burned Negro at the Stake," *Austin Statesman and Tribune*, July 31, 1915.

64. "Temple Quiet Following Its Tragedy," *The Dallas Daily Times Herald*, July 31, 1915.

65. "Lots Drawn for Souvenirs of Lynched Negro's Anatomy," *Baltimore Herald*, October 19, 1921, reprinted in Ginzburg, *100 Years of Lynchings*, 155.

66. Article and letter sent to President Franklin D. Roosevelt, December 25, 1933, Department of Justice Central Files, Straight Numerical Files, Box 1278; "'100 Years of Lynchings' A Shocking Documentary of Racial Violence in America," *Baltimore Afro-American*, 14 July 1962; Akers, *Flames After Midnight*, 70; "N.A.A.C.P. Writes U. S. Senators On Kirvin [sic], Texas, Burning At Stake," 12 May 1922, Papers of the NAACP, Series A, Part 7, reel 20; "Texas Troops Guard Waco," *New York Times*, 28 May 1922; "Temple Quiet Following Its Tragedy," *Dallas Time Herald*, 31 July 1915; "Texas 1915," *Crisis* (January 1916) in NAACP Papers, Series A, Part 7; "Race Riot Feared in Texas Over Burning Young Negro," *Cordova Daily Times* (Cordova, AK), May 27, 1922.

67. "Frank Majors," *Austin American Statesman*, August 9, 1905; Equal Justice Initiative, "EJI Partners with Shelby County, Texas, Community To Install Historical Marker," December 28, 1918, EJI Partners with Shelby County, Texas, Community To Install Historical Marker; "Negro, Charged With Murder, Is Lynched in Texas," *The Town Talk*, May 21, 1928.

68. *The Facts in the Case*, 69.

69. *The Facts in the Case*, 69; Hale, 229; "Governor Hogg's Action," *Galveston Daily News*, February 3, 1893.

70. Young, Harvey, *Embodying Black Experience: Stillness, Critical Memory, and the Black Body* (Ann Arbor: University of Michigan Press, 2010), 170.

71. Young, *Embodying Black Experience*, 171.

72. Jacqueline Goldsby, "The High and Low Tech of It: The Meaning of Lynching and the Death of Emmett Till," *Yale Journal of Criticism* 9(2) (Fall 1996), 274. See also Goldsby, Jacqueline, *A Spectacular Secret: Lynching in American Life and Literature* (Chicago: University of Chicago Press, 2006).

73. Goldsby, "The High and Low Tech of It," 274.

74. Ida. B. Wells-Barnett, *Crusade for Justice: The Autobiography of Ida B. Wells*, Alfred M. Duster, ed. (Chicago: University of Chicago Press, 1970), 85; *Hull-House Bulletin* 5, no. 1, Semi-Annual 1902, 6.

75. Wells-Barnett, *Crusade for Justice*, 85.

76. Wells-Barnett, *Crusade for Justice*, 85.

77. Litwack, *Trouble in Mind*, 292.

78. "A Suggestion: Why Not have a Texas Lynching Reproduced by Kinetoscope?" *New York Times*, October 6, 1905.

79. "A Suggestion: Why Not have a Texas Lynching Reproduced by Kinetoscope?" *New York Times*.

80. "A Suggestion: Why Not have a Texas Lynching Reproduced by Kinetoscope?" *New York Times*.

81. John H. Slate, "Film Industry," *Handbook of Texas Online* http://www.tsha online.org/handbook/online/articles/ecf01 (uploaded on June 12, 2010). Published by the Texas State Historical Association; Burnes St. Patrick Hollyman, "The First Picture Shows: Austin, Texas, 1894–1913," in John L. Fell, ed., *Film Before Griffith*, (Berkeley: University of California Press, 1983), 188.

82. Burdett, *A Test of Lynch Law*, 17; Stadler, Gustavas, "Never Heard Such a Thing: Lynching and Phonographic Memory," *Social Text 102*, Spring 2010, 88.

83. Burdett, *A Test of Lynch Law*, 17.

84. Burdett, *A Test of Lynch Law*, 17.

85. Bill Lohse, "Dr. Samuel Burdett (1849 – ?)," www.blackpast.org; Burdett, *A Test of Lynch Law*, 17; "History of the Cylinder Phonograph," Library of Congress, https://www.loc.gov/collections/edison-company-motion-pictures-and-sound -recordings/articles-and-essays/history-of-edison-sound-recordings/ history-of-the-cylinder-phonograph/.

86. Burdett, *A Test of Lynch Law*, 17.

87. Burdett, *A Test of Lynch Law*, 89.

88. Burdett, *A Test of Lynch Law*, 18.

89. Burdett, *A Test of Lynch Law*, 18.

90. Burdett, *A Test of Lynch Law*, 18–19.

91. Burdett, *A Test of Lynch Law*, 19.

92. Burdett, *A Test of Lynch Law*, 19.

93. "Cleanse the County Fairs," *The Manchester Democrat* (Manchester, IA), September 19, 1900.

94. "Prize Drill Yet To Come," *Omaha Daily Bee*, March 30, 1901.

95. "To Judge Duncan," *Daily Gesperian* (Gainesville, TX), October 31, 1895.

96. "The Wonderland," *Boston Globe,* March 31, 1896, from Lynching in Texas Staff, "Lynching of Robert Henson Hilliard," *Lynching in Texas*, http://www .lynchingintexas.org/items/show/355.

97. "The Wonderland," *Boston Globe*.

98. Amy Louise Wood, *Lynching and Spectacle: Witnessing Racial Violence in America, 1890–1940* (Chapel Hill: University of North Carolina Press, 2009), 75.

99. Wood, *Lynching and Spectacle*, 75.

100. Vance, *The Facts in the Case*, 19.

101. NAAPC, *Years of Lynching*, 12; "Lynchings," Papers of the NAACP, Series A, Part 7, reel 18.

102. "Breckenridge & Scruggs," stereographs.

103. "Breckenridge & Scruggs," stereographs.

104. "Breckenridge & Scruggs," stereographs.

105. *Thirty Years of Lynching*, 12; "Lynchings," Papers of the NAACP, Series A, Part 7, reel 18.

106. "Cutting Her Throat," in "Breckenridge & Scruggs," stereographs.

107. "The Body as Found," in "Breckenridge & Scruggs," stereographs.

108. "The Body as Found," in "Breckenridge & Scruggs," stereographs.

109. "In the Hands of the Mob," "9-Building the Scaffold," "10-Praying on the Scaffold," "11-Binding to the Stake," in "Breckenridge & Scruggs," stereographs;

Thirty Years of Lynching, 12; "Lynchings," Papers of the NAACP, Series A, Part 7, reel 18.

110. Sarah Swofford and Garrett R. Herring, Oral History Interviews with Garrett R. Herring, February 1980, audio recording, {1980–02–07,1980–02–14}; https://texashistory.unt.edu/ark:/67531/metapth845088/m1/, University of North Texas Libraries, The Portal to Texas History, https://texashistory.unt.edu; crediting Lee College; Lynching in Texas Staff, "Lynching of Burl Smith," *Lynching in Texas*, https://www.lynchingintexas.org/items/show/481.

111. George Miller, and Dorothy Miller, *Picture Postcards in the United States: 1893–1918* (New York: Clarkson N. Potter, Inc., 1976), 18.

112. Miller and Miller, 20; Bernadette A. Lear, "Wish They Were Here: Old Postcards and Library History," *Libraries & the Cultural Record* 43.1 (2008) 77–100, 78; Smithsonian Institute Archives, "Postcard History," http://si archives.si.edu/history/exhibits/postcard/postcard-history.

113. Goings, *Black Collectibles*, 40–43; Wayne Martin Mellinger, "Postcards from the Edge of Color Line: Images of African Americans in Popular Culture, 1893–1917," *Society for the Study of Symbolic Interaction* 15, no. 4 (Winter 1992), 413–33; Maniskas, Judith Stoltz, *The Hocking Hills: 1900–1950* (Charleston, SC: Arcadia Publishing, 2015), 7.

114. Brown, Nikki L. M. and Barry M. Stentiford, *The Jim Crow Encyclopedia: Greenwood Milestones in African American History* (Westport, CT: Greenwood Press, 2008), 629.

115. See Goings, *Black Collectibles*; also see Mellinger, "Postcards from the Edge."

116. "Texas Mob Lynches Negro in Jail Yard: Batter Steel Doors and Wreck Steel Cell to Get Man Accused of Murdering White Woman," *New York Times*, August 3, 1920; National Association of the Advancement of Colored People, *Report of the National Association of the Advancement of Colored People for the Years 1917 and 1918: Eighth and Ninth Annual Reports, A Summary of Work and an Accounting* (New York: National Association for the Advancement of Colored People, 1919), 37; Lynching in Texas Staff, "Lynching of Lige Daniels," *Lynching in Texas*.

117. James Allen, John Littlefield, et al., *Without Sanctuary: Photographs and Postcards of Lynching in America* (Santa Fe, NM: Twin Palms, 1999).

118. Allen and Littlefield, *Without Sanctuary*.

119. Allen and Littlefield, *Without Sanctuary*.

120. "Decency's Law Should Apply," *The Dallas Times Herald*, 8 March 1910.

121. "Mob Takes Negro From Court House, Burns Him At Stake," *Waco Times*, May 16, 1916; "15,000 Witness Burning of Negro in Public Square," *New York World*, May 16, 1916, reprinted in Ralph Ginzburg, *100 Years of Lynchings* (Baltimore: Black Classic Press, 1962), 103; "Gildersleeve" is printed on the back of the postcard. He was the photographer.

122. "The Burden," *Crisis* 11, no. 3, January 1916, 145.

Chapter 5

1. "Thousands Visit Sherman Sunday," *Sherman Daily Democrat*, May 11, 1930.

2. "Thousands Visit Sherman Sunday," *Sherman Daily Democrat*.

3. "Thousands Visit Sherman Sunday," *Sherman Daily Democrat*.

4. "Women Clap Hands at Sight of Negro," *Daily News-Telegram* (Sulphur Springs, TX), May 11, 1930.

5. Waldrep, Christopher, ed., *Lynching in America: A History in Documents* (New York: New York University Press, 2006), 23.

6. Handbook of Texas Online, George C. Werner, "Railroads," http://www.tsha online.org/handbook/online/articles/eqr01.

7. *New York Sun*, February 2, 1893, Reprinted in Osofsky, Gilbert, *The Burden of Race: A Documentary History of Negro-White Relations in America* (New York: Harper and Row, 1967), 181–84.

8. Vance, *The Facts in the Case*, 60.

9. Vance, *The Facts in the Case*, 41.

10. Vance, *The Facts in the Case*, 41.

11. Vance, *The Facts in the Case*, 41.

12. Vance, *The Facts in the Case*, 41.

13. Vance, *The Facts in the Case*, 41.

14. "The Corsicana Negro Burned at the Stake," *Daily Times Herald* (Dallas, TX), March 13, 1901.

15. "The Corsicana Negro Burned at the Stake," *Daily Times Herald*.

16. "The Corsicana Negro Burned at the Stake," *Daily Times Herald*.

17. Lynching in Texas Staff, "Lynching of Robert Henson Hilliard," *Lynching in Texas*, http://www.lynchingintexas.org/items/show/355.

18. Grace Elizabeth Hale, "Spectacle Lynching," in Christopher Waldrep, ed., *Lynching in America: A History in Documents* (New York: New York University Press, 2006), 23.

19. "'Can a Dead Man Be Lynched?' If so, George Johnson, Negro, Was Lynched on the Afternoon of May 16, 1930, at Honey Grove, Fannin County, Texas," *Signal-Citizen* (Honey Grove, TX), as quoted in Mary Elizabeth Estes, "An Historical Survey of Lynchings in Oklahoma and Texas" (MA Thesis, University of Oklahoma, 1942), 100.

20. Estes, "An Historical Survey of Lynchings in Oklahoma and Texas," 100.

21. Estes, "An Historical Survey of Lynchings in Oklahoma and Texas," 100; "Mob Violence Near Sherman," *Sweetwater Sunday Reporter*, May 18, 1930.

22. "Can a Dead Man Be Lynched? If so, George Johnson, Negro, Was Lynched on the Afternoon of May 16, 1930, at Honey Grove, Fannin County, Texas," *Signal-Citizen* (Honey Grove, TX), as quoted in Estes, "An Historical Survey of Lynchings in Oklahoma and Texas," 100.

23. Estes, "An Historical Survey of Lynchings in Oklahoma and Texas," 100; "Mob Violence Near Sherman," *Sweetwater Sunday Reporter*, May 18, 1930; "Honey Grove Burns Negro: Mob Takes Body Of Black In Front Of Church In Mad Orgy," *Brownsville Herald* (Brownsville, TX), May 17, 1930.

24. "Mob Burns Three Negroes At Dawn of Day of Kirvin," *Dallas Morning News*, May 7, 1922.

25. "Lynching Record for 1934" Papers of the NAACP, Series A, Part 7, reel 20.

26. For examples of victims of lynch mobs who were affixed to a car and dragged to the Black sections of the nearest towns, see "Local Man With Dynamite on Person is Held," *Sherman Daily Democrat*, May 11, 1930; "A Throwback to Savagery," *Houston Post*, August 12, 1933, newspaper clipping Papers of Jesse Daniel Ames, folder 4, University of North Carolina, Chapel Hill; "Heart and

Genitals Carved from Lynched Negro's Corpse," *New York World Telegram*, December 8, 1933, article reprinted in Ginzburg, *100 Years of Lynchings*, 211–12.

27. For examples of victims of lynch mobs who were affixed to a car and dragged to the Black section of town, see "Local Man With Dynamite on Person is Held," *Sherman Daily Democrat*, 11 May 1930; "A Throwback to Savagery," *Houston Post*, 12 August 1933, newspaper clipping in Papers of Jesse Daniel Ames, folder 4, University of North Carolina, Chapel Hill; "Heart and Genitals Carved From Lynched Negro's Corpse," *New York World Telegram*, 8 December 1933, article reprinted in Ginzburg, *100 Years of Lynchings*, 211–12; Lynching of Arthur brothers in Paris, Texas, "Their charred smoking bodies were then chained to an automobile and dragged for hours through the streets, particularly in sections inhabited by our Race. For examples of lynch mobs dragging mobs but not taking them to any particular place, see "Lynching Record for 1934," Papers of the NAACP, Series A, Part 7, reel 20.

28. "Two Negroes Pay for Act on Tree Limb," 1935, article in Papers of the NAACP, Series A, Part 7, Reel 8.

29. "That's Why Henry Davis was Sent to the Hereafter on Nothing but a Confession," *The Fort Worth Daily Gazette*, July 14, 1889.

30. "That's Why Henry Davis was Sent to the Hereafter on Nothing but a Confession," *The Fort Worth Daily Gazette*.

31. "Crime and Criminals: The Lynched Rapist at Robinson Will Rest Unavenged," *The Galveston Daily*, July 17, 1889; "McLennan County: Former Sheriffs," https://www.co.mclennan.tx.us/205/Former-Sheriffs.

32. Alexis McCrossen, *Holy Day, Holiday: The American Sunday* (Ithaca: Cornell University Press, 2000), 79.

33. McCrossen, *Holy Day, Holiday*, 79.

34. "The Hanging at Henderson," *Palestine Daily Herald*, November 14, 1905, and "Negroes Condemn Negroes," *Liberty Vindicator*, November 17, 1905, from Lynching in Texas Staff, "Lynching of Robert Askew," *Lynching in Texas*, http://www.lynchingintexas.org/items/show/74.

Chapter 6

1. W. E. B. Du Bois, ed., "The Waco Horror: A Report on Lynching," the *Crisis* 12 (July 1916), supplement, 3; "Mob Takes Negro From Court House, Burns Him At Stake," *Waco Times*, May 16, 1916.

2. "Mob Takes Negro From Court House, Burns Him At Stake," *Waco Times*; "15,000 Witness Burning of Negro in Public Square," *New York World*, May 16, 1916, reprinted in Ginzburg, *100 Years of Lynchings*, 103.

3. Du Bois, "The Waco Horror," 4.

4. Du Bois, "The Waco Horror," 4.

5. Du Bois, "The Waco Horror," 4.

6. Du Bois, "The Waco Horror," 1.

7. "How the Sum of $10000.00 Could Be Used By The N.A.A.C.P. Towards The Prevention of Lynching," Papers of the NAACP, Series A, Part 7, reel 1.

8. Du Bois, "The Waco Horror," 8.

9. Du Bois, "The Waco Horror," 8.

10. Du Bois, "The Waco Horror," 8.

11. "A Texas Diversion," *Cleveland Advocate*, September 4, 1915. www.dbs.ohio history.org.

12. "A Texas Diversion," *Cleveland Advocate*.

13. "A Texas Diversion," *Cleveland Advocate*.

14. "A Texas Diversion," *Cleveland Advocate*.

15. "A Texas Diversion," *Cleveland Advocate*.

16. "A Texas Diversion," *Cleveland Advocate*.

17. Baaki Brian, "White Crime and the Early African American Press: Elements of Reprinting and Reporting in New York's Freedom's Journal," *American Periodical*, 2019 29 Issue 2, 121–34; Simmons, Charles A., *The African American Press: A History of News Coverage During National Crisis, with Special Reference to Four Black Newspapers, 1827–1965* (Jefferson, NC: McFarland & Company, Inc., 2005). For a study on African American women of the Black press, see Roger Streitmatter, *Raising Her Voice: African-American Women Journalists Who Changed History* (Lexington: University of Kentucky Press, 1994).

18. Walter White, *Rope and Faggot: A Biography of Judge Lynch*, 180; W. E. B. Du Bois, "Race Relations in the United States, 1917–1947," *Phylon (1940–1956)* 9, no. 3 (1948), 234, 236.

19. "Town Hall Meeting," March 1, 1922, Papers of the NAACP, Series A, Part 7, reel 20.

20. "A Sheriff Led the Mob," *Herald* (Austin, TX), 1892.

21. "A Sheriff Led the Mob," *Herald*.

22. "A Sheriff Led the Mob," *Herald*.

23. For examples of victims of lynch mobs whom were affixed to a car and dragged to the Black section of town, see "Local Man With Dynamite on Person is Held," *Sherman Daily Democrat,* May 11, 1930; "A Throwback to Savagery," *Houston Post*, 12 August 1933, newspaper clipping in Papers of Jesse Daniel Ames, folder 4, University of North Carolina, Chapel Hill; "Heart and Genitals Carved From Lynched Negro's Corpse," *New York World Telegram*, 8 December 1933, article reprinted in Ginzburg, 211–12; Lynching of Arthur brothers in Paris, Texas, "Their charred smoking bodies were then chained to an automobile and dragged for hours through the streets, particularly in sections inhabited by our Race. For examples of lynch mobs dragging mobs but not taking them to any particular place, see "Lynching Record for 1934," Papers of the NAACP, Series A, Part 7, reel 20.

24. "A Sheriff Led the Mob," *Herald* (Austin, TX), January 7, 1892; Hullen Owens, May 19, 1922, Texarkana, Texas, "Lynchings May, 1922," Papers of the NAACP, Series A, Part 7, reel 20; see appendix for list of Texas lynchings and modes of death.

25. See, for example, "Judge Lynch as an Educator," *Nation*; see also *Crisis*; "Lynching Pastime," *Dallas Express,* November 29, 1919, Dallas Public Library; Journalists frequently used the word "parade" to describe the ritualistic dragging of a body and the "procession" that followed.

26. For a listing of Texas segregation legislation, see *Complete Texas Statutes* (Kansas City, MO: Vernon Law Book Company, 1920); Jack Temple Kirby, *Darkness at the Dawning: Race and Reform in the Progressive South* (Philadelphia: J. B. Lippincott, 1972); also see C. Vann Woodward, "Progressivism--For Whites

Only," in *Origins of the New South, 1817–1913* (Baton Rouge: Louisiana State University Press, 1951); John Dittmer, *Black Georgia In the Progressive Era: 1900–1920* (Urbana: University of Illinois Press, 1977); Arthur Link and R. McCormick, *Progressivism* (Wheeling: Harlan Davidson, 1983); Patricia A. Schechter, *Ida B. Wells-Barnett and American Reform, 1880–1930* (Chapel Hill: University of North Carolina Press, 2001); Lasch-Quinn, Elizabeth, *Black Neighbors: Race and the Limits of Reform in the American Settlement House Movement* (Chapel Hill: University of North Carolina Press, 1993); see also Sernett, Milton, *Bound For the Promised Land: African American Religion and the Great Migration* (Durham: Duke University Press, 1997). For additional information on the struggles and accomplishments of Black Dallasites during the Progressive Era, see Marsha Prior and Terry Anne Schulte, "Tragedy and Triumph: Progressive Era Reforms And African Americans in Dallas," in Duane Peter et al. eds., *Freedman's Cemetery: A Legacy of a Pioneer Black Community in Dallas, Texas* (Austin: Texas Department of Transportation, 2000); Carole Lynn Stewart, *Temperance and Cosmopolitanism: African American Reformers in the Atlantic World* (University Park, PA: Penn State University Press, 2018).

27. Postcard to Captain J. J. Sanders, Roy Wilkinson Aldrich Papers, [AR 83-10-253B], Dolph Briscoe Center for American History, The University of Texas at Austin; "Five Men Hanged at Tombstone," *Frontier Times* 5, no. 10, July 1923.

28. Katy Electric Studio, 1916, Wikimedia Commons.

29. Arthur Raper, *Tragedy of Lynching* (Chapel Hill: University of North Carolina Press, 1933).

30. Untitled article, *New York Times*, November 10, 1896.

31. "Texas Celebrates the Armistice," *Pittsburgh Courier*, November 27, 1926.

32. "Texas Celebrates the Armistice," *Pittsburgh Courier*.

33. "Texas Celebrates the Armistice," *Pittsburgh Courier*.

34. "Nab 5 After Mob Quiz: Lynchers of 3 Will Face Murder Trial," *Chicago Defender*, November 20, 1926; "History of Veteran's Day," Office of Intergovernmental Affairs, US Department of Veterans Affairs, http://www .va.gov/opa/vetsday/vetdayhistory.asp.

35. Michael Chesterman, Janet Chan, and Shelley Hampton, "Managing prejudicial publicity: an empirical study of criminal jury trials in New South Wales (Sydney, Law and Justice Foundation of NSW: 2000).

36. As quoted in Patricia Bernstein, *The First Waco Horror: The Lynching of Jesse Washington and the Rise of the NAACP* (College Station: Texas A&M University Press, 2005), 22. See Bernstein for additional information related to the lynching of Sank Majors.

37. Ida B. Wells Barnett, *On Lynchings* (New York: Humanity Books, 2002), 42.

38. James Weldon Johnson, *The Autobiography of An Ex-Coloured Man* (Wilder Publications, 2008), original publication date, 1912, 35–36. Although Johnson's text is a thinly fictionalized account of race in early twentieth century America, it is informed by historically accurate social phenomena.

39. Johnson, *The Autobiography*, 68–69; White, 181–82.

40. White, *Rope and Faggot*, 176.

41. W. E. B. Du Bois, "Race Relations in the United States, 1917–1947," *Phylon* 9, no. 3 (1948), 237; "Opinion," *Crisis* 7, no. 3 (January 1914), 125; "Views and Reviews," *The Pittsburgh Courier*, February 19, 1927.

42. White, *Rope and Faggot*, 174.

43. Richard M. Perloff, "The Press and Lynchings of African Americans," *Journal of Black Studies* 30, no. 3 (January 2000), 316–17.

44. Perloff, "The Press and Lynchings of African Americans," 320.

45. "Black Brutes' Awful Deeds: Would Be Criminal Assaulter Shot to Death Near Henderson," *Houston Chronicle and Herald*, August 22, 1903, Houston Public Library, Houston, Texas; "Assaulted by a Negro," *Galveston Daily News*, August 27, 1895.

46. "Brute's Crime; A Mob's Vengeance," *Dallas Times Herald*, March 3, 1910 (Dallas Public Library).

47. "Go the Whole Way of Law Against The Lyncher," *San Antonio Express*, 24 January 1919, on file at San Antonio Public Library, San Antonio, Texas. For examples of white reporters in Texas who condemned lynchers, see *San Antonio Express*. The newspaper regularly printed articles that condemned the act of lynching; "Lynchers Must Go," *San Antonio Inquirer*, 18 August 1918; untitled newspaper article, *Goliad Guard*, 3 February 1893, San Antonio Library. No instances were found in which a local newspaper reporter criticized a lynching that occurred in his or her town.

48. "Mob of 500 Burned Negro at the Stake," *Austin Statesman*, July 31, 1915, Austin, Texas.

49. "Burning of Texas Negro," *El Paso Morning News*, July 31, 1915, in Papers of the NAACP, Series A, reel 7, 1.

50. "Burning of Texas Negro," *El Paso Morning News*.

51. White, *Rope and Faggot*, 175–76.

52. White, *Rope and Faggot*, 175–76.

53. White, *Rope and Faggot*, 176.

54. "Lynching, Not Bull Fights, Are Allowed in Texas," *Cleveland Advocate*, 1920. www.dbs.ohiohistory.org.

55. "The Lynching in Texas," *Cleveland Advocate*, August 14, 1915.

56. "The Lynching in Texas," *Cleveland Advocate*.

57. "The Lynching in Texas," *Cleveland Advocate*.

58. "Tragedy of Temple Now Old History," *Dallas Times Herald*, August 1, 1915.

59. "Tragedy of Temple Now Old History," *Dallas Times Herald*.

60. "Tragedy of Temple Now Old History," *Dallas Times Herald*; "The American Mob," *The Pittsburgh Courier*, January 17, 1931.

61. "Hale Bros. Index Diagram of the World's Columbian Exposition" Hale Bros. Map Publishers, Chicago, 1892, www.chicagohs.org.

62. Thomas C. Holt, *Children of Fire: A History of African Americans* (New York: Hill and Wang, 2010),190. For an excellent and insightful discussion of African Americans efforts to have Black achievement highlighted in the Chicago World's Fair, see Holt, 185–204.

63. Holt, *Children of Fire*, 193–94, 197; Major Ben. C. Truman, "1893 History of The World's Fair being A Complete and Authentic Description of the Columbian Exposition From Its Inception" (Philadelphia, PA: J. W. Keeler & Co.), 592, http://people.tamu.edu/~louhodges/RPTS-320/readings/Texas%20 House.pdf.

64. *Dallas Express*, July 12, 1919, 4, as quoted in William Douglas Turner, Jr., *The*

Dallas Express As A Forum on Lynching, 1919–1921 (Dallas: Southern Methodist University), Master's Thesis, 49.

65. Turner, *The Dallas Express*, 35, 51–52; see *Dallas Express*, on file at Dallas Public Library, Dallas, Texas.

66. Holt, *Children of Fire*, 196; Frederick Douglass, "Why Is the Negro Lynched?" in Philip S. Foner, ed., *Frederick Douglass: Selected Speeches and Writings* (Chicago, Lawrence Hill Books, 1999), 752.

67. Foner, *Frederick Douglass*, 752; Frederick Douglas, "Lynching Black People Because They Are Black," *Christian Educator* (1894), 96.

68. Booker T. Washington, "A Protest Against the Burning and Lynching of Negroes," *The Sacred Heart Review*, Volume 31, Number 10, 5 March 1910, originally published in Birmingham *Age Herald*, 29 February 1904, http://newspapers.bc.edu/cgi-bin/bostonsh?a=d&d=BOSTONSH19040305-01.2.13.

69. "Civilized Savages" *Chicago Defender*, February 21, 1921.

70. "Civilized Savages" *Chicago Defender*.

71. "Civilized Savages" *Chicago Defender*.

72. "Civilized Savages" *Chicago Defender*.

73. "When Texas Lynches," *Chicago Defender*, June 30, 1934.

74. "When Texas Lynches," *Chicago Defender*.

75. "Texas Man and Maiden," *Cleveland Journal*, December 2, 1905.

76. Lawrence W. Levine, *Highbrow Lowbrow* (Cambridge: Harvard University Press, 2002, original publication 1988), 15–16.

77. Richard Posner, "When Is Parody Fair Use?" *Journal of Legal Studies* 21, no. 1 (January 1992), 67–78, 67.

78. "Since Lynching Must Go On In America," *Chicago Defender*, December 11, 1916.

79. Metz T. P. Lochard, "The Negro Press in Illinois," *Journal of the Illinois State Historical Society (1908–1984)* 56, no. 3, Emancipation Centennial Issue (Autumn, 1963), 570–91, 572, 573, 577; "The Lynching Party," *Chicago Defender*, February 19, 1938; "While Lynching Goes On," *Chicago Defender*, July 4, 1936; "The Annual Dixie Classic," *Chicago Defender*, January 12, 1935; "The Latest Lynching Implements," *Chicago Defender*, October 18, 1924; "College Sports," *Chicago Defender*, May 12, 1923.

80. White, *Rope and Faggot*, 178–79.

81. White, *Rope and Faggot*, 178–79.

82. "Little Letters from the South," William Cowart to Mr. Villiard, April 1, 1911, *Crisis* 2, no. 1 (1911), 32.

83. "How the Sum of $10000.00 Could Be Used By The N.A.A.C.P. Towards The Prevention of Lynching," Papers of the NAACP, Series A, Part 7, reel 1.

84. "Opinion," *Crisis* 7, no. 3 (January 1914), 125.

85. "The Lynchings Industry," *Crisis* 13, no. 5, 237.

86. "Our Lynching Culture," *Crisis* (October 1916), 283.

87. See, for example, "The Decline of Lynching," *Crisis* 8, no. 1 (May 1914), 20; "The Lynchings Industry," *Crisis* 13, no. 5, 237.

88. Du Bois, "The Waco Horror," 8.

89. "How the Sum of $10000.00 Could Be Used By The N.A.A.C.P. Towards

The Prevention of Lynching," Papers of the NAACP, Series A, Part 7, reel 1, University of Texas, Austin.

90. Sara E. Parsons, Boston, Massachusetts, to Spingarn, New York, New York, July 12, 1916, *Crisis* (September 1916), 220.

91. *Crisis* (September 1916), 220.

92. *Crisis* (September 1916), 219.

93. Memo, 24, Papers of the NAACP, Series A, Part 7, reel 1.

94. Report of N.A.A.C.P. Investigator, Papers of the NAACP, Series A, Part 7, reel 18.

95. Report of N.A.A.C.P. Investigator, Papers of the NAACP, Series A, Part 7, reel 18.

96. Du Bois, W. E. B., "Opinion," *Crisis* 18, no. 2, June 1919, 59.

97. Du Bois, "Opinion," 59.

98. Du Bois, "Opinion," 59.

99. Memorandum for NAACP Branches, Papers of the NAACP, Part 7, Series A, Reel 28.

100. Robert L. Zangrando, *The NAACP Crusade Against Lynching, 1909–1950* (Philadelphia: Temple University Press, 1980), 37.

101. Zangrando, *The NAACP Crusade Against Lynching*, 37.

102. Memorandum for NAACP Branches, Papers of the NAACP, Part 7, Series A, Reel 28.

103. Zangrando, *The NAACP Crusade Against Lynching*, 37.

104. Zangrando, *The NAACP Crusade Against Lynching*, 37.

Epilogue

1. Some pundits have refuted that James Byrd Jr. was lynched, at times citing the supposed public lack of community support for the act. Overt community support was not necessarily required for an act of murder to qualify as a lynching. If this was a necessary component, then early lynch mobs would not have frequently felt the need to mask their faces when committing the murder. In this study, I have employed a definition of lynching (see the introduction) that wholly qualifies Byrd's murder as a lynching.

2. Joyce King, *Hate Crime: The Story of the Dragging in Jasper, Texas* (Holt Paperbacks Books, 2003), prologue.

BIBLIOGRAPHY

Primary Sources
Manuscript and Archival Collections

DALLAS COUNTY RECORDER'S OFFICE, DALLAS, TEXAS

Dallas County Deed Records

DALLAS CITY HALL, DALLAS, TEXAS

Minutes of the City Council, City Secretary's Office

DALLAS PUBLIC LIBRARY, DALLAS TEXAS

Dallas City Directories
Marion Butts Collection
Murphy and Bolanz Addition Book I
Standard Certificates of Death, Texas State Board of Health, Genealogy
Papers of John and Ethelyn M. Chisum
Records of Subassistant Commissioner of the 40th District, Bureau of Refugees,
    Freedman, and Abandoned Lands
Sanborn Insurance Maps of Dallas

DALLAS HISTORICAL SOCIETY, DALLAS, TEXAS

Elmer Scott Collection
Bartholomew, Harland, A Master Plan for Dallas, Texas, vols. 1–12 (St. Louis:
    Harland Bartholomew and Associates, 1943–1945)
Kessler, George, A City Plan for Dallas (Dallas, 1913)

EAST TEXAS RESEARCH CENTER, RALPH W. STEEN LIBRARY,
STEPHEN F. AUSTIN STATE UNIVERSITY, NACOGDOCHES, TEXAS

Clippings, Upshur Echo

LIBRARY OF CONGRESS, WASHINGTON DC

Papers of the National Association for the Advancement of Colored People, Branch
    Files
"Series of fifteen stereographs relating to the murder of a woman in Tyler, Texas,"
    photographs by C. A. Davis, published by Breckenridge and Scruggs company,
    LOT 11782 (F) [P&P], Prints and Photographs Division, Library of Congress
    (series referred to as "Breckenridge & Scruggs").
United States Work Projects Administration, Federal Writers' Project, Library of
    Congress, Interview with Edward W. Riley, Sheldon F. Gauthier (interviewer),

Tarrant County, Texas, Folklore Project, Life Histories, 1936–39 MSS55715: BOX A734.

PERSONAL INTERVIEWS

Carter, Evelyn, 1999 (interview now in possession of African American Museum, Dallas, Texas)

NATIONAL ARCHIVES AT COLLEGE PARK, MARYLAND

Department of Justice Files

TEXAS STATE LIBRARY & ARCHIVES DIVISION

Prints and Photographs
Papers of Governor J. D. Sayers

UNIVERSITY OF ILLINOIS, CHICAGO

Sanborn Maps of Chicago

UNIVERSITY OF TEXAS AT AUSTIN, DOLPH BRISCOE CENTER
FOR AMERICAN HISTORY, AUSTIN, TEXAS

Roy Wilkinson Aldrich Collection
Various Texas Newspapers

Newspapers and Periodicals

100% American (Dallas, Texas)
Baltimore Afro-American
Bonham News
Brownsville Daily Herald (Brownsville, Texas)
Bryan Morning Eagle (Bryan, Texas)
Butte Inter Mountain (Butte, Montana)
Abilene Reporter News (Abilene, Texas)
American Quarterly
American Historical Review
Austin Statesman and Review
Birmingham Age-Herald (Birmingham, Alabama)
Bismarck Weekly Tribune
Bridgeport Evening Farmer (Bridgeport, Connecticut)
Chicago Defender (Chicago, Illinois)
Chicago Record-Herald (Chicago, Illinois)
Chicago Daily Tribune (Chicago, Illinois)
Christian Recorder
Christian Educator
Cleveland Advocate
Cleveland Journal
Crisis
Daily Ardmoreite (Ardmore, Oklahoma)
Daily Capital Journal (Salem, Oregon)

Daily Courier-Light (Corsicana, Texas)
Daily Hesperian
Daily News-Telegram (Sulphur Springs, Texas)
Daily Times Herald (Dallas, Texas)
Daily Republican (Wilmington, Delaware)
Dallas Daily Herald (Dallas, Texas)
Dallas Express (Dallas, Texas)
Dallas Morning News (Dallas, Texas)
Dallas Times Herald (Dallas, Texas)
Dallas Weekly Herald (Dallas, Texas)
Detroit Journal (Detroit, Michigan)
Ebony
Eureka Daily Sentinel
Evening Telegraph (Philadelphia, Pennsylvania)
Fort Worth Democrat (Fort Worth, Texas)
Fort Worth Morning Register (Fort Worth, Texas)
Frontier (O'Neill City, Nebraska)
Frontier Times
Gallipolis Journal
Galveston Daily News (Galveston, Texas)
Goliad Guard
Hallettsville New Era (Hallettsville, Texas)
Herald (Austin, Texas)
Hot Springs Star (Hot Springs, Dakota [Dakota Territory, i.e., SD])
Houston Chronicle and Herald
Iola Register
Jefferson Jimplecute (Jefferson, Texas)
Lampasas Daily Leader (Lampasas, Texas)
Los Angeles Herald
Lowell Daily Sun (Lowell, Massachusetts)
Madison Daily Leader (Madison, South Dakota)
Morning Star and Catholic Messenger (New Orleans, Louisiana)
Muskogee Cimeter (Muskogee, Indian Territory, Oklahoma)
Nation
New York Times
New York World
Omaha Daily Bee
Palestine Daily Herald (Palestine, Texas)
Pensacola Journal (Pensacola, Florida)
Pittsburgh Courier (Pittsburgh, Pennsylvania)
Pittsburgh American (Pittsburgh, Pennsylvania)
Portland Daily Press (Portland, Oregon)
Prescott Daily News (Prescott, Arkansas)
Puget Sound Dispatch (Seattle, Washington)
Record and Chronicle (Denton, Texas)
Richmond Planet (Richmond, Virginia)
San Antonio Express (San Antonio, Texas)
San Antonio Evening News (San Antonio, Texas)

San Antonio Inquirer (San Antonio, Texas)
San Marcos Times (San Marcos, Texas)
Shiner Gazette (Shiner, Texas)
Sociological Theory
Southern Enterprise (Greenville, South Carolina)
Southern Mercury
Sunday Gazetteer
Texas Almanac
Texas Republican (Marshall, Texas)
Town Talk (Alexandria, Louisiana)
True Northerner (Paw, Michigan)
Vinita Daily Chieftan (Vinita, Indian Territory)
Waco Times (Waco, Texas)
Waco Daily Examiner (Waco, Texas)
Waterbury Evening Democrat (Waterbury, Connecticut)
Washington Post
Weekly Commercial Herald (Vicksburg, Mississippi)
Weekly Democratic Statesman (Austin, Texas)
Wheeling Register (Wheeling, West Virginia)

Primary Sources, Published

Benjamin, R. O. C., *Southern Outrages: A Statistical Record of Lawless Doings* (Colored Lawyers National Bar Association, 1894).

Brewer, J. Mason, *Heralded Dawn* (Dallas: Superior Typesetting Co., 1934).

Buchanan v. Warley, 245 US 60 (1917).

Burdett, Samuel, *A Test of lynch law: an expose of mob violence and the courts of hell*, 1901.

Constitution of the Republic of Texas.

Department of Interior, *Compendium of the Eleventh Census: Part I, Population* (Washington, DC: Government Printing Office, 1892).

Du Bois, W. E. B., "The Waco Horror" Supplement, *Crisis* 12 (July 1916).

Ellison, Ralph, *Invisible Man* (Vintage International; 2nd edition, 1995).

Equal Justice Initiative, *Lynching in America: Confronting the Legacy of Racial Terror: Report Summary* (Montgomery, AL, 2015).

Hall, Josie Briggs, *Hall's Moral and Mental Capsule* (Dallas: Reverend R. S. Jenkins, Publisher, 1905).

Johnson, James Weldon, *The Autobiography of An Ex-Coloured Man* (Wilder Publications, 2008), original publication date 1912.

National Association of the Advancement of Colored People, *Report of the National Association of the Advancement of Colored People for the Years 1917 and 1918: Eighth and Ninth Annual Reports, A Summary of Work and an Accounting* (New York: National Association for the Advancement of Colored People, 1919).

National Association for the Advancement of Colored People, *Thirty Years of Lynching in the United States, 1889–1918* (New York: Negro Universities Press, 1919).

Papers of the National Association for the Advancement of Colored People, microfilm edition.

Papers of William Edward Burghardt Du Bois. Special Collections and University Archives, University of Massachusetts Amherst Libraries.

Pruden, Durward, "A Sociological Study of a Texas Lynching," Volume 1, Number 1, *Studies in Sociology* (Dallas: The Department of Sociology, Southern Methodist University, 1936).

Records of the Department of State Relating to the Internal Affairs of Mexico, 1910–1929, Frank Pierce's "Partial List of Mexicans Killed in the Valley Since July 1, 1915." National Archives, Microfilm Publication, M274, vol. 51, File No. 812/17186, image number 0175. www.lynchingintexas.org.

Smith, Bolton, *A Philosophy of Race Relations* (Memphis: n.p., 1919).

Terrell Election Law, 1903.

Texas Constitutional Convention, "Report of the Special Committee on Lawlessness and Violence in Texas" (Austin: Office of the Daily Republican, 1868).

Vance, Henry, *The Facts in the Case of the Horrible Murder of Little Myrtle Vance and its Fearful Expiation in Paris, Texas* (Paris: P. L. James, 1893).

Wells, Ida B., *The Red Record: Tabulated Statistics and Alleged Causes of Lynching in the United States* (Chicago: Donohue & Menneberry, 1895).

Secondary Sources

Akers, Monte, *Flames After Midnight: Murder, Vengeance, and the Desolation of a Texas Community Revised Edition* (Austin: University of Texas Press, 1999).

Allen, James, and John Littlefield, *Without Sanctuary: Photographs and Postcards of Lynching in America* (Santa Fe, NM: Twin Palms, 2000).

Aron, Cindy Sondik, *Working at Play: A History of Vacations in the United States* (New York: Oxford University Press, 1999).

Ayers, Edward L., *Vengeance and Justice: Crime and Punishment in the19th-Century American South* (New York, 1984).

Barr, A., *Black Texans: A History of African Americans in Texas, 1528–1995* (Norman: University of Oklahoma Press, 1996).

Baum, Dale, *Counterfeit Justice: The Judicial Odyssey of Texas Freedwoman Azeline Harris* (Baton Rouge: Louisiana State University Press, 2009).

Bernstein, Patricia, *The Waco Horror: The Lynching of Jesse Washington and the Rise of the NAACP* (College Station: Texas A&M University Press, 2005).

Bills, E. R., *Black Holocaust: The Paris Horror and a Legacy of Texas Terror* (Fort Worth: Eakin Press, 2015).

Block, W. T., "Milltowns and Ghost Towns: East Texas Before the Great Sawmilling and Logging Era," East Texas Research Center, Ralph W. Steen Library, Stephen F. Austin State University.

Boyle, Kevin, *Arc of Justice: A Saga of Race, Civil Rights, and Murder in the Jazz Age* (Holt Paperbacks, 2005).

Brewer, J. Mason, *Negro Legislatures of Texas and Their Descendants* (Austin: Jenkins Publishing, 1970).

Brown, Nikki L. M. and Barry M. Stentiford, *The Jim Crow Encyclopedia: Greenwood Milestones in African American History* (Westport, CT: Greenwood Press, 2008).

Brundage, W. Fitzhugh, *Lynching in the New South: Georgia and Virginia, 1880–1930* (Urbana: University of Illinois Press, 1993).

Carrigan, William D., *The Making of a Lynching Culture: Violence and Vigilantism in Central Texas, 1836–1916* (Urbana: University of Illinois Press, 2006).

Casdorph, P. D., *Republicans, Negroes, and Progressives in the South, 1912–1916* (Tuscaloosa: University of Alabama Press, 1981).

Cash, W. J., *The Mind of the South* (Vintage, 1991, first published 1941).

Cohen, C. S., "Elmer Scott and the Civic Federation of Dallas" (Master's Thesis, Southern Methodist University, 1979).

Crouch, Barry A., *The Freedman's Bureau and Black Texans* (Austin: University of Texas Press, 1999).

Cutler, James E., *Judge Lynch: An Investigation into the History of Lynching in the United States* (London and Bombay: Longmans, Green, and Co., 1905).

Delfino, Susanna, Michele Gillespie, and Louis M Kyriakoudes, eds., *Southern Society and Its Transformations 1790–1860* (Columbia: University of Missouri Press, 2011).

Dittmer, John, *Black Georgia in the Progressive Era: 1900–1920* (Urbana: University of Illinois Press, 1977).

Du Bois, William Edward Burghardt, *Dark Waters: Voices from Within the Veil* (New York: Harcourt, Brace and Howe, 1920).

Du Bois, W. E. B., *The Suppression of the African Slave-trade to the United States of America 1638–1870* (Casimo Classics, reprinted 2007).

Du Bois, W. E. B., "Race Relations in the United States, 1917–1947," *Phylon* 9, no. 3 (1948): 234–47.

Equal Justice Initiative, *Lynching in America: Confronting the Legacy of Racial Terror: Report Summary* (Montgomery, AL, 2015).

Dray, Philip, *At the Hands of Persons Unknown: The Lynching of Black America* (The Modern Library, New York, 2002).

Eatman, Megan, *Ecologies of Harm: Rhetorics of Violence in the United States* (Columbus: Ohio State University Press, 2020).

Equal Justice Initiative, "Reconstruction in America: Racial Violence after the Civil War, 1865–1876" (2020).

Estes, Mary Elizabeth, *An Historical Survey of Lynchings in Oklahoma and Texas* (Master's Thesis, University of Oklahoma, 1942).

Fanon, Frantz, translated by Charles Lam Markman, *Black Skins, White Masks* (Grove Press, 1968).

Foner, Philip S., ed., *Frederick Douglass: Selected Speeches and Writings* (Chicago, Lawrence Hill Books, 1999).

Foucault, Michel, *Discipline and Punish: The Birth of the Prison* (Vintage Books: 2nd edition, 1995).

Gelber, Steven M., *Hobbies: Leisure and The Culture of Work in America* (New York: Columbia University Press, 1999).

Giddings, Paula J., *Ida, A Sword Among Lions: Ida B. Wells and the Campaign Against Lynching* (New York: Amistad, 2008).

Gilmore, Glenda, *Gender and Jim Crow: Women and the Politics of White Supremacy in North Carolina, 1896–1920* (Chapel Hill: University of North Carolina Press, 1995).

Ginzburg, Ralph, *100 Years of Lynchings* (Baltimore: Black Classic Press, 1962).

Glasrud, Bruce A., ed., *Anti-Black Violence in Twentieth-Century Texas* (College Station: Texas A&M University Press, 2015).

Goldbeck, J. Helen, ed., *A Survey of the Black's Response to Lynching* (New Mexico Highlands University Medial Materials Center, 1973).

Goings, Kenneth, *Black Collectibles and American Stereotyping* (Bloomington: Indiana University Press, 1994).

Goldsby, Jacqueline, "The High and Low Tech of It: The Meaning of Lynching and the Death of Emmett Till," *Yale Journal of Criticism* 9, no. 2 (Fall 1996): 245–82.

Hale, Grace Elizabeth, *Making Whiteness: The Culture of Segregation in the South, 1890–1940* (New York: Pantheon Books, 1998).

Hall, Josie Briggs, *Hall's Moral and Mental Capsule* (Dallas: Reverend R. S. Jenkins, Publisher, 1905).

Hirsch, Arnold R., *Making the Second Ghetto: Race and Housing in Chicago, 1940–1960* (Chicago: University of Chicago Press, 1998).

Holt, Thomas C., *Children of Fire: A History of African Americans* (New York: Hill and Wang, 2010).

Holt, Thomas C., "Marking: Race, Race-making, and the Writing of History," AHA Presidential Address, *American Historical Review* 100, no. 1 (February 1995): 1–20.

Howell, Kenneth W., *Still the Arena of Civil War: Violence and Turmoil in Reconstruction Texas, 1865–1874* (Denton, TX: University of North Texas Press, 2012).

Ignalls, Robert P., "Lynching and Establishment Violence in Tampa, 1858–1935," *Journal of Southern History* 53, no. 4 (November 1987): 613–44.

Jones, William Powell, *The Tribe of Black Ulysses: African American Lumber Workers in the Jim Crow South* (Urbana: University of Illinois Press, 2005).

Kirby, Jack Temple, *Darkness at the Dawning: Race and Reform in the Progressive South* (Philadelphia: J. B. Lippincott, 1972).

Kousser, J. M., *The Shaping of Southern Politics Suffrage, Restriction and the Establishment of the One-Party South, 1880–1910* (New Haven: Yale University Press, 1974).

Lear, Bernadette A., "Wish They Were Here: Old Postcards and Library History," *Libraries & the Cultural Record* 43, no. 1 (2008): 77–100.

Lemons, J. Stanley, "Black Stereotypes as Reflected in Popular Culture, 1880–1920," *American Quarterly* 29, no. 1 (Spring 1977): 102–16.

Levine, Lawrence W., *Highbrow Lowbrow* (Cambridge: Harvard University Press, 2002, original publication 1988).

Link, Arthur and R. McCormick, *Progressivism* (Wheeling: Harlan Davidson, 1983).

Litwack, Leon, *Trouble in Mind: Black Southerners in the Age of Jim Crow* (New York: Vintage Books, 2010).

Litwack, Leon, *Without Sanctuary: Lynching Photography in America* (Santa Fe, NM: Twin Palms, 2000).

Lochard, Metz T. P., "The Negro Press in Illinois" *Journal of the Illinois State Historical Society (1908–1984)* 56, no. 3 (Fall 1963): 570–91.

Madison, James H., *A Lynching in the Heartland: Race and Memory in America* (New York: Palgrave, 2003).

Mahar, William J., *Behind The Burnt Cork Mask: Early Blackface Minstrelsy and Antebellum American Popular Culture* (Urbana: University of Illinois Press, 1999).

Marquart, James W., Ekland-Olson, Sheldon, and Jonathan R. Sorensen, *The Rope, The Chair, and the Needle: Capital Punishment in Texas, 1923–1990* (Austin: University of Texas Press, 1994).

Martin, Edward Dean, *The Behavior of Crowds* (New York: Harper and Brothers, 1920).

Matthews, Donald G., *At the Altar of Lynching: Burning Sam Hose in the American South* (Cambridge: Cambridge University Press, 2018).

McDonald, W. L., *Dallas Remembered: A Photographic Chronicle of Urban expansion, 1870–1925* (Dallas: Dallas Historical Society, 1978).

McKnight, Mamie, *African American Families and Settlements of Dallas: On the Inside Looking Out. Exhibition, Family Memoirs, Personality Profiles and Community Essays*, vol II (Dallas: Black Dallas Remembered, 1990).

McMillen, Neil R., *Dark Journey: Black Mississippians in the Age of Jim Crow* (Urbana: University of Illinois Press, 1990).

Montgomery, Cora, *Eagle Pass, Or, Life on the Border* (New York: G.P. Putnam and Company, 1852).

Murphy, Edgar Gardner, *The Basis of Ascendancy* (New York, 1909).

Nevels, Cynthia Skove, *Lynching to Belong: Claiming Whiteness Through Racial Violence* (College Station: Texas A&M University Press, 2009).

Neumeyer, Martin H. and Esther R. Neumeyer, *Leisure and Recreation: A Study of Leisure and Recreation in Their Sociological Aspects* (New York: The Ronald Press Company, 1958).

Ogden, F., *The Poll Tax in the South* (Tuscaloosa: University of Alabama Press, 1958).

Osofsky, Gilbert, *Harlem: The Making of a Ghetto: Negro New York, 1890–1930* (New York: Harper & Row, 1963).

Pfeifer, Michael J., "At the Hands of Persons Unknown? The State of the Field of Lynching Scholarship," *The Journal of American History* 101, no. 3 (December 2014): 832–60.

Pfeifer, Michael J., *The Roots of Rough Justice: Origins of American Lynching* (Urbana: University of Illinois Press, 2011).

Posner, Richard, "When Is Parody Fair Use?" *Journal of Legal Studies* 21, no. 1 (January 1992).

Prince, Robert, *A History of Dallas: From a Different Perspective* (Nortex Press, 1993).

Prior, Marsha and Terry Anne Schulte, "Freedman's Town/North Dallas: The Convergence and Development of an African American Community," in Peter, Duane et al., *Freedman's Cemetery: A Legacy of a Pioneer Black Community* (Austin: Department of Transportation, 2000).

Prior, Marsha and Terry Anne Schulte, "Where Dignity Lives: Freedman's Town/ North Dallas," in Duane E. Peters et al., *Freedman's Cemetery: A Legacy of a Pioneer Black Community* (Austin: Department of Transportation, 2000).

Raper, Arthur, *Tragedy of Lynching* (Chapel Hill: University of North Carolina Press, 1933).

Reynolds, Donald E., *Texas Terror: The Slave Insurrection Panic of 1860 and the Secession of the Lower South* (Baton Rouge: Louisiana State University Press, 2007).

Rice, L. D., *The Negro in Texas: 1874–1900* (Baton Rouge: Louisiana State University Press, 1971).

Senechal de la Roche, Roberta, "Why Is Collective Violence Collective?" *Sociological Theory* 19, no. 2 (July 2001): 126–44.

Smith, Felipe, *American Body Politics: Race, Gender, and Black Literary Renaissance* (Athens: University of Georgia Press, 1998).

No author, "Postcard History," Smithsonian Institute Archives.

SoRelle, James M., "The 'Waco Horror': The Lynching of Jesse Washington, *Southwestern Historical Quarterly* 86, no. 4 (April 1983): 517–36.

Stebbins, Robert, *Amateurs, Professionals, and Serious Leisure* (Montreal: McGill-Queen's University Press, 1992).

Sugrue, Thomas, *The Origins of the Urban Crisis: Race and Inequality in Postwar Detroit* (Princeton: Princeton University Press, 1996).

Texas State Historical Association, *The Handbook of Texas: A Digital Gateway to Texas History*.

Trotter, Joe W., *Black Milwaukee: The Making of an Industrial Proletariat, 1915–1945* (Urbana: University of Illinois Press, 1985).

Truman, Major Ben. C., "1893 History of The World's Fair being A Complete and Authentic Description of the Columbian Exposition From Its Inception" (Philadelphia, PA: J. W Keeler & Co.).

Tuttle, William, *Race Riot: Chicago in the Red Summer of 1919* (New York: Atheneum, 1974).

Waldrep, Christopher, ed., *Lynching in America: A History in Documents* (New York: New York University Press, 2006).

Waldrep, Christopher, "Wars of the World: The Controversy over the Definition of Lynching, 1899–1940," *The Journal of Southern History* 66, no. 1 (February 2000): 75–100.

Weems, Robert, *Desegregating the Dollar: African American Consumers in the Twentieth Century* (New York: New York University Press, 1998).

White, Walter, *Rope and Faggot: A Biography of Judge Lynch* (Notre Dame, IN: University of Notre Dame, 2001), original publication date, 1929.

Wilkinson, J. L., *The Trans-Cedar Lynching and the Texas Penitentiary* (New York: Carlton Press, 1974).

Turner, William Douglas, Jr., *The Dallas Express as a Forum on Lynching, 1919–1921*, Master's thesis, Southern Methodist University, 1974.

Williamson, Joel, *The Crucible of Race: Black-White Relations in the South Since Emancipation* (New York: Oxford University Press, 1984).

Wallace-Sanders, Kimberly, *Mammy: A Century of Race, Gender, and Southern Memory* (Ann Arbor: University of Michigan Press, 2008).

Wood, Amy Louise, *Lynching and Spectacle: Witnessing Racial violence in America, 1890–1940* (Chapel Hill: University of North Carolina Press, 2009).

Woodard, C, Vann, *Origins of the New South, 1877–1913* (Baton Rouge: Louisiana State University Press, 1951).

Zangrando, Robert L., *The NAACP Crusade Against Lynching, 1909–1950* (Philadelphia: Temple University Press, 1980).

INDEX

University of Texas Law School, 152
Upshur, Texas, 33, 60
urbanization, 9, 13, 22, 121, 145, 170, 202, 219
Urban League, 219

vagrancy ordinance, 145
Vance, Henry, 79, 81–82
Vance, Myrtle, 79–82, 85, 166–67
Veal, Bert, 187
Virginia, 14, 42
Vitascope, 182
voting. *See* suffrage

Waco (Texas), 3–8, 30–31, 98–100, 113–15, 117, 119, 178, 236, 280; chief of police, 6; city hall, 29; public square of Waco, 213; Waco Avenue Bridge, 114; Waco High School, 6; Waco Horror, 31, 214, 235, 235
Waco Morning News, 31, 34, 69
Waco Times, 6, 220
Wagner, Robert F., 109
Waldrep, Christopher, 24
Wallace-Sanders, Kimberly, 174
War Department, 47
Washington, Booker T., 227
Washington, Jesse, 3–7, 25, 29–31, 97–100, 213–14, 234–35; coerced confession, 98; death certificate, 97; trial of, 3–5, 100
Washington, Martha, 97
Washington County, Texas, 48
Watt Street, 131
Weatherford, Texas, 93
Weaver, C. C., 89
Weekly Herald, 93
Weems, Robert, 163
Wells, Annie, 106
Wells, George, 106
Wells, Ida B., 45, 78–80, 87, 106, 180, 221

West Virginia, 11
Wheeling Daily Register, 11
White, George Henry, 111
White, Walter Francis, 16, 42, 46, 80, 106, 110, 120, 171, 217, 221, 223, 231
White, Alexander, 66
White, Esseck, 95
Whitehall, Texas, 70
White, John, 38
Whitesboro, Texas, 93–94
Wichita, Kansas, 95, 120
Wickersham, George Woodward, 104
Wilder, Abe, 74, 93–94
Williams, Bragg, 105–6, 108
Williams, Frank, 41
Williams, Thomas, 32
Williamson, Joel, 20, 55
Wilson, Woodrow, 104–7
Winn, Alex, 71
Winn, John, 48
Winters, Joe, 229
Witt, M. W., 93–94
Wood, Amy Louise, 13, 185
Wolfe City, Texas, 167
Woodard, C. Vann, 16, 170, 218
World's Columbian Exposition, 225
World War I, 105–9, 117, 137, 230
World War II, 161, 244–45
Wright, Richard, 29,
Wyoming, 246

xenophobic expressions, 215

Yoakum Seed Company, 159
Young, Dave, 242
Young, Harvey, 179
Younger, Conway, 90
Younger, Valle, 87–88, 90, 205

Zangrando, Robert L., 236
zoning measures, 138

TERRY ANNE SCOTT is associate professor of American history and chair of the History Department at Hood College. She is the editor of *Seattle Sports: Play, Identity, and Pursuit in the Emerald City.*